P9-CKE-270

Atlas of South Asia

About the Book and Authors

This up-to-date atlas includes maps, figures, and narratives that provide comprehensive coverage of political, physical, economic, historical, and cultural aspects of South Asia. India is given primary attention, with a secondary emphasis on Pakistan and Bangladesh. Sri Lanka, Nepal, and Bhutan receive briefer treatment. Although the maps are the main focus, the accompanying text explains and interprets the visual materials.

The authors examine such topics as climate, religion, physical features, and historical setting for the subcontinent as a whole in the chapter on South Asia. In subsequent country chapters, the authors deal with political and administrative systems, agriculture and industry, natural resources, trade, transportation, and demographic characteristics. Based on the most recent census and other current data, the atlas will be useful as a supplementary text for courses dealing with South Asia and as a basic reference work for all who are interested in the region.

Ashok K. Dutt is professor in the Department of Geography, University of Akron, where **M. Margaret Geib** is resident cartographer.

Fully Annotated

Atlas of South Asia

Ashok K. Dutt

Professor of Geography and Urban Studies,
The University of Akron

M. Margaret Geib

Cartographer, Department of Geography
The University of Akron

Westview Press / Boulder and London

Copyright © 1987 by Westview Press, Inc.

Published in 1987 in the United States of America by Westview Press, Inc.; Frederick A. Praeger, Publisher; 5500 Central Avenue, Boulder, Colorado 80301

Library of Congress Catalog Card Number: 86-051422
ISBN: 0-8133-0044-4
ISBN: 0-8133-0045-2 (pbk.)

Composition for this book was provided by the authors.
This book was produced without formal editing by the publisher. The publisher submitted the book for the usual peer review.

Printed and bound in the United States of America

The paper used in this publication meets the requirements of the American National Standard for Permanence of Paper for Printed Library Materials Z39.48-1984.

6   5   4

Dedicated to our deceased parents
Dr. Sashanka S. and Subala S. Dutta
and
Arleigh L. and Mary L. Geib

Contents

Preface

Atlas of South Asia is an introduction to the Indian subcontinent from a spatial point of view and it includes topics from disciplines such as geography, geology, history, political science, linguistics and economics. Thus, an effort has been made to deal with spatial aspects of the subcontinent both comprehensively and with a multi-disciplinary approach. Explanation of political, physical, historical, economic, social and cultural characteristics are the main subject matter of this *Atlas*.

Though maps are made the main focus of this *Atlas*, written materials explain the background of and interpret the spatial features. With the use of a combination of map and explanation many features are revealed more closely than with a single graphic presentation. Photographs and sketches have also been added for the same purpose. Considering the wide range of information in the *Atlas*, only the pertinent aspects are explained with the use of maps. For unity of organization the book is arranged in seven chapters.

After the publication of *India in Maps* in 1976 by the authors and S. P. Chatterjee, there remained a need for a similar book dealing with the entire subcontinent. The present volume is intended to fill that gap and in addition, it updates the Indian maps and explanations using the latest available data. The *Atlas* places primary emphasis on India. Bangladesh and Pakistan have received secondary treatment, while Sri Lanka, Nepal, and Bhutan are dealt with less detail. Though a few maps have been reproduced from *India in Maps* with the permission of the publisher and the copyright owners, most maps and almost all textual materials are either new or revised.

Ashok K. Dutt

M. Margaret Geib

Conversion Table

To change	To	Multiply by
acres	hectares	.404
centimeters (cm)	inches	.393
feet (ft)	meters	.304
gallons, U.S.	liters	3.785
hectares	acres	2.471
inches (in)	millimeters	25.400
inches	centimeters	2.540
kilograms (kg)	pounds	2.204
kilometers (km)	miles	.621
liters	gallons, U.S.	.264
meters (m)	feet	3.280
metric tonnes	tons	.984
millimeters (mm)	inches	.039

Acknowledgments

Many individuals have rendered valuable help in preparing this Atlas. Zeenat Hasan, Mohammad Haq, Karen Shauri, Randall Neugenbauer, Susmita Roy, Andrew Vargo, and Ramesh Vakamudi, graduate assistants of the departments of Geography and Urban Studies, The University of Akron, have not only helped in researching for the textual part of the book, but have prepared some of the initial drafts of maps and diagrams.

Assistance has been given in typing and retyping the manuscript by Mrs. Hilda Kendron, secretary of the Geography Department, and by Lisa Dipzinski, Jennifer Turner and Alexis Williams, her student assistants. Their help is gratefully acknowledged. Miss Linda Rogers and Barbara Hajek are especially thanked for the typesetting and Mrs. Deborah Phillips-King's assistance in design and layout of the book is gratefully acknowledged. Dr. Rinku Dutt and Mrs. Jhumku Dutt Kohtz are thanked for drawing the temple sketches for the book.

Dr. Allen G. Noble, Professor and Head of the Department of Geography, The University of Akron and Dr. Norton Ginsburg, Professor of Geography, University of Chicago are thanked for going through the entire manuscript and making valuable suggestions. Similar help rendered by Dr. Ramesh Dhussa of The University of Akron, Mr. Abdullah M. Khan of Kent State University, Dr. Mohan Shrestha of Bowling Green State University, Dr. Lester Panditratna, Vice-Chancellor, Paradenia University, Sri Lanka and Mr. Bimal K. Paul of Kent State University is also gratefully acknowledged.

Grateful acknowledgments are also expressed to Dr. Asok Mitra, Professor Emeritus, Jahawarlal Nehru University, Dr. Mushtak Rahaman, Department of Earth Sciences, Iowa State University, Mr. Charles M. Heyda of the U.S. State Department, and the Embassies of India and Pakistan in Washington D. C. for providing valuable statistical and graphic materials.

Ashok K. Dutt

M. Margaret Geib

List of Maps and Diagrams and Their Captions

(In most cases, the maps and diagrams have been identified by their numbers at the top-left corner; numbers have been put at other corners only when it was not possible to place them at the top-left.)

CHAPTER 4 PAKISTAN

CHAPTER 7 BHUTAN

1. SOUTH ASIA GENERAL

South Asia is a realm of one of the oldest civilizations in the world, where people from all races and religions have coexisted, displaying a multitude of cultures that have a parallel only in Europe. Negroids, Australoids, Mongoloids and Caucasoids have peopled the realm layer after layer, and the religious faiths of the Hindus, Buddhists, Jains, Christians, Jews, Zoroastrians, Moslems and Sikhs have ebbed and flowed throughout the centuries. Though the predominant linguistic families are Indo-European and Dravidian, Austric, Sino-Tibetan and Negroid families are also to be found in specific regions. The different parts of the realm developed over such a long time period, often in isolation, as to give rise to a kaleidoscope of varied and deeply rooted regional cultures.

The appellations South Asia and the Indian subcontinent are synonymous. The area was usually referred to as Britain's Indian Empire or Raj prior to 1947. Most geographers, such as Sir Dudley Stamp, called it the Indian subcontinent because of its physical separation from the rest of the Asian landmass by a nearly continuous barrier of mountain ranges. These mountains to the north have worked as a barrier to normal inter-realm human migration and cultural interchange and have, thus, enabled the subcontinent, through the ages, to develop its own civilization in relative isolation.

The six independent countries of the realm: India, Bangladesh, Pakistan, Nepal, Sri Lanka and Bhutan, bear the imprints of this great civilization, but all the countries in turn share regional cultures with centrally located India.

Maldives, another independent country, is also considered by some as the seventh nation of the subcontinent.

LOCATION

The first Asian Nobel laureate, Rabindranath Tagore, wrote in a poem almost half a century ago that *Bharatbarsha* (an ancient name for the subcontinent) has absorbed different racial and ethnic groups: Aryans, Dravidians, Mongoloids, Sakas, Huns, Afghans and Mughals. He also rightly pointed out that the doors of the Indian subcontinent were open to the West from where gifts, in the form of ideas and knowledge, were pouring in and that the Indians ought to welcome them in exchange for their own.

South Asia's location at almost the southern extremity of the Eurasian continent is a factor in its racial/ethnic mixture. Continental access is mainly from the west through passes such as the Khyber and the Bolan, difficult but not impossible to cross. Through these passes the Aryans and possibly the Dravidians came to inhabit the land 1500 and 3500 years ago, respectively. Others since, of different cultures and races, have come and, in the words of Tagore, 'they got absorbed in one Indian body polity'. Moreover, being a physiographic *cul-de-sac*, the subcontinent became the easternmost extension of Caucasoid racial spread. To the east and north there simply are no easy land routes through the mountains and jungles into the area of present-day China and Burma. The reverse is also true, so that only on the fringes of South Asia is there any Mongoloid influence in culture or race.

South Asia's location bordering the Indian Ocean opened it to maritime trade over 3000 years ago. It was the European colonists, starting with the landing of the Portuguese Vasco

1

da Gama in 1498, who took the greatest advantage of such maritime linkage. Eventually, sagacious British diplomacy was able to oust almost all European competition from the area and establish the Crown Colony of the Indian Empire. Britain, in its effort to maintain firm control over its colonies, spread throughout the world, turned the Indian Ocean into a *British Lake* by colonizing all the entrance points along its waters, including the important islands. The British occupation of South Asia was an important element in controlling this *British Lake* as a vital part of the greater *British Lifeline*. Starting in London, the *Lifeline* passed through Gibralter, Malta, the Suez Canal and Aden, then on to Bombay, Colombo, Singapore and Hong Kong, all owned and controlled by the British. Britain's East African colonies were reached by this trade route, as were Australia and New Zealand. Colombo, the capital of Sri Lanka, and Bombay, the western gateway to the subcontinent, were

indispensable mid-points along the *Lifeline*.

The immediate neighbors of South Asia are Burma, China, Afghanistan, Iran and the U.S.S.R. They have varied political systems and their motives toward South Asia are also different. The U.S.S.R. is separated from South Asia by an approximately 25-mile wide stretch of Afghan territory, which gave Afghanistan a buffer status in the 19th and the first half of the 20th centuries between the great Russian and British Indian empires. As a part of their general world outlook, the U.S.S.R. is definitely interested in subverting the subcontinent to communism. All communists in the subcontinent derive their inspiration from the U.S.S.R.

Burmese foreign policy is based on neutralism and Burma maintains a relative isolation from international power politics. However, the seeming treatment of Burmans of Indian origin as second-class citizens since the early 1960s, and the subsequent migration of some of them to India, have created dif-

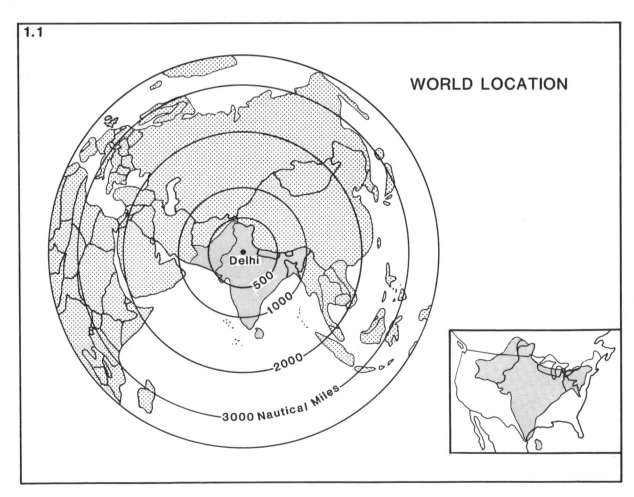

ficulties in Indo-Burmese relations. Burma's military dictatorship has counterparts in South Asia, too. Like Burma, both Bangladesh and Pakistan started as democracies immediately following independence, but soon became military dictatorships.

Both China and the U.S.S.R. are communist countries; the former is allied to the military dictatorship of Pakistan and the latter to the western-style democracy of India. China, in 1962, invaded India, and since then has occupied the northeastern tip of Kashmir, creating a serious problem between the two countries. The U.S.S.R., on the other hand, not only makes military alliances, such as with India, but considers all of South Asia as a realm that needs "deAmericanization." Befriending democratic India, therefore, suits the Soviet game plan quite well. India, basically unfriendly with both China and Pakistan, who are also inimical to the U.S.S.R., finds Russia to be a natural "ally" in many ways. The U.S. has had strong military ties with Pakistan and tries to use the country as an anti-Soviet base and staging ground for supporting Afghan anti-communist rebels. The U.S. maintains a general friendship with all other South Asian countries.

Iran, after the formation of a hard-line Islamic rule in 1979, expected its neighboring Moslem countries, such as Pakistan, to follow its lead. Pakistan, already an Islamic Republic, felt the pressure, but the tradition of liberalism of many Pakistanis has prevented the country from becoming totally hard-line with a Khomeini-type leader.

South Asia's triple communist neighbors (U.S.S.R., China, and Afghanistan) to the north and northwest make it a strategic realm in the world of power politics between the U.S.-led western nations and the U.S.S.R.-led communist world. The fact remains that no South Asian country has a communist government, and all of them basically practice free enterprise. In the strategy to establish world communism, the South and Southeast Asian realms are the most vulnerable because of their common borders with communist countries

and poverty-stricken economies. The Free World in general, and the western nations in particular, are deeply concerned with keeping the South Asian realm from falling under communism. It is an area where major confrontations between the two ideologies could come about in the future.

PHYSICAL FEATURES AND MOUNTAINS

The Indian subcontinent has many diverse physical characteristics. The three basic geomorphological divisions are: a) the Deccan Plateau, a portion of a great land mass from early geologic times (Pre-Cambrian), a part of ancient Gondwanaland; b) the Northern Mountain rim including the Himalayas dating back to a more recent geological era (Tertiary); and, c) the great Indo-Gangetic Plain from the latest geological periods (Pleistocene and Recent). All three not only give rise to different landforms, but produce varied human response to the use of land and resources in each division.

The Deccan Plateau consists of several mountain ranges (Aravalli, Vindhya, Satpura, Western Ghats, Eastern Ghats and the outlier of the Assam Range), mesa-like Deccan Lava country, and scarplands and rift valleys.

The Aravalli Range is the oldest mountain range in South Asia, resulting from mountain building activity during the Pre-Cambrian period. A prolonged period of erosion following the uplift has turned the Aravalli into a worn-down range, forming a virtual peneplain. Erosion left resistant quartzites which form bold ridges which trend NE-SW from Delhi to Gujarat. The Aravalli extends for a distance of 800 km or 497 miles. The highest point is Mt. Abu (1158 m or 3799 ft), on which is located a sacred Jain temple and a former western hill station used by the British.

The Vindhya Range, composed of massive sandstone and limestone beds, traverses nearly the entire width of peninsular India in an east-west direction for 1050 km (652 miles) with an average elevation of 300 m (984 ft). Along the Narmada and Son Valleys, the Vindhya forms scarplands.

South of the Vindhya Range and nearly parallel to it rises the Satpura Range which separates the Narmada and Tapti River valleys. The range extends from Ratanpur on the west to Amarkantak on the east, a distance of 900 km (599 miles). Several of its peaks rise above 1000 m (3281 ft) and few peaks of the range are below 500 m (1640 ft). The range is triangular in shape with the two sides parallel to the Narmada and Tapti rivers. The Satpura consists of a number of parallel ridges which enclose extensive flat-topped lava plateaus. The highest peak of the Satpura is Dhupgarh (1350 m or 4,429 ft). The eastern part is known as the Maikala Plateau. This area marks the site of an ancient shoreline and may have prevented lava flow in the Deccan Trap period. The Vindhya and Satpura Ranges are considered the dividing line between the Deccan Plateau and northern India and historically have acted as a north-south barrier for territorial and cultural extensions.

The Western Ghats (Sahyadri) run for 1600 km (994 miles) along the western border of the Deccan from the mouth of the Tapti River to Cape Comorin. The average elevation is 1200 m (3,937 ft). The Western Ghats are not truly mountains but are the faulted edge of an upraised plateau with scarp-like features to the west, steep-sided valleys, and narrow gorges and waterfalls and a youthful geological landscape. The Ghats (beginning in the north) consist of horizontal sheets of lava, and become granitoid to the south. The highest peak is Doda Betta (2,637 m or 8,651 ft). *The Eastern Ghats* border the peninsular plateaus on the east. Similar to the Western Ghats they are not true mountains but uplifted plateaus belonging to no single geological formation.

The Meghalaya (or Shillong) Plateau includes the Garo, Khasi, and Jaintia hills which run east-to-west. It is a disconnected portion of the ancient Deccan Plateau. The area between it and the main Plateau subsided, making it an outlier. The northern part is composed of ancient granites, gneisses, schists, and quartzites while the southern part is Sylhet limestone and other Tertiary strata. The highest peak is Shillong (1,961 m or 6,434 ft).

A large part of the northwestern Plateau is

1.3

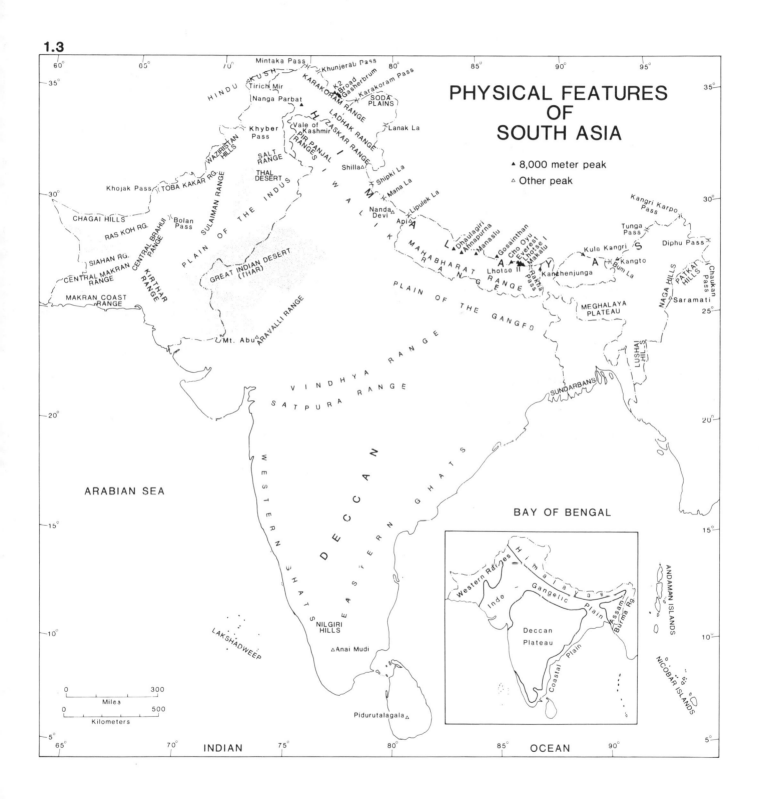

PHYSICAL FEATURES
OF
SOUTH ASIA

▲ 8,000 meter peak

△ Other peak

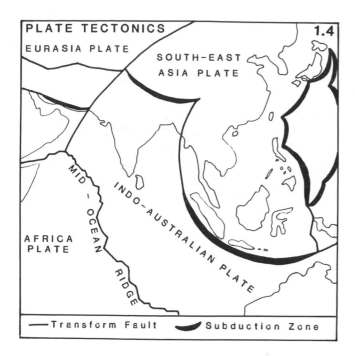

Longitudinally, the Himalayas are classified into 3 parallel zones which differ in orographical, hydrographical and vegetational features:

1) *Great Himalayas*: perpetual snow, average height 6,000 m or 19,685 ft (Everest, 8,848 m or 29,029 ft),
2) *Middle Himalaya*: related to and bifurcate the Great Himalayas, mean elevation 3,700 - 4,500 m or 12,139 - 14,764 ft, and
3) *Outer Himalaya* (or *Siwalik*) intervene between Middle Himalaya and the plains of the Indus and Ganges. Form a series of foothills with an average height of 900 -1,200 m (2,953 - 3,937 ft).

The Western Ranges are found in Pakistan and trend in a general NE to SW direction roughly parallel to each other. The Sulaiman and Kirthar Ranges are nearest to the Indus Valley, whereas the Toba Kakar Range is adjacent to Afghanistan and the Siahan penetrates into Iran. Between Sulaiman and Kirthar lies the famous Bolan Pass, northeast of which is situated Quetta, the capital of Baluchistan. The Vale of Peshawar is situated between the Sulaiman and Hindu Kush. The city of Peshawar, the capital of Pakistan's Northwest Frontier Province, guards the eastern entrance to the historic Khyber Pass.

The Assam-Burma Ranges consist of several hill systems such as Patkai, Naga and Lushai and they only occasionally exceed 2,100 m (6,890 ft) though their highest peak, Saramati, attains a height of 3,925 m (12,880 ft). East-west travel across the ranges is difficult despite the existence of several passes.

The Indo-Gangetic Plains lie between the Northern Mountains and the Plateaus. Spate and Learmonth point out that 'the great crescent of alluvium from the delta of the Indus to that of the Ganga represents the infilling of a foredeep warped down between the Gondwana block and the Himalayas.' The depth of alluvium exceeds 1,829 m (6,000 ft) at places and the Plain is characterized by an almost level, gently-sloping landform, in which the only changes are caused by the rivers and the features created by them, such as bluffs, natural levees, slopes of the broad interfluves, flood plains, ox-bow lakes, and islands (or *diars*) in the middle of the rivers. Travel across the Plain is easy.

covered by *Deccan Lava or Traps* which cover about 518,000 sq. km (200,000 sq. miles) with mesa-like landforms. These step-like formations have been caused by fluvial erosion of horizontal basaltic outpourings, which covered the area during the early Tertiary era.

The Northern Mountains may be divided into three distinct divisions: the central part with the lofty Himalayas with 20 of the highest peaks of the world, the Western Ranges bordering Afghanistan, and the Assam-Burma Ranges.

The Himalaya mountains rose from the floor of the sea, called Tethys, as a result of pressure from the Indian Plate moving northward and colliding with the Asian Plate. Most of the rocks date from the Upper Carboniferous to the Eocene. The Himalayas were formed by three distinct and widely separated phases of uplift: post-Eocene (found in Kashmir and western Tibet); the Miocene epoch which formed the middle Himalayas; and post-Pliocene giving rise to longitudinal Siwalik deposits.

The Himalayas are 2,400 km (1,491 miles) long and are not a continuous chain but are a series of parallel or converging ranges intersected by enormous valleys and extensive plateaus. Other ranges intersecting the Himalayas include the Hindu Kush, the Karakoram, the Kunlun, and the Tien Shan.

1.5

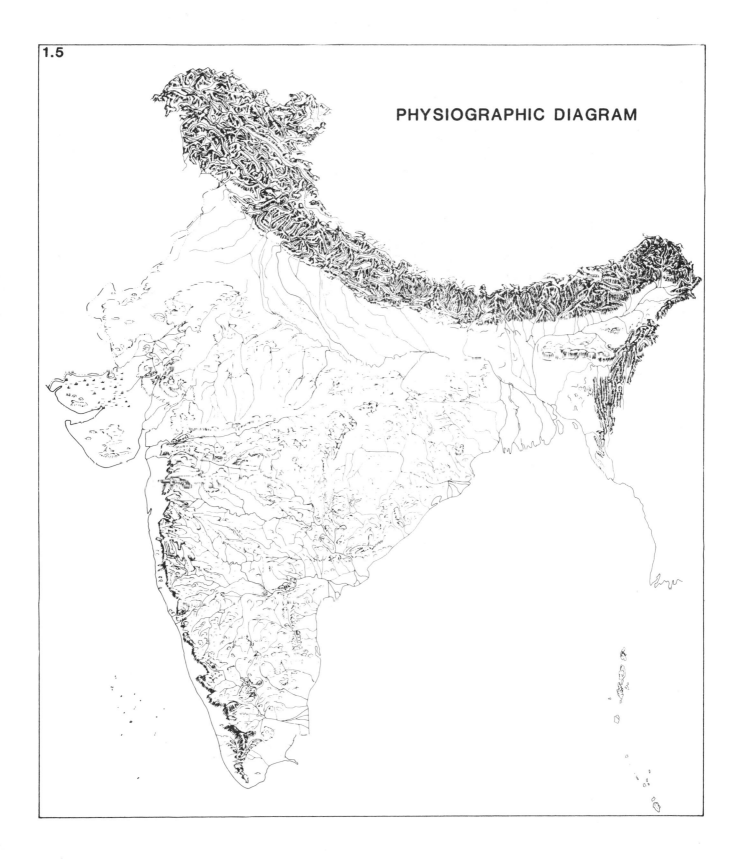

PHYSIOGRAPHIC DIAGRAM

RIVERS

The rivers of South Asia have sources either in the Himalayas or in the Deccan Plateau. The rivers of the Himalayas are new compared to those of the Plateau and have rapidly flowing streams that are still engaged in widespread downcutting, giving rise to V-shaped valleys in the mountainous part of their courses. The most important systems from the mountains are those of the Indus, Ganges and Brahmaputra. The Plateau rivers, on the other hand, are generally characterized by an older or more mature stage with wide valleys, flowing down gentle slopes. The Mahanadi, Godavari, Krishna and Cauvery are the principal east-flowing rivers of the Plateau and all of them at their coastal stage have given rise to wide and fertile agricultural plains and/or deltas. However, the small streams that originate from the Western Ghats and terminate in the Arabian Sea are still in a juvenile stage with swiftly flowing rapids because, before the beginning of the Tertiary Era, the Plateau east of the Western Ghats tilted eastwards causing a new scarp-like feature at the western side. The Narmada and the Tapti are west-flowing plateau rivers and they do not give rise to wide plains or deltas as they are on structural faults. Moreover, the rivers originating from the Himalayas are snow-fed and, therefore, perennial, whereas the Plateau rivers become a mere trickle during the dry season (April-June). During the rainy season (June-September), the rivers all over the subcontinent are susceptible to floods.

The Indus. The Indus River is one of the world's great rivers measuring 2800 km from its source to the sea. The major tributaries of the Indus are the Kabul and Swat Rivers(from the west) and the Jhelum, Chenab, Ravi, Beas, and Sutlej (from the east). These tributaries have a total length of 5600 km. The annual flow of the Indus is 209,697 million cubic meters, about double the flow of the Nile. The Indus has a drainage area of 1,178,440 square km., but only 453,250 sq. km. lie in the Himalayas. The Indus basin includes northwest India, Pakistan, eastern Afghanistan, and southern Tibet.

The Ganges. The five source rivers of the Ganges (Ganga), Bhagirathi, Mandakini, Alaknanda, Dhauli Ganga, and Pindar, are found in Uttar Pradesh and join at Devaprayag to form the Ganges which emerges on the plains at Rishikesh. The drainage area of this portion of the river is 97,902 sq. km. The Yamuna is the first major tributary which joins the Ganges from the right at Allahabad. The Yamuna has a drainage basin measuring 371, 871 sq. km. The Ghaghara River flows from the Himalayas, runs along the left bank of the Ganges, and joins at Chapra, Bihar. The Kosi and the Gandak Rivers join from the north and the Son River from the south. Beyond Rajmahal Trap, the Ganga River enters its vast delta (58,752 sq. km.).

The importance of the Ganga in Indian history and spiritual life has been immense. Nehru says in *The Discovery of India* 'The Story of the Ganga from her source to the sea, from old times to new, is the story of India's civilization and culture, of the rise and fall of empires, of great and proud cities, of the adventure of man and the quest of the mind which so occupied India's thinkers, of the richness and fulfillment of life as well as its denial and renunciation, of ups and downs, of growth and decay, of life and death'.

The Brahmaputra. The third great Himalayan river is the Brahmaputra. The Brahmaputra, which in Hindi means 'son of Brahma', travels 2900 km. through Tibet, India, and Bangladesh. It rises from a glacier in the northern Himalayas in Tibet where it is known by various names. The river flows eastward, parallel to the Himalaya for 1800 km. before turning south into India where initially it is called the Dihang. It becomes known as the Brahmaputra in the Assam Valley, where it turns westward then southwards into Bangladesh. Here it is joined by its most important tributary, the Tista. Further south,the Brahmaputra joins the Ganges at Goalondo. Rivers are considered sacred in India and many shrines can be found on their banks. Most of the rivers of South Asia,both large and small, were of historic importance. Their importance lies in South Asian future development. The potential for using the rivers for economic and agricultural growth is unlimited. Most rivers have been used for navigation and irrigation and some are being utilized for hydroelectric generation, a use of great potential. Despite the great economic potential of South Asia's rivers, their place in the spiritual life of the Hindus can never be overshadowed.

1.6

RIVERS OF SOUTH ASIA
AND MARITIME FEATURES

CLIMATE

A monsoon type of climate, characterized by wet summers and dry winters, generally prevails over all South Asia. The word monsoon originates from the Arabic "mousim" which means season. A monsoon climate really is a seasonal climate and to understand the reasons for this seasonality one has to take into consideration certain factors occurring beyond the subcontinent. During the summer when the sun is directly over the subcontinent, the central Asian land mass warms, creating a low-pressure center, while the Indian Ocean water-mass remains relatively cool, generating a high-pressure center. Such differential heating and cooling causes the moisture-laden air from the ocean to move toward the Indian subcontinent; from high-pressure to low. As all winds are deflected toward the right in the northern hemisphere, these winds become the southwest (SW) monsoon. During the winter, pressure systems reverse because the polar cold air mass moves southward and Tibet and the areas north of it become a high-pressure center, whereas the Indian Ocean, over which the sun's rays now fall directly, turns into a low-

pressure center. Thus, the wind directions are reversed, becoming the northeast (NE) Trade Winds of the winter.

There is another factor, i.e., the situation of the upper level jet streams that direct the onset or disappearance of the summer monsoon in the subcontinent. When a high, latitudinal mountain system like the Himalayas lies in its path, the westerly jet stream divides into two branches (south and north of the Himalayas). These two branches remain prevalent from November through April. The disappearance of the jet stream south of the Himalayas in April-May results in the sudden appearance of monsoon rains and, therefore, it is often called the "break" of the monsoon. Similarly, the reappearance of the jet stream south of the Himalayas in November causes the sudden "retreat" of monsoon rains from the subcontinent. During the months of July and August there is an easterly jet stream running over the middle of the peninsula.

The SW winds, during the summer, produce most of the rainfall over all the subcontinent. These winds, however, miss the Rajasthan or Thar Desert and western Pakistan because they are deflected by the earth's rotation toward the northeast and, therefore, the northwestern part of the subcontinent remains

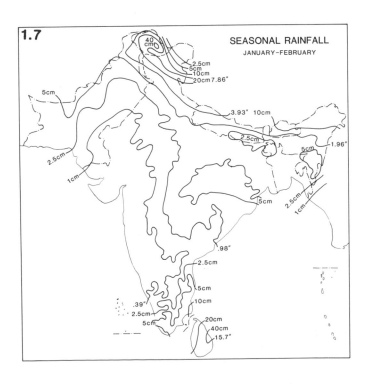

1.7 SEASONAL RAINFALL JANUARY–FEBRUARY

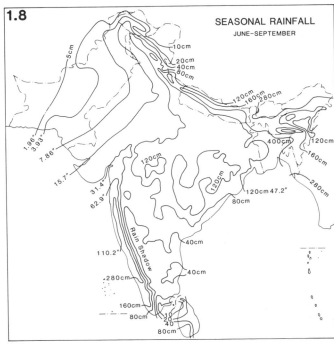

1.8 SEASONAL RAINFALL JUNE–SEPTEMBER

relatively dry. Thus, there are only 20 rainy days in Kachchh, whereas some places of the Rajasthan (Thar) Desert have fewer than 5 rainy days. Jaisalmer, in the heart of the desert, receives only 178 mm (7") annual rainfall, and Karachi, at the southern tip of the desert receives only 195 mm (7.7") annually.

The moisture-laden winds from the Arabian Sea cause heavy rainfall on the windward side

(west) of the Western Ghats, whereas the bulk of the Plateau receives minimal rainfall as it is located in a "rain shadow." Bombay, on the windward side of the Western Ghats, receives an annual rainfall of 1,805 mm (71"), whereas Pune, less than 100 miles from Bombay and on the leeward side of the Ghats, receives only 661 mm (26") annually. Similarly, the southern Assam Hill area and the southern Himalayas

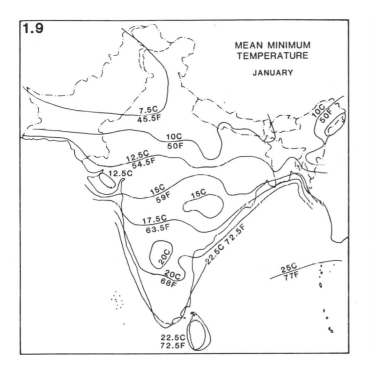

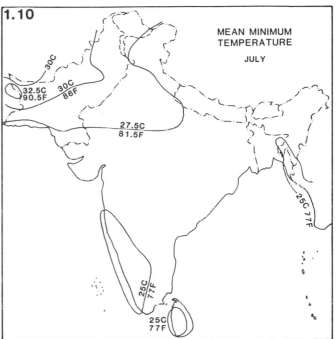

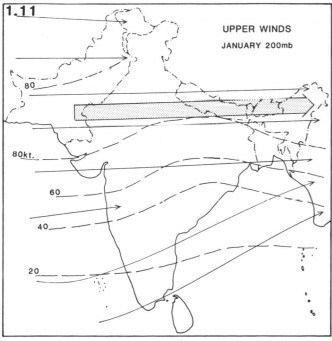

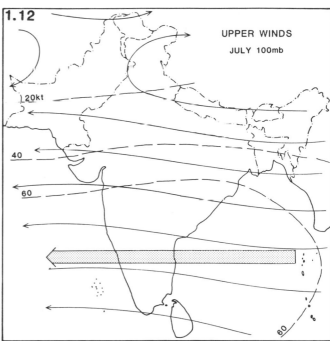

receive heavy rainfall. The southern slopes of the Assam Hills, lying on the windward side of the Bay of Bengal, receive heavy rainfall. Cherrapunji receives as much as 10,869 mm (427") and has 160 rainy days annually, the highest annual rainfall in the world. On the contrary, Shillong, on the northern slopes and leeward side of the Assam Hills, receives only 2,425 mm (95").

As one moves from the Ganges Delta to the Punjab Plains, rains diminish gradually as the winds start to lose the moisture carried from the Bay of Bengal and the Arabian Sea. Dhaka and Calcutta, in the Ganges delta, receive 1,879 mm (74") and 1,625 mm (64"), respectively; Patna, 400 miles west of Calcutta, receives 1,148 mm (45"), while Amritsar and Lahore in

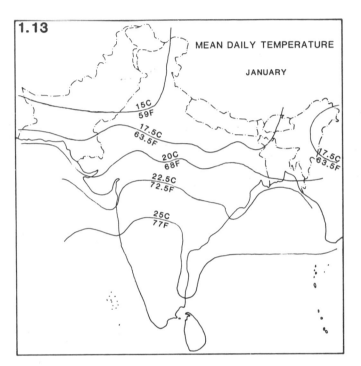

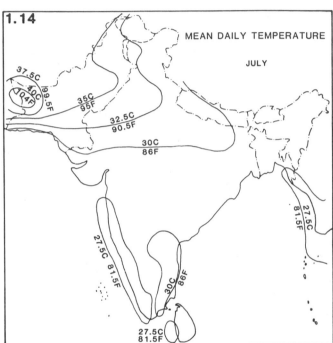

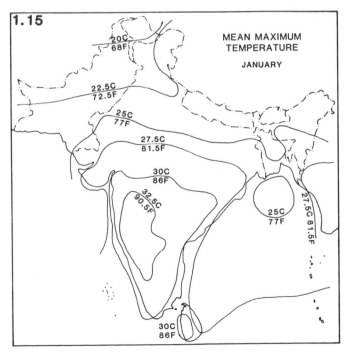

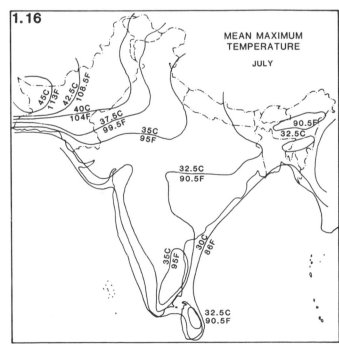

Punjab only 563 mm (22") and 482 mm (19"), respectively.

During the winter, the NE Trade Winds bring rain to the southeastern coast of the peninsula and to northern Sri Lanka. The city of Madras receives 1,316 mm (51") of rain, most of it coming October-December. The northwestern part of the subcontinent is affected by the passage of low-pressure systems of Mediterranean origin, which cause rainfall in the months of December through April. Srinagar, 658 mm (25"), and Quetta, 228 mm (9") receive most of their precipitation during this time. It is dur-ing these months that the bulk of the snow ac-cumulation takes place in the Himalayas.

Sri Lanka is characterized by a Wet Zone in the southwestern segment of the country, where the annual rainfall is above 2,500 mm. The remaining parts of the country lie in the Dry and Intermediate Zones. Most of the rain-fall in the Wet Zone falls during the southwest monsoon because the zone is on the windward side of the mountains. The intermonsoonal rainfall (October-November) is also sizeable in the Wet Zone. The eastern and northern parts of the island lie in a rain shadow during the

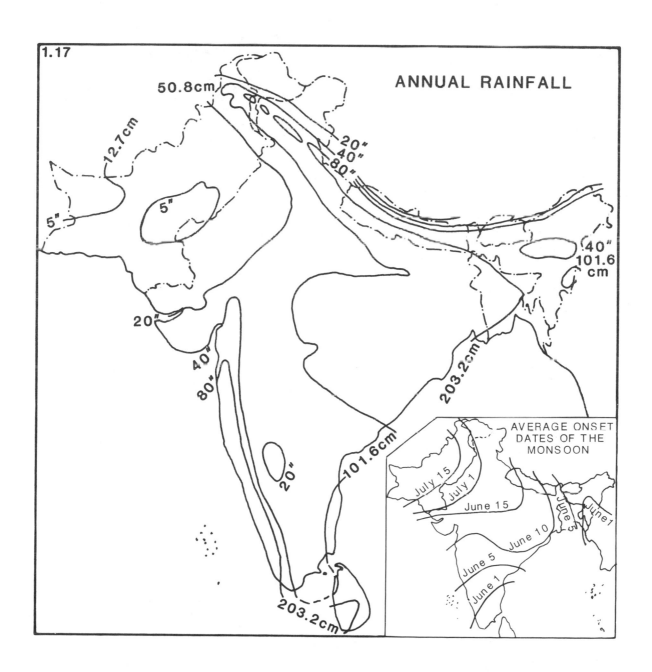

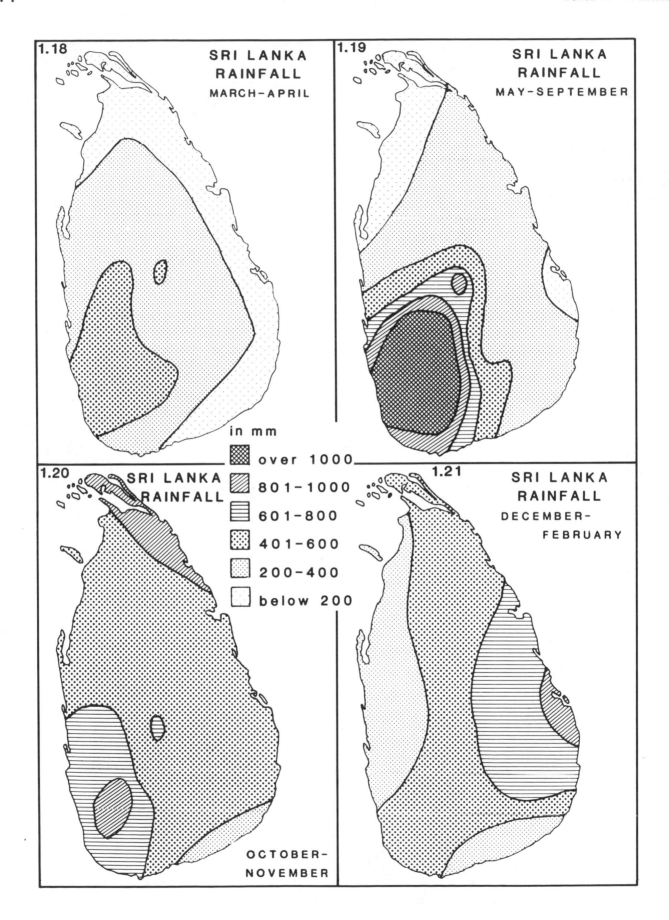

1.18 SRI LANKA RAINFALL MARCH–APRIL

1.19 SRI LANKA RAINFALL MAY–SEPTEMBER

in mm
- over 1000
- 801–1000
- 601–800
- 401–600
- 200–400
- below 200

1.20 SRI LANKA RAINFALL OCTOBER–NOVEMBER

1.21 SRI LANKA RAINFALL DECEMBER–FEBRUARY

southwest monsoon but are to the windward side during the northeast monsoon (December through February), at which time the east receives its greatest rainfall. The north receives its greatest in the intermonsoonal period of October-November.

The monsoon is very important to South Asian life because agriculture is dependent on its arrival. The advent of the summer monsoon is eagerly awaited by the farmers because that is when they sow their rice, maize and other crops. As the amount, timing and duration of the monsoon is highly unpredictable in large parts of the subcontinent, the farmers are quite uncertain of their future. If the monsoon is highly irregular, it may cause drought or flood, and either is ruinous to crops. Such extreme conditions often caused famines, resulting in millions of deaths. With the establishment of better communication networks, especially railroads, grain can be moved into deficit regions from different parts of the country or from abroad, thus averting famine. It is no wonder that the people of this subcontinent have become fatalists. The monsoon rains, which give life as well as take it, are uncontrollable and, therefore, it is believed that fate alone ultimately decides the well-being of the people.

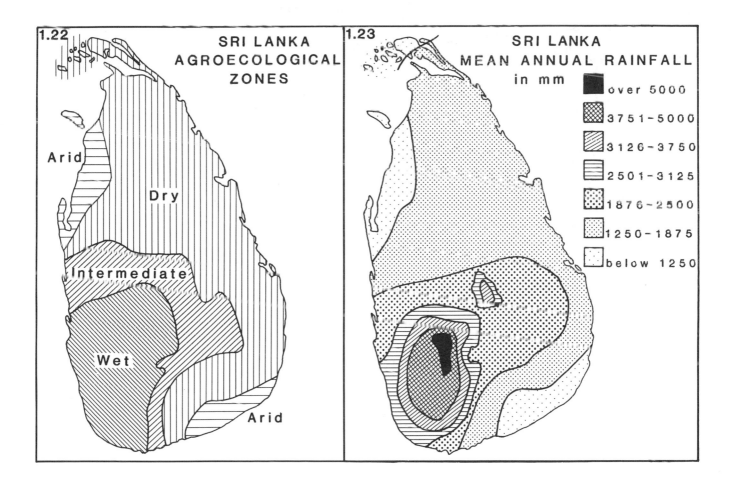

HISTORICAL SETTING

The Indian subcontinent is full of imprints cast by diverse racial, religious, and cultural groups who have either immigrated to the land or have come into contact with it. The history of the subcontinent is generally divided into five periods: Indus Valley (3000 B.C. to 1500 B.C.); Aryan or Hindu (1500 B.C. to A.D. 1206); Moslem (1206 to 1757); British (1757 to 1947); and post-colonial (1947 to the present). During these periods the traces left by the various groups have produced unique characteristics on the landscape and in the social life of the Indian subcontinent.

Probably the first group of people to inhabit the country were a group of aborigines racially akin to the Negritos and Australoids. It is difficult to trace their origin. They now reside in the hills and plateaus where they were driven by the advancing Dravidians and Aryans. The Dravidians first occupied the fertile northwestern plains, followed by the Aryans. The aborigines have their primitive way of life and their religion based on animism.

The Indus Valley Period. The origins of the Dravidians are as obscure as those of the aborigines. Numerous historians and archeologists regard them as being racially similar to the Mediterranean peoples. The Dravidians are basically of dark complexion and short stature. They developed an urban-based culture which flourished in the Indus Valley crescent between 3000 B.C. and 1500 B.C. The prime force behind the growth of their cities was a surplus of agricultural products. Their capital cities, Mohenjodaro and Harappa, the sites of which are situated in present day Pakistan, were also based on the prosperous agricultural economy in the Indus Valley. It has been determined that, at that time, the climate of the Indus Valley was more moist. In addition, the farmers utilized irrigation to increase production. Mohenjodaro and Harappa conducted trade by sea with Mesopotamia. No other ancient civilization, until the Romans almost 2,000 years later, enjoyed the luxuries of civic facilities of the Indus Valley civilization. Mohenjodaro, situated on the Indus proper, and Harappa, on the Ravi, a tributary of the Indus, were established as planned cities as early as 3000 B.C. Though there were several other cities along the Indus Valley crescent, those two were the largest and the most developed. Both Mohenjodaro and Harappa had rectangular road systems and large elevated areas (citadels). Mohenjodaro was covered by sedimentary deposits of the Indus River and the first excavations began in 1921. The excavations revealed the following features of the city: i) a carefully constructed citadel, ii) an open-air bath, *hammam*, iii) numerous well-built, spacious houses of burnt brick, iv) street crossings at right angles forming blocks 400 feet by 200 feet (111 m by 122 m), v) drainage and sewage systems for the streets with connections from inside the houses, vi) baths and toilets inside houses, vii) a street garbage system, and viii) a schematic plan of the city consisting of five main streets, three of which were north-south and two east-west. The demise of the Dravidian civilization was possibly the result of the Aryan incursions which began as gradual migrations into the Indus Valley and then developed into full-scale invasions.

The above view of the origin and characteristics of the Indus Valley civilization is held by most western and Indian archeologists and historians, but some scientists of the Soviet Institute of Ethnography have raised alternative views during their conference in October, 1985. They suggest that the high-level Indus Valley civilization existed 5000 years before the arrival of the Aryans, and that the demise of the civilization was the result of earthquakes that changed the course of rivers creating a dry environment.

After the establishment of Aryan supremacy over the Indus Valley and north India, a large number of Dravidians were pushed into south India where they developed a remarkably distinct Dravidian civilization with their own languages, which are fundamentally different from Aryan Sanskrit-based tongues. The Dravidians, at different stages, accepted various religions (Hinduism, Buddhism and Jainism) that diffused from the Aryan north. Eventually, most adopted Hinduism.

The Hindu Aryan Period. The Aryans of Indo-European Caucasoid stock were fair-skinned, tall, and had sharp facial features. They originally inhabited the steppe lands of central Asia and practiced nomadic pastoralism. Formidable warriors who utilized horses and chariots, the Aryans had no difficulty in driving out the comparatively peaceful Dravidians. The Aryan conquerers felt no affinity for urban living. The Dravidian cities were abandoned after 1500 B.C. The Aryans had brought with them their religion, later known as Hinduism, which was based on the sacred *Vedas*, which not only set the basis of the Hindu religion, but affected the thought processes and the way of life of the South Asians. Sun worship is very prominent in the Veda. As the discovery of fire was a very significant step in the history of human civilization, the *Rig Veda*, one of the first four Vedas, considers *Agni* (fire) to be a god; 'priest of gods and god of priests.' Indra, the hero and leader of the Vedic Aryans and responsible for the victories and conquest of the Indus Valley, is regarded as the most prominent divinity in the *Rig Veda*. Indra made a primeval sacrifice and destroyed the demon Vritra, who had enclosed the rains and sun, and thus released the essentials of life. This is how the universe originated according to the Veda. The functionally based four-caste system governed the social life of the Vedic Aryans; *Brahmins* (priests), *Kshatriyas* (nobility and warriors), *Vaishyas* (traders and farmers), and *Sudras* (serfs and hard manual laborers).

While a segment of the Dravidian population was driven by the Aryans to the regions of the south and farther to the east, a sizeable number of the conquered people were enslaved and eventually absorbed into the Hindu society as serfs and slaves. They were relegated to the lowest rank of the social castes, the Sudras.

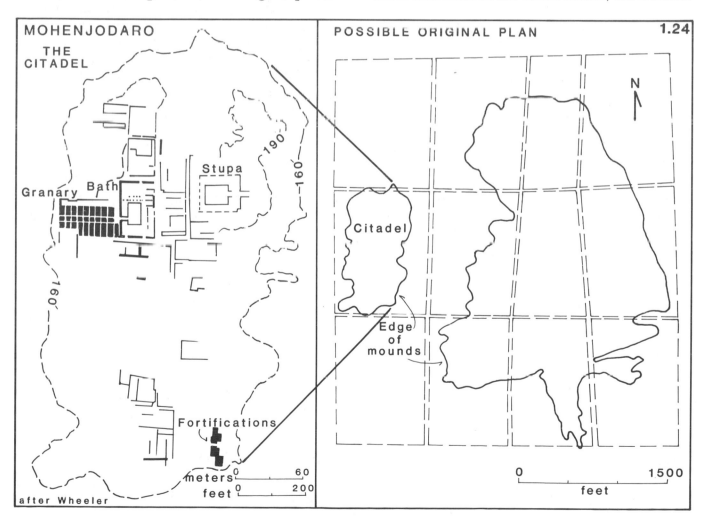

In south India, where Brahmins from the north intruded into the society at a much later stage of history, the Dravidians in general maintained much better social status than that of the north.

Alexander the Great, of Greece, in his pursuit of a Eurasian empire, invaded India in 327 B.C. and occupied the Punjab area after subjugating Afghanistan and Persia. The Greek campaign lasted only for two years. For a while after the campaign, Greek troops occupied the northwestern part of the subcontinent and a number of Greek settlers were eventually assimilated into the local population. The movement of the Greek army from Europe to India opened the doors for further trading and exchange of ideas.

The Aryans organized into a national state in 322 B.C., and founded the historic Maurya Dynasty. The greatest of the Maurya kings, Asoka (269-232 B.C.), who eventually adopted Buddhism as the state religion, succeeded in unifying almost all of India under his leadership. Asoka's, and his father Bindusara's kingdoms were also significant for the fact that they were the first to bridge the political gap between north and south India. After witnessing the horrors of the brutal war in Kalinga (Orissa), Asoka became a Buddhist and an exponent of non-violent philosophy. Royal hunting was given up; he himself became a vegetarian, and hospitals were established. His messages: obedience to parents, respect for teachers and Buddhist monks, toleration toward all religions, charity to the needy, the leading of a truthful life, living in moderation, and warnings against jealousy, cruelty and laziness, were inscribed on pillars, rocks and cliffs. Huge sandstone pillars, known as Asoka *stambha*, containing his Buddhist messages, were erected throughout the country. Some of these pillars contained numerals, known to the present-day world as Arabic numerals, that became the basis of advanced mathematics during the Gupta period. He also sent missions to spread Buddhism to Sri Lanka and other Asian countries. Beatrice Lamb rightly states that 'if there is an Indian ruler whom most modern Indians can agree to revere, it is Asoka.' After India's independence in 1947,

the country officially adopted Asoka's lion-seal. Beginning with Chandragupta, grandfather of Asoka and the first emperor of the Indian subcontinent with sizeable territory, Pataliputra (modern Patna) became the capital. Situated on the right bank of the Ganges in the Middle Ganges (or Eastern) Plain, Pataliputra was planned by Chandragupta's minister, Chanakya, author of *Arthasashtra*, which is recognized as the first treatise on economics in the world. The city remained the capital of the dominating kingdoms of the subcontinent intermittently through the 6th century. Pataliputra presented spatial characteristics typical of an Aryan Hindu capital city. It had an oblong shape, a massive timber wall which had 64 gates and 570 towers, surrounded by a moat, the king's palace with gardens and a lake at the center, with the four castes settled around the center, virtually separated from each other.

Soon after Asoka's death, political conditions in the country became chaotic and the central administration disintegrated. The disorganization was further aggravated by additional invasions by new Aryan migrants (Sakas, Parthians, and Kushans) from the northwest. It was not until the Imperial Gupta Age (A.D. 320-550) that all of north India was again united under one centralized administration. During the Gupta Period, which is also known as the Golden Age, the arts, sciences, mathematics, and literature flourished. The so-called Arabic numerals, which are used widely throughout the world, were further developed during this period and transmitted to the West by the Arabs. Aryabhata was the first to solve some basic problems of astronomy in A.D. 499 as he calculated pi to 3.1416 and the length of the solar year as 365.358605 days. To him, the earth was round and it rotated on an axis, and the lunar eclipse was caused by the shadow of the earth falling on the moon. Kalidasa, called the Indian Shakespeare, wrote outstanding verses in Sanskrit. The code of administrative and popular ethics developed by Yajnavalkya in the early Gupta period and the *Lawbook of Manu* in the first century B.C. gave an integrated philosophy of life and helped establish a disciplined social organization. Fa-Hsien, a

HINDU PERIOD

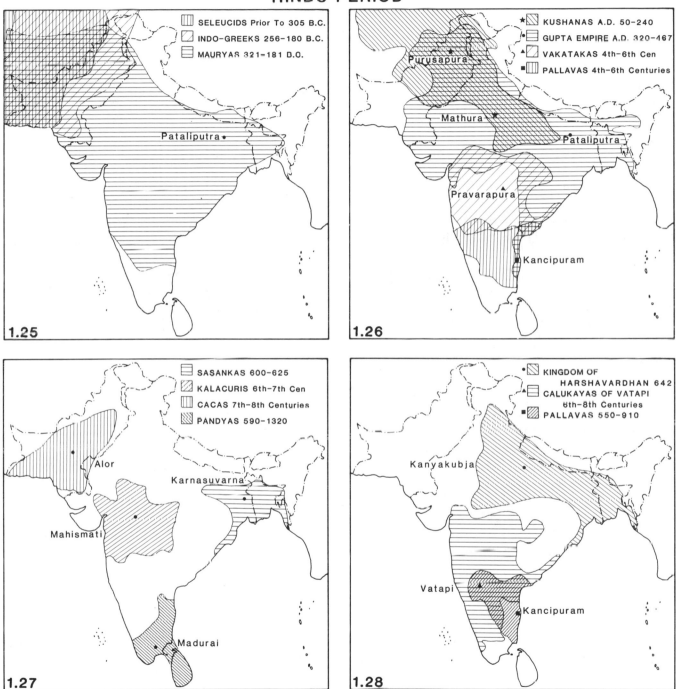

1.25

SELEUCIDS Prior To 305 B.C.
INDO-GREEKS 256-180 B.C.
MAURYAS 321-181 D.O.

Pataliputra •

1.26

★ KUSHANAS A.D. 50-240
• GUPTA EMPIRE A.D. 320-467
▲ VAKATAKAS 4th-6th Cen
PALLAVAS 4th-6th Centuries

Puruṣapura ★
Mathura ★
Pataliputra ▲
Pravarapura ▲
Kancipuram ■

1.27

SASANKAS 600-625
KALACURIS 6th-7th Cen
CACAS 7th-8th Centuries
PANDYAS 590-1320

Alor •
Karnasuvarna •
Mahismati •
Madurai •

1.28

• KINGDOM OF
  HARSHAVARDHAN 642
▲ CALUKAYAS OF VATAPI
  6th-8th Centuries
■ PALLAVAS 550-910

Kanyakubja •
Vatapi ▲
Kancipuram ■

The boundaries on the maps on pages 19,
21 and 23 are mainly based on Schwartzberg (1978)

Chinese Buddhist visitor to India during the Gupta period, found that a) the Gupta kings were Hindus, but Buddhism flourished in the country, b) people enjoyed freedom and lived in peace and prosperity, c) travel was safe and d) capital punishment was rare. The Guptas operated from their capital in Pataliputra, but soon after their fall, the center of activity moved westwards to Kanuaj (Kannakubja), Mathura and the Delhi-Agra region.

In the second half of the seventh century India again faced political disintegration. Not being organized into one cohesive central system, the country was divided into principalities and small states. The four maps that indicate the extent of the kindgoms from the sixth through the early fourteenth century A.D. show only a few that are representative of the time. Harshavardhan's domain in north India is the only exception, where in the 7th century, he ruled a considerable territory. There was constant warring among and between all these small kingdoms. Such a condition continued until the Moslem occupation of India in 1206.

The Moslem Period. The Moslem invasion of India dates back to A.D. 711 when Sind (presently in Pakistan) was conquered by the Arabs. Actual occupation of the territory in general, however, began in 1206 when Qutbuddin established himself as Sultan of Delhi. Thus began the group of dynasties known as the Turko-Afghan Sultans. The principal reason for the success of the Moslem occupation of India was the religious fervor of Islam which inspired its followers to conquer non-Islamic lands. A contributing cause, in addition, was the division and enmity among the indigenous Indian kingdoms in the eleventh and twelfth centuries. The Sultans as a rule controlled only north India, but Sultan Mohammad Tughluq (1325-51) succeeded in expanding his empire southward all the way to include present-day Kerala. Soon after his death, however, his huge kingdom disintegrated. The Islamic Mughals displaced the weak Sultans in 1526. Babur, the first Mughal, operated from the Delhi-Agra Core. The greatest of the Mughals was Akbar (1556-1605) who attempted in vain to reconcile the differences between the Hindus and the Moslems. Akbar expanded

his kingdom southward, a trend which was continued both by his grandson, Shah Jahan (who had the Taj Mahal built), and his great-grandson, Aurangzeb (1659-1707), who was a religious fanatic and an arch enemy of all followers of non-Islamic religions. As during the times of Asoka and Mohammad Tughluq, the greater part of India was again united under one political rule. Over-expansion, high taxation imposed on Hindus, and the parochial policies pursued by Shah Jahan and Aurangzeb eventually resulted in the demise of the Mughal Empire.

Under Moslem rule, migrants from Afghanistan, Persia and Central Asia introduced their culture, literature, architecture and military practices to the subcontinent. India's trade link with the Middle East was further crystallized. The input of polite Persian culture enriched the already high level of native civilization. European traders first visited India during the Moslem period, with the landing of the Portuguese explorer Vasco da Gama in 1498. The Moslem rulers, not too enthusiastically, let Portuguese, Dutch, French, Danish and British traders establish maritime outposts in different parts of the subcontinent. Goa, Chittagong, Colombo, Madras, Bombay and Calcutta were early European outposts.

During the five hundred and fifty years of Moslem rule, a new element in the form of Islam was introduced into Indian society. Before Moslem rule, both Hinduism and Buddhism prevailed in India, but the fanatic Moslem rulers not only tried to destroy all visible symbols of other religions, but public display of non-Islamic religions was forbidden. High public offices were offered to Moslems only and Hindus paid higher taxes (*Zijya*) compared to the Moslems. With the destruction of its monasteries, the Buddhist religion, which was largely dependent upon monastery-based services, virtually disappeared from India. Hinduism survived because of its tenacious popular beliefs, non-institutionalized form and adaptability for worship in homes. About one-fourth of the population of the subcontinent was converted to Islam both by direct and indirect force. However, the continued persecution of the Hindu religion was much more

LATE HINDU AND EARLY MOSLEM PERIODS

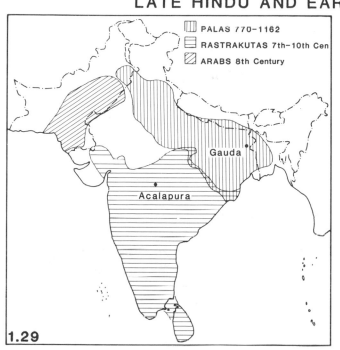

Legend for 1.29:
- ▨ PALAS 770-1162
- ▤ RASTRAKUTAS 7th-10th Cen
- ▧ ARABS 8th Century

Gauda

Acalapura

1.29

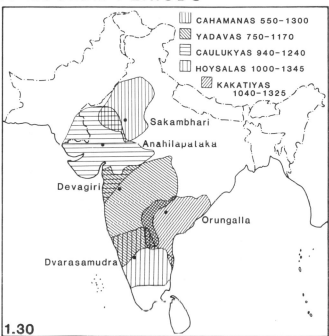

Legend for 1.30:
- ▥ CAHAMANAS 550-1300
- ▨ YADAVAS 750-1170
- ▤ CAULUKYAS 940-1240
- ▦ HOYSALAS 1000-1345
- ▧ KAKATIYAS 1040-1325

Sakambhari

Anahilapataka

Devagiri

Orungalla

Dvarasamudra

1.30

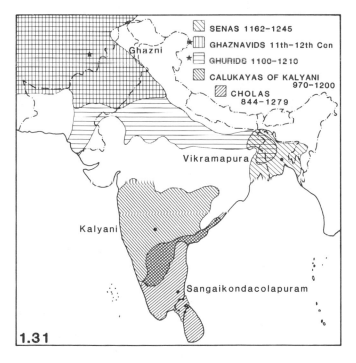

Legend for 1.31:
- ▧ SENAS 1162-1245
- ★▦ GHAZNAVIDS 11th-12th Cen
- ★▤ GHURIDS 1100-1210
- ▤ CALUKAYAS OF KALYANI 970-1200
- ▨ CHOLAS 844-1279

Ghazni

Vikramapura

Kalyani

Sangaikondacolapuram

1.31

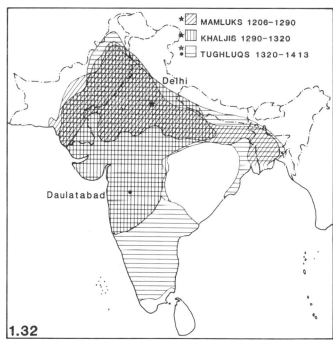

Legend for 1.32:
- ★▨ MAMLUKS 1206-1290
- ★▦ KHALJIS 1290-1320
- •▢ TUGHLUQS 1320-1413

Delhi

Daulatabad

1.32

severe in north India than in the south. This is perhaps a reason, according to many India experts why social tensions are more intense in north India than in the south. In Sri Lanka, however, no Moslem king ever ruled the country, but a substantial proportion of the coastal population there was converted to Islam, a result of sea-borne trade conducted by Moslems from the Middle East and the west coast of India. Most Indian converts to Islam, then, resulted from 'forced and voluntary diffusion' while in Sri Lanka only the 'voluntary diffusion' was in operation.

The South Indian Scene. While empire building and dynastic changes were occurring in north India during the Aryan and Moslem periods, the south was also experiencing similar developments. Of its many regional kingdoms Pallavas (A.D. 30-897), Pandyas (A.D. 590-920), Cholas (590-920) and Vijaynagar (1398-1525) were particularly eminent.

The main centers of political control were historically located in north India (mainly the Ganges-Yamuna plains). No south Indian kingdom, except the Marathas for a brief period in the eighteenth century, ever reigned over north India. South India kingdoms compensated for this by pursuing ocean-based trading with Southeast Asia, and, at times, by politically subjugating Sri Lanka and Burma.

The Indo-Gangetic Plain always had resources (both human and agricultural) superior to those of south India and thus was able to maintain powerful core areas which succeeded in effectively controlling parts or all of the southern region. Nevertheless, at times when those northern core areas became weak through mismanagement, disorganization, and lack of vision on the part of the kings and their counselors, the peripheral regions (south India was always on the periphery in relation to the north Indian core) declared their independence or strengthened their independent status.

The Indian subcontinent encompasses a huge amount of land. The southern region is hilly and mountainous and was not conducive to centralized administration. Therefore it was not always possible for the northern kingdoms to maintain easy control over the entire coun-

try, particularly given the cumbersome, slow-moving modes of transport: horse carts, foot travel, and primitive sailing craft. The very nature of Indian geography caused occasionally powerful and united national kingdoms to alternate with small, but numerous, independent regional kingdoms during the Aryan and Moslem periods.

The British Period. When the British established their occupation of India in 1757 by defeating one of the regional kings in Bengal, the region was already seriously fragmented with incessant interregional conflicts. The British took advantage of the internal divisions and subdued most of the regional native kingdoms by playing one against the other in an admirable display of a traditional British diplomacy: *Divide and Rule.* By 1857, the indigenous population understood the British policy and joined together to fight India's first war of independence (known through the writings of British historians as the Sepoy Mutiny) which was ruthlessly crushed by the occupation forces. From 1857 to 1947 British supremacy remained virtually unchallenged. The two-century old British system affected the region in many ways. First, the British introduced English into the administration and education system. Second, an extensive railroad network was established. Third, a westernized bureaucratic civil service was introduced, which even now perpetuates a self-generating, corrupt administrative apparatus. Fourth, a new group of native elites was created, trained in the westernized colonial system of education. They were unable to adapt to a developmental directed economy and nationalistic oriented social needs after independence. Finally, the British succeeded in uniting the entire area under its own colonial rule. One basic result of two hundred years of colonial rule in India was the creation of a mass psychology of slavery, which takes generations to overcome. Moreover, whatever the British did for development and education was essentially meant for efficiency and perpetuation of the colonial administration. For example, a) the railroads were built to effectuate efficient movement of commodities to and from the ports, which imported finished goods from and exported raw materials to Britain, b) the same railroads were used for speedy troop movement whenever necessary and c) the English education system produced junior-level support personnel (clerks, drivers, machine-operators, lawyers, civil servants, engineers and doctors) to man the colonial system, while highest level positions were occupied by the British. No wonder Mahatma Gandhi designated the British-created schools and colleges as 'Slave Producing Machines.' One-third of the area was allowed to be governed by *Native States*, whose suzerainty, however, remained in British control. These Native States depended on the British for defense, foreign relations, and modern means of communication: railroads, post and telegraph, and so forth.

MOSLEM PERIOD

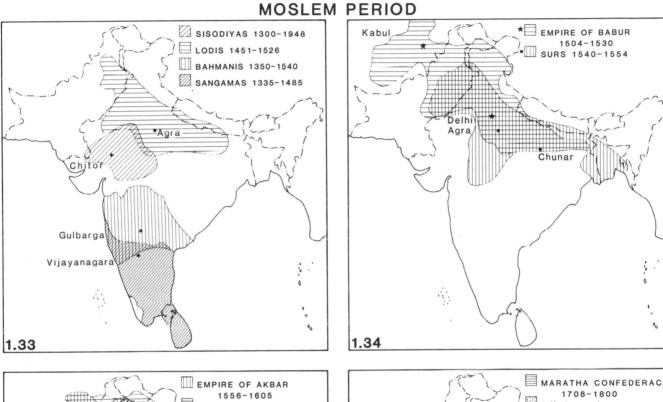

1.33

SISODIYAS 1300-1948
LODIS 1451-1526
BAHMANIS 1350-1540
SANGAMAS 1335-1485

Agra
Chitor
Gulbarga
Vijayanagara

1.34

★ EMPIRE OF BABUR 1504-1530
SURS 1540-1554

Kabul
Delhi
Agra
Chunar

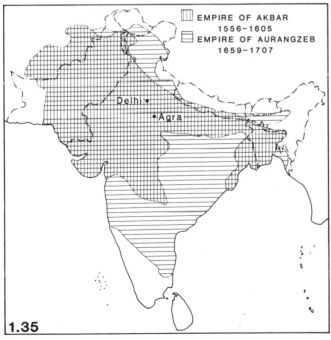

1.35

EMPIRE OF AKBAR 1556-1605
EMPIRE OF AURANGZEB 1659-1707

Delhi
Agra

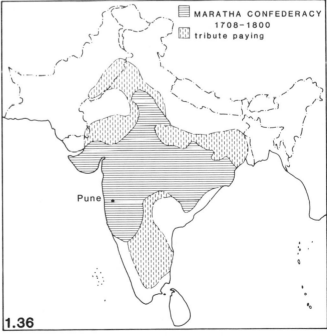

1.36

MARATHA CONFEDERACY 1708-1800
tribute paying

Pune

The Post-Colonial Period. The British were obliged to terminate their occupation of the subcontinent in 1947. The movie "Gandhi" directed by Richard Attenborough, an English liberal, and many other scholars interpreted this termination to be the result of the moral force exerted by Mahatma Gandhi's non-violence movement. In actuality, the growing violence and mass agitation for freedom during 1945-47, convinced the British that unless they withdrew in a peaceful transfer of power, their future economic interests would be jeopardized. They had already sensed that the Indians would soon force India's independence. Therefore, the British made a deal for the transfer of power with the native liberals, the Indian National Congress and the Moslem League.

The Native States (numbering 562) which had never joined India's struggles for independence in the twentieth century, were reluctant to join the Indian Union. Eventually those states were incorporated into the Indian Union either voluntarily or, in some instances, by force. The entire country was then reorganized into states, the basis of which was primarily linguistic. The boundaries of the older Native States, in most cases, were obliterated to facilitate the formation of new administrative boundaries.

East and West Pakistan, also independent in 1947, were separated by about 1200 miles, with India between its two wings: Bengali-culture-based East Pakistan and multi-cultural West Pakistan. After a bitter civil war, East Pakistan seceded from the West in 1971 and proclaimed itself independent Bangladesh. Like India, both Pakistan and Bangladesh have done away with their native states, integrating their territories with provincial and district boundaries. Sri Lanka, independent in 1948, has not fought any wars with its neighbors, while India fought three wars with Pakistan: one in 1947-48 over the Kashmir issue, another over border disputes in 1965 and the third one over the independence of Bangladesh in 1971. Another war was fought with the Peoples Republic of China in 1962, from which time the latter maintains control over sizeable portions of Indian territory in Kashmir. At the present time the core country of India holds the central power in the subcontinent, while Pakistan, Bangladesh, Sri Lanka, Nepal and Bhutan are relatively diminutive powers located at the periphery.

BRITISH PERIOD

1.37

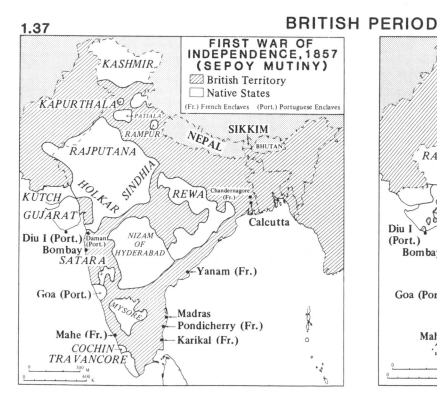

FIRST WAR OF INDEPENDENCE, 1857 (SEPOY MUTINY)
- British Territory
- Native States

(Fr.) French Enclaves   (Port.) Portuguese Enclaves

1.38

ON EVE OF INDEPENDENCE, 1947
- British Territory
- Native States

(Fr.) French Enclaves   (Port.) Portuguese Enclaves

The Kashmir Dispute. The Native State of Kashmir, ruled by a Hindu king with a Moslem majority had the option, in 1947, according to the agreements of the transfer of power with Britain, to either join India or Pakistan. For two months the Hindu ruler hesitated to make a decision. Pakistan then sponsored an armed raid into the native state, the "raiders" claiming that Kashmir deserved to belong to Pakistan because both had a Moslem majority. When the "raiders" had reached the Vale of Kashmir and were within striking distance of the state capital, Srinagar, the Kashmir ruler, in late October of 1947, used his legal perogative to accede to India. After India's ac-

ceptance, Kashmir legally became a part of India. Moreover, Kashmir's popular Peoples' Conference, led by a secular nationalist leader, Sheikh Abdullah, supported the decision to join secular India rather than Islamic Pakistan. Air-borne Indian army troops were sent to the area, saving Srinagar and a large part of Kashmir for India. After about 14 months of battle, a United Nations sponsored cease-fire was established on January 1, 1949 and since then, the land of Kashmir has remained divided; west of the cease-fire line unofficially becoming a part of Pakistan while the area east of the line became a state of India. On the cease-fire front, battles were also fought in 1965 and 1971 between India and Pakistan leading to a slight change in the actual position of occupation. Though the U.N. proposed a plebisite in 1949 to decide the final accession of Kashmir either to India or Pakistan, the plebisite never took place. India claims all of Kashmir while Pakistan claims more than it occupies now. Naturally, maps prepared in India and Pakistan show different boundaries of Kashmir. The United States State Department considers the whole state to be a disputed area and shows it on its maps as such. As of 1985, there was an intra-departmental suggestion that the U.S. accept the actual line of control in Kashmir as the border between India and Pakistan. To complicate things further, Pakistan has ceded part of Kashmir to China though it had no legal right to do so. While all these legal and mapping disputes continue, Kashmiri land and culture remain divided leaving the possibility that tensions could flare between the two countries at any time. As a matter of fact, in 1985, both the Indian and Pakistani military were exchanging gunfire on the border.

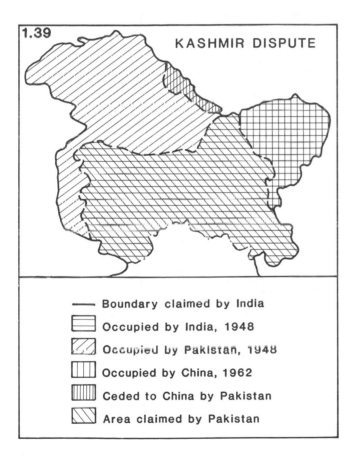

1.39 KASHMIR DISPUTE

—— Boundary claimed by India

☐ Occupied by India, 1948

▨ Occupied by Pakistan, 1948

▥ Occupied by China, 1962

▦ Ceded to China by Pakistan

▧ Area claimed by Pakistan

RELIGION

Although Hinduism has been prevalent in South Asia, the "Land of the Hindus" or "Hindustan," for almost 3,500 years, the aboriginal or animist religious groups are even older. These groups, who worship spirits and nature forces, are found in hilly and other inaccessible areas which the followers of Hinduism and Islam did not later penetrate.

Hinduism is by far the predominant religion in India and Nepal. Even before the partition of India, in 1947, when most Moslem-dominated areas were formed into the newly created country called Pakistan, as much as three-fourths of the population of British India was Hindu.

Although god figures are numerous and widely worshipped, the major Hindu gods are Vishnu and Siva. In contrast to most other religions, Hinduism lacks a single founder and an organized dogma and hence is tolerant of divergent views and practices. The religion is based upon sacred books, the *Vedas*. Hinduism is a way of life in which *karma* (a deed or performance of the existing life) is based on *dharma* (a good work or one which conforms to the

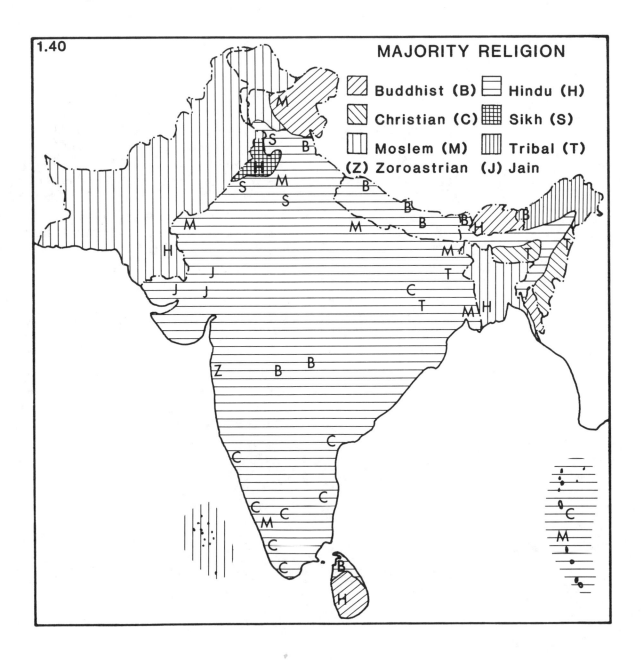

tenets of the religion); thus, good *karma* enables the individual to achieve salvation without facing the evils of reincarnation. The Aryans who brought the Hindu belief from the northwest succeeded in spreading it throughout India. The priest caste, the *Brahmins*, were the main agents of the diffusion of Hinduism, which eventually spread into the Dravidian south.

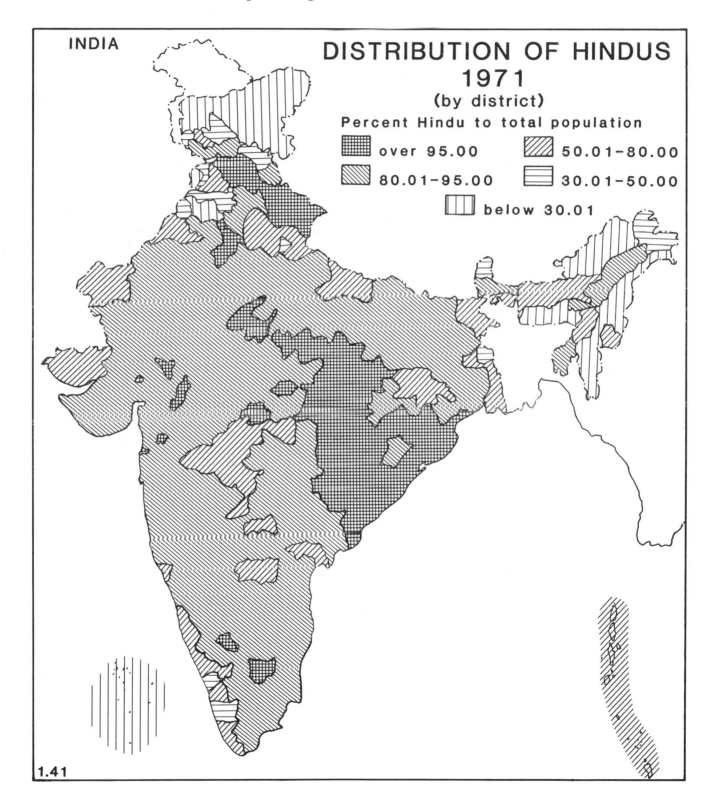

INDIA

DISTRIBUTION OF HINDUS
1971
(by district)
Percent Hindu to total population
over 95.00   50.01-80.00
80.01-95.00   30.01-50.00
below 30.01

1.41

Buddhism and Jainism, which originated in Bihar in the sixth century B.C., also spread widely in India. Originating as protest reform movements, both religions are similar to Hinduism. Jainism never became a main religion in India primarily because the religion prescribes a difficult way of life for its adherents. Still, it is practiced by less than half of one percent of the Indian population, particularly in the central part of western India. Buddhism, at one point in history (second century, B.C. through fifth/sixth century A.D.), almost superseded Hinduism in importance because of its castelessness and its optimistic outlook. The

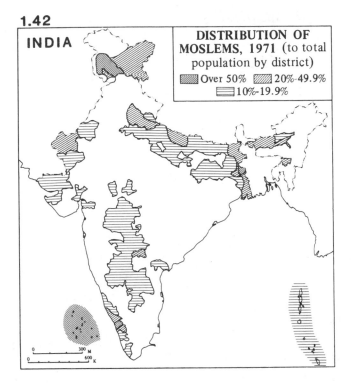

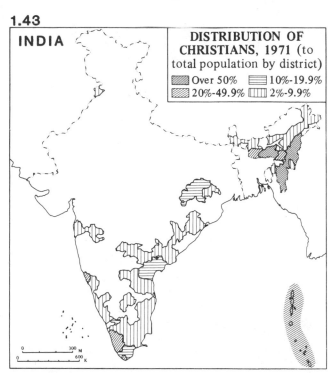

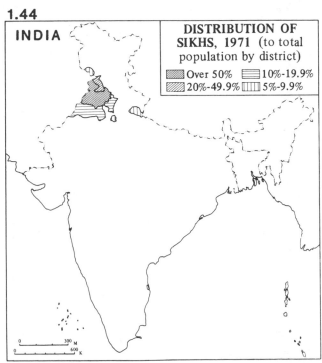

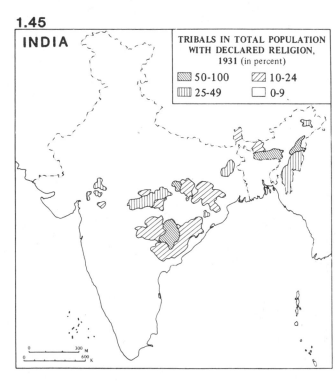

fanatic Moslem sheiks, beginning in 1206, systematically attempted to destroy all visible symbols of every religion excepting Islam. With the destruction of the Buddhist monasteries which had been the main seats of this organized religion, Buddhism eventually lost its remaining popular ground in India. It virtually disappeared from India, but a revival movement, led by B. R. Ambedkar in Maharashtra during recent times, has augmented the number of followers; less than one percent of the Indian population is Buddhist. The northern and eastern frontiers of India have a considerable Buddhist population because of their closeness to Tibet and Burma, whose people have been long-time adherents of this religion. The majority of the people in Sri Lanka and Bhutan are Buddhist.

Islam, the predominant religion of Pakistan and Bangladesh, is the second most important religion in South Asia. Since India is a secular state, the followers of Islam practice their religion openly. In fact, the Indian Republic has had two Moslem presidents. Pakistan is officially an Islamic state, while Bangladesh adheres to a semi-official Islamic rule. Islam began to gain strength in South Asia after 1206 when Delhi was occupied by Moslem Sultans. Sind in Pakistan, turned to Islam in A.D. 756 and parts of west Pakistan in the 11th century. Islam, probably the most uncompromising of all the religions, did not have the institution of caste system. The regional impacts of the spread of Islam in the subcontinent were (a) the conversion of the Hindus of the western parts, including Kashmir, by force; (b) voluntary conversion of low-caste Hindus who had been maltreated by the upper castes, particularly in Bengal; (c) conversion of the peoples of Lakshadweep and the southwestern coast through seaborne contact with Moslem traders who operated out of the Middle East; (d) conversion of large numbers of Hindu believers in the Ganges Plain, where the effects of Moslem-core areas were direct; and (e) a contiguous stretch of Moslem population in the central Deccan, reflecting the effects of regional Moslem kings, such as the Nizam of Hyderabad and the Sultan of Mysore.

Christianity, which was probably introduced

in the subcontinent during the third century or even earlier, became more active in the years after western occupation. The aborigines and other scheduled tribes, who did not have a firmly-based religion, accepted Christianity in large numbers in Nagaland, Meghalaya, Mizoram, and the Chotanagpur Plateau. In

1.46

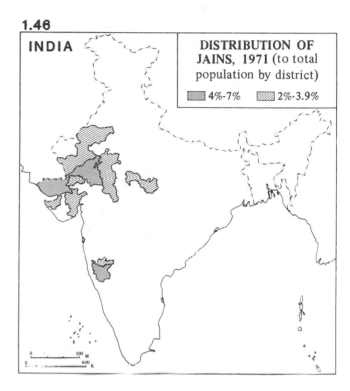

1.47

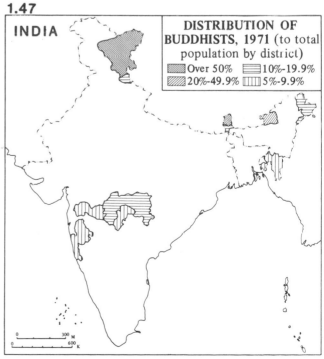

BANGLADESH

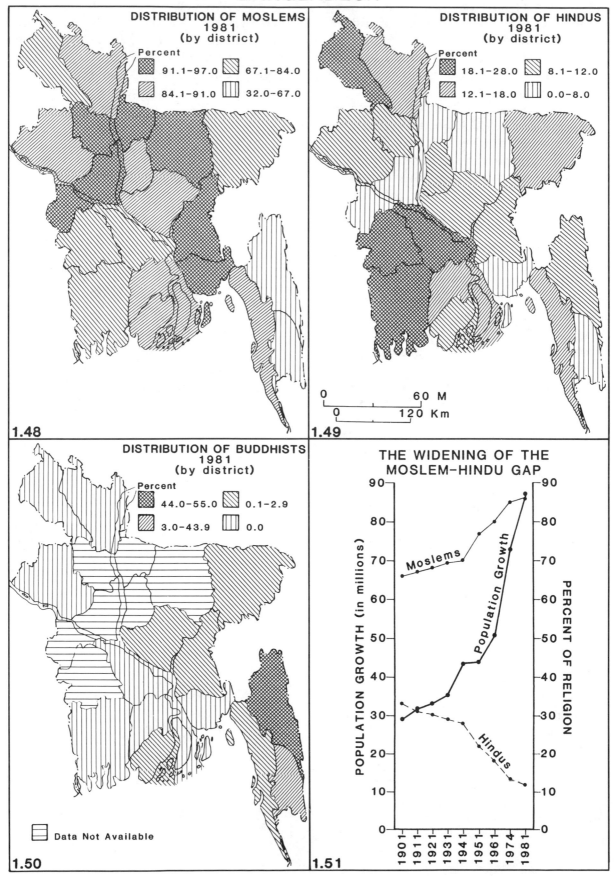

DISTRIBUTION OF MOSLEMS
1981
(by district)
Percent
91.1–97.0   67.1–84.0
84.1–91.0   32.0–67.0

1.48

DISTRIBUTION OF HINDUS
1981
(by district)
Percent
18.1–28.0   8.1–12.0
12.1–18.0   0.0–8.0

0   60 M
0   120 Km

1.49

DISTRIBUTION OF BUDDHISTS
1981
(by district)
Percent
44.0–55.0   0.1–2.9
3.0–43.9   0.0

Data Not Available

1.50

THE WIDENING OF THE
MOSLEM–HINDU GAP

Moslems
Population Growth
Hindus

POPULATION GROWTH (in millions)
PERCENT OF RELIGION

1901 1911 1921 1931 1941 1951 1961 1974 1981

1.51

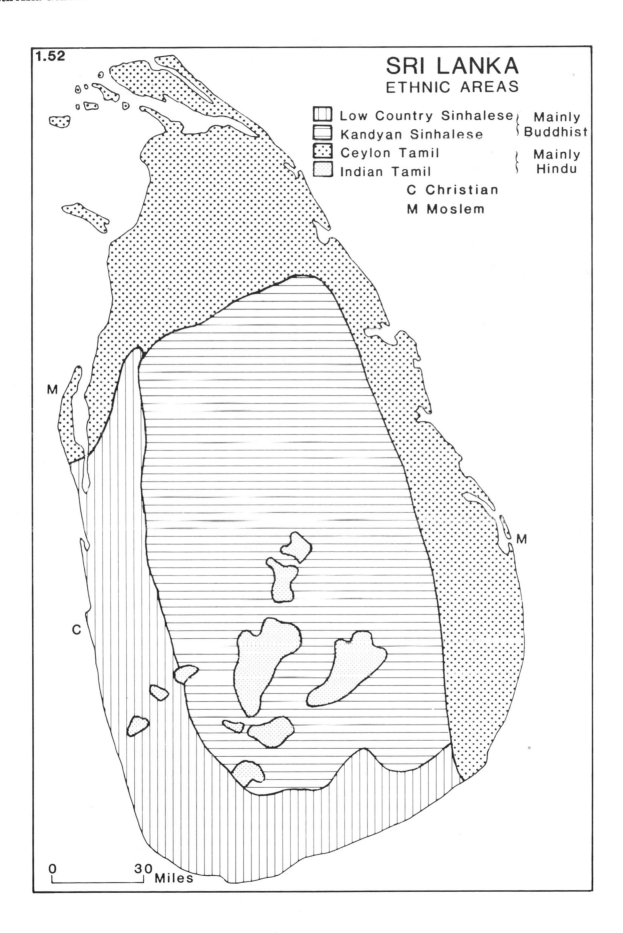

1.52

SRI LANKA
ETHNIC AREAS

- Low Country Sinhalese ⎫ Mainly
- Kandyan Sinhalese ⎬ Buddhist
- Ceylon Tamil ⎫ Mainly
- Indian Tamil ⎬ Hindu

C Christian
M Moslem

M

M

C

0   30 Miles

Kerala, Goa, and other parts of the south Indian coast, western seaborne contact has
caused Christianity to gather a sizeable following. Christianity also was accepted by some
socially deprived low-caste Hindus, because
through conversion they believed they had
gained more status. Moreover, during the
western colonial period a large number of

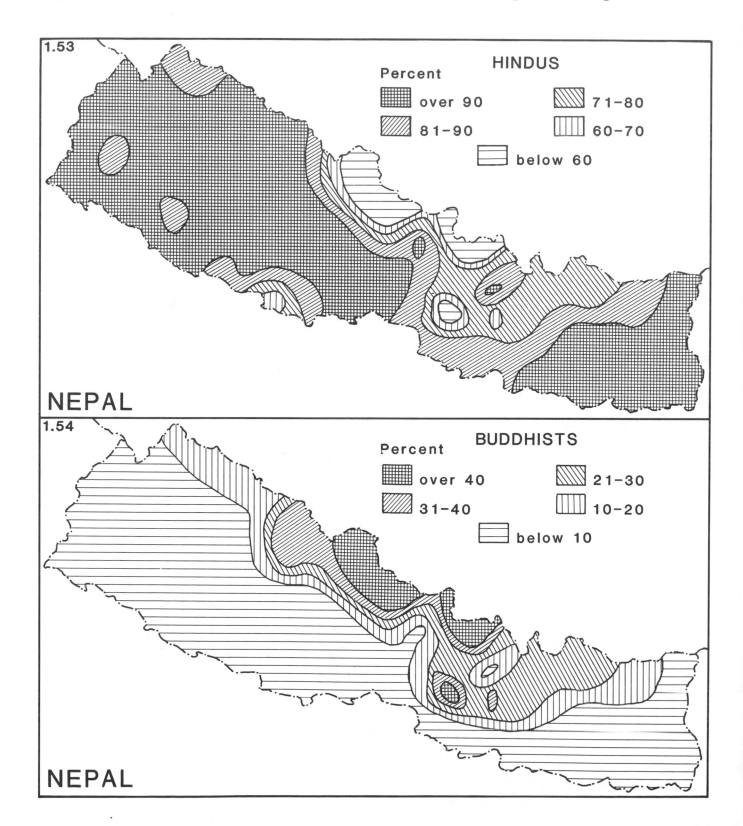

Christian males from Europe married native girls and gave rise to a new community of Christians, the Anglo-Indians. In addition to Goa, the cities of Bombay and Calcutta have large Anglo-Indian communities.

Sikhism, a religion limited mostly to the state of Punjab where it was founded by Guru Nanak in 1499, contains elements of both Hinduism and Islam. Sikhs tend to be more

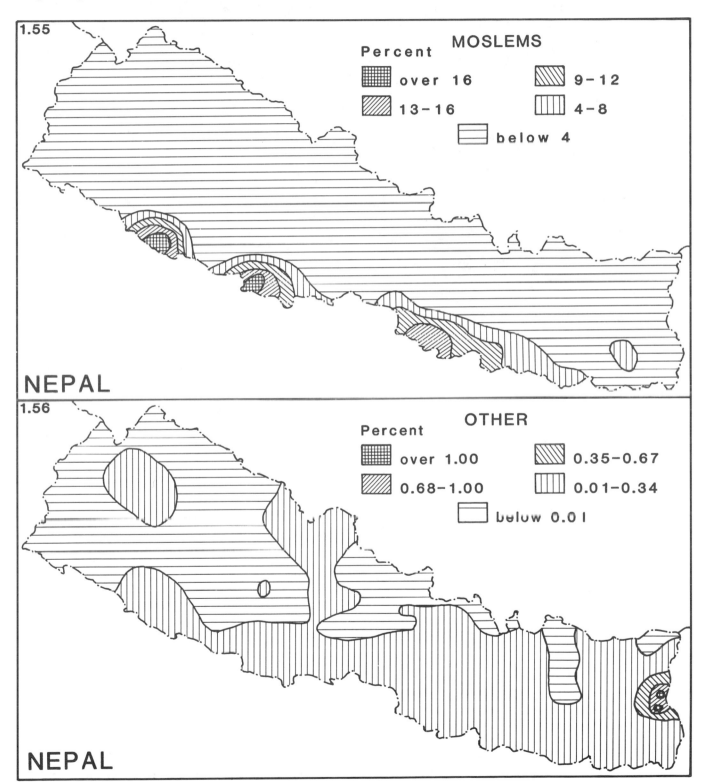

amenable to Hinduism than to Islam because, in historical times, Moslem kings, especially Aurangzeb, persecuted their religion ruthlessly. A detailed account of origin and expansion of Sikhism has been given at the end of this section. Parsees are numerically very small, but are an influential and wealthy group of people. They are believers of the Zoroastrian religion, who escaped to India after the Islamic conquest of Persia and settled on the west coast of India, mainly in Gujarat and Bombay.

Nepal, Bhutan and Sri Lanka have specific distributional characteristics of different religious groups. In Nepal, the northern high mountain fringe is Buddhist, primarily affected by Tibetan Buddhism, while traces of

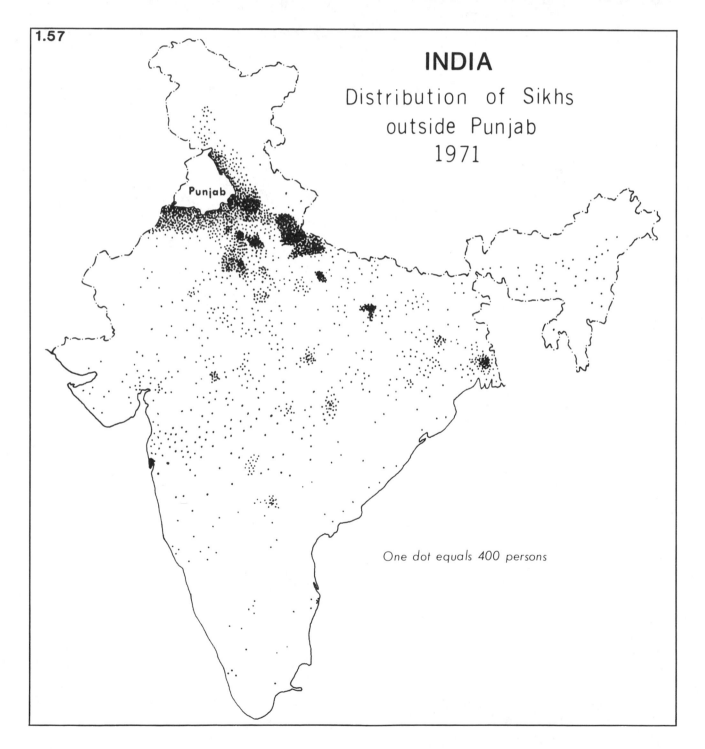

1.57

INDIA
Distribution of Sikhs outside Punjab 1971

Punjab

One dot equals 400 persons

Islam are found at the southern fringe where Moslems have penetrated from India's Middle Ganges Plain. Nonetheless, 87% of Nepal is Hindu. It is the only Hindu kingdom left in the world. The country is likely to remain Hindu, as religious conversion is unlawful. In Bhutan, the reverse is true. Perhaps 20% or more of the population is Nepali Hindu, most of whom live in the southern border area. The bulk of the population is Buddhist with a strong Tibetan influence. Sri Lanka, on the other hand, is a nation of Buddhists (66%), Hindus (18.5%), Christians (8.4%) and Moslems (6.8%). Among the South Asian countries, it has decidedly the highest religious diversity. All Tamil Sri Lankans, living in the northern part of the island, are Hindu, while the most densely populated southwestern area around Colombo is essentially Buddhist.

Pakistan has 1% Hindu and no Sikh is left there since the partition. It has some Christian and tribal population, who are the main non-Islamic people. From a religious point of view it is the most homogeneous country in South Asia. In Bangladesh, about 12% of its population is Hindu and they are distributed throughout the country.

Whatever his religion, the average South Asian tends to follow it seriously in belief and in practice. The geography of the area is partly responsible for such seriousness. First, the irregular nature of the monsoon rains prevented farmers from much needed effective cropping, which is so important for subsistence and, thus, belief in rain gods grew as such irregularity continued generation after generation. Second, calamities such as flood, drought, destructive storms, epidemics, and earthquakes, which occurred regularly in one or more parts of the area could not be checked by human efforts, leading to a belief in fate and the God's different ways of punishment. Finally, short life expectancy of the average person continued to take a toll of dear ones for centuries in spite of the human desire to live through to old age. Such conditions further strengthened beliefs in fatalism. Clinging rigidly to religion is a tradition rooted deeply in South Asia's geographical environment. Any change in such environment through human efforts, which has already

started to take place, will eventually moderate such beliefs.

Origin and Diffusion of Sikhism. A more detailed treatment of Sikhism is given here because it is not only a religion unique to South Asia, but in recent times a great deal of tensions were caused in India concerning the rights of Sikhs. Some militant Sikhs went so far as to demand an independent Sikh state, Khalistan.

Sikhism had its origin in Punjab at the end of the 15th century in a reform movement initiated by Nanak, the guru of the Sikhs. The custom of accepting a person as guru by a number of people, who in turn designate themselves as disciples, is an age-old tradition. Nanak's ideas can be summarized as follows: the unity of God, God is formless, therefore, no idol worship; God is both truth and reality and to him all human beings are equal, therefore, a casteless society; a belief in human will, therefore denial of fate or predestination; the detachment of a *yogi* while living among his fellow beings, therefore not a life of ascetic isolation (like Hinduistic *Vanaprastha*) nor one of torturing of one's body (like Jain *Itavara*) but one of tempered moderation.

Historically, no religion has ever thrived without political support of some kind. The best opportunity for a religion to consolidate and expand occurs when that particular religion offers a fresh spiritual idea which the people find attractive, peaceful conditions prevail, and the administrators support the religion either directly or indirectly. Occurrence of all three conditions together in a *spatial crossroads* such as the Punjab Plains proved to be difficult because of (i) continuous Moslem incursions from northwestern India, Afghanistan, and Persia, (ii) occasional onslaughts from the Moslem emperors of Delhi and their governors stationed at Lahore during the 17th and 18th centuries, (iii) rivalry, especially in the 18th century, among the numerous subregional Sikh chiefs in the Punjab area, (iv) invasion by Hindu rulers in adjacent regions and by the Gurkhas from the Himalayan region, particularly after the decline of the central Mughal power with the death of Aurangzeb in 1707, and (v) British colonial interests resulting in the subjugation or 'protection' of Punjab beginning in the period from 1845–1848 and lasting a full century, ending in 1947 with India's independence.

As a result of such hindrances to consolidation and expansion, the survival of the Sikhs as a separate religious community was more dependent upon pragmatic approaches. In adopting such approaches, the Sikhs and their leaders did not deviate from the basic tenets of their religion.

Initial political patronage was obtained during the second half of the 16th century when Akbar, the powerful Mughal Emperor of Delhi provided royal patronage to the religion by granting some hundred hectares of land for the erection of a tank (pond) at the present site of Amritsar, which was to become in time, a sacred site. This century-long period of uninterrupted growth established the Sikhs on a firm footing in Punjab.

One of the first problems of survival arose when the Mughal emperors succeeding Akbar began to persecute the Sikhs by imprisoning and executing the gurus, and by imposing "fines." The Mughal governors stationed at Lahore, in the heart of Punjab, had no difficulty in initiating punitive action against the Sikhs, when directed to do so. The easy ac-

cessibility of the Punjab Plains brought success to the vindictive Mughals who also had a superior army. However, a century of suppression resulted in certain adjustments by the Sikhs.

Fearing for their very existence, the Sikhs sought a political accommodation with the powerful Mughals, who in turn saw in the Sikhs a resource which could be useful in an effort to extend the Empire. On two occasions Sikh gurus accompanied the Mughal armies. Sikh representatives were stationed at the Mughal court of Delhi. During the 19th century, when the British became a powerful political force in North India, Ranjit Singh, a powerful Sikh king from 1799 to 1839, not only avoided any armed confrontation with the British, but allowed a British emissary in his capital city, Lahore, to keep a close watch on all activities.

Because the Punjab Plains were so readily accessible to invading Mughal armies, the Sikhs, as directed by their gurus, moved their headquarters to the Siwalik foothills at Kiratpur, where a retreat and a fort were built by guru Hargovind. The Sikhs bought horses and organized an army and fought the Moslems whenever necessary. In spite of the fact that Sikhism is in part Islamic in content, the Sikhs,

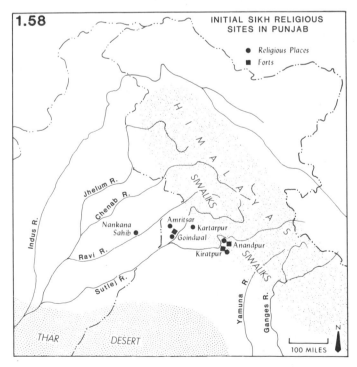

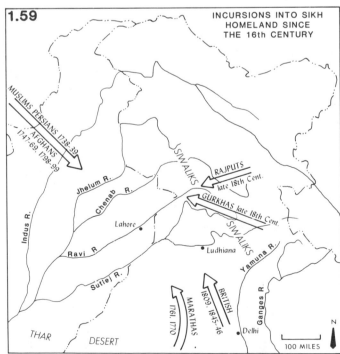

in reaction, turned against the Moslems thereby generating an anti-Islamic spiritual tradition that continues to the present.

One of the primary reasons for Sikhism's persistence as a religion was its superior social vision compared to caste-based Hinduism. To the average Hindu in the Punjab, lacking the privileges accorded a Brahmin, Sikhism was attractive. Sikh beliefs did not deviate from Hinduism in many of the fundamentals, and thus the Hindus' attraction to Sikhism, in the face of ruling Islamic onslaughts, was a militant alternative. Sikhism was a means for many Hindus to cling to their beliefs, the militant nature of this religion allowing them the opportunity to do so with great zeal and tempo. There were but few Moslem converts to Sikhism, in part because they, unlike Hindus, were not confronted with any political persecution during Moslem rule in India.

Sikhism had its initial beginnings in the Punjab and remained confined to that area in the two centuries that followed. The reasons are several. Although the nine gurus succeeding Nanak operated from different places (Khadur, Goindeval, Amritsar, Kiratpur, and Anandpur), these were, however, either in the Punjab Plains or nearby Siwalik Hills. Most gurus were chosen in accordance with family lines thus, restricting the possible diffusion of Sikhism outside of the Punjab area. A new writing script known as *Gurmukhi* (from the mouth of the Guru) was used for writing Nanak's teachings; it was introduced by the middle of the 17th century. Though this script and the eventual development of a full-fledged Punjabi language (in which all Sikh religious literature came to be written) acted to give a degree of individuality to the Punjabi Sikhs, they further confined Sikhism to the Punjabi speaking area. Finally, the almost constant preoccupation of the Sikhs and their gurus with Mughal emperors during the 18th century turned Sikh attention to internal survival rather than external expansion.

Possibilities for expansion were best when Ranjit Singh, an ardent Sikh, proclaimed himself the Maharaja of Punjab in 1801, and started to organize the Sikhs into a well-organized political force. His powers were strong enough to militarily keep the Afghans out of his tribute-paying area and confined the British through treaties, to the area east of the Sutlej River. Ranjit was so pragmatic that he ruled his territory without any motive of religious proselytism even though the majority of his subjects were not Sikhs. They consisted of Moslems, Hindus, and some Buddhists; his aim being not "to set up a Sikh Kingdom, but a Punjabi state . . .". The very fact of the existence of a Sikh king gave a significant boost to the consolidation of Sikhism in the area of its original development, with only limited expansion in the tribute paying areas through a migration of Sikhs to the urban centers of Ranjit's kingdom. These Sikhs held positions of social advantage.

The British occupied Punjab in 1848, and unlike some of the Mughal rulers, did not persecute the Sikhs because of their religious persuasion. The Sikhs enjoyed a religious freedom which at least removed their former fear of extinction. After 250 years of existence the Sikhs could worship in peace. The unity of British India under one political system and the introduction of railroads throughout the country from the middle of the 19th century, gave the Sikhs the opportunity to migrate to different parts of India, many of whom did, settling in various urban centers.

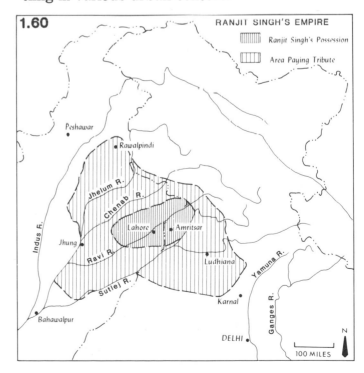

1.60 RANJIT SINGH'S EMPIRE
Ranjit Singh's Possession
Area Paying Tribute

Peshawar
Rawalpindi
Jhelum R.
Chenab R.
Indus R.
Jhung
Lahore
Amritsar
Ravi R.
Ludhiana
Sutlej R.
Yamuna R.
Karnal
Bahawalpur
Ganges R.
DELHI

N
100 MILES

2. INDIA

POLITICAL AND ADMINISTRATIVE SYSTEM

The Indian political system is unique in many respects. The Indian government, following independence, adopted certain socialistic policies: target-oriented national plan, nationalization of banks and coal mines, state ownership of the railroad and major bus transportation operations, new steel mills, many machine making factories, armament and other military equipment-making installations, etc. Nonetheless, private enterprise coexists with these socialistic government policies. Almost all of the agricultural land, most of the urban property, large numbers of industrial operations, and most of the retail and wholesale businesses, are privately owned.

In the midst of poverty and scarcity, India has undertaken the difficult task of developing and maintaining a democratic system of

---

India at a Glance

Name: Republic of India

Borders with: Bangladesh, Burma, Bhutan, China, Nepal, Pakistan

Area: 1,269,420 mi^2 (3,287,782 km^2)

Population: 730,572,000 (1983 est.)

Capital: New Delhi (Delhi)

Other Cities: Calcutta, Bombay, Madras

Monetary Unit: Rupee (March 1986: 12.25 = 1 U.S. $)

Chief Products: Agriculture - Rice, Wheat, Coffee, Sugarcane, Tea, Spices, Cotton, Copra, Jute, Linseed

Industries - Textile, Steel, Processed Food, Cement, Machinery, Chemicals, Fertilizers, and Consumer Appliances

Minerals - Chromium, Coal, Iron, Manganese, Mica

Per Capita G.N.P.: $260 (1982)

Religion: Hinduism, Islam, Christianity, Sikhism, Buddhism

Languages: Hindi (official), English (alternative official), Assamese, Marathi, Oriya, Punjabi, Sindhi, Tamil, Telugu, Bengali, Gujarati, Kannada, Kashmiri, Malayalam, Urdu

Railroads: (1983-84) 61,640 km (38,303 mi)

Roads: (1983-84) 1,770,000 km (1,104,834 mi)

---

government based on free voting rights for individuals over the age of twenty-one. Developing countries in Asia and elsewhere, including most of India's immediate neighbors, after being freed from colonial rule, generally turned to military or dictatorial forms of government. India has clung to a kind of federally-based parliamentary democracy, with national elections taking place at least once every five years.

2.1

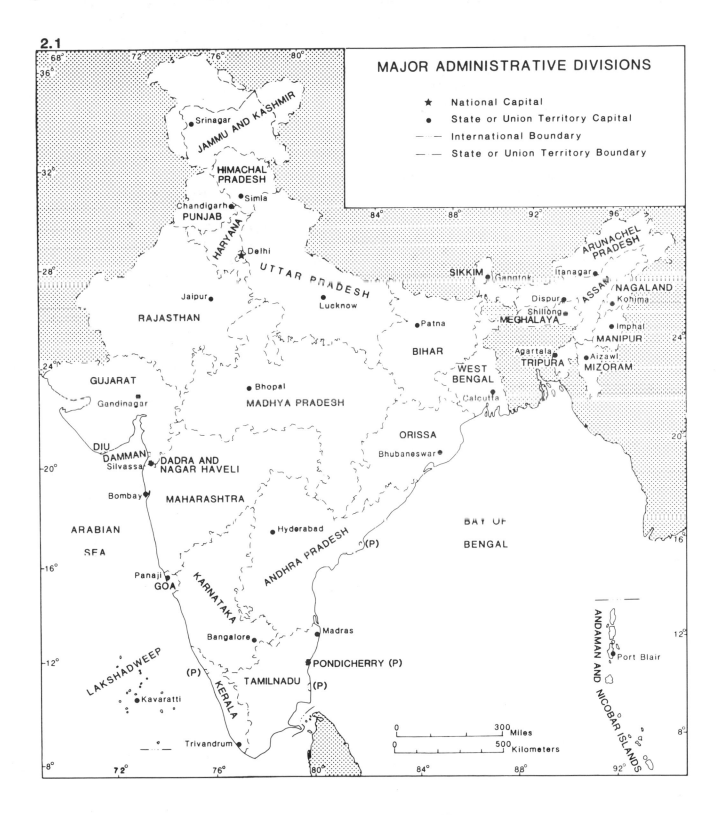

The first general election was held in 1952, about two years after the official commencement of the Indian constitution (January 26, 1950, which date is also celebrated as Republic Day). Since then eight elections were held until 1984, when Rajiv Gandhi was elected prime minister. Only once in 1975-77, a national emergency was declared and the then prime minister, Indira Gandhi, became virtually a dictator after dissolving the Parliament. This was one of the darkest periods of Indian democracy and is not apt to be repeated, particularly because of extreme popular resentment against such a dictatorship. Though Indian elections are considered relatively free and fair, it is the *Hindi Belt* (the six Hindi speaking states of north-central India) that plays the dominant role in Indian politics; in all the eight elections the majority of voters of this belt determined the ruling party; when Mrs. Indira Gandhi's Congress Party was thrown out of power in 1977 as a result of her 'excesses' during the emergency, the Hindi Belt solidly disavowed the Congress Party and voted for the Janata Party. Similarly, when Mrs. Gandhi returned to power in the 1980 elections, it was the Hindi Belt that solidly backed her Congress Party. Again from 1947 through 1986, four of the five prime ministers (Nehru, Shastri, Mrs. Gandhi, and Rajiv Gandhi) who stayed in office at least for one year, represented one central state (Uttar Pradesh) of the Hindi Belt. Morarji Desai was the only prime minister from outside the belt, in office 1977-79. The Hindi Belt, with 44% of the country's population and 42% of the national Parliament members, may be called the nerve center of Indian politics. Though democracy seems to be well entrenched in India, dynastic lineage in the country's ruling power continues on because since India's independence only for about five years (1964-66 and 1977-79) prime ministers were in office from outside the Nehru family. Jawaharlal Nehru, his daughter Indira Gandhi and her son Rajiv, have held the prime minister's office almost 90% of the time during the 39-year post-independence period. Also except for the 3-year Janata Party rule (1977-79) the Nehru-family-led Congress Party has been the ruling party in the central government.

The current political system in India is based on a constitution adopted on January 26, 1950, the basis of which is democracy, secularism, and equality. Women have equal rights; "un-

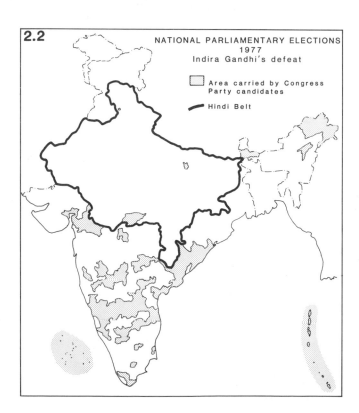

2.2

NATIONAL PARLIAMENTARY ELECTIONS
1977
Indira Gandhi's defeat

☐ Area carried by Congress Party candidates

▬ Hindi Belt

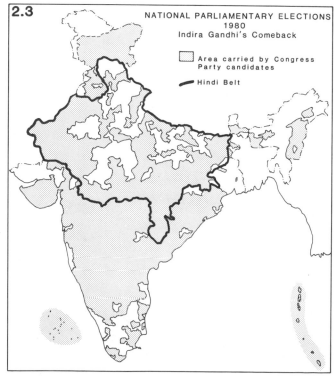

2.3

NATIONAL PARLIAMENTARY ELECTIONS
1980
Indira Gandhi's Comeback

☐ Area carried by Congress Party candidates

▬ Hindi Belt

touchables," who were traditionally considered as a lowly caste, are equal to other men under the law. The official name of the nation, designated by the constitution, is the Republic of India. The national animal is the tiger, with the peacock the national bird.

In practice, the democracy attempts to include within its power base a broad spectrum of the society. Though India is predominantly Hindu, two presidents of the country were Moslems and one a Sikh. In spite of the Hindi Belt dominance of Indian politics, three presidents were from South India. Moreover, the Council of Ministers, which is headed by the prime minister and the chief *de facto* executive body of the government, always consists of members from Hindu, Moslem, and Sikh religious groups, scheduled castes, and from north and south India. One woman, Mrs. Gandhi, remained the prime minister for 14 years.

India has a federal system of government similar to the United States but its central government has more power in comparison. The President of India, who is elected in an indirect way by members of the central legislature (parliament) and state legislatures, is a figurehead like the British Crown. The principal executive power resides in the office of the Prime Minister who is the majority party leader of one of the houses in the national parliament, Lok Sabha, 544 members of which are directly elected by the people. The other house of parliament, Rajya Sabha, is indirectly elected by the members of the state legislatures. Real legislative power resides in the Lok Sabha. The first Prime Minister of India was Pandit Jawaharlal Nehru, who held the office for 17 years. He was also one of the leaders of the nonaligned, third-world group of countries. As of 1986, his grandson, Rajiv Gandhi, holds the office of Prime Minister. The headquarters of the central government is in Delhi, the capital of India.

Until recently, the country was divided into 21 states which have elected legislatures and,

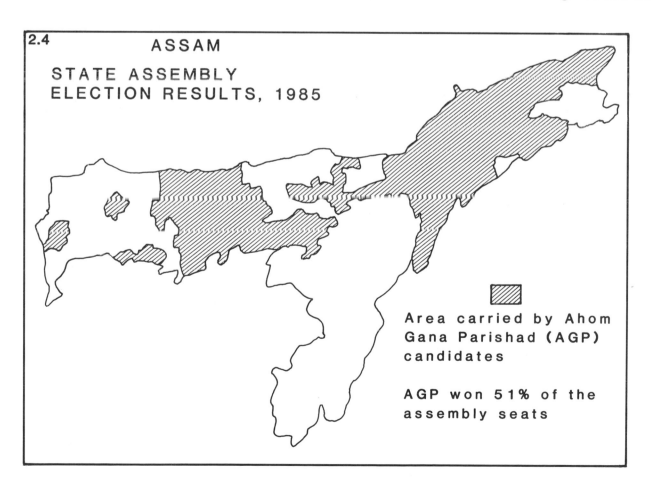

2.4
ASSAM

STATE ASSEMBLY
ELECTION RESULTS, 1985

Area carried by Ahom Gana Parishad (AGP) candidates

AGP won 51% of the assembly seats

in many administrative matters, autonomy. Nine union territories, directly governed by the central (or union) government through their local legislatures have some limited powers. Sikkim, a protectorate inherited from British times, was incorporated into India in April of 1975. Sikkim, thus, is India's 22nd state.

The states and the union territories are divided into districts which in 1981 totaled 408. A district is governed by a group of appointed civil servants headed by a District Magistrate responsible to the respective state and union territory governments. In terms of administrative hierarchy, the districts are comparable to counties in the United States. One of the primary differences between the district and the county organizations lies in the fact that the Indian district administrators are not elected, whereas the U.S. county officials are. A strongly-knit bureaucratic apparatus exists in India from the federal level down to state, district, and still lower levels of administration. At the village, town, and city levels, local self-government exists which in the villages is known as *Panchayat*, in towns and comparatively smaller cities, as *Municipality*; and in larger cities, as *Corporation*. These local governments are elected by the people for terms of four to five years. However, they do not have as much responsibility or power as American civic governments. The local governments in India, for example, are not responsible for the police, high school education, or judiciary functions.

Though India is called a country of 'unity in diversity,' its national integrity is often questioned by separatist movements in the peripheral states, such as Tamilnadu, Punjab and Assam. Though Tamilnadu separatism, very active in the 1960s, has now stabilized with a regional political party in power in the state legislature, the separatism in Assam and Punjab reached its peak in 1985, when the prime minister, Rajiv Gandhi, reached compromise solutions for these problems. As a result, separatist movements in Punjab and Assam greatly disappeared with the erstwhile

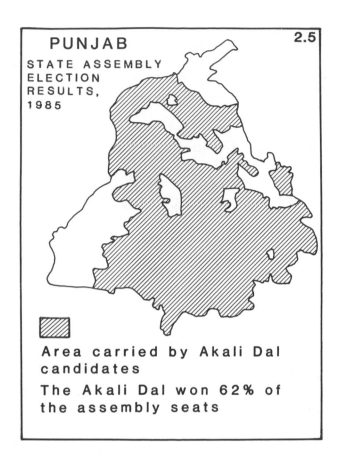

regional separatist groups adhering to more moderate positions as well as winning new state elections. In 1985, the Punjab government was headed by the Sikh moderates, the Akali Dal, while Assam was ruled by a newly formed regional party; Ahom Gana Parishad (AGP). India's cultural, religious and regional diversity is definitely an asset in creating a rich and diverse heritage, but at times, it may also strike at the very base of the national unity. Punjabi and Assamese problems seem to have been 'solved'; at least that is the picture one gets in early 1986, but no one can predict with any certainty that they or a separatist issue in another region might not surface again.

The states, union territories, and districts have been listed and their locations have been identified on the map. They are based on the 1981 census.

LIST OF STATES, UNION TERRITORIES, AND DISTRICTS

I. JAMMU & KASHMIR

1. Kupwara
2. Baramula
3. Srinagar
4. Badgam
5. Pulwama
6. Punch
7. Anantnag
8. Rajauri
9. Udhampur
10. Jammu
11. Kathua
12. Doda
13. Kargil
14. Ladakh

II. HIMACHAL PRADESH

15. Chamba
16. Kangra
17. Hamirpur
18. Una
19. Bilaspur
20. Mandi
21. Kulu
22. Lahul & Spiti
23. Simla
24. Solan
25. Sirmaur
26. Kinnaur

III. PUNJAB

27. Gurdaspur
28. Amritsar
29. Firozpur
30. Ludhiana
31. Jalandhar
32. Kapurthala
33. Hoshiarpur
34. Rupnagar
35. Patiala
36. Sangrur
37. Bathinda
38. Faridkot

IV. HARYANA

39. Ambala
40. Kurukshetra
41. Karnal
42. Jind
43. Sonipat
44. Rohtak
45. Faridabad
46. Gurgaon
47. Mahendragarh
48. Bhiwani
49. Hisar
50. Sirsa

V. UTTAR PRADESH

51. Uttarkashi
52. Chamoli
53. Tehri Garhwal
54. Dehra Dun
55. Garhwal
56. Pithoragarh
57. Almora
58. Nainital
59. Saharanpur
60. Muzaffarnagar
61. Bijnor
62. Meerut
63. Ghaziabad
64. Bulandshahr
65. Moradabad
66. Rampur
67. Budaun
68. Bareilly
69. Pilibhit
70. Shahjahanpur
71. Aligarh
72. Mathura
73. Agra
74. Etah
75. Mainpuri
76. Farrukhabad
77. Etawah
78. Kanpur
79. Fatehpur
80. Allahabad

81. Jalaun
82. Jhansi
83. Lalitpur
84. Hamirpur
85. Banda
86. Kheri
87. Sitapur
88. Hardoi
89. Unnao
90. Lucknow
91. Rai Bareli
92. Bahraich
93. Gonda
94. Bara Banki
95. Faizabad
96. Sultanpur
97. Pratapgarh
98. Basti
99. Gorakhpur
100. Deoria
101. Azamgarh
102. Jaunpur
103. Ballia
104. Ghazipur
105. Varanasi
106. Mirzapur

VI. BIHAR

107. Patna
108. Nalanda
109. Nawada
110. Gaya
111. Aurangabad
112. Rohtas
113. Bhojpur
114. Saran
115. Siwan
116. Gopalganj
117. Paschimi Champaran
118. Purbi Champaran
119. Sitamarhi
120. Muzaffarpur
121. Vaishali
122. Begusarai
123. Samastipur
124. Darbhanga

125. Madhubani
126. Saharsa
127. Purnia
128. Katihar
129. Munger
130. Bhagalpur
131. Santhal Pargana
132. Dhanbad
133. Giridih
134. Hazaribag
135. Palamu
136. Ranchi
137. Singhbhum

VII. WEST BENGAL

138. Koch Bihar
139. Jalpaiguri
140. Darjiling
141. West Dinajpur
142. Malda
143. Murshidabad
144. Nadia
145. Twenty Four Parganas
146. Calcutta
147. Haora
148. Hugli
149. Medinipur
150. Bankura
151. Puruliya
152. Barddhaman
153. Birbhum

VIII. SIKKIM

154. North
155. East
156. South
157. West

IX. ASSAM

158. Goalpara
159. Kamrup
160. Darrang
161. Lakhimpur
162. Dibrugarh
163. Sibsagar
164. Karbi Anglong
165. Nowgong
166. North Cachar Hills
167. Cachar

X. NAGALAND

168. Kohima
169. Phek
170. Wokha
171. Zanheboto
172. Mokokchung
173. Tuensang
174. Mon

XI. MANIPUR

175. Manipur North
176. Manipur West
177. Manipur South
178. Tengnoupal
179. Manipur Central
180. Manipur East

XII. TRIPURA

181. West Tripura
182. North Tripura
183. South Tripura

XIII. MEGHALAYA

184. Jaintia Hills
185. Bast Khasi Hills
186. West Khasi Hills
187. East Garo Hills
188. West Garo Hills

XIV. RAJASTHAN

189. Ganganagar
190. Bikaner
191. Churu
192. Jhunjhunun
193. Alwar
194. Bharatpur
195. Sawai Madhopur
196. Jaipur
197. Sikar
198. Ajmer
199. Tonk
200. Jaisalmer
201. Jodhpur
202. Nagaur
203. Pali
204. Barmer
205. Jalor
206. Sirohi

207. Bhilwara
208. Udaipur
209. Chittaurgarh
210. Dungarpur
211. Banswara
212. Bundi
213. Kota
214. Bhalawar

XV. GUJARAT

215. Jamnagar
216. Rajkot
217. Surendranagar
218. Bhavnagar
219. Amreli
220. Junagadh
221. Kachchh
222. Banas Kantha
223. Sabar Kantha
224. Mahesana
225. Gandhinagar
226. Ahmadabad
227. Kheda
228. Panch Mahals
229. Vadodara
230. Bharuch
231. Surat
232. Valsad
233. The Dangs

XVI. MADHYA PRADESH

234. Morena
235. Bhind
236. Gwalior
237. Datia
238. Shivpuri
239. Guna
240. Tikamgarh
241. Chhatapur
242. Panna
243. Sagar
244. Damoh
245. Satna
246. Rewa
247. Shahdol
248. Sidhi
249. Mandsaur
250. Ratlam
251. Ujjain
252. Shajapur
253. Dewas
254. Jhabua

2.6

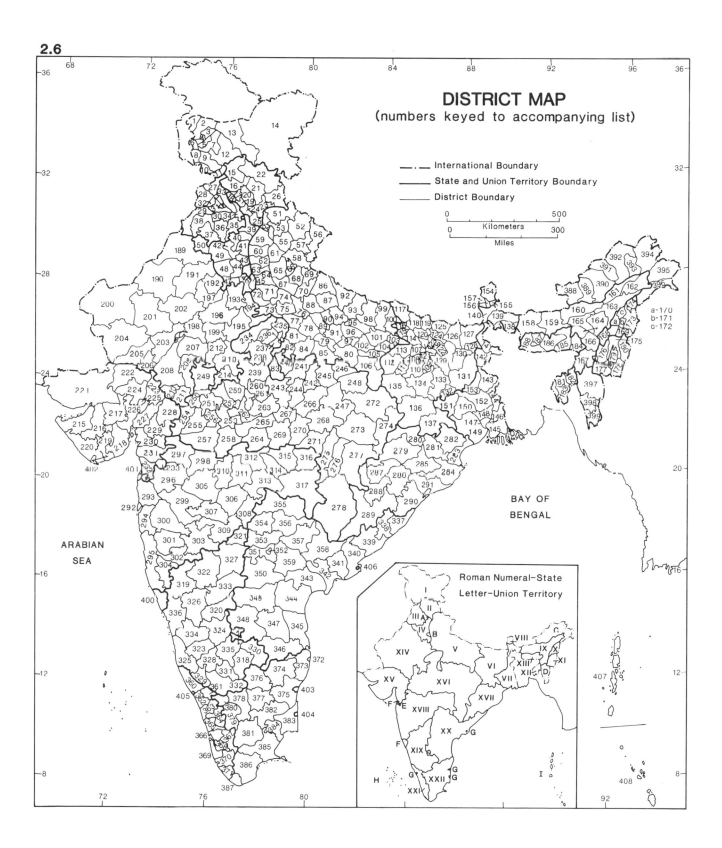

DISTRICT MAP
(numbers keyed to accompanying list)

_ . _ International Boundary
_____ State and Union Territory Boundary
_____ District Boundary

Kilometers
Miles

ARABIAN
SEA

BAY OF
BENGAL

Roman Numeral-State
Letter-Union Territory

255. Dhar
256. Indore
257. West Nimar
258. East Nimar
259. Rajgarh
260. Vidisha
261. Bhopal
262. Sehore
263. Raisen
264. Betul
265. Hoshangabad
266. Jabalpur
267. Narsimhapur
268. Mandla
269. Chhindwara
270. Seoni
271. Balaghat
272. Surguja
273. Bilaspur
274. Raigarh
275. Rajnandgaon
276. Durg
277. Raipur
278. Bastar

XVII. ORISSA

279. Sambalpur
280. Sundargarh
281. Keonjhar
282. Mayurbhanj
283. Baleshwar
284. Cuttack
285. Dhenkanal
286. Baudh Khondmals
287. Balangir
288. Kalahandi
289. Koraput
290. Ganjam
291. Puri

XVIII. MAHARASHTRA

292. Greater Bombay
293. Thane
294. Kulaba
295. Ratnagiri
296. Nasik
297. Dhule
298. Jalgaon
299. Ahmadnagar
300. Pune
301. Satara
302. Sangli
303. Solapur

304. Kolhapur
305. Aurangabad
306. Parbhani
307. Bir
308. Nanded
309. Osmanabad
310. Buldana
311. Akola
312. Amravati
313. Yavatmal
314. Wardha
315. Nagpur
316. Bhandara
317. Chandrapur

XIX. KARNATAKA

318. Bangalore
319. Belgaum
320. Bellary
321. Bidar
322. Bijapur
323. Chikmagalur
324. Chitradurga
325. Dakshin Kannad
326. Dharwad
327. Gulbarga
328. Hassan
329. Kodagu (Coorg)
330. Kolar
331. Mandya
332. Mysore
333. Raichur
334. Shimoga
335. Tumkur
336. Uttar Kannad

XX. ANDHRA PRADESH

337. Srikakulam
338. Vizianagaram
339. Vishakhapatnam
340. East Godavari
341. West Godavari
342. Krishna
343. Guntur
344. Prakasam
345. Nellore
346. Chittoor
347. Cuddapah
348. Anantapur
349. Kurnool
350. Mahbubnagar
351. Rangareddy
352. Hyderabad
353. Medak

354. Nizamabad
355. Adilabad
356. Karimnagar
357. Warangal
358. Khammam
359. Nalgonda

XXI. KERALA

360. Cannanore
361. Wynad
362. Kozhikode
363. Malappuram
364. Palghat
365. Trichur
366. Ernakulam
367. Idukki
368. Kottayam
369. Alleppey
370. Quilon
371. Trivandrum

XXII. TAMIL NADU

372. Madras
373. Chengalpattu
374. North Arcot
375. South Arcot
376. Dharmapuri
377. Salem
378. Periyar
379. Coimbatore
380. Nilgiri
381. Madurai
382. Tiruchirappalli
383. Thanjavur
384. Pudukkottai
385. Ramanathapuram
386. Tirunelveli
387. Kanniyakumari

UNION TERRITORIES

A. CHANDIGARH

B. DELHI

C. ARUNACHAL PRADESH

388. West Kameng
389. East Kameng
390. Lower Subansiri
391. Upper Subansiri
392. West Siang
393. East Siang

PHYSICAL CHARACTERISTICS

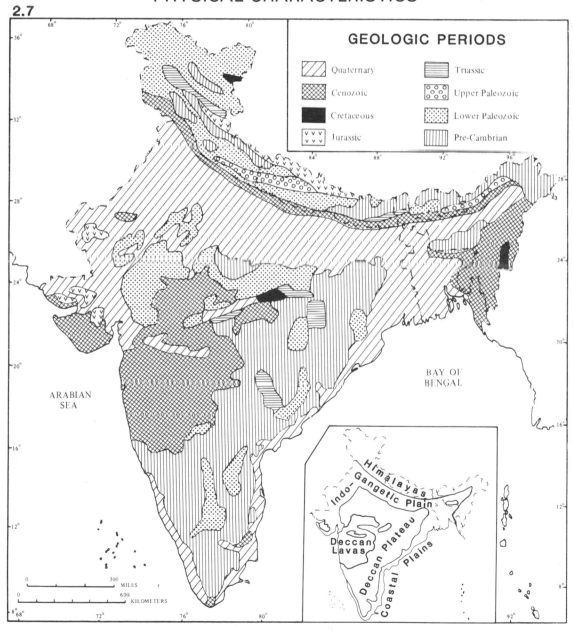

2.7

GEOLOGIC PERIODS

- Quaternary
- Cenozoic
- Cretaceous
- Jurassic
- Triassic
- Upper Paleozoic
- Lower Paleozoic
- Pre-Cambrian

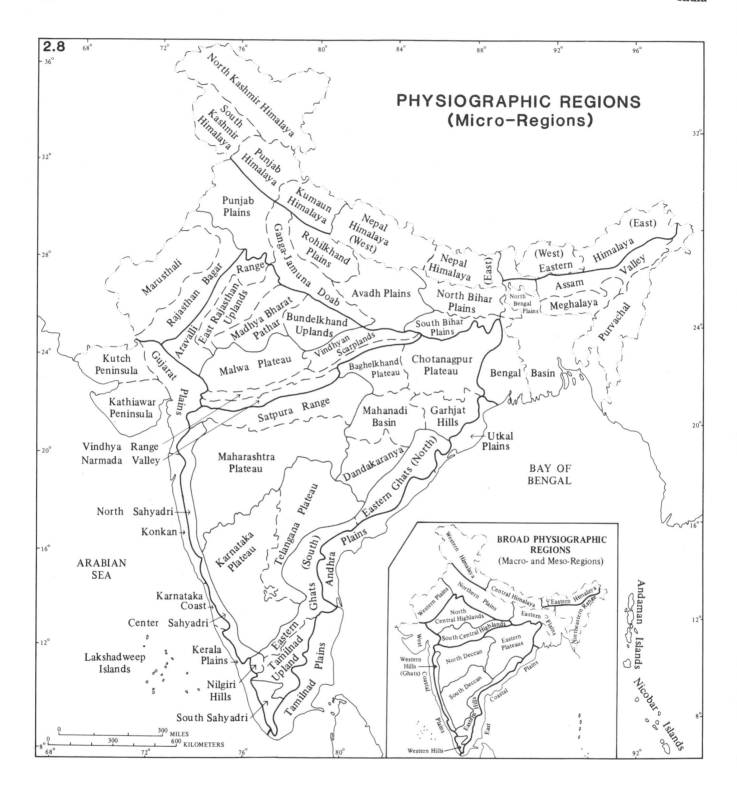

PHYSIOGRAPHIC REGIONS
(Micro-Regions)

Though India is traditionally divided into four principal (Supermacro) regions: a) the Deccan Plateau, b) the Himalayas, c) the Indo-Gangetic Plain, and d) the Coastal Plains, physiographically it is subdivided into 7 macro-regions, 20 meso-regions and 58 micro-regions. Each region has distinctive landform characteristics which reveal their economic potential as well.

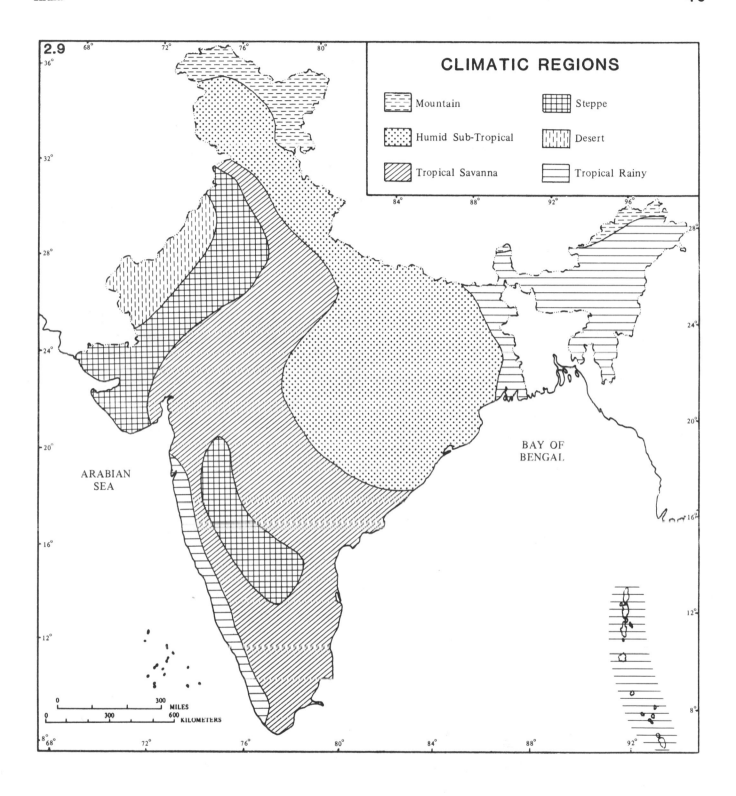

Three main climatic regions of India are tropical rainy, humid subtropical and tropical, and tropical savanna. In the greater part of the tropical rainy region the mean annual temperature ranges from 25°C (77°F) to 27°C (80°F) and the rainfall averages from 200 cm (78 in) to 400 cm (156 in). Tropical semi-evergreen forests are the typical vegetation of this region. This region also has a 'very high' rainfall reliability, which makes this region less dependent on irrigation.

The humid subtropical and tropical region,

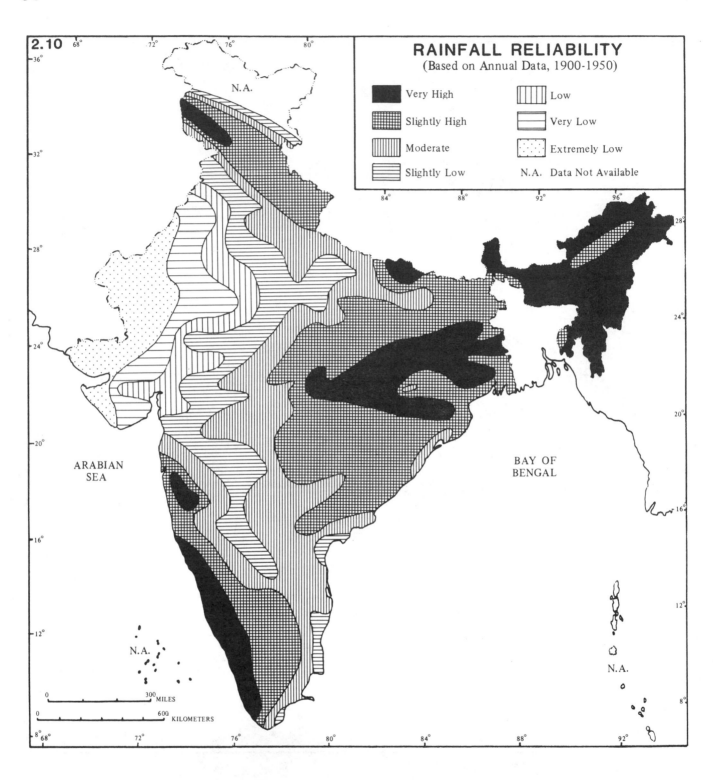

2.10

RAINFALL RELIABILITY
(Based on Annual Data, 1900-1950)

Very High   Low

Slightly High   Very Low

Moderate   Extremely Low

Slightly Low   N.A. Data Not Available

N.A.

ARABIAN
SEA

BAY OF
BENGAL

N.A.

N.A.

0   300
MILES

0   600
KILOMETERS

where annual precipitation is from 100 cm (39in) to 200 cm (78 in) and mean temperature between 20°C (68°F) and 25°C (77°F), has tropical moist deciduous (or monsoon) forests in most parts. The rainfall reliability in this region is generally 'slightly high' and irrigation is necessary for guaranteed crop-output.

The tropical savanna region with an annual rainfall range from 60 cm (24 in) to 80 cm (32 in) and the mean annual temperature of 25°C (77°F) mainly falls in tropical dry deciduous forest zone. Long-rooted small trees, often arm-

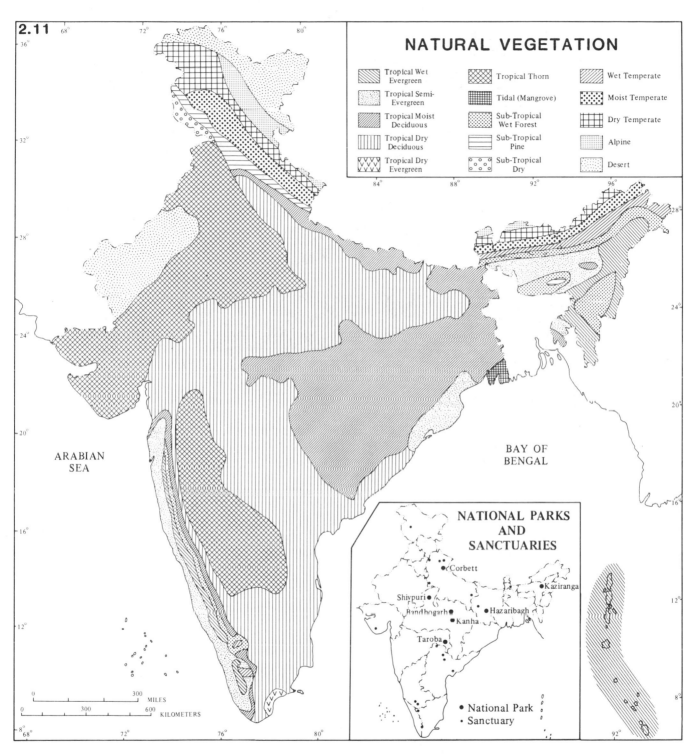

2.11

NATURAL VEGETATION

Tropical Wet Evergreen	Tropical Thorn	Wet Temperate
Tropical Semi-Evergreen	Tidal (Mangrove)	Moist Temperate
Tropical Moist Deciduous	Sub-Tropical Wet Forest	Dry Temperate
Tropical Dry Deciduous	Sub-Tropical Pine	Alpine
Tropical Dry Evergreen	Sub-Tropical Dry	Desert

ARABIAN SEA

BAY OF BENGAL

NATIONAL PARKS AND SANCTUARIES

- Corbett
- Kaziranga
- Shivpuri
- Bandhogarh
- Hazaribagh
- Kanha
- Taroba

● National Park
· Sanctuary

MILES
KILOMETERS

ed with sharp thorns, are characteristic of the natural vegetation of this region. As rainfall reliability is 'moderate' to 'slightly low', irrigation is a necessity for continued success in agriculture.

Steppe climatic region with low annual rainfall has bunch grass and thorny bushes as its typical natural vegetation. As the rainfall reliability is low irrigation is highly desirable for cropping.

The desert region with very scanty rainfall has tropical thorn and desert type of natural vegetation. The rainfall reliability is 'very low' to 'extremely low' and virtually no agriculture is possible without irrigation.

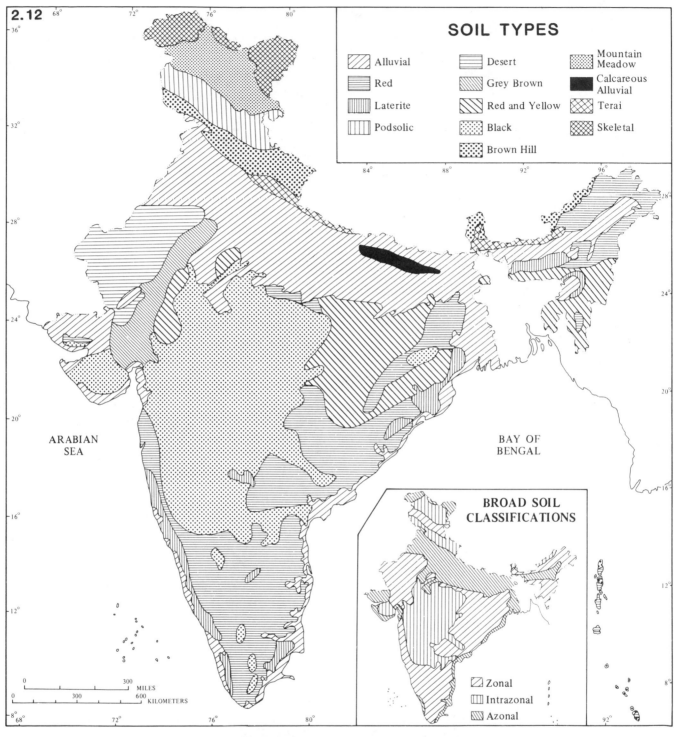

2.12

SOIL TYPES

Alluvial

Red

Laterite

Podsolic

Desert

Grey Brown

Red and Yellow

Black

Brown Hill

Mountain Meadow

Calcareous Alluvial

Terai

Skeletal

ARABIAN SEA

BAY OF BENGAL

0   300   MILES
0   300   600   KILOMETERS

BROAD SOIL CLASSIFICATIONS

Zonal

Intrazonal

Azonal

Zonal, Intrazonal, and Azonal, three major soil groups of the world are present in India. Zonal soil types represented in India are five (Desert, Red, Red/Yellow, Grey-Brown, and Podsolic); Intrazonal soil types, three (Black, Brown Hill, and Mountain Meadow); Azonal soil types, five (Alluvial, Calcareous Alluvial, Terai, Laterite, and Skeletal). Of these 13 different types three (Alluvial, Red and Black) are dominant. The alluvial soils are rich in potash but deficient in nitrogen and organic matter and are attractive agriculturally. The black soils, rich in potash, iron and lime but deficient in nitrogen, phosphates and organic matter, are also suitable as good agricultural land. The red soils, light in texture and easily drained, are deficient in organic matter and are not as attractive agriculturally as the alluvial and black soils.

LAND USES

Indians have maximized the use of land suitable for agriculture. All of the plain lands, except western Rajasthan which is a hot desert, are cultivated. The higher elevations, steep slopes, and mountain country are permanently snowclad, forested, or wasteland. Conventional land uses are practiced on the level plains and lower elevations with adequate rainfall, which are generally under agriculture; mountains, rugged plateaus and steep slopes, and areas of very low rainfall usually preclude

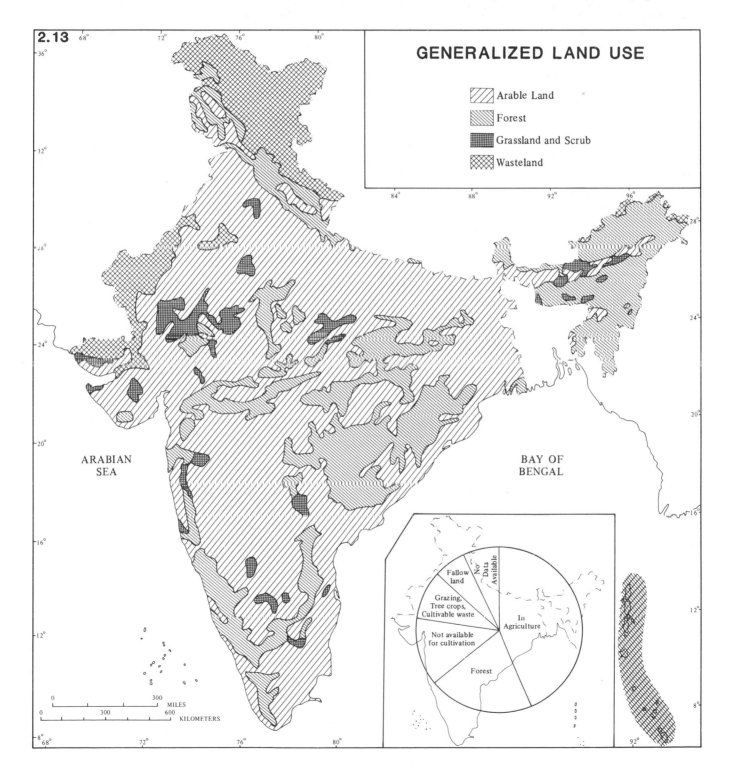

habitation as well as the practice of agriculture.

Land-use data is available for 92% (1978-79) of the country's area; 43% of the land was cultivated compared to 42% in 1968-69. However, compared to 1950-51, when the net cultivated area was 1.19 billion hectares, the area increased by 20% in 1978-79. Though there had been a consistent decline in the area of land devoted to foodgrains, the food production has consistently increased because of higher yields. The 557,117 villages and 3,949 towns (1981) also occupy a certain proportion of land. Though the area of operational agricultural holdings in the villages is increasing slightly, the average size of such holdings is declining, 2.3 hectares in 1970-71 to 2 hectares in 1976-77. Population pressure, in-

heritance laws and land fragmentation are responsible for this decline. Forests occupied 22% of the land in 1976-79, up 60% compared to 1950-51.

Though the average size of a farm holding was 2 hectares (4.92 acres), 72.6% of the farm holders operated on less than 2 hectares and they farmed only 23.5% of the country's cultivated area. However, 3% of the farm holders owned farms of over 10 hectares (24.71 acres) and they farmed 26.3% of the cultivated area.

With the increase in population pressure, land is intensively cultivated more than once a year (commonly referred to as double-cropped or triple-cropped land). A case study of one of the villages in the South Bihar Plains is given here.

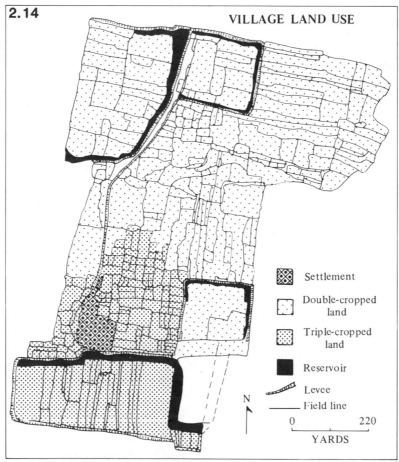

Source: N. Ali, *Masautha Khurd Landuse and Socioeconomic Survey*, Masters Village Survey, Department of Geography, Magadh University. (unpublished)

VILLAGE-BASED PRIMARY ECONOMIC ACTIVITIES
CROPS

India is an agricultural country. Sixty percent of its work force draws its livelihood from agriculture, and about 40% of the national income is derived from it. The principal food grains produced in India are, in order of importance: rice, wheat, pulses, *jowar*, maize, and *bajra*. In 1984-85, the total Indian food-grain production was 151 million tons, although in 1972-73, the production was only 95 million tons.

The food-grain production in India is primarily the result of man's adjustment to the environment. Rice, which constitutes 41% of India's food production, is grown wherever the physical conditions are favorable: alluvial soil, level land, rainfall above 45'' (115 cm) per annum, and warm temperatures during the growing season. Such conditions are prevalent in the eastern half of India and along the western coastal plain. Wheat is the second most impor-

tant crop and constitutes about 24% of the nation's food-grain production. Wheat also demands fertile, alluvial soil, and level land, but it can be grown in lesser rainfall areas, i.e., 25'' (64 cm) to 50'' (127 cm) per annum. Moreover, the contrast between wheat and rice lies in the fact that rice is more suitable to a high rainfall, warm monsoon climate while wheat grows better under comparatively drier conditions and with lower winter temperatures. The white rice grain is covered by a hard shell (kernel) which prevents the grain inside from rotting in spite of outside moisture. The wheat grain grows unprotected by any outer covering, and therefore any sizeable amount of moisture will cause the grain to rot.

Approximately 84° E longitude forms the eastern margin and 25° N latitude forms the southern margin of traditional wheat cultivation. The recent introduction of Green Revolution techniques in India have increased the wheat yield by approximately three times on farms which have substituted the high-yielding varieties for the more traditional variety.

PRODUCTION OF FOODGRAINS

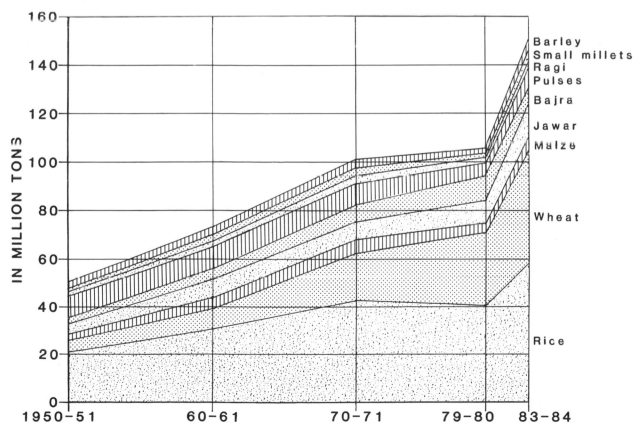

FOODGRAINS

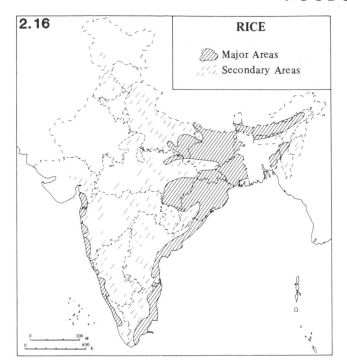

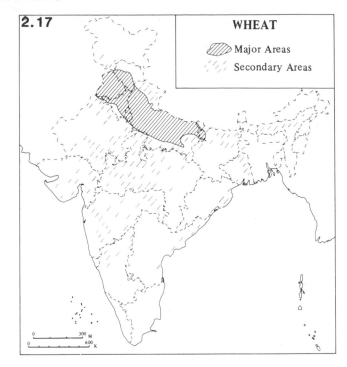

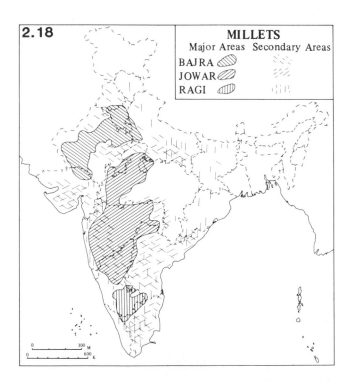

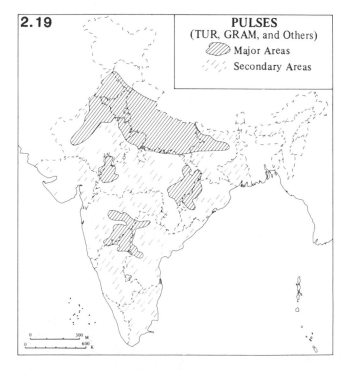

However, the high-yielding varieties of wheat are now introduced outside the traditional growing area: in the northern plains of Bihar and the plains of western Bengal, Assam, and Orissa, as a dry, winter-season, second crop (*rabi*) based on current levels of irrigation.

Although rice or wheat form the main staple of the Indian diet, south India does not pro-

duce much wheat. Nor did Bengal, Assam, and Orissa in the east produce any wheat as a matter of traditional preference. Hence, the eating habits of the population have adjusted in accordance with the food-growing customs of the locality: for example, the northwestern part of India is bread-eating, while the eastern and southern parts are rice-eating. However, the increasing population needs more interregional trade of grain. Only wheat is available in surplus amounts for such trade. Rice is primarily consumed in the areas where it is grown because rice-producing plain areas are generally over-populated. As a result, the food deficit of the rice-producing areas is met by wheat. Thus wheat-made bread or *chapaties* are being introduced into the traditionally rice-eating diets of eastern and southern India.

The three forms of millet (*bajra, jowar,* and *ragi*) are grown in the western half of India in the less favorable areas: hilly tracts, less fertile soil, and where the average annual rainfall is less than 25" (64 cm). These dry crops are less productive and less preferred as food; hence, they are known as poor man's food, although their nutritional content is actually greater than that of rice.

Pulses, consisting of peas, beans, lentils, and similar legumes are used to supplement rice and bread diets in the form of gravylike substances, commonly known as "dal" in north India. They are grown in the drier parts of India as a *rabi* crop with a principal concentration in the Northern Plains.

In the wake of modern improvements resulting from the Green Revolution, it is the wheat crop which has benefited most because of various technological and environmental advantages. As a result, 76% of India's wheat sown in 1983-84 was of the high-yielding varieties (HYV). The lack of favorable environmental conditions for HYV rice has, up until now, prevented its widespread introduction in the traditional rice-growing areas. As a result, only 54% of the rice fields in 1983-84 were sown with the new variety. Even more adverse conditions have prevented the further introduction of HYV in maize, *jowar*, and *bajra*, resulting in less than 35% of the area sown in these crops being of HYV.

Cash crops (the commercial crops) such as sugarcane, oilseeds (ground nut and coconut inclusive), cotton, tea, and jute, are produced in India under different environmental conditions. Wheat is primarily grown in northwest India, whereas ground nuts (peanuts) are found in southern India. (Ground nuts are made into cooking oils.) Coconuts also have a large-scale concentration in the southwestern coastal plains. In addition to the use of its shell for ropes and housing material, the coconut fruit is pressed to obtain cooking oil. Jute and cotton reflect contrasting geographical regions in terms of the location of their production. Jute is favorably grown in the eastern section of India, in the *alluvial* plains which have an average annual rainfall of over 60" (154 cm); cotton production, however, is primarily concentrated in the northwestern part of the Deccan Plateau where dry conditions and the especially suitable black (regur) soils of igneous origins provide an ideal growing situation for the crop. The production of tea in north India and coffee in the south (both in high-rainfall areas of hilly or mountainous regions) has contributed in different regional beverage drinking habits. People in north India principally drink tea, whereas, the south Indians drink coffee. Probably earlier British influence and their occupation of north India beginning from the eighteenth century, began the popularization of tea-drinking. The French influence and occupation of parts of south India during and before the nineteenth century, attributed to the spread of coffee-drinking in that region.

Among the cash crops, tea and jute (particularly burlap and other jute textiles) are most important, because India produces a sizeable proportion of the world production of these two items and also is responsible for supplying them to the world market. Jute and tea, of all the agricultural production, are India's highest foreign exchange earners. Although India is one of the world's largest sugarcane producers (traditionally grown in the northern part of the Ganges Plain), the country's overall yield produced little beyond her own needs that could be exported. Rubber production, which is concentrated in the hills of the southeastern part of India, is adequate only for the country's own demands.

On the whole, agriculture production in India is undergoing a great deal of change. Increase in productivity is the main goal in all fields and is resulting into a considerable social, economic, contractual, legal, and infrastructural modernization in the country.

COMMERCIAL CROPS

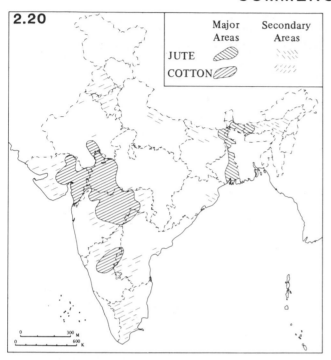

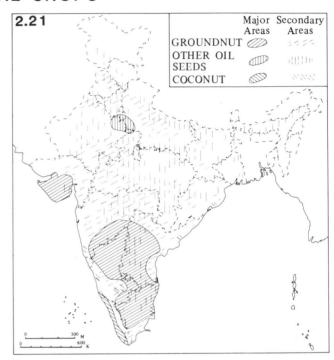

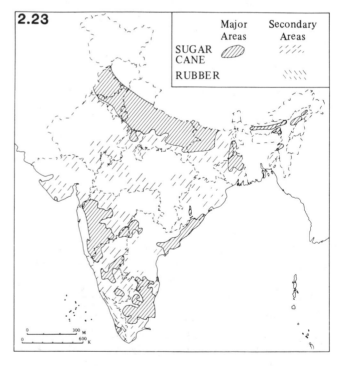

IRRIGATION

Expansion of irrigation has already determined the fate of the Indian population in terms of starvation or an adequate diet. India cannot only feed itself, but has an exportable surplus of food grains. The Food and Agriculture Organization has predicted that India can feed triple the size of her 1985 population by the year 2010. One of the essential factors in the success of the high-yielding varieties (HYV) of seeds is the regulation of water. Therefore, HYV is more fruitful in the areas where irrigation is utilized. Indian rains are primarily seasonal; the rainy season, therefore, is more productive than the dry season. Thus, the increase in productivity of agricultural crops is very closely aligned to the practice of irrigation. Since irrigation assures an area of a sufficient supply of water, it is particularly important to the drought-prone sections of the country.

By the beginning of the 1970s, it was estimated that three-quarters of India's cultivated land could be irrigated ultimately from surface and groundwater resources. Surface water irrigation consists of canals and tanks, while groundwater irrigation is obtained by tube-well pumps or traditional wells.

Canal irrigation is more widely practiced in areas where water can be obtained either directly from the rivers or from storage reser-

voirs. Since canal water flows by natural gravity it is the level plain regions which profit most from this kind of irrigation. Canal irrigation, therefore, is most prevalent in the Northern and Eastern Plains, along the Eastern Coastal Plains, and along the narrow valleys of the Deccan rivers. The recent efforts to irrigate the margins of the Rajasthan desert compares well with southern Californian canal irrigation systems.

Tank irrigation is prevalent primarily in the southern part of the Deccan Plateau. Tanks cover small catchment areas per unit, whereas a canal may cover thousands of acres in its supply area. Tank irrigation requires a hilly surface to create natural storage areas. Rains that fall during the monsoon season are stored in the reservoirs to be used during times when rainwater is not available.

Tube-well irrigation is a recent innovation which has resulted from modern technology and the dispersion of electricity to the rural areas. This type of irrigation is prevalent where subsoil regions do not encounter any rocky surfaces. Moreover, the availability of groundwater at a reasonable depth is another necessary factor in the use of tube-well. The Northern and Eastern Plains provide the best physical conditions for tube-well irrigation.

There had been an increasing gap in the 'utilization' of irrigation potential in the country; of the major and medium irrigation projects during the First Five-Year Plan, 12.2

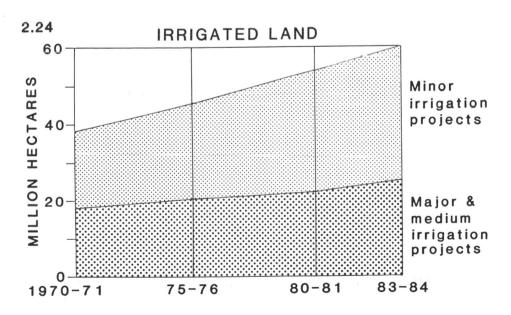

2.24
IRRIGATED LAND

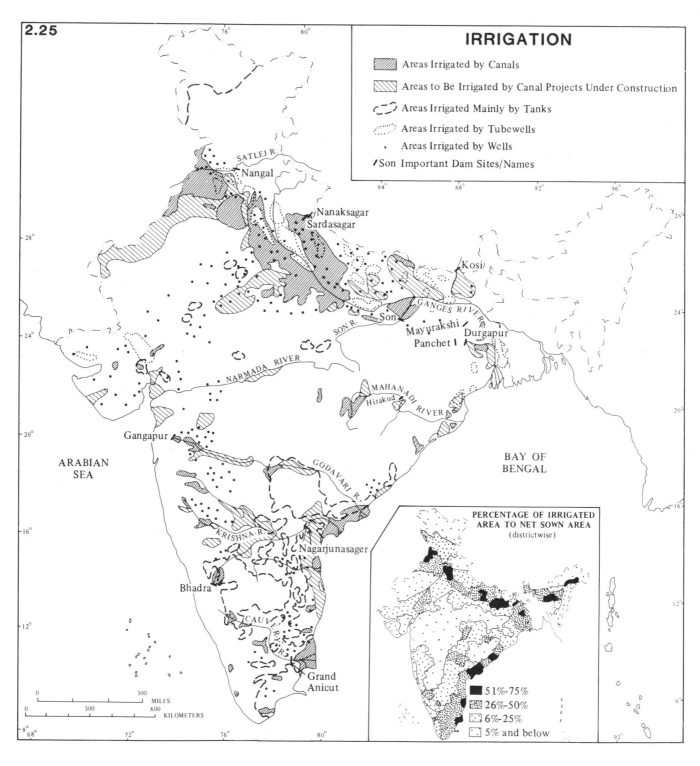

2.25

IRRIGATION

- Areas Irrigated by Canals
- Areas to Be Irrigated by Canal Projects Under Construction
- Areas Irrigated Mainly by Tanks
- Areas Irrigated by Tubewells
- Areas Irrigated by Wells
- Son Important Dam Sites/Names

SATLEJ R.
Nangal
Nanaksagar
Sardasagar
Kosi
GANGES RIVER
SON R.
Son
Mayurakshi
Panchet
Durgapur
NARMADA RIVER
MAHANADI RIVER
Hirakud
Gangapur
ARABIAN SEA
GODAVARI R.
BAY OF BENGAL
KRISHNA R.
Nagarjunasager
Bhadra
CAUVERI R.
Grand Anicut

0   300
MILES
0   300   600
KILOMETERS

PERCENTAGE OF IRRIGATED AREA TO NET SOWN AREA
(districtwise)

- 51%-75%
- 26%-50%
- 6%-25%
- 5% and below

million hectares of irrigation potential, as much as 90% was utilized; during the Fifth Plan, of the 24.7 million hectares of potential only 86% was utilized; in 1983-84 of the 30 million hectares of potential only 83% was utilized. Silt deposits, evaporation and seepage, water loss due to inadequate water channels, poor management, lack of maintenance and suboptimal cropping patterns are the reasons for such an under-utilization of the irrigation potential of capital-intensive major and medium projects. However, the minor irrigation schemes, are not only less capital-intensive, but they utilize 100% of their potential. Of the 35.6 million hectares of potential from minor irrigation schemes in 1983-84, all were utilized. As these schemes are primarily based on groundwater, their success is not only dependent on pumping of the resources economically, but on rural electrification. Of the 60.5 million hectares of India's irrigated area in 1983-84, 58.8% was under the minor schemes, showing their importance in the total agricultural productivity. There had been an increasing emphasis given by the government to the minor schemes, which can be completed in a shorter time compared to the major projects and which are also dependent on farmers' private initiative. During the period 1971-71 to 1983-84, the area irrigated under minor schemes has increased by 72% compared to only 44% in major and medium projects. Moreover, the expansion of minor irrigation is also a part of the government's 'removal of poverty' strategy.

Of all the foodcrops, the land under wheat (70% in 1980-81) is the most irrigated, followed by barley (50%) and rice (41%). The traditional wheat areas are in a dry climate, but have fertile soils. Moreover, the presence of perennial rivers and availability of groundwater resources make it possible to develop both major and minor irrigation schemes there. The traditional rice areas fall in high rainfall areas and the rice is also grown during the time when the rainfall is high. Therefore, rice does not require irrigation to the extent that wheat does. During the 1971-72 to 1980-81 period, irrigated wheat acreage increased by 49% compared to only 16% in rice. Nevertheless, both wheat and rice are increasingly produced outside their traditional areas as second crops.

The irrigation system of India, therefore, is based on utilization of various types which are suitable for different conditions. By the mid '70s, about 40% of India's potentially irrigable acreage had been brought under irrigation. Most likely by the turn of the century all potential areas will have been brought under irrigation.

INTENSITY OF CROPPING

The only means by which India can feed its people is by increasing the yield of its crops and by cultivating the same land more than one time each year (multiple cropping). Intensity of cropping refers to how often a piece of land is used for cultivation in one year. Agricultural land could be used two, three, and sometimes four times a year, depending on the availability of labor, water, capital, fertilizer, the selection of crops, and their marketability, because almost all of India, except the mountainous regions, has a year-round growing season.

A comparison of the intensity of irrigation to the intensity of cropping reveals a very significant correlation. Generally one crop a year, based on monsoon rains, is possible over almost all of India. The availability of irrigation not only assures the success of that crop during drought years, but also helps to grow crops in the dry winter and spring seasons. Therefore, it is understandable that most irrigated areas grow more than one crop a year. Such areas are, for example, the Indo-Gangetic Plains, the Eastern Coastal Plains, the upper Mahanadi Valley, and the irrigated areas of Rajasthan and Madhya Pradesh. Furthermore, in the southern portion of the western coast, the Brahmaputra Valley of Assam, the hilly areas of Himachal Pradesh and Kashmir where the annual rainfall exceeds 70'' (178 cm), a second, and sometimes a third, crop is grown without irrigation.

According to the statistics for the late 1960s, less than 20% of the sown area of the country was sown more than once a year, but with expansion of irrigation, the multi-cropped area has increased considerably in the 1980s. As a matter of geographical corrrelation, the regions which are densely populated and have physical characteristics such as flood plains, deltas, and coastal plains, are most intensively cultivated for the reasons that adequate water is obtained either by irrigation or from rainfall, and also the pressure of the population demands an increase in farm output through the intensive use of land. Areas of low intensity of cropping

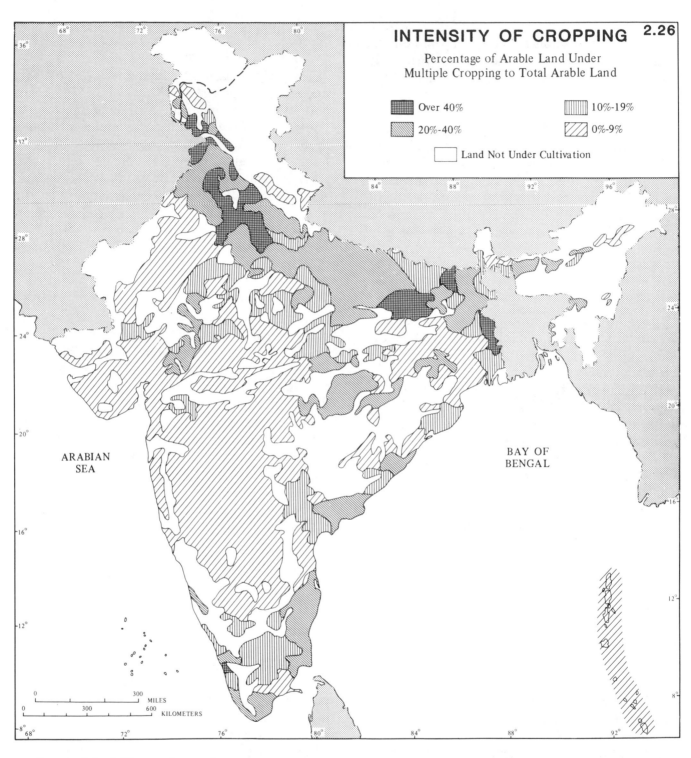

Percentage of Arable Land Under
Multiple Cropping to Total Arable Land

Over 40%   10%-19%
20%-40%   0%-9%
Land Not Under Cultivation

ARABIAN
SEA

BAY OF
BENGAL

0   300
                    MILES
0   300   600
                    KILOMETERS

are located in hilly regions, desert areas, and the Deccan Plateau due to the difficulty of obtaining water for irrigation and/or soils not being suitable for intensive cropping.

Recently, the Government of India, through its Indian Agricultural Research Institute, introduced a new program of multiple cropping, relay cropping, and dry farming to increase the earnings of the middle and small farmers who lack sufficient capital for the purchase of inputs. This program is known as crop cafeteria. In areas where dependable rainfall or assured irrigation occur, the small farmer can, through this program, grow up to four crops a year and increase his earnings from $40 per hectare on a single crop basis to $130 per hectare on a multiple crop basis. In fact, the farmers of Bihar, near the city of Patna, have been utilizing this technique for a long time, relying on monsoon rains and traditional well irrigation. They raise wheat, potatoes, sugarcane, mustard, and vegetables, in combination with poultry and cattle. The crops are well planned and are alternated in a system of relays, maximizing the use of both inputs and the land. The cattle and poultry thrive on wastes of the farm and homestead. The produce is either sold in the city of Patna or is shipped elsewhere, given the easy accessibility in the area by rail, road, and water transportation. A similar technique has been devised by the Institute for the drier areas employing efficient use of fertilizers, bacterial cultures, water management practices, new technology of direct-seeded rice which minimizes crop losses, improved means to counteract disease and pests, and cross-breeding of cattle.

The wealthy farmers have taken great advantage of the recently developed Green Revolution techniques. After learning the profitability of farm output in the market-place, they make every effort to increase their farm's productivity, and the most common technique used is multiple cropping. For example, a farmer in Punjab produces wheat, gram, and oilseeds or fodder in the same field because he has expendable income which he can invest in inputs such as tractors, fodder threshers, chemical fertilizers, hybrid seeds, water pumps, diesel oil, and labor costs. Therefore, a rich farmer in the plains with existing irrigation facilities is likely to turn to multiple cropping on his own without much direct assistance from the government, whereas, the middle and poor farmers do need external help. As the irrigation system of the country expands, multiple cropping will also be extended. In addition, the dry farming technique will help further the utilization of intensity of cropping in appropriate areas.

The concept of multiple cropping is not unknown in the United States, but its most widespread use is limited mainly to truck farming where as many plantings of vegetables are made as the season will allow. Large-scale multiple plantings of field crops (grains, soybeans, etc.) are virtually nonexistent for three reasons. The first and main reason is availability of extensive arable land. Second is climatic limitations; the short (compared to India) frost-free growing season. Lastly, the American farmer has never faced a burgeoning population that would necessitate growing every ounce of food within his capabilities. Thus we see two sides of the coin: the Indian farmer producing all he can and the American farmer often paid not to grow anything, a practice incomprehensible to most Indians. Perhaps as the world food picture turns even grimmer in the future, American agriculture will force itself into greater production. Then multiple cropping may enter the American scene, always limited, however, by climatic considerations.

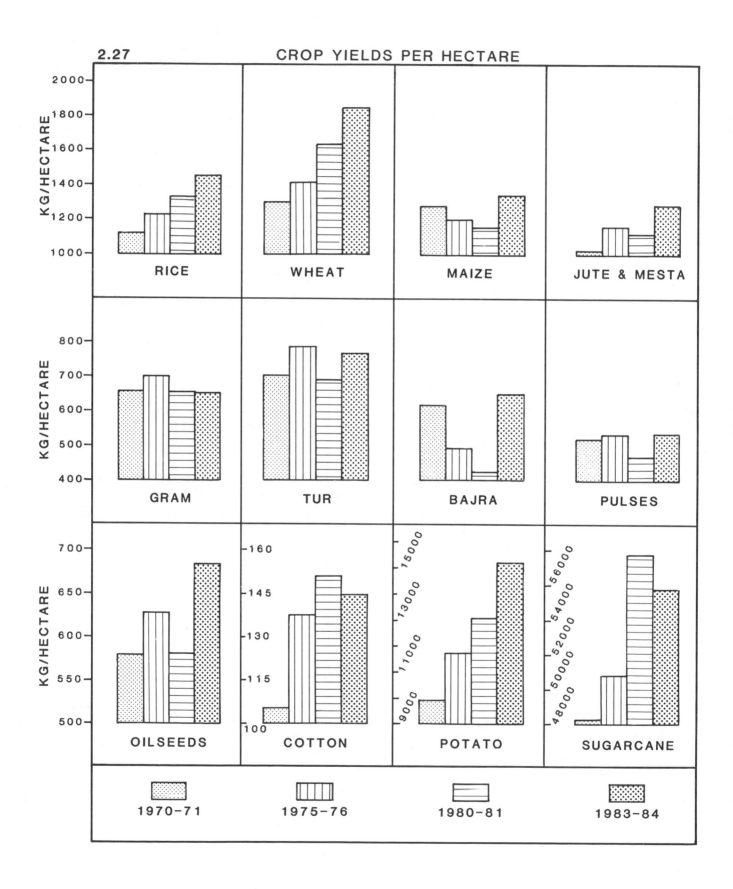

CROP YIELDS PER HECTARE

GREEN REVOLUTION

The Green Revolution in India was initiated in 1966 when high-yielding varieties (HYV) of wheat and rice were introduced. The basic components of the Green Revolution are i) the use of HYV seeds, ii) controlled water through irrigation, iii) plant protection measures by using pesticides and iv) adequate and balanced use of fertilizers. The basic research for HYV wheat, known as Mexican Dwarf variety, was conducted by Nobel Prize Winner Norman Borlaug. The HYV rice was introduced by the International Rice Research Institute in the Philippines. Indian scientists modified the primary HYV types to suit Indian climatic and topographic conditions and developed a number of native varieties as well.

There is a wide regional variation in the diffusion of the Green Revolution techniques. In the case of wheat, the states of Punjab, Haryana, and western Uttar Pradesh, where irrigation is a certainty, have benefited most and there, the wheat yield (1200 kg per acre) is over double compared to the rest of India. These three states account for over two-thirds of the country's acreage in HYV wheat. It is noteworthy that Punjab, Haryana and western Uttar Pradesh, traditionally a non-rice region, have taken significant advantage of the Green Revolution technique because of marketing profitability and have increased their rice production from 2.5 million in 1970-71 to 7.2 million tonnes in 1981-82, an annual growth rate of 10.93% compared to only 2.39% for the country; rice yields increased at an annual rate of 5.66% compared to 1.55% nationally. Punjab's rice yield (1240 kg per acre) in 1983-84 was 2 1/2 times higher than the eastern states consisting of east U.P., Bihar, West Bengal, Orissa and Assam.

Andhra Pradesh, Jammu and Kashmir, Tamilnadu, and Kerala have also profited from the HYV rice considerably. The initial center for the diffusion of HYV rice was Tamilnadu in 1966. Wherever HYV rice is successful, irrigation is necessarily a concomitant factor. The high rainfall areas of West Bengal, Bihar, Assam, and Orissa, which experience a great deal of daily and seasonal variation in the

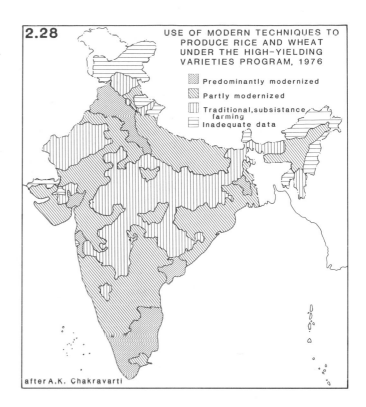

2.28 USE OF MODERN TECHNIQUES TO PRODUCE RICE AND WHEAT UNDER THE HIGH-YIELDING VARIETIES PROGRAM, 1976

Predominantly modernized
Partly modernized
Traditional, subsistence farming
Inadequate data

after A.K. Chakravarti

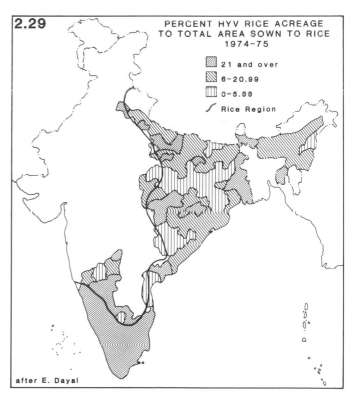

2.29 PERCENT HYV RICE ACREAGE TO TOTAL AREA SOWN TO RICE 1974-75

21 and over
6-20.99
0-5.99
Rice Region

after E. Dayal

amount of precipitation, have not adopted the HYV rice to any great degree. This is due primarily to the fact that in high rainfall areas water control during the monsoon season is extremely difficult and a more sophisticated system of controlled irrigation and drainage is necessary for HYV rice compared to HYV wheat. As a compensation, during the dry winter season a *rabi* crop (dry season winter crop) in the form of HYV wheat is becoming more prevalent. Thus, West Bengal, Assam, and Orissa which formerly produced very little wheat, have begun to devote a sizeable area of *rabi* crop to wheat. In West Bengal alone, almost 10% of the total foodgrain production was wheat in the mid-1980s. Of this figure, almost ninety percent was HYV wheat. The proportion of HYV wheat to total wheat areas in Assam, Orissa, and Andhra Pradesh is also very high because most wheat production in these states and West Bengal is new, made practicable only by the new HYV seeds of the "green revolution."

High-yielding varieties, provided with regulated applications of fertilizer, water, pest control techniques, and so forth, are capable of producing greatly increased yields. The wheat yield can be tripled, and the rice yield doubled. This capacity for increasing production is very encouraging, particularly viewing the future problems posed by increasing population and inadequate food supply. Indian farmers are hardworking. Moreover, there is no dearth of labor. If management, organization, and the required inputs in the form of HYV seeds, an adequate supply of water and fertilizers (both chemical and organic) are utilized efficiently, there is reason to believe that India will continue to feed herself.

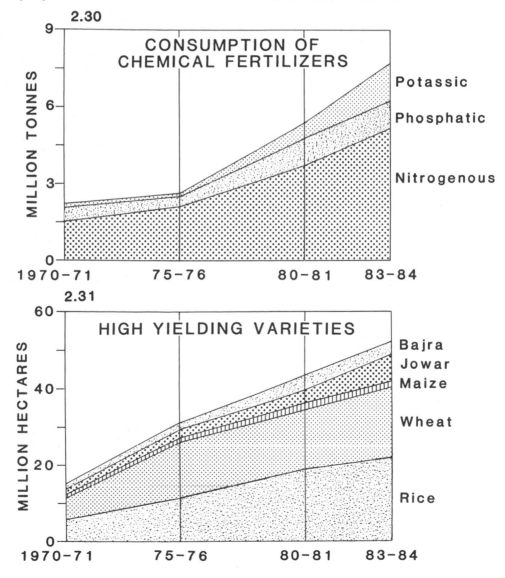

LIVESTOCK AND POULTRY

With 178 million head of cattle (cows and oxen) and 57 million buffaloes, India has nearly one-fourth of the world's horned livestock. It also has the world's largest domesticated bovine population. Cattle in India are primarily concentrated in the hot and humid areas of the east, whereas buffaloes are primarily concentrated in the drier northwestern regions. The cow is a sacred, but little cared for animal. The bovines have probably been considered, from time immemorial, the lifegivers by the agriculturalists of India. Oxen are used as plow animals and beasts of burden; cows provide milk. Cow dung, which is collected regularly, is a multiple-use product: for example, the dried cakes provide fuel, and, when made into a paste it becomes a waxlike substance for smoothing the mud floors and walls. Further, in rural areas cow dung-based gas plants (gobar gas plants) are becoming increasingly prevalent. The cow is very much tied to the well-being of the Indian farmer. Its conservation has, therefore, always been much desired and sought after.

Since very little land in India is available for open grazing and fodder production, the maintenance of cattle as a commercial endeavor is not developed as extensively as in Denmark, Australia, and the United States where cattle raising in itself is a commerical venture. As a result, livestock account for only 8% of India's national income.

Neither bullocks nor cows are very efficiently utilized in India. It has been estimated that, on the average, a pair of bullocks is used for cultivating only 10 acres of land per year. The average milk production per cow is also very low, although the she buffalo accounts for a higher yield. She buffaloes constitute only 45% of the total breeding bovine population, but account for 55% of the milk production; their milk has a higher butterfat content than that of the cow. India produced 38.8 million tonnes of milk in 1984-85 (about 50 kg per capita) and by the end of the Seventh Plan (1990) it is targeted to be raised to 51 million tonnes.

The main problems regarding India's bovine population are those of an acute shortage of feed and fodder and the lack of better breeds. The government is conscious of these problems and has initiated steps to solve them through several Five-Year Plans; intensive cattle-development projects which aim at selective breeding and crossbreeding, and developing high-yielding milk animals. In 1971-72, 529 key villages were selected to operationalize intensive cattle-development projects.

Chickens and ducks are inhabitants of a moist and year-round warm climate. In 1982, there were 35 million chickens in India. The southern states (Karnataka, Andhra Pradesh, Maharashtra, Kerala and Tamilnadu, in order of importance) produce 57% of the country's eggs. The native chicken is raised primarily in the backyards of the village houses. Those who practice domestic chicken-farming are the Moslems, Christians, Tribals, and some low-caste Hindus; upper-caste Hindus do not raise chickens as a matter of tabu. Organized poultry farming oriented towards serving metropolitan markets is a post-World War II development. The commercialization of the chicken and egg trade based on commercial chicken farms has resulted in a rise in the number of birds. Egg production in 1973-74 was 7.7 billion, but in 1984-85 it rose to 13.4 billion. Improved breeds of poultry have been used increasingly. As in the United States, it is the feed for the chicken which accounts for most of the input. The feed alone accounts for 70% of the cost of egg production and 60% of the chicken and duck meat. Domestically-raised chickens live on household wastes and therefore, cost virtually nothing to feed.

Sheep and goats numbered 42 million and 64 million, respectively. Both are used for meat, but sheep also yield India's wool supply. The average sheep produces only 0.9 kg of wool per annum which is almost one-fifth of that of a sheep in Australia, New Zealand, or the United Kingdom. India produced 37 million kg of wool in 1984-85 and the Seventh Plan target is to raise it to 43 million kg. The Indian climate is partly responsible for the low wool output and its inferior quality. However, in the northern temperate climate of Kashmir, Himachal Pradesh, and Uttar Pradesh, better breeds yield increased output. Currently, only 10% of the total wool produced in India is used for ap-

LIVESTOCK

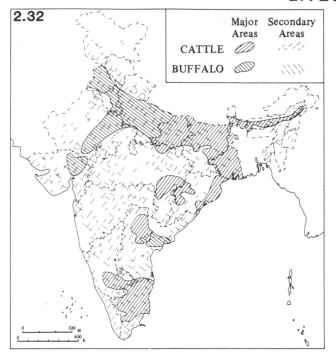

2.32

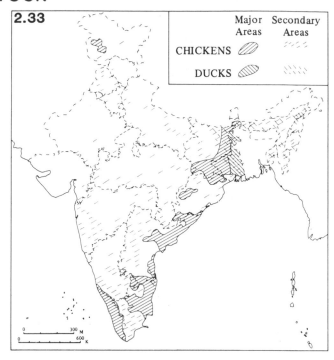

2.33

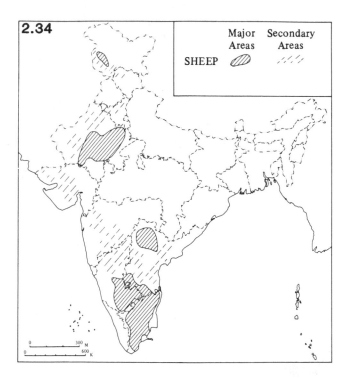

2.34

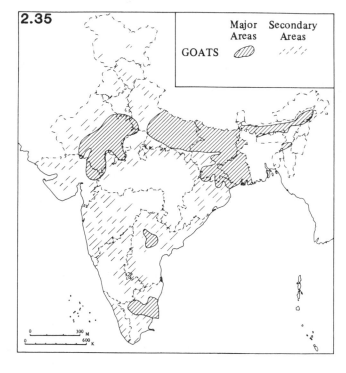

2.35

parel making; the remainder is used for carpets and blankets.

On the whole, animal husbandry in India is at a low ebb. Nonetheless, its improvement is very closely linked to the improvement in living standards, per capita income of the farmer, and in the protein content of the Indian diet.

FISHERIES

To many Hindus in India, the fish is an auspicious sign. Although it is widely eaten, approximately 30% to 50% of Indians do not, because of some type of religious belief or tabu. The principal content of the average Indian diet consists of carbohydrates and is significantly deficient in protein and other nutrients. Such deficiencies can result in various diseases and types of retardation. Since fish contains a considerable amount of protein and could provide a good part of the protein requirement for a healthy diet, the general view is that the development of fisheries in India is very closely intertwined with the improvement in the quality of the Indian diet.

Although India ranks seventh in world fish production its percentage of the total world catch is a mere 2.4. The country's production of 2.4 million tonnes (1981) is insufficient to meet the demands of the people. For adequate nourishment, nutrition experts recommend intake of 40 grams (1.4 ounces) of animal protein per day; if only fish in considered, on the average every individual in India consumes as little as six grams per day.

There are enormous resources of inland and marine fish available to India. The total culturable area of tanks and ponds is 1.6 million hectares, of which only .6 million hectares are currently being utilized. There are 16,767 miles (27,000 km) of rivers and 70,173 miles (113,000 km) of irrigation canals. From these sources, a total of .8 million tons of freshwater fish is obtained. On the average, per hectare fish production in the tanks and ponds is low, only 1,320 lb (600 kg). Marine sources are responsible for 1.4 million tonnes per annum; almost 60% of the country's fish catch is obtained from the sea. Further, not only does India have an extensive coastline, but along its continental shelf lies a potentially vast, unexplored reserve of fish. Currently, the Indian Ocean accounts for only four percent of the world's fish catch.

The principal difficulty of the Indian fishing industry is its lack of modernization. The inland fisheries do not have scientifically-bred fish fry and fingerlings which are capable of large-scale growth. As a result, based on the utilization of the traditional fry, the yield is low. Recently, the Central Inland Fisheries Research Institute has undertaken research into the breeding of Indian and foreign fish. Based on such culture, yields of up to 6,600 lb (3,000 kg) per hectare have been obtained. The application of such Green Revolution type fish is bound to substantially increase the fish production. This and other new methods of fish culture need to be popularized. In addition, more area needs to be devoted to the extension of culturable swamps, ponds, reservoirs, etc.

In marine fishing, traditional nonmechanized fishing methods account for almost 60% of the marine catch. It is in this kind of fishing that the great majority of Indian fishermen earn their living. These fishermen constitute one of the poorest and most deprived sectors of the Indian population; their needs were overlooked by the government until the Fifth Five-Year Plan. Beginning in 1974, a plan was developed to improve the condition of the marine fishermen. Elements of the plan included streamlining the design of the boats, improving the quality of the sails, providing outboard motors to increase efficiency, installing onboard storage facilities, providing mechanized facilities for fishing by traditional methods and making ice available at docking areas. The target fish production in the Sixth Five-Year Plan was 3.5 million tons, but in 1984-85 only 2.28 million were produced. The Seventh Plan has earmarked its target for 4 million tons.

Another kind of sea fishing is classified as coastal but mechanized. Previous Plans, as well as the Fifth and Sixth Five-Year Plans, have greatly assisted this method of fishing primarily by supplying mechanized boats. Deep-sea fishing, which requires trawlers and more efficient vessels, is gaining increasing support. The Sixth Five-Year Plan intended to use 350 large vessels for deep sea fishing. The Plan foresees that the proportion of the total production of marine fishing vis-a-vis inland fishing will remain the same.

Of the maritime states of India, Kerala and Maharashtra are the leading producers of fish. Jointly, they are responsible for almost half of

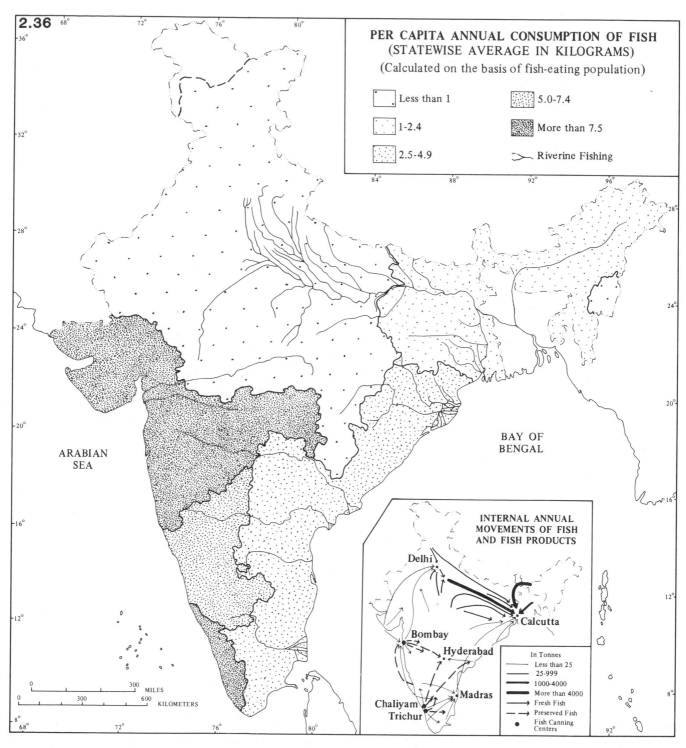

2.36

PER CAPITA ANNUAL CONSUMPTION OF FISH
(STATEWISE AVERAGE IN KILOGRAMS)
(Calculated on the basis of fish-eating population)

Less than 1

1-2.4

2.5-4.9

5.0-7.4

More than 7.5

Riverine Fishing

ARABIAN SEA

BAY OF BENGAL

MILES
KILOMETERS

INTERNAL ANNUAL MOVEMENTS OF FISH AND FISH PRODUCTS

Delhi

Bombay

Hyderabad

Calcutta

Chaliyam Trichur

Madras

In Tonnes
Less than 25
25-999
1000-4000
More than 4000
Fresh Fish
Preserved Fish
Fish Canning Centers

the total production of maritime fish in the country. On the whole, the western coast of India produces double the amount of the east. This fact is well reflected in the greater per capita consumption of fish (based on fish-eating population) in the states of the west coast as compared to those of the east. However, much greater proportion of people in the east, particularly in West Bengal, eat fish; even the *Brahmins* of West Bengal consider fish to be a part of their regular diet, whereas a south Indian or a Gujarati Brahmin will seldom touch it. Regarding the internal movement of fish in the country, the greatest percentage is directed to the markets of Calcutta. This is due to the fact that not only is fish an essential part of the daily Bengali diet, but also because the yield of the northeastern coast is not sufficient to meet the local demand. In fact, the states of West Bengal and Orissa supply only 5% of the country's marine fish catch.

If the predominant religious group of India, the Hindus, did not have a tabu against eating beef, it is conceivable that the current protein deficiency problem could be solved with a regional strategy utilizing a meat-based protein diet in the north, and a fish-based diet in the south. As such a belief is more likely to continue, it is realistic to concentrate in the north on milk and goat meat for protein intake, and in the south on fish and mutton.

ENERGY AND MINERAL RESOURCES

The development of energy sources is fundamental to the modernization of India. The Seventh Five-Year Plan had given the highest priority in allocation of its public funds because it considered energy availibility to be basic both for industrial and agricultural development and for ensuring a 5% annual growth rate for the country. Energy sources consist of the traditional types such as fuel wood, dry cattle dung, vegetable wastes, and modern sources such as coal, hydel (hydroelectric power), petroleum, and atomic power. Most of the modern energy sources, except those used in the transportation sector, are converted into electricity.

The traditional sources of energy are essentially non-commercial, their use primarily restricted to the home. It has been estimated that 91% of the rural domestic fuel use and 75% of the urban fuel use are derived from traditional sources: fuel wood constituting 70%, dry dung 15%, and vegetable wastes 10% to 15%. Fuel wood is obtained from community and waste lands, trees that grow on the farms, and from the forests near villages. There is increasing demand for wood from both the burgeoning population and industrial users. Thus, depletion of the supply of trees is increasing at a rapidly accelerating rate. Four hundred million tons of wet cattle dung are

converted annually into 60 to 65 million tons of dry cattle dung (equal to 25 million tons of coal) for domestic fuel use. If this supply of dung were used as fertilizer it would amount to eight times the present production of the Sindri fertilizer plant. Thus, the farmers are faced with a critical dilemma; whether to utilize the cow dung as fuel or as fertilizer. Unless fuel needs are met by alternative sources, the possibility of the extensive use of dung as fertilizer is remote.

Of the total installed capacity of power generation in India (about 42 million kilowatts in 1985), 61% comes from thermal sources, 37% from hydel, and approximately 2% from the development of nuclear resources. Thermal sources are abundant in the coal-rich eastern region of India. Hydel sources predominate in the coal-deficient south and are important in the north. The northeast, which is least industrialized and therefore requires minimal power supplies, consumes little thermal or hydel power.

The principal source of modernized energy is coal. Proven reserves of coal as computed by the Geological Survey of India in 1972 are 21.36 billion tons; estimated total reserves amount to about four times that figure. In rank order, the prinicpal consumers of coal are electric power stations, steel mills, and the railroads. Together, they constitute about two-thirds of the total coal usage in the country. With 1983-84 production at 145 million tons, and anticipating an increase in future production, coal reserves can last at least until the end of the next century. The country is deficient, however, in large reserves of coking coal, which is a necessary input for the continuing manufacture of steel.

Good quality coal occurs in the northeastern part of the Deccan Plateau, specifically the Damodar and Mahanadi Valleys. This region is responsible for the overwhelming portion of India's supply of coal. Naturally, movements of coal within India emanate from these areas, principally by railroad. Due to the shortage of hopper cars in recent years and the inability of the railroads to make the necessary transfers, the states that are distant from the Damodar and Mahanadi regions receive less coal than their demands require.

ENERGY

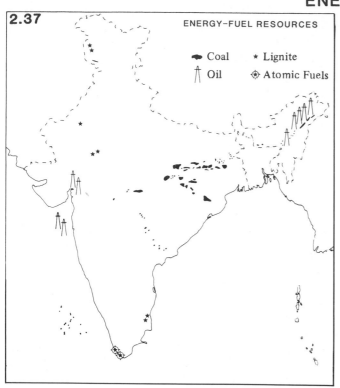

2.37 ENERGY-FUEL RESOURCES

- 🐟 Coal   ★ Lignite
- ⚔ Oil   ⊛ Atomic Fuels

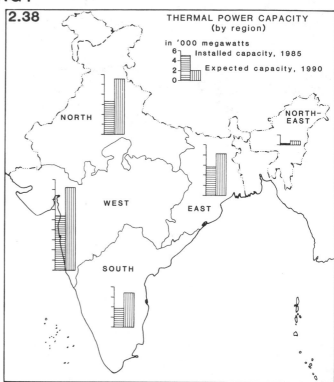

2.38 THERMAL POWER CAPACITY
(by region)

in '000 megawatts

6
4
2
0
Installed capacity, 1985

Expected capacity, 1990

NORTH

NORTH-EAST

WEST   EAST

SOUTH

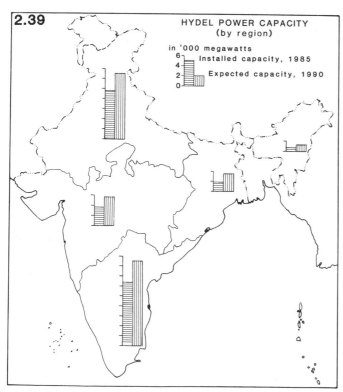

2.39 HYDEL POWER CAPACITY
(by region)

in '000 megawatts

6
4
2
0
Installed capacity, 1985

Expected capacity, 1990

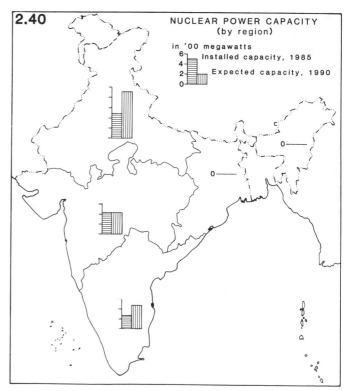

2.40 NUCLEAR POWER CAPACITY
(by region)

in '00 megawatts

6
4
2
0
Installed capacity, 1985

Expected capacity, 1990

0

0

Hydel-power potential is abundant and is possible in many parts of the country. Of the total potential of 75,000 mw, only 11,394 (1980) of installed capacity have been developed due to various factors: the problems involved with managing such large-scale capital investment; the lack of large, perennially flowing rivers in the Deccan Plateau area; seasonal variations in the amount of precipitation which necessitate the construction of reservoir facilities; and the unresolved problems arising from drought years. Still, when compared with hydel capacity at the time of independence, the country's capacity has increased about thirteen times with a total of seventy-nine major hydel-power stations. The abundance of coal in the eastern region of India has not necessitated a sizeable hydel-power development there, whereas the south and the north particularly have developed a greater hydroelectric capacity.

India, at present, has limited petroleum resources. Production, restricted to Assam in the northeast and to Gujarat in the west, is able to supply only one-half of the nation's internal consumption of petroleum. Thus, there is great dependence on foreign producers for the vital mineral. The government has now implemented a policy which restricts the use of petroleum to such unavoidable consumers as automobiles, diesel railroad engines and petro-chemical industries. Direction of the future energy supply is toward thermal power based on coal, hydel, and atomic sources.

The first atomic power station at Tarapur (Maharashtra) began to supply power in 1969 and has a 420 mw capacity. A similar facility with a capacity of 440 mw has been developed near Kota in Rajasthan. A third installation, at Kalpakkan in Tamilnadu with a capacity of 235 megawatts. A fourth one at Nararo in Uttar Pradesh with two 235 mw units is under construction. These four stations have been

2.41 MINERAL PRODUCTION 1951-79

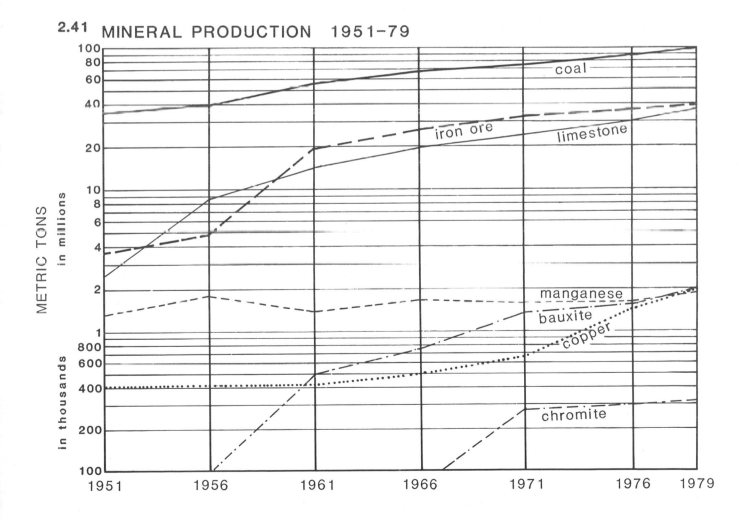

located so as to supply power in coal-deficient areas.

India is fortunate to possess the world's largest reserve of thorium, an atomic ore: 500,000 tons of ore containing approximately eight to ten percent thorium. The ore is located along the beaches of Kerala and Tamilnadu for a distance of about twenty miles. The two main centers of deposit are Chavara in Kerala and Manavia Kurichi in Tamilnadu.

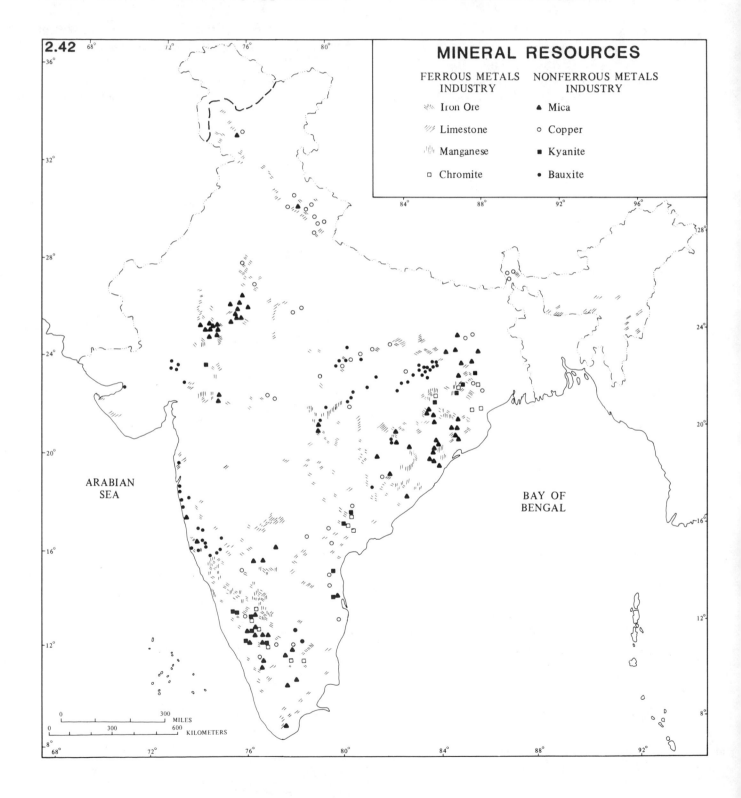

MINERAL RESOURCES

FERROUS METALS INDUSTRY

- Iron Ore
- Limestone
- Manganese
- □ Chromite

NONFERROUS METALS INDUSTRY

- ▲ Mica
- ○ Copper
- ■ Kyanite
- • Bauxite

ARABIAN SEA

BAY OF BENGAL

MINERAL BASE

India is rich in minerals. Of the leading minerals, the country is self-sufficient in coal and limestone. It has an exportable surplus of iron ore, manganese, mica, kyanite, and chromite. It is deficient in and therefore must import petroleum, copper, zinc, and tin. The principal location of minerals is in the Deccan Plateau in association with rocks of the Pre-Paleozoic Era. Areas of specific concentration are the northeastern Deccan Plateau and the southern half of south India. A significant number of mineral-based industries are, as a result, located in those areas.

The iron ore reserves of India are the largest in the world. Of this reserve, 8.1 billion tons are estimated to contain over 55% iron content (Fe), which is indicative of high quality ore. Thus, the quantity of the resource not only meets the entire internal needs of the country, but also provides a sizeable quantity for exportation. Of the 1982-83 production of 42 million tons, 59% was exported.

One of the principal barriers to large-scale exportation has been the general occurrence of ore deposits (except in Goa) in the inaccessible interior, and the lack of efficient transport connections with a seaport. Concerted efforts have been made, however, to construct railroad facilities to provide linkages from mineral deposit to port, such as in Paradip (Orissa) and Visakhapatnam.

India not only has abundant manganese reserves, but it exports most of its production. In fact, it is the second largest exporter of manganese in the world. Chromite, kyanite, and mica are mined mainly for exportation. India produces 75% of the world's mica and almost all of the kyanite. Mica deposits are located principally in the Kodarma area of south Bihar. Limestone, used primarily in the cement industry, is also an essential raw material for steel making. Although the Vindhyan quarries of the Son Valley have extensive high-quality deposits, limestone also is found in other locations on the Indian peninsula. The reserves of bauxite, a raw material utilized in the aluminum industry, are ade-

quate. Bauxite is mined principally in the Lohardaga region of south Bihar, but there are additional deposits in other areas of the Deccan Plateau.

On the whole, India is quite well endowed with mineral resources. Of the vitally important minerals, petroleum is the principal deficiency. The discovery of offshore oil in Bombay High in early 1975 and other discoveries have brightened the country's oil picture because these and other sources account for almost 50% of the country's total consumption. On the whole, the country has the requisite raw materials for an extensive development of mineral-based industries such as iron and steel, aluminum, and coal-based fertilizer.

DAMODAR VALLEY CORPORATION

The Damodar River, like the Huang Ho of China, was known as a "River of Sorrow." Annual flooding caused by the Damodar in West Bengal was notorious and frequent. As a result of the severe flood of 1943, the British government decided to harness the river's flow. Each year as the river flooded, swamps and marsh areas formed, providing breeding grounds for the malaria carrying Anopheles mosquitoes.

The flood control program of the Damodar River was intended to control the flow of water both in the main river and its tributaries such as the Konar and the Barakar. Dams and reservoirs were built to reserve water during the monsoon rains and to eventually release the water when the rains end. The reservoir sites at Tilaya, Panchet Hills, and Maithon were used for hydroelectric generation. A 2,262' (692 meter) long barrage was constructed near Durgapur from where canals were dug to irrigate parts of southern West Bengal. The total length of the irrigation canals is 1,673 miles (2,695 km) with an irrigation potential of .51 million hectares. The DVC has an installed power-generating capacity of 1,181 mw, of which 91% is made up of thermal power and 9% hydel. One canal meets the Hooghly River and was expected to be used for navigation though this has been impeded by lack of ade-

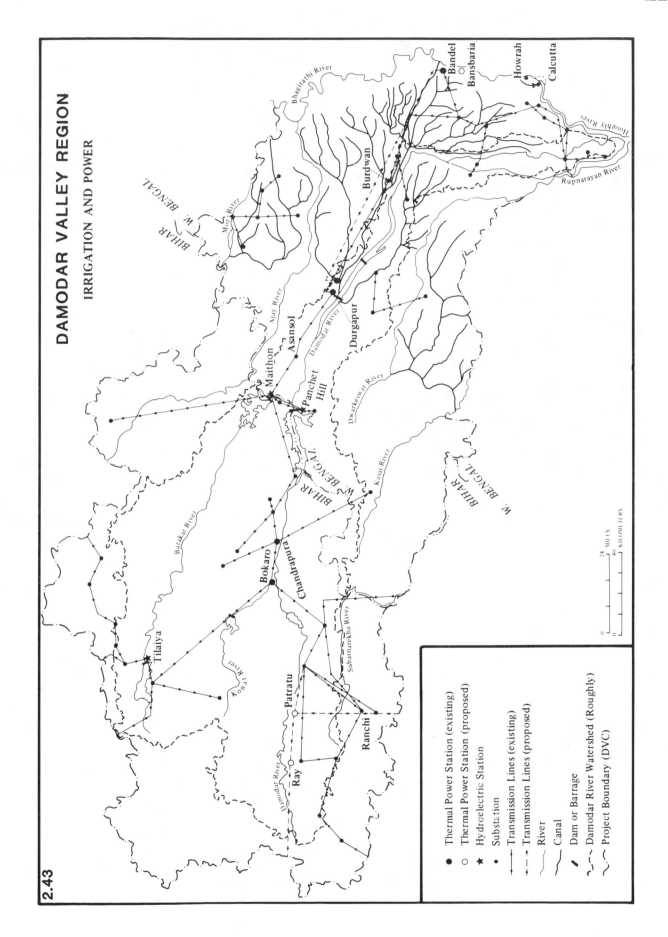

DAMODAR VALLEY REGION

IRRIGATION AND POWER

2.43

- ● Thermal Power Station (existing)
- ○ Thermal Power Station (proposed)
- ★ Hydroelectric Station
- • Substation
- —•— Transmission Lines (existing)
- ---•--- Transmission Lines (proposed)
- ⟋ River
- ⟋ Canal
- ▸ Dam or Barrage
- —··— Damodar River Watershed (Roughly)
- ⟋⟋ Project Boundary (DVC)

quate water flow.

The entire Damodar Valley system with its 1,181 megawatts installed power generating capacity, has an interconnected electrical transmission line system. Sometimes the irregularity of monsoon rains lowers reservoir levels and causes insufficient electrical generation affecting industries in the Damodar Valley as well as in the Calcutta region. Nevertheless, based on the power supply of both DVC electricity and Damodar Valley coal, a large number of industries have been attracted to this region particularly since the 1950s. It is also one of the five major industrial regions of the country.

The Damodar Valley Corporation (DVC) is essentially a multipurpose river-valley project designed by an American engineer, William Voorduin, who was brought to India from the Tennessee Valley Authority in the United States. The TVA formed the model on which Voorduin based the DVC at its formal inception in 1948. The DVC Board consists of three representatives; one each from the states of Bihar, West Bengal, and the central government. It was involved in implementing the first river basin plan in India that encompassed the jurisdiction of more than one state. The DVC functions within its own jurisdiction independently from participating governments. However, the success of tripartite governmental cooperation depends primarily on the at-

titude of the participants. In this connection, a disagreement began in 1956 when the government of West Bengal refused to fund more than four dams and, as a result, state electric power boards were established both in West Bengal and in Bihar. These boards virtually challenged the jurisdiction of the DVC in matters of electrical generation in both states. Despite continued controversy, the presence of a central government representative on the DVC Board has worked as a neutralizing factor and the DVC continues to function as a separate, independent, and effective organization.

India benefited from the DVC experience and this has been extremely important as the project became an effective guideline in both its good and bad points for other multipurpose river-valley projects such as the Bhakra-Nangal, Mahanadi Valley, and Kosi. Voorduin began his project in 1945 with insufficient data, such as over-estimating water availability, which resulted in inadequate water supply for canals in West Bengal in the dry season, January through June. Also, a large-scale cultivation of winter *rabi* crops based on canal water was found to be impossible. Nevertheless, the overall benefits of the DVC in the expansion of land-use productivity, flood control and in the developmental experience have outweighed the shortcomings of the project.

INDUSTRIES
MANUFACTURING REGIONS

Industries in India are concentrated in specific regions based on the economics of location. During the process of industrial evolution, some regions developed more advantageously from a locational point of view, growing into clusters of industrial complexes, such as Greater Bombay and Calcutta-Hooghlyside. The industrial regions have been divided by Karan (1964) into five first-order districts, 14 second-order districts, and 12 third-order districts based on the numbers of workers. A description of the characteristics of the five first-order industrial districts follows.

Calcutta-Hooghlyside Region. This region, which is also known as the Calcutta Metropolitan District (CMD), is the most important in the country. Jute processing and metal works (engineering) are the main industrial activities of the CMD. This region has stagnated economically. The primary causes for this were: (1) congestion of surface transportation within this district; (2) a decline in Calcutta's port activity due to a gradual silting of the Hooghly River and relegating into the fifth ranked port of the country which handled 10.3 million tonnes in 1983-84, i.e., only 11% of India's export-import trade; (3) hardships created by the political imposition of the partition in 1947 when jute-growing areas went to East Pakistan, now Bangladesh, cutting off the very base of Calcutta's jute mills in terms of raw material supply (which difficulty was partly circumscribed in the 1950s by encouraging jute production in West Bengal and other parts of India); (4) undercapacity of city services including water supply and sewage; (5) political anarchy created by extreme leftist groups (*naxalites*) between 1967 and 1972; (6) frequent failures of the power supply (electricity) because of the inadequacy and inefficiency of the power-generating plants; and finally (7) the Marxist leftist government of the state being unable to attract new capital investments. This region, however, has some inherent advantages such as: (1) nearness to the Damodar Valley coal supply, and Chotanagpur steel-making centers, (2) riverine location, (3) command of a hinterland covering almost a quarter of India and a third of the country's population, (4) rejuvenation of riverine routes inland through the Farakka Barrage Scheme, completed April, 1975, and (5) the advantages of an early industrial start (since the early 19th century).

Bombay-Pune Region. This region includes Greater Bombay, Pune, and the Bombay-Pune corridor. Greater Bombay specializes in cotton textiles, general engineering, and chemicals. Cotton textiles accounts for 40% of the workers employed. Since 1947, industrial growth has taken place primarily in chemical, engineering, and capital-intensive electronic industries. The 120 mile corridor between Pune and Bombay is developing rapidly with numerous industrial establishments. Greater Bombay's locational advantages are: (1) excellent natural port facilities, (2) good transportation linkages in both railroads and roads for collecting raw materials and marketing manufactured products, (3) availability of basic utilities, and (4) command of a well-established hinterland covering a large part of west and northwestern India. The port of Bombay is India's largest port where 1369 ships entered and which handled 24.98 million tonnes in 1983-84. It accounted for 25% of the country's exports and imports. Moreover, the Maharashtra State government has been giving special impetus to the Bombay region to facilitate growth.

Ahmadabad-Vadodara Region. This region falls in Gujarat. Cotton textiles is the most important industry of this region, employing about three-quarters of its total industrial work force. Being in the heart of the principal cotton-growing region in India provides an unprecedented locational advantage. A large public sector petrochemical complex has been set up in Vadodara since 1974-78, which in 1982-83 made a profit of $66.6 million. The Gujaratis, one of the main business communities of India, have in recent times started to pump a considerable amount of capital into their own state. The nearby port of Kandla has also contributed to the growth of the area as it is not only the second ranked port in the country, but it handles 14% of India's foreign trade. Moreover, several port locations—including

Surat, at the mouth of the Tapti River, and Bharuch, at the mouth of the Narmada River— are ancient sites which flourished for over 1,500 years. These ports conducted sea-borne trade with East and Southeast Asia and the Middle East. Traditionally, this area falls at the oceanic end of the "historical corridor" originating from the Delhi-Agra-Kanauj core areas of ancient times.

Madurai-Coimbatore-Bangalore Region. This region is a combination of three distinctive industrial complexes. As a whole, they specialize in cotton textiles employing almost one-half of the total industrial workers. Although Coimbatore and Madurai are largely oriented to cotton textiles, Bangalore has developed an in-

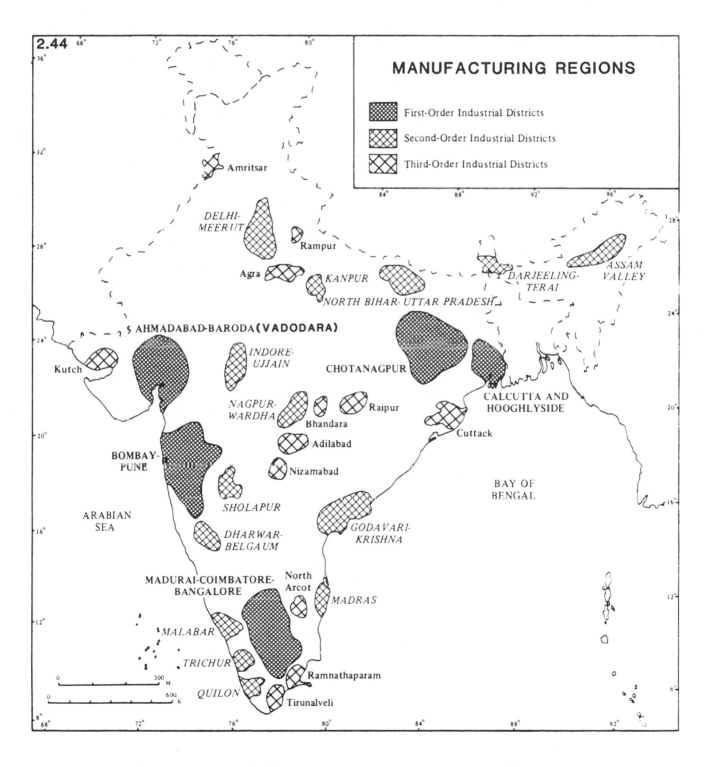

dustrial mixture of cotton textiles, electronics, machine building, aircraft, electric goods, and telephone industries. Out of the twenty-four most important industries in Bangalore, fourteen are state owned, signifying large-scale public enterprise investments in the city.

Chotanagpur Region. This region has developed an industrial complex consisting of iron and steel, heavy machines, explosives, cement, aluminum, locomotives, and diesel trucks. The most important centers in this region are Jamshedpur, Rourkela, Bokaro and Ranchi. The primary factor in attracting such an industrial complex is the occurrence of coal in large quantities and in association with a variety of minerals. Additional factors are the cheap DVC electric power, the availability of water from streams and reservoirs, and the nearness of Calcutta's market and port.

TEXTILES

As long ago as the eighteenth century, India was world-famous for its production of fine handwoven muslins and silks. The introduction of the factory manufacturing of textiles, however, began just over a century and a half ago. The first cotton mill was established near Calcutta in Fort Gloster in 1818, and a jute mill, also near Calcutta in Rishra in 1859.

By the beginning of this century, both the cotton and jute industries had localized near their raw-material sources: cotton in the Bombay-Ahmadabad region and jute in the Calcutta metropolitan area along the Hooghly River. By the 1960s, the cotton industry had expanded north and south following both local raw material availability and market demand. The eastern region of India, where the wet climate is unsuitable for cotton cultivation, has developed only a few cotton manufacturing centers such as Calcutta. In the case of jute, however, the Calcutta area has remained the principal center with over 90% of the nation's mills. Jute cultivation has remained mainly concentrated in the Ganges delta because of the region's particular climatic, soil, and hydrologic suitability.

Cotton textile mills numbered 803 in 1982. The cotton industry is the largest in the country employmentwise, with a work force of almost one million. Currently, this industry is divided into two types, the mill and decentralized handloom clothmaking. The latter type is most often located in villages and conducted by families as small, localized units, often using mill-made yarns. Since independence, the rate of growth of the decentralized operation has exceeded that of the mill, primarily because handwoven cloth is less expensive to purchase than the manufactured cloth. Mill-made yarn production has almost doubled during the same period, however, because a sizeable portion of the output is utilized by handlooms. The principal problem faced by mill operators is obsolete machinery which retards effective productivity and occasional, but prolonged labor strikes.

The jute industry, which experienced a catastrophe after partition, when the prime jute-producing areas were incorporated into East Pakistan, has now reestablished its base with raw jute growing areas developed in West Bengal and other neighboring states. In 1982, there were 69 jute mills operational. Jute is primarily an export product of India and accounts for about 30% of the world's jute-goods exports. Its manufacture in India has been either almost static or on the decline for the past thirty-five years because world demand has not increased significantly. Further depressing the Indian jute situation is the fact that the Bangladesh mills are more modern and are located nearer to a better raw material supply base.

Other textiles produced in India include woolens, rayon, silk, and coir. Woolen manufacturing is concentrated primarily in the drier northwestern part of India where sheep-raising occurs. The manufacture of coir, a by-product of the coconut husk, is concentrated in the principal coconut-growing region of Kerala. In terms of rate of production, rayon, which began with a very low base in 1950-51, has witnessed the most spectacular growth because of increasing demand.

TEXTILES

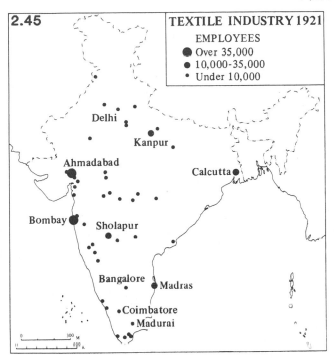

2.45 TEXTILE INDUSTRY 1921
EMPLOYEES
● Over 35,000
● 10,000-35,000
· Under 10,000

Delhi
Kanpur
Ahmadabad
Calcutta
Bombay
Sholapur
Bangalore
Madras
Coimbatore
Madurai

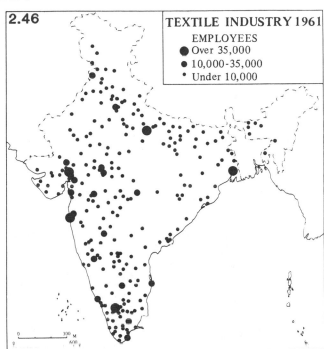

2.46 TEXTILE INDUSTRY 1961
EMPLOYEES
● Over 35,000
● 10,000-35,000
· Under 10,000

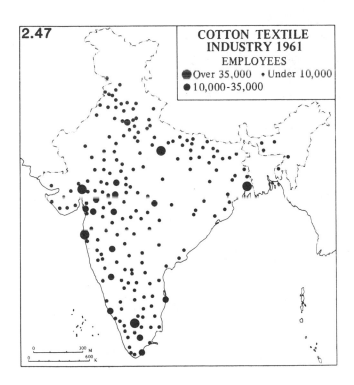

2.47 COTTON TEXTILE
INDUSTRY 1961
EMPLOYEES
● Over 35,000 · Under 10,000
● 10,000-35,000

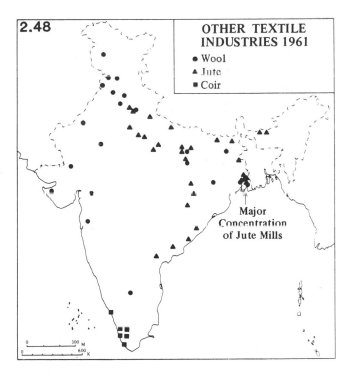

2.48 OTHER TEXTILE
INDUSTRIES 1961
● Wool
▲ Jute
■ Coir

Major
Concentration
of Jute Mills

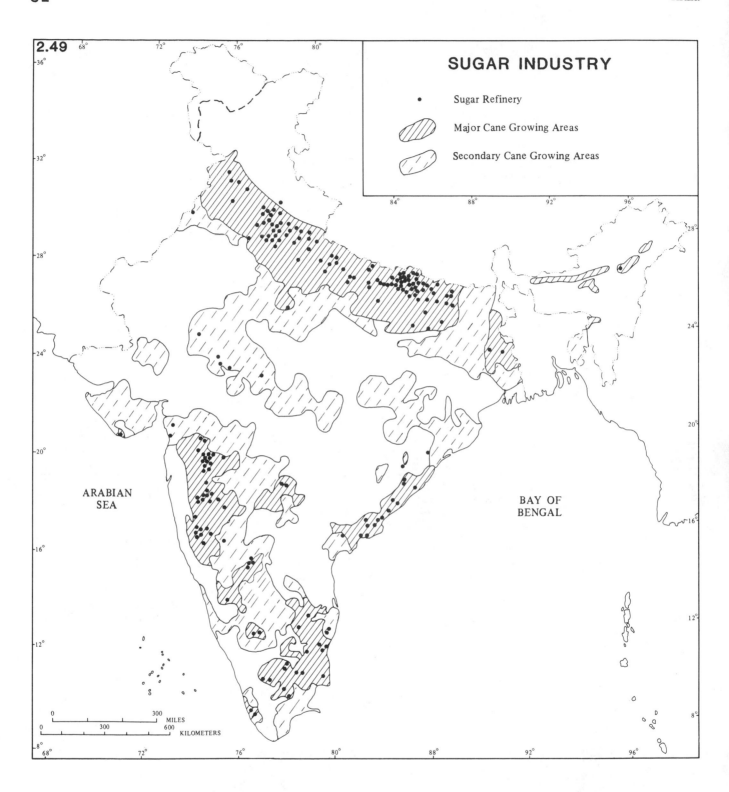

SUGAR INDUSTRY

- Sugar Refinery
- Major Cane Growing Areas
- Secondary Cane Growing Areas

SUGAR INDUSTRY

In terms of location, sugar refineries are basically raw-material oriented. First, it is vital that the sugarcane reaches the refinery immediately after harvesting, otherwise it loses its sucrose content, resulting in an inferior sugar-generating potential. Best results are obtained if the transfer of the cane is effected within twenty-four hours of cutting. Second, as cane is a bulky raw material (as much as ten tons is required to produce one ton of white sugar granules), costly transportation costs are avoided by locating the refineries in close proximity to the producing areas.

The Northern Plains and parts of the Eastern Plains are the traditional and most important sugarcane-producing areas. The industry first originated and became localized in these regions after the imposition of a protective tariff in 1932, which virtually eliminated the importation of cheaper sugar from Java. In 1931-32, Uttar Pradesh and Bihar accounted for over ninety percent of the country's total production of refined sugar. Climatically, however, this traditional area is not the best for maximum yield. The climate of south India is more favorable, and there has been a tendency toward a southward shift of sugarcane production. Currently, south Indian refineries, which are more modern and which can operate year-round because of the availability of fresh cane, have nearly overtaken the production of the north where cane is available for only four to five months.

The refined Indian sugar has had difficulties in competing on the world market because of high production costs. As a result, a very small proportion of the national production (2.7% on the average) had been exported in the sixties and the early seventies. The increased demand and price of sugar in the world market in the 1970s resulted in a special incentive for increased sugar production. Thus, another agro-based item of importance was added to the list of potentially important exports. Though sugar production has risen about 125% during 1970-71 to 1982-83, the exports in the early 1980s leveled to about 0.2 million tonnes only because of increased internal consumption.

However, increased production of sugar, through the use of high-yield varieties, is a necessary prerequisite to the growth of the industry because it assures cost reduction and minimizes the competition with food grain production in terms of competing land uses.

STEEL AND OTHER METAL-BASED INDUSTRIES

Metal-based industries have progressed at a rapid rate since independence, principally to satisfy the country's own needs resulting from accelerated industrialization. Beginning with the Second Five-Year Plan (1956-61), there has been an increasing emphasis on heavy industry with particular reference to steel-making. While steel is the most important of the metal-based industries, the aluminum and copper industries are also significant.

The availability of bauxite in the Chotanagpur Plateau, Salem in Tamilnadu and in the vicinity of Goa has given rise to the establishment of large-scale aluminum smelting industries in Jaykaynagar (Burdwan district) based on thermal power and in Hirakud and Alwaye based on hydroelectricity; new smelters are being planned at Korba and Ratnagiri. Copper smelting is concentrated in the region where it is mined, in Ghatsila (Singhbhum) and Khetri (Rajasthan).

The iron and steel industries are mainly concentrated in the northeastern region of the Deccan Plateau where iron ore, coal,

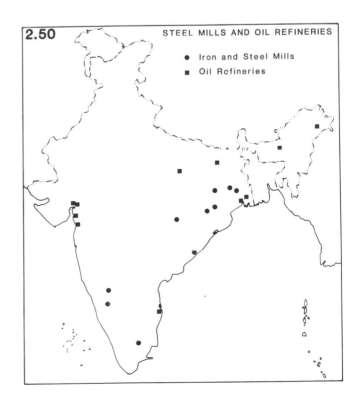

2.50   STEEL MILLS AND OIL REFINERIES

● Iron and Steel Mills

■ Oil Refineries

METAL-BASED INDUSTRIES

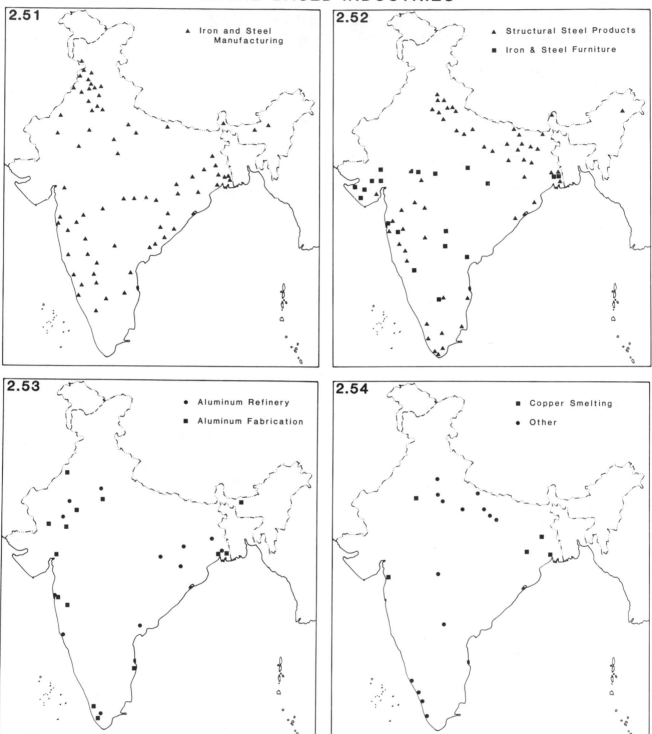

manganese, and limestone are found in close proximity. While the location of this industry is primarily raw material oriented, the large market of Calcutta is a definite plus factor in attracting the industry to this region.

Although the first steel mill (the Tata Iron and Steel Company in Jamshedpur) went into operation in 1911 as a private enterprise effort, only two additional factories were established by independence in 1947 when the total steel ingot production for the country was 2 million tons. The post-independence period, however,

OTHER INDUSTRIES

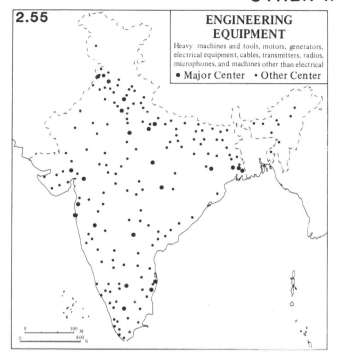

2.55

ENGINEERING EQUIPMENT
Heavy machines and tools, motors, generators, electrical equipment, cables, transmitters, radios, microphones, and machines other than electrical
● Major Center •Other Center

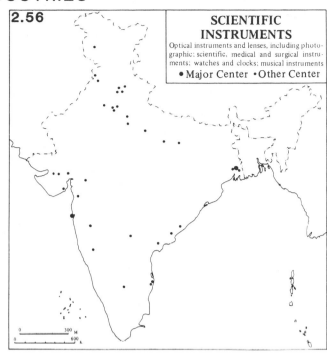

2.56

SCIENTIFIC INSTRUMENTS
Optical instruments and lenses, including photographic; scientific, medical and surgical instruments; watches and clocks; musical instruments
● Major Center •Other Center

2.57

LEATHER INDUSTRIES
Tanneries, shoe factories, and other leather products
● Major Center •Other Center

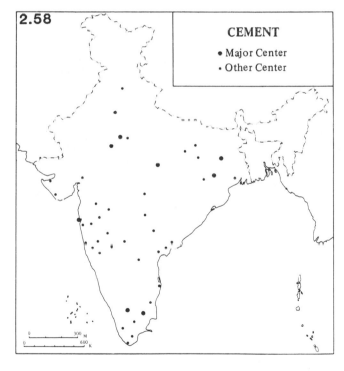

2.58

CEMENT
● Major Center
• Other Center

has witnessed not only the expansion of the old mills at Jamshedpur, Burnpur-Kulti, and Bhadravati, but the opening of new state-owned mills in Durgapur (with British collaboration), Rourkela (with West German collaboration), Bhilai and Bokaro (both with Russian collaboration). Apart from the seven large

integrated steel mills, 169 (in 1982-83) mini steel mills are also in operation. In 1983-84, India produced 10.48 million tonnes of steel ingots, of which about 80% came from the seven large mills and the remaining 20% was contributed by the mini steel plants.

The three new mini steel plants in south In-

TRANSPORT INDUSTRIES

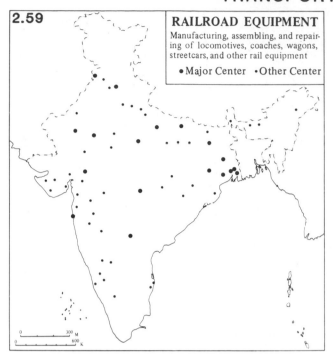

2.59

RAILROAD EQUIPMENT
Manufacturing, assembling, and repairing of locomotives, coaches, wagons, streetcars, and other rail equipment
• Major Center •Other Center

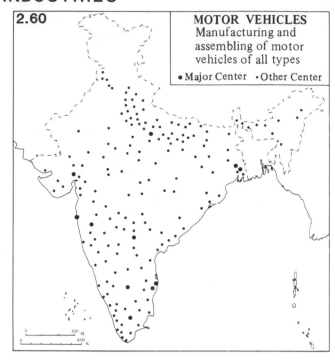

2.60

MOTOR VEHICLES
Manufacturing and assembling of motor vehicles of all types
• Major Center •Other Center

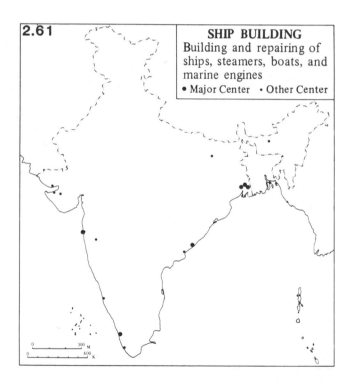

2.61

SHIP BUILDING
Building and repairing of ships, steamers, boats, and marine engines
• Major Center • Other Center

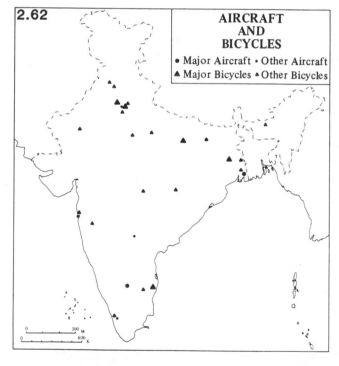

2.62

AIRCRAFT AND BICYCLES
• Major Aircraft •Other Aircraft
▲ Major Bicycles ▲Other Bicycles

dia (Visakhapatnam, Vijaynagar, and Salem) are central government projects and are intended to serve south Indian demands. Though these south Indian mills ease the regional imbalance in steel production to some extent, the overall location of steel mills in the country remains concentrated in the areas of iron and coal deposits. Though substantial compensations have been made in balancing steel mill locations beginning with the Second Five-Year Plan, even reasonable balancing of location will probably never be achieved. The geographical advantage of raw-material location will continue to be an overriding factor in the future.

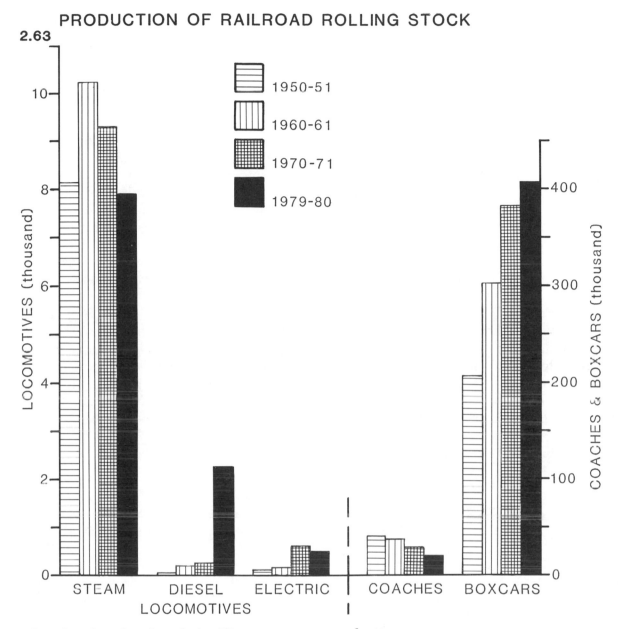

PRODUCTION OF RAILROAD ROLLING STOCK

2.63

Legend:
- 1950-51
- 1960-61
- 1970-71
- 1979-80

LOCOMOTIVES (thousand)

COACHES & BOXCARS (thousand)

STEAM DIESEL ELECTRIC | COACHES BOXCARS

LOCOMOTIVES

While Bombay has developed significant production capacity for structural steel products, steel furniture, and the manufacture of other steel products primarily based on Bhilai and Bhadravati steel ingots, the principal locational factor remains regional demand.

Bhadravati steel ingots and alloy serve the demands of nearby Bangalore which has developed into an important metallurgical center where the famous Hindustan Machine Tools Factory is located.

Small-scale, decentralized steel manufacturing based on iron and steel from distantly located steel mills has developed in the Punjab, Haryana, and Delhi regions. Delhi's market attracts a large concentration of structural steel products.

During the past several years additional problems have retarded growth in production in the steel industry, among which are the underutilization of steel-mill capacity, a coal supply problem, an insufficient power supply, good quality coking coal availability from internal sources, inefficient management of the six large public sector steel mills, and inadequate transportation linkages. Unless sufficient effort is put forth by the responsible agencies to solve these problems, India will not be able to meet its domestic production targets of the Seventh Plan, 18.10 million tonnes capacity and 15.38 million tonnes production of steel ingots by 1990.

CHEMICAL INDUSTRIES

Chemical industries, insignificant before India's independence, have now become important in the wake of increasing internal requirements for industrial chemical products, consumer goods, and pharmaceuticals. No other industry provides a more vivid example of rapid growth than drugs and pharmaceuticals; its value of production in 1982-83 was 50 times the 1947 figure. In 1984-85, the value of drugs and pharmaceuticals produced in India was $18 billion. India is not only self-sufficient in the manufacture of modern drugs, but the country is consistently increasing its exports in recent years. India's pharmaceutical industry is ahead of any other developing country in the world.

The chemical industries produce the basics (acids and alkalies), petrochemicals (methanol, formaldehyde, and styrene), and coal derivatives (coal tar and carbon black). There are three principal areas of manufacturing concentration: (1) the Calcutta-Durgapur-Sindri region in the east; (2) the Bombay-Vadodara-Pune region in the west; and (3) the southern

part of south India.

Though there were 12 petroleum refineries, all in the public sector, in India in 1982 processing 30 million tonnes annually, only two large petrochemical complexes (one in Vadodara and the other in Bongaigaon in Assam) were in operation. Rubber and plastic products are the most important in Calcutta. Bombay's specialities are medicinals, cosmetics, coal chemicals, rubber, and basic industrial chemicals. Basic chemical and soap manufacturing are also concentrated in the Greater Bombay area specifically to serve the textile industries of the region. In the case of both Calcutta and Bombay, the location of the chemical industries was based on proximity to the market.

Individual cities in south India do not have large concentrations of manufactures; instead, they are decentralized into small- and medium-size centers, the most important being Ernakulam, Bangalore, Madras, and Ramanathpuram. The main reasons for locating the industries in this area are the availability of cheap hydroelectricity and labor in association with a sufficiency of raw

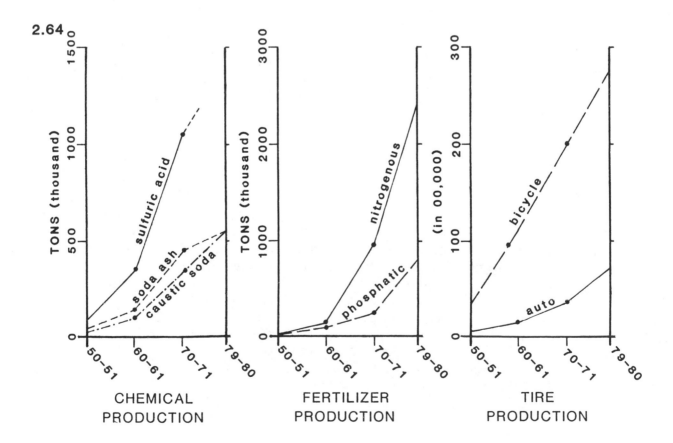

2.64

CHEMICAL PRODUCTION

FERTILIZER PRODUCTION

TIRE PRODUCTION

materials such as coconut oil, rubber, sea salt, and softwoods from the forests.

Fertilizers have recently developed into an important branch of the chemical industry due to the increased demands for them by the agricultural sector. India has made spectacular progress in fertilizer production since the early fifties when only one factory at Sindri was in operation. In 1983, India had 35 major and 36 small fertilizer plants in operation with a capacity of 6.5 million tonnes annually; the fourth largest in the world. The country still must import the product to fulfill its current needs; the import valued at $213 million in

CHEMICAL INDUSTRIES

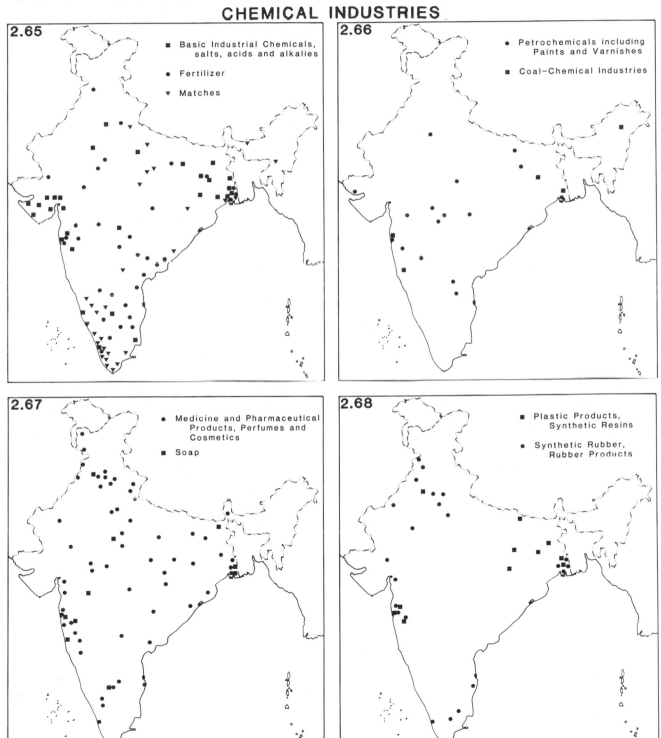

1983-84. Imports are expected to decline with a targeted production increase of 8.8 million tonnes in 1989-90. The public sector is more important in the country's fertilizer production than the private, but both face the identical problem: the unavailability of raw materials. Rock phosphate, sulphur, and petroleum, which are among the raw material requisites, must be imported in substantial quantities and at high cost.

Government policy has been to locate the fertilizer factories throughout the country. At one time the slogan of the Planning Commission was: "One fertilizer factory in each state." This planned decentralization helps reduce the transport cost per unit of fertilizer delivered to the farmer.

TRANSPORT SYSTEM

RAILROAD

The transport system in India, as in other countries, provides the essential infrastructure to serve agriculture and industry and also to stimulate regional socioeconomic development. Consisting as it does of railroads, highways, inland water routes, ports, and airways, the transport system was developed as the consequence of investments which have long-range implications and are essential to the successful completion of any type of development the public or private sector initiates.

Railroads play a dominant role in India's transport system. This point, well recognized by the government, is reflected in the fact that about 47% of the investment in the transport sector of the Sixth Five-Year Plan (1980-85) had been allocated to the railroads; in the Seventh Plan (1985-90) it was raised to 54%. The railroad system, a public undertaking, owned and operated by the central government, is the largest nationalized complex in the country. India's railroad network is the largest in Asia, whereas in the world it ranks fourth.

The railroad system as developed from 1853 to 1947 (approximately 31,050 miles or 50,000 km of tracks by 1947) was built to facilitate the political and economic endeavors of the British. With the extension of the railroad

system, which operated on Indian coal, the British were guaranteed (a) swift and efficient administrative control, (b) the movement of police and the military throughout the country, and (c) access to ports for shipment of raw materials destined for the industries of Great Britain. The same port and railroad system also allowed the distribution of manufactured goods which were received from England. Thus did the massive development of the railroad system perpetuate the strength of the British colonial system both politically and economically.

Following independence in 1947, constant endeavor was made to extend the system for the benefit of national economic development. By 1982, the railroad network extended over 38,048 miles (61,230 km) of tracks and with 7,012 stations. The system transported 3.7 billion passengers and 245 million tonnes of freight in 1981-82.

The pattern of railroad density shows great regional variation. In general, the Northern and Eastern Plains have a dense network. The Deccan Plateau has an uneven density indicating areas of greater activities centered around a large number of nuclei, whereas the Northern and Eastern Plains show a rather even distribution of economic activities with a few major nodes. The Himalayan region is almost devoid of railroad linkages because of rugged topography, sparse population, and lack of any significant economic activity.

There are six principal nodes or clusters within the railroad system. Five occur in the Northern and Eastern Plains, whereas the sixth is in the Gujarat-Ahmadabad-Vadodara-Surat region, nucleated around the country's largest cotton-textile center. Among the centers in the north and east Indian plains, most prominent are Calcutta-Dhanbad and Kanpur-Lucknow, both associated with the country's leading industrial activities. In the plateau region, the areas of least density are associated with undulating and rugged topography and a minimal level of economic activity. In Rajasthan and the Rann of Kutch, desert and swampy conditions respectively account for low density.

On the whole, railroads have now spread into

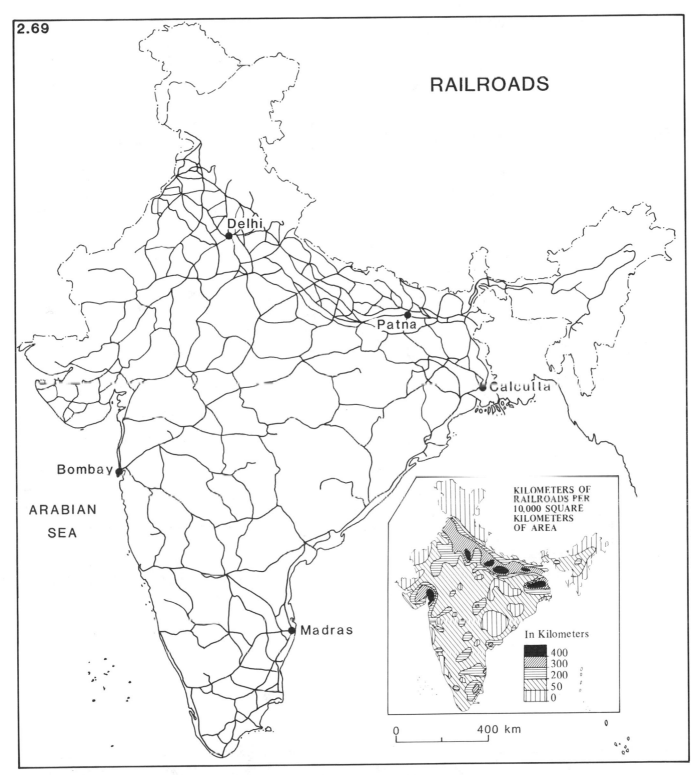

2.69

RAILROADS

Delhi

Patna

Calcutta

Bombay

ARABIAN SEA

Madras

KILOMETERS OF RAILROADS PER 10,000 SQUARE KILOMETERS OF AREA

In Kilometers
400
300
200
50
0

0   400 km

regions where they are necessary and possible. Recognizing this fact, the Seventh Five-Year Plan intends to modernize and make more efficient the existing system rather than increase its track mileage; highest priority has been given to replacement of obsolete rolling stock, box-cars, passenger coaches and renewal of tracks. Currently three trends are worth noting. The busy arterial rail tracks, which constitute only about 25% of the route mileage, are responsible for almost 75% of the traffic. The second trend is the sizeable increase in the

ROUTE LENGTH OF RAILROADS

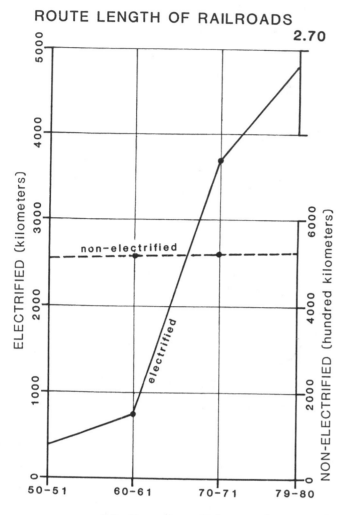

2.70

GROWTH IN TRANSPORT OF PASSENGERS & GOODS BY RAILROAD

2.71

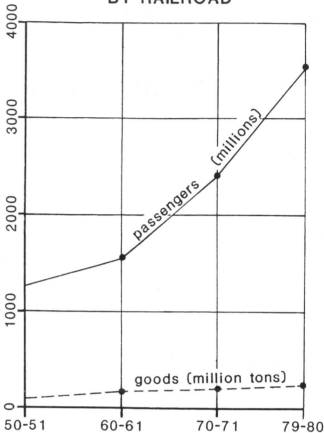

movement of bulk commodities such as coal, iron and steel, ores, stone, cement, fertilizers, food grains, and petroleum products. The third is the stabilization of railroad freight at a 66% level compared to 34% by road since 1965; for the passengers such stability occurred since 1971 with 60% by road and 40% by railroad. The Seventh Five-Year Plan not only more than doubled its financial allocation to the railroads compared to the Sixth Plan, but envisaged an increase of revenue-earning freight traffic from 240 million tonnes in 1985 to 320 million in 1990.

The railroad system undoubtedly has become the country's most important mode of transport. In spite of diesel fuel shortages, the railroads are likely to thrive based on large-scale electrification, for which the principal sources of energy (coal and water power) are available in adequate amounts within the country.

ROAD TRANSPORT

Road transportation, an important mode in modern India, has long historical roots. During the sixteenth century the first national highway, the Grand Trunk Road, was constructed from Calcutta to Peshawar. Currently, the significance of road transport is expressed by the fact that the total mechanized freight traffic increased from 5.5 billion in 1950-51 to 81 billion tonne/km in 1978-79 and passenger/km from 23 billion to 270 billion. To meet the needs of such large volumes of traffic, the country has developed and will continue to develop an extensive network of highways which consist of national highways, border highways, state highways, and other roads. Although in 1947, the country already had a sizeable road network of .38 million km, of which less than half had concrete or brick surfaces, by 1979 the

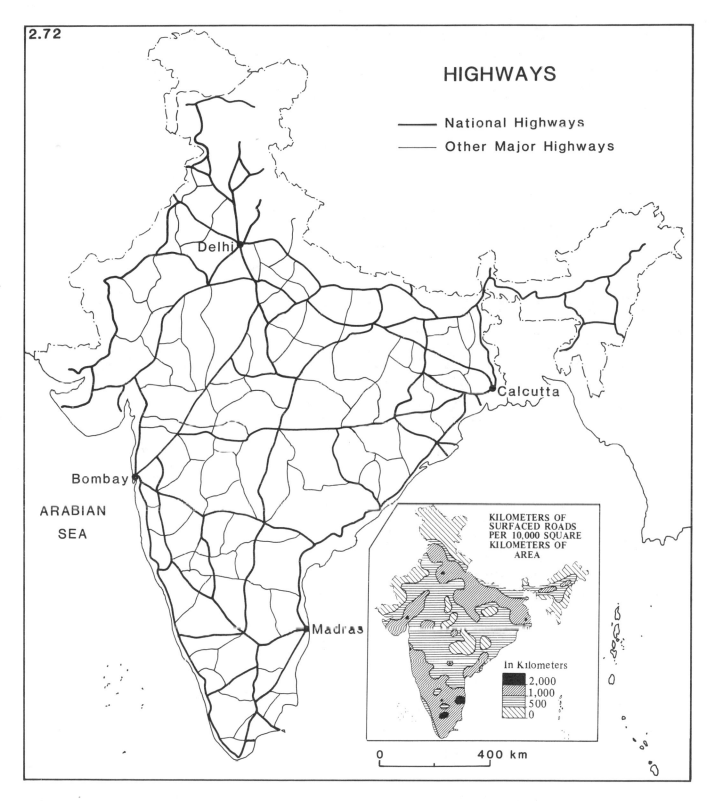

total length of roadways had been increased to 1.6 million km of which only 39% was concrete-brick surfaced. The national highway system, which is important for interstate traffic, had only 13,049 miles (21,000 km) in 1947; by 1979 it had increased to 18,220 miles (29,340 km); it carried about 25% to 30% of the total road transportation load.

As a matter of national policy, an integrated system of rail and road is considered a part of the infrastructure development. Railroads are intended to serve long-distance traffic, while roads are planned to act as local feeders to the railroads. Therefore, the current emphasis is (a) to widen the existing national highway system to four-lane rather than extend it; (b) to complete the missing links and bridges; and (c) to construct by-passes. Increased emphasis is given to the construction of rural roads. The Seventh Five-Year Plan plans to link all villages with a population of 1,500 and 50% of the villages with populations between 1000-1500 with all-weather roads; for reaching these targets, 24,000 additional villages need to be connected by roads. The railroad, then, will concentrate in the future on the movement of specific bulk commodities for long distances, while road transportation will handle local collection and distribution.

The motor vehicle count in 1980 was 4.1 million, of which 46% was motor cycles and scooters, 22% automobiles and 6% buses. The substantial demand of metropolitan traffic is met by buses. Calcutta is the only city in India with an underground railroad system for commuters. Non-mechanized road transport is particularly important in India. There are 80 million work animals including 70 million bullocks and 13 million bullock carts. Animals carry 10 billion tonne/km of the freight traffic annually.

Another aspect of the recent Five-Year Plans relates to the future use and conservation of energy. Individual ownership of automobiles has been given a low priority because automobiles are the least efficient means of passenger transport. Production of passenger buses, on the other hand, has been given high priority. Scooters, autorickshaws, and taxi cabs, as means of personalized transport have also been given a high priority. Thus, production priorities and the transport pattern have been synchronized with the future energy costs and availability within the framework of a general policy objective in transport planning.

Considering the country as a whole, a particular density of roads occurs within the suburban fringe of very large cities such as Calcutta, Bombay, Delhi, Madras, Hyderabad, Ahmadabad, Bangalore, and Coimbatore.

PROPORTION OF VEHICLES ON ROAD 1979

2.73

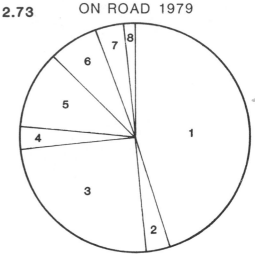

1 Two wheelers
2 Three wheelers
3 Cars, jeeps, taxis
4 Buses
5 Trucks
6 Tractors
7 Trailers
8 Others

These cities are nodal centers and, as all roads once led to Rome, the roads from the surrounding areas coverge at the nodes. A particular concentration of roads is found in a large area of the Northern and Eastern Plains, and in the south and northwestern parts of the Deccan Plateau, both reflecting the combination of high population densities and sizeable agricultural and industrial activities.

However, areas of low road density occur between the two above mentioned regions, and in the Himalayas. In the north, the Himalayan region is not only physically difficult to traverse but also has virtually no population to serve. Therefore, any access route of importance in this region serves one of the following functions: as a strategic border road, or connecting hill stations like Darjeeling, Nainital, Simla or Srinagar. In recent years, a few roads have been constructed in the mountains to provide access to religious places. Most of the hilly and/or dry Deccan Plateau and western desert areas have little need for connecting routes. In the northern Deccan Plateau, particularly, the least populated areas have not developed an extensive highway network.

AIRWAYS, INLAND WATERWAYS AND PORTS

Air transport in India, as in most other nations, has developed significantly since the Second World War. For example, Indian Airlines flew 3.7 million miles (6 million km) in 1971 compared to 1.2 million miles (2 million km) in 1947. In 1979-80, Indian Airlines, the only domestic carrier, had 5,771 million available seat/kms and by 1985 it was planned to increase by 52%. Air transport accounts for passenger as well as cargo traffic within the country. Civil aviation for scheduled flights is state owned. The Department of Civil Aviation operates the civil airports. The four international airports (Delhi, Calcutta, Bombay, and Madras) have been managed by the International Airports Authority since 1972. Two agencies manage the operation of flights: Air India for international flights, and Indian Airlines for national flights with connections also to Nepal and Bangladesh. In addition to the four international airports, there are nine other customs airports: Ahmadabad, Patna, Delhi (Safdarjung), Tiruchirapalli, Varanasi, Jodhpur, Bhuj, Port Blair, and Amritsar. Altogether there are 85 working airfields in India.

As might be expected, the Ganges Plain, with its high density of population, has the largest number of airfields. Not all the airfields are regularly used for scheduled flights, however. Only important cities and tourist locations have regular flight connections; others are used only occasionally.

Flying in India is a luxury which few people can afford; only a few select business people, professional individuals, government officials,

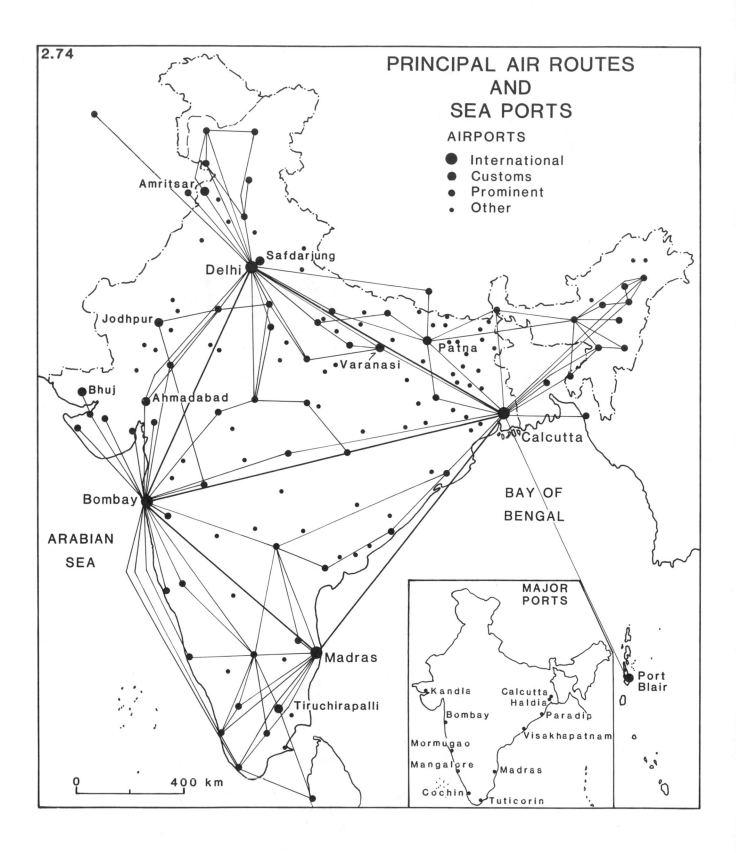

2.74

PRINCIPAL AIR ROUTES
AND
SEA PORTS

AIRPORTS
● International
● Customs
● Prominent
• Other

Amritsar

Safdarjung
Delhi

Jodhpur

Patna
Varanasi

Bhuj
Ahmadabad

Calcutta

Bombay

BAY OF
BENGAL

ARABIAN
SEA

MAJOR
PORTS

Madras

Tiruchirapalli

Port
Blair

Kandla   Calcutta
             Haldia
   Bombay   Paradip

Mormugao   Visakhapatnam

Mangalore   Madras

  Cochin   Tuticorin

0   400 km

top politicians, and foreign tourists are able to take advantage of it.

Water transport has played a significant role for over 2,000 years; Indian merchants traded with Southeast Asian countries, China, and the ancient Romans. Within the nation, inland shipping was particularly well developed in the north where perennial rivers make navigation possible throughout the year. In southern India, because of the many rapids and the nonperennial character of the rivers, stream transport never extended much beyond the deltaic areas. British occupation of the Ganges Delta, with headquarters in Calcutta on the bank of one of the distributaries of the Ganges River, made possible the control of all north India. At that time river transport was the most efficient and convenient means of long-distance inland traffic. The introduction of railroads in 1853 caused a sharp decline in inland waterway transport. Only in the Ganges and Brahmaputra arterial river system is water transportation still significant. One important waterway system was the Calcutta-Assam network which extends through Bangladesh and the Sunderbans, but this system was closed in 1965 after the India-Pakistan War. With the creation of an independent Bangladesh in 1971, it again became operational. Of about 3,231 miles (5,200 km) of major Indian rivers, navigable by mechanized boats, only 33% was utilized in the early 1980s. Water canals are insignificant because only 206 miles (331 km) are in use by mechanized crafts.

Along a coastline of approximately 3,536 miles (5,690 km), India has ten major and 139 working ports. The major port traffic increased from 19 million tonnes in 1950-51 to 107 in 1984-85. Among the major ports, Bombay, Calcutta, Cochin, Madras, and Visakhapatnam had already attained major port status before 1947. Bombay, the largest port, handles about 25% of the nation's foreign trade. The main cargo consists of petroleum products and dry cargo. Calcutta commands the largest and richest hinterland in the country; Haldia is Calcutta's deep-water subsidiary port, fully equipped with containerized berths. Calcutta handles diversified cargo; Haldia, petroleum products and dry cargo. Visakhapatnam is the port location where the first shipbuilding yard was constructed. This port exports sizeable quantities of iron ore to Japan. Cochin, which has one of the best natural harbors, completed the construction of a shipbuilding yard in collaboration with the Mitsubishi Company of Japan in 1974. It handles mainly petroleum products, fertilizers and general cargo. Madras, serving the southeast, has an artificial harbor and it mainly handles general cargo. Five new major ports, Kandla, Paradip, Mormugao, Mangalore, and Tuticorin were added after independence as part of the national plan to allocate at least one major port to every maritime state. Kandla, in Gujarat, was to compensate for the loss of Karachi and to relieve pressure on Bombay as well. Kandla became a Free Trade Zone in 1965. Petroleum products and fertilizers are its principal cargo. Paradip, in Orissa, is primarily an iron ore exporting center similar to Mormugao and Mangalore. Mangalore, in the state of Karnataka, has been recognized as a major port since 1974. Mormugao, originally a port for the Portuguese Colony of Goa, largely exported iron ore to Europe as it still does. It has been recognized as a major port since 1963, and in terms of total tonnage handled is the nation's third largest port. The most recently created major port of Tuticorin handles mainly salt, coal, oil and dry cargo. An eleventh major port, Nheva Sheva is being constructed as a project of the Seventh Plan, which has targeted to increase the major port traffic capacity to 164.45 million tonnes in 1990.

FOREIGN TRADE

Prior to 1947, the foreign trade of India was largely restricted to the exchange of goods with Britain and other Commonwealth countries. Exports consisted mainly of agricultural products such as jute, tea, spices, and leather; minerals such as mica and manganese; and some agriculture-based industrial items as cotton textiles and jute goods. Imports were largely manufactured items including a great volume of consumer products. India had a

favorable balance of payments because, as a little-industrialized colony, it did not need to import large quantities of industrial machinery, or raw materials which were available in the colony itself. This condition changed, however, in the 1980s, as a result of the continued process of decolonization of the economy and the realignment of the country's international relationships.

In terms of exports and imports, the United States ranks first as a trading partner with 11% and 14% of the country's total export and import value in 1983-84, respectively. In the

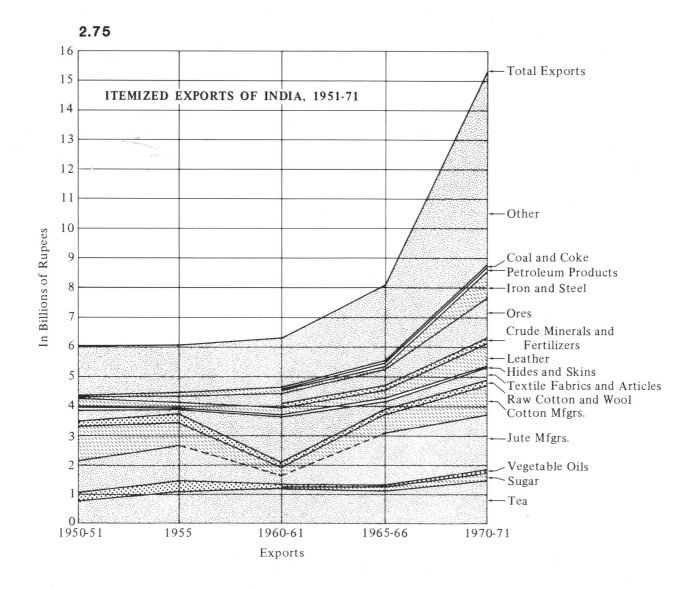

2.75

early 1950s, when India was in the process of altering the base of its former colonial economic structure, Britain was its principal supplier of imports. By 1983-84, however, India's American foreign trade was twice as much. The new economic relationship with the United States is primarily the result of large-scale imports of capital goods, fertilizers, vegetable oil and other aid goods. Meanwhile, Indian exports to the United States (jute, manganese, and handicraft items in particular) had increased considerably, but in the 1980s it is witnessing a weakening tendency.

The Soviet Union and Communist East European nations have become new markets and sources of goods. Imports from these countries in 1950-51 constituted less than 1% of India's total trade. These Eastern Block nations in 1983-84 contributed 12% of India's total imports and 16% of her exports. Indian imports consist primarily of industrial support items, whereas exports are the traditional tea, jute, cotton textiles, leather, and leather goods. The Soviet Union ranks second as India's trading partner.

Japan is another new entrant on India's

2.76

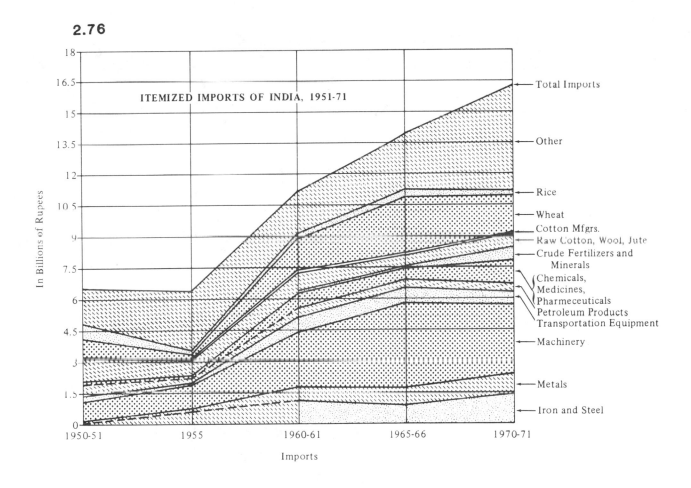

foreign trade roster. In 1983-84, it ranked as the third largest purchaser of Indian exports (8%); one out of every six tons of iron ore consumed in Japan comes from India. Thus, from dependence on British Empire trade during the colonial era, India's trade now follows multidirectional routes.

As a result of increased industrial growth and economic self-reliance, India requires more sophisticated and specialized types of manufactures. Thus, 26% of Indian imports consist of iron and steel, capital goods including machinery and transport equipment, and chemicals. Since the mid-1970s, India's im-

ports far exceeded exports because of a) needs for development, b) slow growth of exports resulting from larger internal consumption, and c) steep hike in the prices of imported petroleum. The population explosion, combined with frequent drought and other climatic vagaries, had necessitated massive food imports from the United States and Canada until the mid-1970s, but in 1981-82 food imports were less than 2% of the country's total. Other significant imports are petroleum (obtained primarily from the Middle East countries) and petroleum products. Almost 36% of India's imports consisted of

2.77

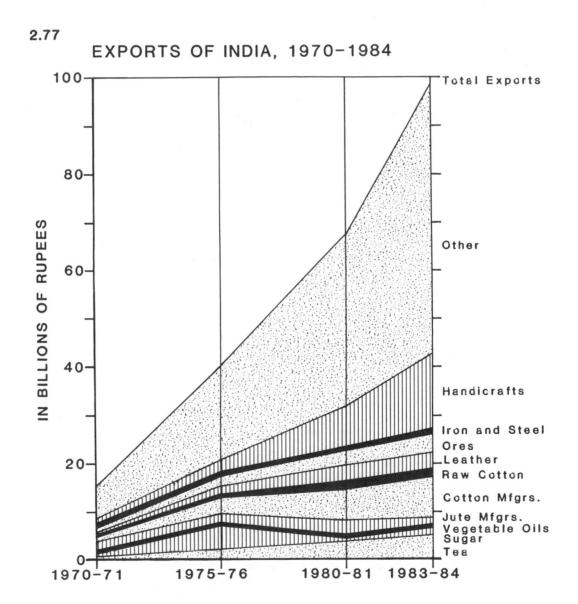

EXPORTS OF INDIA, 1970-1984

petroleum between 1978 and 1984.

While agricultural products and live animals have declined in significance as exports, manufactured goods have risen to account for 56% of the total in 1981-82. With the modernization of industry, exports of iron and steel engineering manufactures and electronic goods are increasing at a faster rate than that for the traditional goods such as jute and cotton. In the area of raw materials, iron ore is the leading export earner, followed by leather.

India's share of world exports in the 1950s and 1960s grew very slowly. Between 1950 and 1970, India's exports increased only 2.5 times while the figure for the world was nine times.

India, in 1970, exported only 0.62% of the world's export commodities in value, and this was further down to 0.46% in 1982. India's balance of trade, due to the country's need for specialized products and food stuffs, had been consistently in the red since independence: in the last years of the 1960s food imports to India reached their highest level; since the 1970s the development requirements have accentuated the imports. By the middle of the 1980s, the export-import imbalance continued to deepen and the extensive development projects of the Seventh Plan will need even greater import of specialized capital goods from abroad.

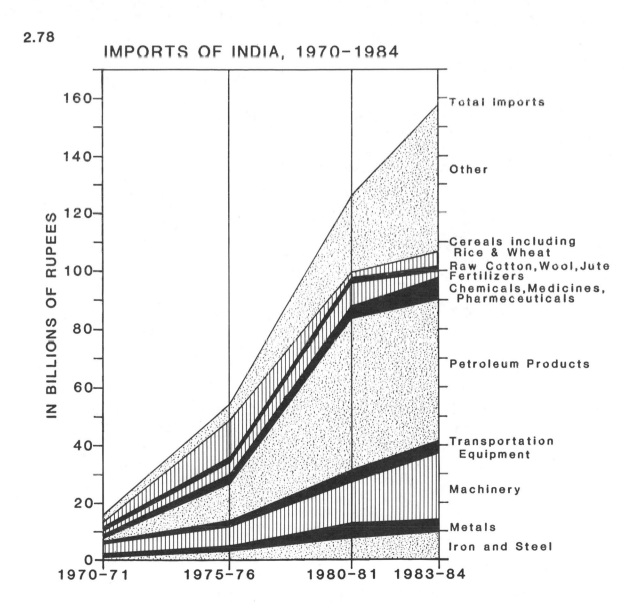

2.78

IMPORTS OF INDIA, 1970-1984

CULTURAL SETTING

TEMPLES

Temples, in India, are places of worship and repositories of cultural heritage. They are not necessarily Hindu but could belong to any of the other India-based religions such as Buddhist, Jain, or Sikh. Idol worship, as a general rule, is practiced in all of the above religions except Sikhism.

Although India's civilization is more than 5,000 years old, temple-building flourished for the most part between A.D. 900 and A.D. 1600. Many of the temples constructed prior to 900 A.D. were of impermanent materials, such as wood, and therefore perished with time.

Indian temples are subject to regional variation in architecture as well as to the types of construction materials utilized. There is, however, a similarity of form to the temples throughout most of India. The chancel of the Hindu temple, known as the *garbha griha*, is a dark, small, square cell carved in stone. The *garbha griha* is the place where the main deity is installed, and immediately above it rises the roof of the cell, called the *Sikhara* or tower. The doorway of the *garbha griha* always faces towards the east. It opens into another chamber which is known as the *antarala* or vestibule. Beyond the vestibule is the *mandapa*, the pillared hall where the worshippers gather. (There are no separate rooms for worship for men and women, but during the actual

Kerala's indigenous temple style is reflected here by the gabled roof-design, for both the main temple and its protruded entrance. The roof consists of tiles which are made according to processes laid down in the ancient treatises. These processes were probably developed to combat the effects of the heavy monsoon rains. The wall material is of laterite bricks. (Sketch by Jhumku Dutt)

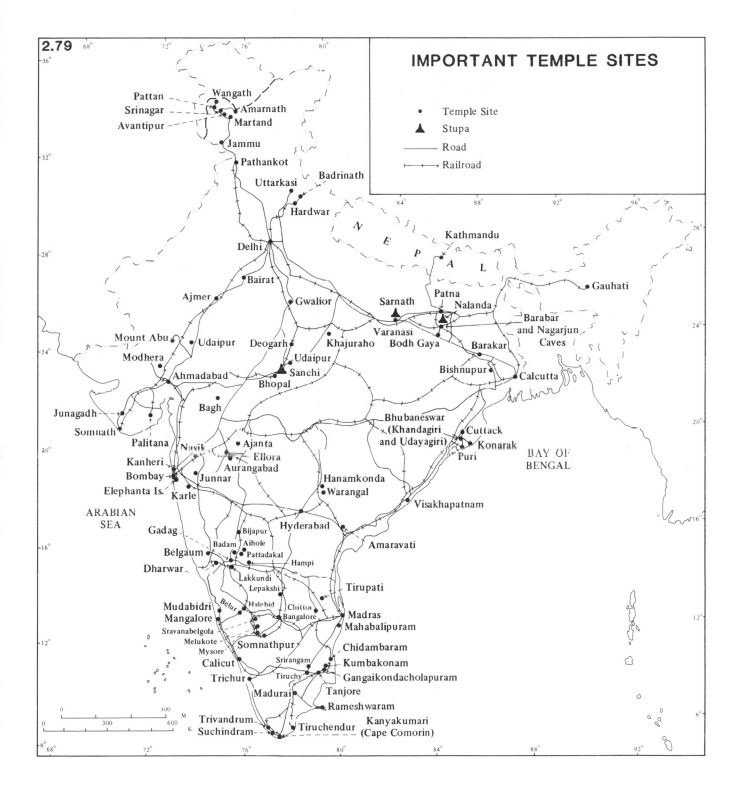

2.79

IMPORTANT TEMPLE SITES

- • Temple Site
- ▲ Stupa
- —— Road
- —+— Railroad

time of prayer the two sexes generally segregate.) The *mandapa* is entered through a porch called the *half-mandapa*. The dominant feature of the temple itself is the tower, which like its Gothic counterpart rises in the sky to a considerable height. The tower generally forms a cone or a cylinder which tapers at the top, although occasionally it does take some other shape.

Temples have been constructed in caves. This type of architecture was practiced widely in the northern and western Deccan plateau because of the existence of naturally suitable rock formations. Most of the cave temples have been well preserved. From a case study of Ajanta and Ellora, sites of cave temples, one can discern the great variety of religious influences. The Thiravada Buddhist chapels of Ajanta date back to the second and first centuries B.C. Four hundred years later, in that same Ajanta cave, Mahayana Buddhist murals were added, the earliest surviving paintings in the whole of Asia, save for prehistoric art. The nearby Ellora caves house Hindu temples which were constructed along Brahminical lines. Of these, Kailasa is the most famous. "Stupas," artificial domelike hills covering relics of the Buddha or Buddhist saints are Buddhist religious forms, which stand impressively at Sanchi, Sarnath (both second century B.C.), and Nalanda (about third/fourth century A.D.).

After the Moslem occupation of India in the thirteenth century which witnessed the planned destruction of Indian temples by the orthodox Moslem rulers, most of the north Indian temples were razed. As a result there are very few surviving north Indian temples of great importance. The "Stupas," however, stood as they were as there was no viable structure to be destroyed. The central Indian temple complex of Khajuraho, which was built during the tenth and eleventh centuries, survived almost in its original form because of its inaccessible location in a remote hilly and forested area. The famous Vishvanath Temple in Varanasi was built as recently as the eighteenth century. On the same site had been an older temple, built before the thirteenth century. It was demolished by the first Moslem

ruler of India, Qutbuddin, and the Razia mosque, for the followers of Islam was erected in its place. Varanasi is probably the most sacred place for a Hindu, even though it does not have any impressive temples. It is the presence of the sacred Ganges River which gives Varanasi the aura of being the center of divine inspiration.

Many temples south of the Vindhya Mountains had not been subjected to the Moslem onslaught and, consequently, have had uninterrupted growth. In many instances, except for damage caused by natural forces, the temples have been preserved in their original form.

The north Indian temples, in terms of adding new concepts of architecture, ceased to develop after the Moslem invasion. The temples of south India, however, not being affected by this movement, made significant gains in the area of design, the most remarkable of which was the erection of massive, ornate, ridged gates which open to the holy place of worship. The gently sloping edges of the ridges are filled with statues which depict stories of the gods and from mythology. The temple designs of Orissa, dating from the ninth and tenth centuries, were very influential and were widely copied all over eastern India. The arrangement and motifs of the exquisite Lingaraja temple of Bhubaneswar were often repeated.

In Bengal there exists an indigenous folk architecture which derives its form from the locally common, thatched bamboo hut. The special feature of this type of temple is the upturned cornice and eave; the bending of the tops is an adjustment to the heavy rainfall. Similarly, although most south Indian temples developed particular Dravidian forms, there is an indigenous variety from Kerala. The focal point of the Kerala temples is the roof, which assumes a conical, pyramidal, or ridged form, and sometimes rises several stories with varying levels of sloped, elongated eaves. Again, the heavy rainfall in Kerala is reflected in such roof designs. Some classical Hindu and Buddhist temples, built prior to the thirteenth century, exhibit European influences originating from ancient Greek occupation in that the capitals of the pillars which support the cor-

One of the gateways to the Ranganatha temple of Srirangam (Tamilnadu), which is the largest Dravidian temple complex. It is situated on an island of the Cauvery River and is famous for the architectural marvels of the seven concentric walls and their gateways, surrounding the main shrine. Within the forewalls of the complex has developed a township, not only consisting of the holy shrine, but also residential quarters and retail stores. The temple enshrines the god *Ranganathar,* which in north India is known as *Vishnu.* (Sketch by Rinku Dutt)

The great Lingaraja temple of Bhubaneswar (Orissa) was built about 1100 A.D. The city of Bhubaneswar is considered sacred because it contained the holy Bhubaneswar Lake, around which was built thousands of shrines; of those about 500 still exist. Lingaraja temple is the most impressive of those shrines. The temple consists of a *Sikhara,* 127' high, constructed without using mortar; in front lies square-shaped and pyramidal roof-designed *mandapa.* The image of Tribhubaneswar (the Lord of Three Worlds) or Lingaraja and Siva *linga* (phallic symbol indicating fertility and creation) are enshrined at different parts of the temple. (Sketch by Rinku Dutt)

nices are Doric.

Temples, regardless of affiliation with a particular religion, are frequented by worshippers as a holy place. Buddhist, Jain, Sikh, or Hindu might be found praying together in the same temple. Indian temples are maintained with gifts of charity and, through historic practice, by their own designated property. They are not only religious places but are centers of great cultural significance.

Dakshineswar temple of Calcutta has a folk architectural design from southern Bengal, originating from the local thatched bamboo hut with curved cornice and eave. The temple is situated by the side of the Hooghly River, one of the distributaries of the holy Ganges. The image of *Kali,* the goddess of power, so commonly worshipped in Bengal is enshrined there. Two great saints and spiritual leaders: Ramkrishna Paramhansa and Swami Vivekananda were very closely associated with this temple. This temple is comparatively recently built. (Sketch by Rinku Dutt)

Taj Mahal, built by Mogul Emperor Shah Jahan (building time being 1624-48) as a tomb for his beloved wife Mumtaj, is one of the greatest architectural triumphs in the world. (Photo A.K. Dutt)

FUSION OF INDO-ISLAMIC ART

Starting from the time of the Moslem conquest of India, Islamic art was fused with Indian art forms through a period of transition and adaptation. This art form is known as Indo-Islamic Art, which has been best demonstrated by the tombs, watchtowers, forts, mosques, royal palaces, and courts constructed by the Moslem emperors. All the Moslem emperors of national stature ruled the country from the Agra-Delhi core area, except for a brief span of time in the fourteenth century when Mohammad Tughluq moved his capital to Deogiri at the northern edge of the Deccan Plateau, only to return to Tughluqabad, a few miles from Delhi. The capital sites of the Agra-Delhi region offered the best geostrategic location for the continentally oriented Moslem rulers. Therefore, most of the remarkable examples of Moslem art forms are found in this core area, though the capitals of the regional Moslem kings, such as Ahmadabad, Golconda (near Hyderabad), and Srirangapattnam (Karnataka) also witnessed some majestic displays of Moslem architecture. Nonetheless, nowhere is this art form so concentrated and chronologically developed as in the Agra-Delhi region.

The most mature stage of Indo-Islamic art was reached in the seventeenth century; two examples being the *Taj Mahal,* the "pearl of the palace," and *Itimaduddaulah* (both in Agra) where octagonal designs, inlaid decorations on soothing white marble, geometrical symmetry, and minarets at the four corners provide a distinctiveness, which often is referred to as Mughal Art of India. Kutub Minar, located in Delhi, built as a watchtower in the form of a minaret, was begun in 1199. The first of the exemplary Indo-Islamic art forms, it displayed typical Moslem construction with ornamental decorations executed by Indian craftsmen. The Tughluq tomb of the fourteenth century is typified by a dome, which during the later Moslem times became not only common, but reached its perfection in the elevated dome design of the *Taj Mahal.* However, after the death of Aurangzeb in 1707, Mughal art reached a stage of decadence with the waning power of the Moslem rulers in Delhi. The Safderjung tomb in Delhi, built in the eighteenth century, represents this decadence in the form of lesser-quality finishings and comparatively inferior elegance.

The lower part of *Kutub Minar,* the construction of which was started by Qutbuddin in 1199, has inscription from the Koran all around its walls; in 1368 and 1503 additions were made; the present height is 238'; it was constructed with locally available red sandstones. (Photo A.K. Dutt)

Tughluq Tombs with slightly slanted walls. (Photo A.K. Dutt)

One of the four octagonal minarets of the *Itimaduddaulah,* a tomb dedicated to the father-in-law of the Emperor Jahangir, son of Akbar. Inlaid work on white marble is exquisitely finished. (Photo A.K. Dutt)

Safderjung Tomb in Delhi. (Photo A.K. Dutt)

LANGUAGES AND LINGUISTIC PROBLEMS

The pattern of languages in India is closely associated with the history of migration in the country. Five major language families —unspecified African, Austric, Sino-Tibetan, Dravidian, and Indo-European—have influenced all the existing Indian languages. Negroid migrants from Africa were probably the first group of people to inhabit India. Only traces of their language are to be found in languages which survived to later times. In India today, no true African language exists either in written or spoken form despite the existence of Negroid races in the Andamans and in remote parts of Tamilnadu.

The Austric family of languages, brought to India by early migrants whose origins were possibly Indochinese, at one time prevailed throughout the country. These languages were eventually absorbed by the Dravidian or Indo-European languages, or were confined to hilly and secluded areas such as the Chotanagpur Plateau (Santali, Mundari, and the Ho language groups), or the Assam Hills (Khasi).

The Sino-Tibetan family of languages, which originated on the Chinese plains, was brought to India by Mongoloid racial groups. In the Sanskrit literature of ancient times these groups were referred to as *Kiratas*. Prior to the influx of the Aryans into India, the Sino-Tibetan languages prevailed over large sections of northern India. Later, this language group, as had happened with the Austric, was absorbed into the expanding Indo-European languages. Sino-Tibetan languages are still found in the relatively inaccessible mountainous regions of the Himalayas and in the eastern hills.

The Dravidians, who inhabited India during the time of the Indus Valley civilization prior to 1500 B.C., evolved their own language. Although ancient tablets and coins bearing Dravidian inscriptions have been found, the language has not yet been satisfactorily deciphered. When the Aryans overpowered the Indus Valley civilization in 1500 B.C., a great number of Dravidian-speaking people migrated southwards. Four states in south India have preserved the Dravidian-family languages: Telugu in Andhra Pradesh, Kannada in Karnataka, Tamil in Tamilnadu, and Malayalam in Kerala. These languages were later greatly influenced by Sanskrit.

The Aryans brought their own language, Sanskrit, which had branched from the Indo-European family; it was widespread in north India beginning in 1500 B.C. While this language also absorbed a great number of Dravidian words, the foundations of the North Indian languages, nevertheless, remained separate from the Dravidian. Like Latin, Sanskrit is no longer a spoken language. Linguists commonly divide the Indo-European languages in India into two groups, Indo-Aryan and Dordic. The latter, greatly influenced by Sanskrit, has been preserved in the form of the Kashmiri language of Kashmir. The Indo-Aryan languages spread all across northern India where various representatives may be found today. Hindi is the most important of these languages today. The generic relationship of Indo-Aryan languages has been represented in a diagram.

The Moslem occupation of India, which began in the north in the thirteenth century, brought with it the influences of the languages of the rulers and administrators, particularly Persian and Arabic. The Sanskrit-based Hindi language incorporated into it a large number of Persian and Arabic words, as did other north Indian languages. Eventually a new language called Urdu developed in India. It is based on the idioms of the Western Hindi dialect, but utilizes a great number of Arabic and Persian words. Urdu gained prestige as "the language of the Exalted Court" of the Mughals. Currently, Urdu is spoken primarily in Delhi, Uttar Pradesh, and the city of Hyderabad. It is also the official language of the State of Kashmir.

The English language, introduced into the Indian school system at the beginning of the last century for the convenience of the British administrators, brought with it influences from the Western World. It is through this language that modern scientific ideas have been conveyed to the Indian elite, for whom English still remains the *lingua franca*. It is the only language spoken throughout India, although

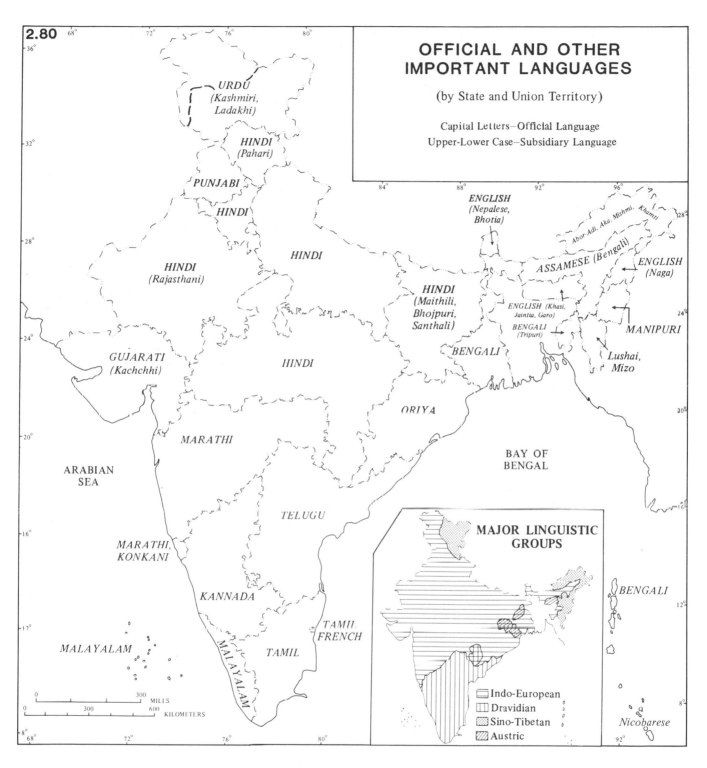

2.80

OFFICIAL AND OTHER IMPORTANT LANGUAGES

(by State and Union Territory)

Capital Letters—Official Language
Upper-Lower Case—Subsidiary Language

URDU
(Kashmiri, Ladakhi)

HINDI
(Pahari)

PUNJABI

HINDI

HINDI
(Rajasthani)

HINDI

ENGLISH
(Nepalese, Bhotia)

Abor-Adi, Aka, Mishmi, Khamti

ASSAMESE (Bengali)

ENGLISH
(Naga)

HINDI
(Maithili, Bhojpuri, Santhali)

ENGLISH (Khasi, Jaintia, Garo)

BENGALI
(Tripuri)

MANIPURI

GUJARATI
(Kachchhi)

HINDI

BENGALI

Lushai, Mizo

ORIYA

MARATHI

ARABIAN SEA

BAY OF BENGAL

TELUGU

MARATHI, KONKANI

KANNADA

TAMIL, FRENCH

MALAYALAM

MALAYALAM

TAMIL

0   300 MILES
0   300   600 KILOMETERS

MAJOR LINGUISTIC GROUPS

BENGALI

Nicobarese

Indo-European
Dravidian
Sino-Tibetan
Austric

the actual number of speakers is small. As a result, mass communication on a nationwide scale is difficult. Hindi, the single most widely understood of the Indian languages, is spoken by over one-fourth of the people, but is not comprehended at all in south India. Though the multilingual character of the country pro-

vides the basis for a regionally differentiated cultural setting, a man to man intercommunication at the national level becomes difficult and sometimes creates regional rivalry.

Only small parts of India are highly homogeneous in terms of languages spoken. Such highly homogeneous areas have different languages and are (1) centered around the Delhi-Agra-Kanauj core on the Northern Plains with Hindi and (2) scattered in the peripheries of the country with regional languages developed during certain times of their cultural history. In those areas over 90% of the people either speak Hindi or one of the respective regional languages. Intraregional communication is easy in those areas.

The main crux of India's linguistic problem lies in the fact that no Indian language is either spoken or understood all over India. English could be regarded as an all-India language but probably less than 2% to 3% of the people can really converse in this language. However, in the wake of anti-British nationalism during the pre-1947 period it was well established in the minds of Indian national leaders that English, the language of the enslavers, should be replaced by a new national language. Moreover, there was a need for a popular-level national language for mass communication. Most Indian political leaders, including those from the non-Hindi-speaking areas such as Gandhi, Rajagopalachari, and Subhas Bose, advocated that only Hindi could be that language. As a result, the Constitution of India, adopted in 1950, declared Hindi to be the official and national language for the Federal (or Union) government, but English would also be used as an official language for fifteen years (until 1965). Fourteen languages were included as major languages; they are known as the "Eighth Schedule languages" because they have been mentioned in the Eighth Schedule of the Constitution. Later, Sindhi was added as a fifteenth major language of the country. Hindi, being one of the Eighth Schedule languages, is both an official language for the nation and state language for six northern states.

Within the fourteen Eighth Schedule languages one finds different scripts, grammar, and pronunciation; knowing one of the languages, it does not necessarily follow that one would automatically know any other. Sanskrit, Hindi, and Marathi have almost the same script. The two through nine languages belong to the Indo-European family and are Sanskrit-based; their common script-base is evident from the organization of the letters. The next four (ten through thirteen), which are Dravidian languages, have a script pattern different from Sanskrit-based languages. Moreover, there are some basic differences in the script pattern within the Dravidian family. Urdu not only has a completely different script (Arabic base) but it is read from right to left, whereas the Sanskrit-based and Dravidian languages

2.81

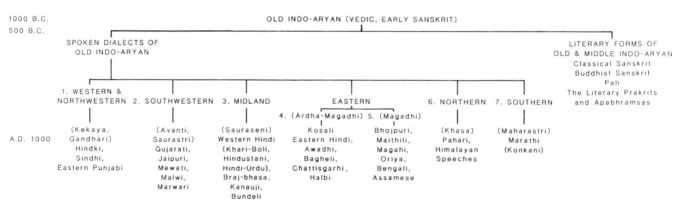

GENETIC RELATIONSHIP OF INDO-ARYAN LANGUAGES

1. Northwest Frontier Province, Punjab, Sind
2. Gujarat and Rajasthan
3. Haryana, Delhi, West Uttar Pradesh, Madhya Pradesh
4. East Uttar Pradesh and East Madhya Pradesh
5. Middle Ganges Plain of Bihar, Orissa, Bengal and Bhramaputra Valley of Assam
6. Northern part of Uttar Pradesh and east Himachal Pradesh
7. Maharashtra and Karnataka coast

(After S. K. Chatterji and S. M. Katre, 1973)

2.82

SCRIPTS USED IN THE EIGHTH SCHEDULE LANGUAGES OF INDIA

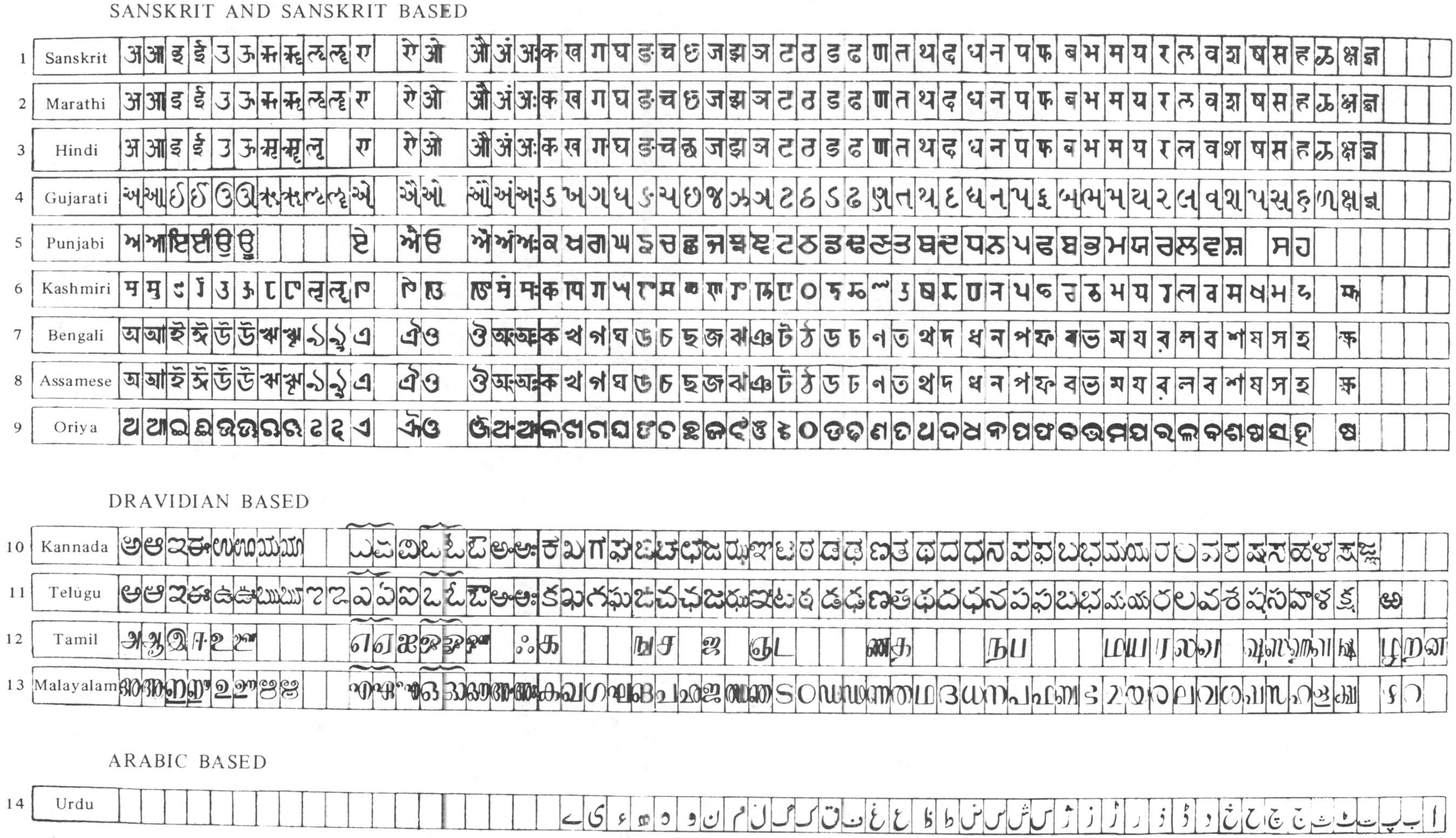

SANSKRIT AND SANSKRIT BASED

1 Sanskrit
2 Marathi
3 Hindi
4 Gujarati
5 Punjabi
6 Kashmiri
7 Bengali
8 Assamese
9 Oriya

DRAVIDIAN BASED

10 Kannada
11 Telugu
12 Tamil
13 Malayalam

ARABIC BASED

14 Urdu

SOURCE: *Report of The Official Language Commission, 1956*, Government of India, 1957, Delhi: Appendix XIV

are read from left to right like English.

Except for Sanskrit, the Eighth Schedule languages are also the major spoken languages. Together they account for about 70% of the people according to the 1971 census, but the same census has recorded the existence of 281 mother tongues in the country, of which 82 have more than 100,000 speakers each. Altogether the prevalence of so many mother tongues and languages creates an extreme kind of regional heterogeneity. Though each state has a state language, there may be one or more subregions in that state where some other language is dominant. In some cases, the official state language is, in fact, a minority language.

With such a diverse situation, the linguistic extremists from Hindi-speaking areas advocate imposition of Hindi throughout India, whereas the extremists from the non-Hindi speaking areas frown upon the spread of Hindi as Hindi imperialism. By the middle of the 1960s, when the time had come to do away with English as an official language, there was extensive resentment in many non-Hindi speaking states, which not only led to riots, arson, and the shooting of protesters by the police, but created a great deal of political instability which threatened the unity of the country. Consequently, a "compromise" was reached; English was continued as an official language, but was given the status of "additional official language." Thus, according to strict semantics Hindi is the official national language, but practically, English continues to have the same status it had in the fifties.

In the end, mass communication remains the principal victim of this diversity of tongues. Although Hindi is generally taught in high schools of non-Hindi speaking states as a non-credit optional language, its progress towards large-scale, interstate communication is very slow. As a result, interstate communication for the great masses of the people remains unresolved.

Classification of Major Linguistic Regions. Based on the nature of the distribution of mother-tongue speakers in each language to total district population, the Indian pattern can be divided into five spatial groups.

i) Hindi and Urdu have a *nation-wide spread.* Both originated and developed in the linguistic heartland of India. The English-speaking population is spread over all of India. Most of the elite or political leaders belong to the English-speaking group.

ii) The *Presidency Town Centered* languages are Marathi, Bengali and Tamil.

iii) *Regionally spread out* languages are Telugu, Gujarati, Punjabi, Oriya, Malayalam and Kannada.

iv) *Limited to their cores* and inner regions are the Assamese and Kashmiri languages, both circumscribed in the extreme eastern and northern ends of the country, in isolation and surrounded by mountains.

v) The only Indian language that has *no core* in India is Sindhi and it has spread into west India through the refugee migrants from Sind in Pakistan entering the Port of Bombay.

Linguistic Heartland. The Punjab-based center of a prestigious Sanskrit language gradually extended its base to the Indo-Gangetic Divide (Delhi region) and western Uttar Pradesh giving rise to a linguistic heartland not only for the Aryan north but also for the Dravidian south.

Capitals were frequently established by the rulers of India in this heartland. The communications requirements of the government resulted in the transmission of the heartland languages (chronologically: Old Sanskrit, Prakrit, Sauraseni Apabhramsa of the Midland, Hindi, especially the Braj Bhasa and Khari Boli forms, and Urdu) throughout the country; most long-distance pilgrims used those languages; many regional administrators and soldiers communicated in them; often official declarations were made in those languages. Moreover, patronage by a king having nationwide sovereignty helped to popularize the language of the heartland.

Hindi. Hindi, the official language of India's Union Government, is the most predominant mother tongue. About 30% of the people speak Hindi. Hindi was established as a language around A.D. 1000 though the actual spoken form was in use by 1300. It emerged from Saurasene Apabhramsa, which was spoken in the region surrounding Delhi (Indo-Gangetic

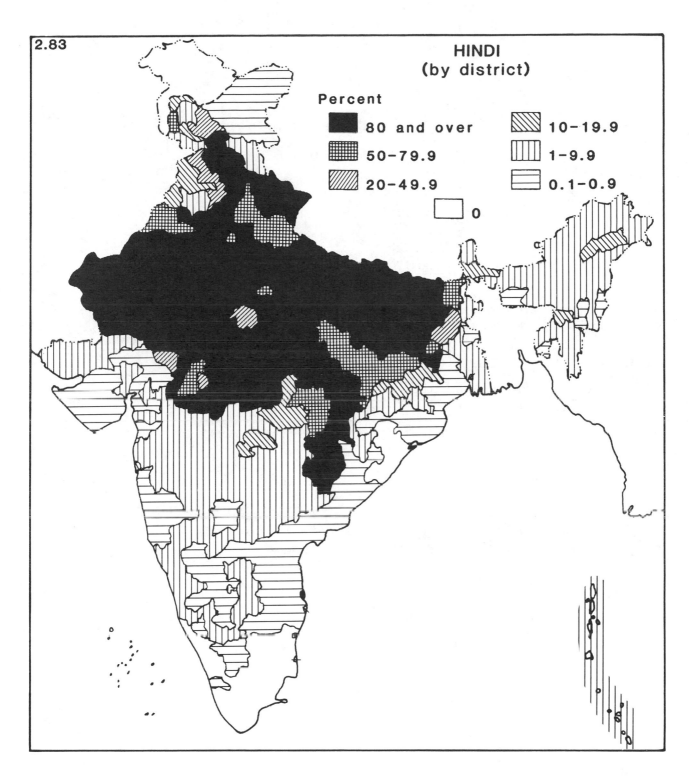

2.83

HINDI
(by district)

Percent

■ 80 and over
▤ 50-79.9
▨ 20-49.9
▧ 10-19.9
▥ 1-9.9
▤ 0.1-0.9
□ 0

Divide) and was influenced by dialects from Punjab, Haryana and western Uttar Pradesh.

There is a sharp dichotomy between the Hindi speaking and non-Hindi speaking regions as the Hindi speakers are concentrated in north-central and west-central parts of the country. This sharp dichotomy does not only coincide with the broad division of the New Indo-Aryan family of languages in the North and Dravidian family of languages in the South, but with other new non-Hindi New Indo-Aryan language areas, such as Gujarat, Maharashtra, Orissa, West Bengal, Assam and Punjab, which have relatively much less a proportion of

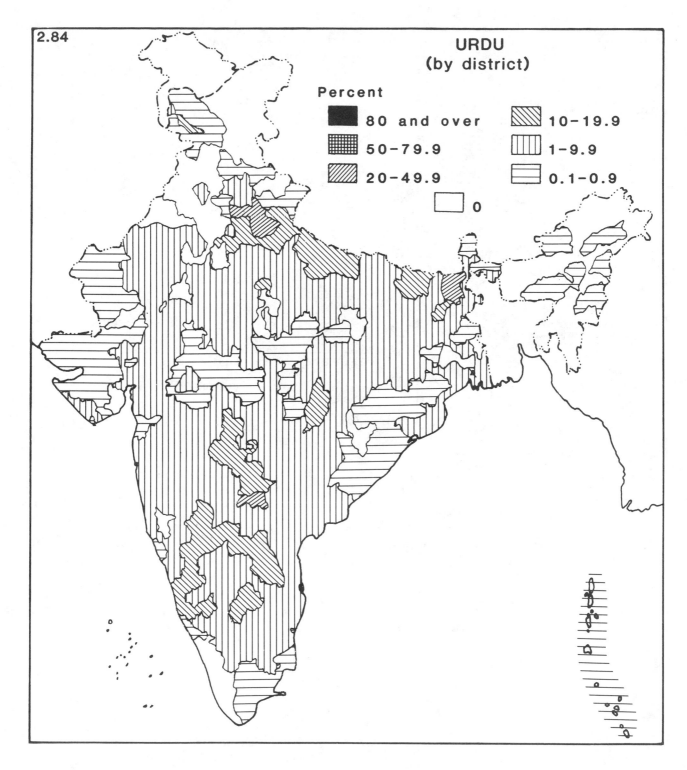

2.84

URDU
(by district)

Percent

■ 80 and over   ▨ 10-19.9
▦ 50-79.9   ▥ 1-9.9
▧ 20-49.9   ▤ 0.1-0.9
□ 0

their district population that have Hindi mother tongue speakers. The southern third of the peninsula, the coasts of Orissa, Andhra Pradesh, Maharashtra, Gujarat and the northern two-thirds of Jammu and Kashmir state have less than 1% mother-tongue Hindi speakers by districts, partly because they are distantly located and/or separated by physical barriers from the historic Hindi core. Mother-tongue Hindi speakers adhere to distance-decay characteristics from the core, surrounded by an intermediate area with a lesser number of Hindi speakers and an outer area with a negligible number.

Urdu. Urdu is considered a "homeless" language by many because it has not been officially adopted as a state language in the states where it has the maximum concentration. The Moslem-majority state of Jammu and Kashmir considers it to be an official language despite the fact that the overwhelming majority of people in that state speak Kashmiri or Ladakhi as mother tongues. Urdu does not have a kind of regional core area where a majority of people in any single state or district speak the language. It is the mother tongue of the majority of the Moslem population in north-central and western India.

Urdu originated as an army language of the 13th and 14th centuries when Turkish and Afghan generals and militia used a language mingled with local dialects, derived from the Hindi of the Delhi region. This mixture gradually developed into a fully grown Urdu language by the 16th and 17th centuries and in the process it was influenced by the rich Persian language. The north Indian Moslem thought Urdu to be a "new discovery", but in actuality this was no more than a Moslem version of Hindi. When the north Indian Moslems established their regional kingdoms or administrative headquarters in the South, they carried with them this language to Hyderabad, Mysore, etc. Urdu adopted the Perso-Arabic script. To north Indian Moslems, Urdu obtained Islamic approval because it is written in the same script as the holy Koran. Urdu lost its position as a royal language with the coming of the British and the consequent spread of English.

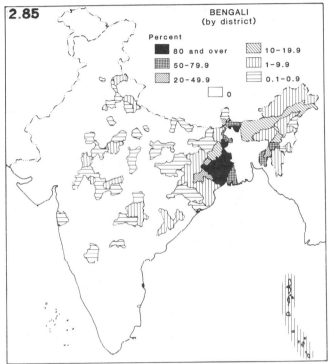

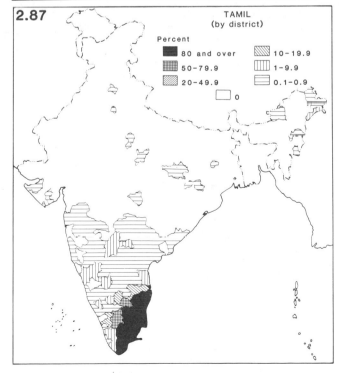

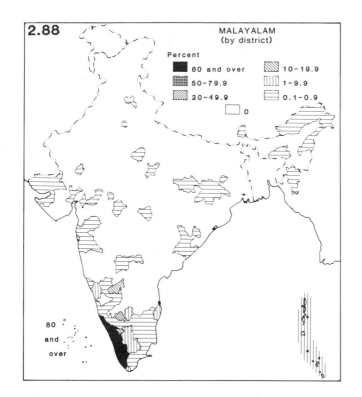

2.88 MALAYALAM (by district)

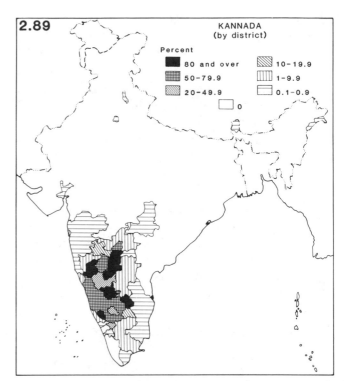

2.89 KANNADA (by district)

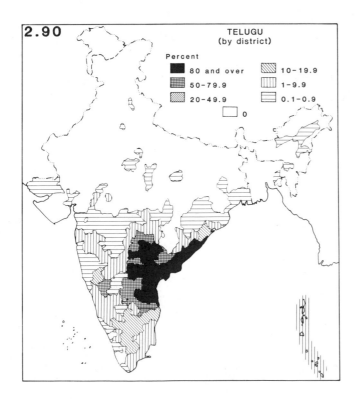

2.90 TELUGU (by district)

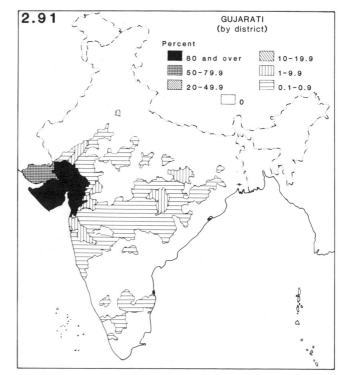

2.91 GUJARATI (by district)

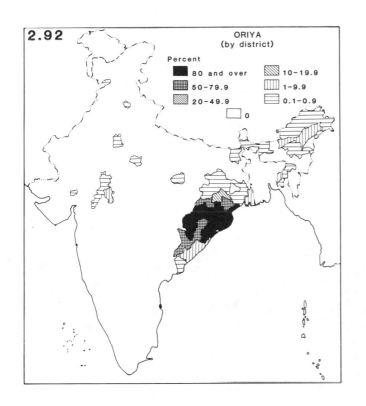

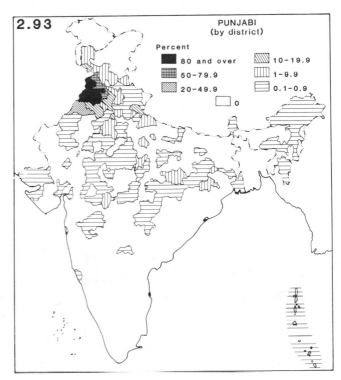

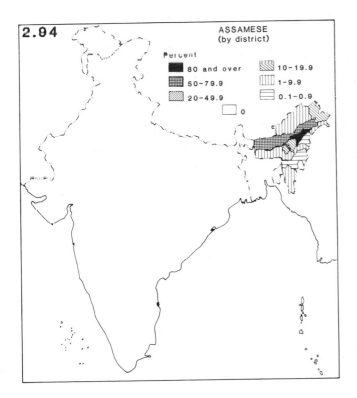

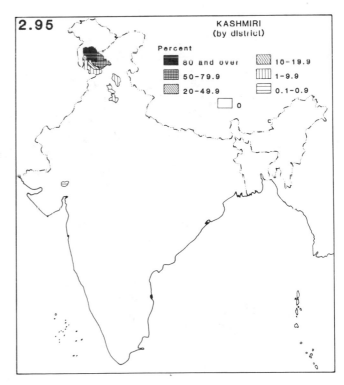

DEMOGRAPHIC CHARACTERISTICS

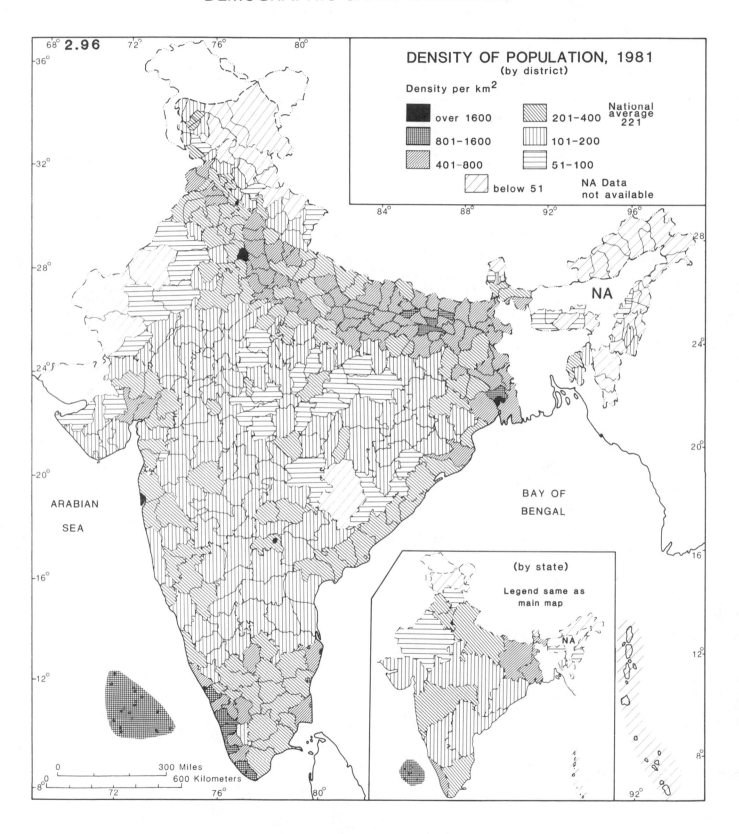

2.96

DENSITY OF POPULATION, 1981
(by district)

Density per km²

- ■ over 1600
- ▨ 201–400 — National average 221
- ▦ 801–1600
- ▥ 101–200
- ▧ 401–800
- ▤ 51–100
- ▨ below 51 — NA Data not available

ARABIAN SEA

BAY OF BENGAL

NA

(by state)

Legend same as main map

NA

0   300 Miles
0   600 Kilometers

POPULATION DENSITY AND GROWTH

According to the 1981 census, the Indian population stands at approximately 658,000,000 (second only to the People's Republic of China in size) with a population density of 514 persons per square mile (or 210 per km²). The growth of India's population had been slow in the beginning of the twentieth century. In 1901, India's population density was only 194 persons per square mile. After 1921, however, the growth rate took a significant turn. Between 1921 and 1951 the nation's population grew by approximately 1.2% annually, whereas, prior to 1911, the growth rate was much lower and sometimes population even declined. Efficient administrative management, eradication of famines, spread of irrigation, health care, and sanitation are responsible for the large-scale net growth of population registered after 1921. However, the most spectacular growth rate of population has occurred since 1951. The annual growth rate between 1951 and 1961 was recorded at 2.2% increasing to 2.5% annually between 1961 and 1971, again declining to 2% during 1971-81 as a result of increasing adoption of family planning. The spectacular growth rate of the Indian population was part of the post-World War II "population explosion," which occurred as the result of sharply declining death rates and only mildy declining birth rates.

The net growth of population has also been accompanied by increased life expectancy. The current life expectancy in India is slightly over 55 years compared to 27 years prior to World War II. Furthermore, the sheer volume and density of the population generates an ever greater national reproduction rate, which further complicates the problem of national economic growth. In addition, the high agricultural density accentuates the rural unemployment problem.

The pattern of population density has remained the same over the last several decades with concentration of population in 1) the Ganges-Brahmaputra plains and the southern coastal plains, 2) the irrigated lands such as the Punjab plains, and 3) the industrial centers of Calcutta, Bombay, and Ahmadabad. The areas of least population density are interior peninsular India (excluding its southern tip), the Rajasthan desert, the swamplands of Kutch and Sunderbans, the Himalayas, and the Assam hills. All of these areas are associated with factors that discourage agriculture: steep slopes, aridity, dense forests, poor drainage, and infertile laterite soils.

Let us take the case of an area where high density is associated with economic backwardness. The Darbhanga district of the North Bihar Plains is primarily agricultural, but has densities as high as 3 1/2 times the national average, with one of the lowest per capita incomes in the nation. In the plains the density is much higher than the national average and because of the great numbers of people, the per capita income generally registers low.

Western European nations with similar population densities do not have such great problems supporting themselves because of their association with manufacturing as opposed to agriculture. Kingsley Davis characterized the Indian population as an oriental agricultural people, long settled in their territory, which they have exploited intensively. As long as such intensive land use remains associated with the traditional subsistence methods of outdated plows and low-yielding seeds, the volume and density of population will remain a burden. However, with the greater expansion of Green Revolution techniques combined with the continued growth of industrialization, the numbers of people may well add to the resources of the country and become an important basis for progress.

LITERACY

Education plays a very important role in nation-building. Literacy means only the ability to read and write simple phrases in any Indian language or in English, and is applied to persons over the age of five years. The strength of the foundation of Indian education must be judged by standards of literacy. When the country became independent in 1947, six of every seven Indians were illiterate. As a result

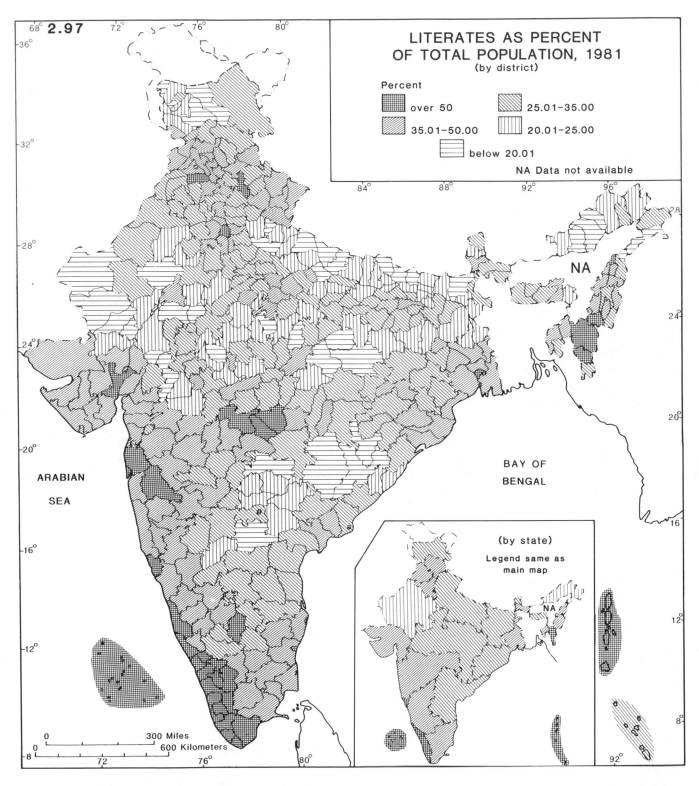

LITERATES AS PERCENT OF TOTAL POPULATION, 1981
(by district)

Percent

over 50

35.01–50.00

25.01–35.00

20.01–25.00

below 20.01

NA Data not available

ARABIAN SEA

BAY OF BENGAL

(by state)
Legend same as main map

NA

0   300 Miles
0   600 Kilometers

2.97

of intensive efforts on the part of the national government, by 1971 the literacy rate had climbed to 29.4%. In 1981, 36% of the Indians were literates, of which 47% were male and 25% female, indicating that a serious imbalance in the education of the sexes exists.

Literacy is of prime importance for the diffusion of modern ideas and technologies. A study of textile workers in Bombay discovered a substantial correlation of job performance and comprehension in groups of literate and illiterate workers, with the literate workers

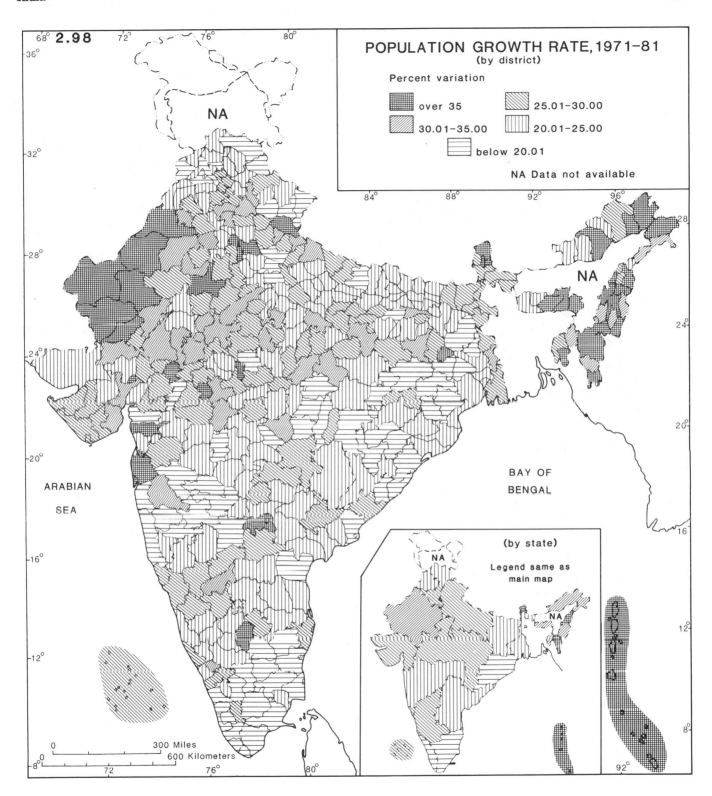

understanding the production process better and having a higher sense of responsibility than their illiterate co-workers. In a different kind of study, literate farm workers were found to use increased amounts of fertilizers which is a precondition for the success of the Green Revolution technique. In this way, literacy and an increased pace of agro-industrial productivity can be correlated. Zachariah found that one of the reasons for the recent success of family planning and fertility decline in Kerala is an increase in female education.

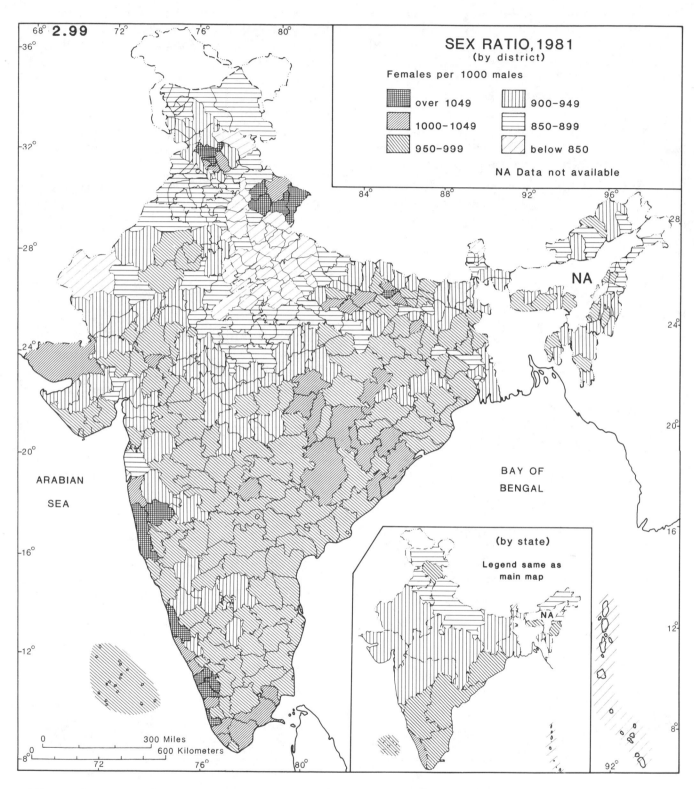

The existence of an enormous national population remaining illiterate was thought by the Indian Planning Commission to be detrimental to national growth. The Fifth Five-Year Plan envisioned a very significant rise in the rate of literacy in order to promote develop-ment. Mass literacy was given top priority, and over 50% of the education budget was invested towards that end.

By the end of the Fifth Five-Year Plan in 1978-79 it was anticipated that almost all the children between the ages of six and eleven would be enrolled in classes. Approximately four-fifths of the children in the above age group were attending primary and junior schools in 1974-75. Programs for adult illiterates were being established through night classes, factory schools, and media instruction, all of which were under national government sponsorship and supervision.

The Sixth Five-Year Plan (1978-83) pointed out that a) low rate of literacy, b) wastage of resources, c) stagnation and low attendence ratios in elementary schools, and d) failure to reach the goal of universal elementary education remained the most serious problems of education in India. This meant that all children between the ages of six and eleven were not attending schools in the early 1980s. The Plan realistically continued to advance the goal of universal education for the age group six-fourteen and proposed that the education system should promote the evolution of a society free of large-scale inequality, poverty and unemployment because they were the principal barriers to the success of universal education.

In general, south India has a higher literacy rate than the north. For example, Kerala has a literacy rate of 71% and Bihar only 26%. This probably may be attributed to greater frequency of contact of India's maritime south with the Western nations. In addition, the western coastal plains of India have a high rate of literacy, probably due also to frequent intercourse with European countries. Also, areas of Christian dominance exhibit high rates of literacy as a result of the influence of the missionaries. Mizoram and the coast of Kerala are examples of this phenomenon. Moreover, in Meghalaya, Nagaland, and south Bihar, Christian influence among the aboriginal and hill tribes has resulted in an increased rate of literacy.

The large metropolitan cities such as Calcutta, Bombay, Delhi, and Madras have a large concentration of literates. According to the 1961 Census, urban literacy reached 54% (in the age group 5-14 years) while rural literacy touched only 24% in the same ages. Similarly, in this age group only 6% of the rural children had primary or junior high school education as contrasted with 19% of the urban children. The figures did improve in 1981, but the overall rural-urban literacy differential is clear with only 30% of the rural population literate in 1981, as against 57% for the urban population.

According to the 1981 Census, Kerala is by far the most literate state in India. Moreover, in the same state there exists more equitable rural-urban rates of literacy (69% rural and 76% urban), and male-female rates of literacy (75% male to 66% female). Bihar has the lowest literacy rate, 38% male literacy and 14% for the females; 23% rural literacy and 52% for the urban areas.

Another area where there is a significant difference in literacy rates is scheduled castes and tribes, traditionally forming the lowest social strata. In 1961, only 10% of the scheduled tribes were literate as compared to the national average in that same year of 24%. The ratio of female literacy was alarmingly low, standing at about 3% for both groups.

Although no data have been available since 1931 on literacy by religion, the 1931 patterns probably have not altered greatly, although percentages must have increased for each group. Parsees, Jains, and Christians had high literacy rates for ages 10 and above of 83%, 38%, and 31%, respectively. Parsees and Christians are not only the most Westernized, but have greater opportunities for Western education as well; Parsees are mostly an urban-dwelling community and Christians are oriented to missionary schools. Jains, in general, are members of rich trading communities and urban dwellers. Therefore, they have more access to higher education. The Sikhs, Hindus, and Moslems each showed less than 10% literacy in the same age group. Moslems had a literacy rate of only 7.2%, and were the least literate of the religious groups. This factor can probably be attributed to their historical antipathy towards Western temporal education. In general, among Hindus, the higher the caste, the greater the degree of literacy.

A significant imbalance in the rate of literacy in India exists not only among regions, religions, and castes, but also between sexes and rural/urban populations.

URBANIZATION AND URBAN CENTERS

RURAL/URBAN CHANGE IN INDIA

Rural/urban change in India is evidenced in the increasing proportion of urban population to the total population: between 1941 and 1971 this proportion almost doubled. In 1971, 20.22% of India's population lived in urban areas. During 1971-81, the urban population grew by 46%, while the rural population registered a growth of 19%. The rate of change has shown a remarkable increase particularly between 1941 and 1951, a reflection of the trends of urbanization in the years following World War II and the independence of India. Since 1951, urbanization has increased at a low but steady rate, a result of consistent migration from rural to urban areas and the natural increase of the urban population itself.

Most of the migrants move to urban centers for economic reasons such as employment, but some are attracted by the "lure" of the city, and its amenities: piped water, sewerage, modern schools, movie theaters, and so forth.

The migration causes an influx to the cities of rural males who eventually save enough money to send back to their wives, children, or other relatives on a regular basis. Through such remittances, rural areas become financially dependent on the urban areas.

Additionally, rural unemployment, which arises from an increasing birth rate and a static amount of cultivable land, is compelling villagers to migrate to the cities to seek work. A large number of these rural migrants are unwelcome additions to an already inflated urban unemployment situation. This is especially true in view of the recent adoption of automation in urban industries which has decreased the utilization of unskilled labor. Thus, the dichotomy of increased productivity through automation on the one hand, and the need for increased employment opportunities for the rural migrants on the other is polarizing Indian labor.

Socially, the rural/urban change is resulting in the withering away of the joint or extended family system which has existed in traditional Indian society for 5,000 years. Let us examine some factors of such withering. First, frequently an urban male must go to another city to seek employment. Thus, a family with four sons may see them scattered to four different areas. Second, traditionally the father commanded the highest respect in the village economy, not only because he was the head of the family but also because he was the head of the farm. His authority was unquestioned. In an urban economy, however, while the son lives in the house of his father, his wages may be equal to, and sometimes greater than, his parents. The father's authority is thereby diminished. Third, since there is no Social Security or few retirement plans in India, after retirement the parents in urban areas generally are dependent on their sons for food, clothing, and other necessities. As a result, parental command is losing its effectiveness. This is another manifestation of the clash between modernism and traditionalism.

The urban areas are invariably the centers of government where the administrators, politicians, and other leaders of society usually reside. Generally speaking, the members of the political power groups were educated in a school system initiated by the British. They tend to be more enlightened, modernized, and open-minded than the rural folk. Indian democracy, which is the largest democracy in the world, has given equal voting rights to urban and rural citizens, literates and illiterates alike. The overwhelming proportion of the Indian population lives in rural areas where illiteracy is very high. Thus, the rural/urban dichotomy in synthesizing the attitudes of the recognized leaders on one hand, and the mass of the people on the other, remains most often unresolved.

Spatially, the district containing, or in the vicinity of, metropolitan areas, such as Calcutta, Bombay, Delhi, Ahmadabad, Kanpur, and Hyderabad, has the largest concentration of urban people. Moreover, it is evident from the map that the western half of the country is more urban than the east.

Physically, rural/urban change is reflected in

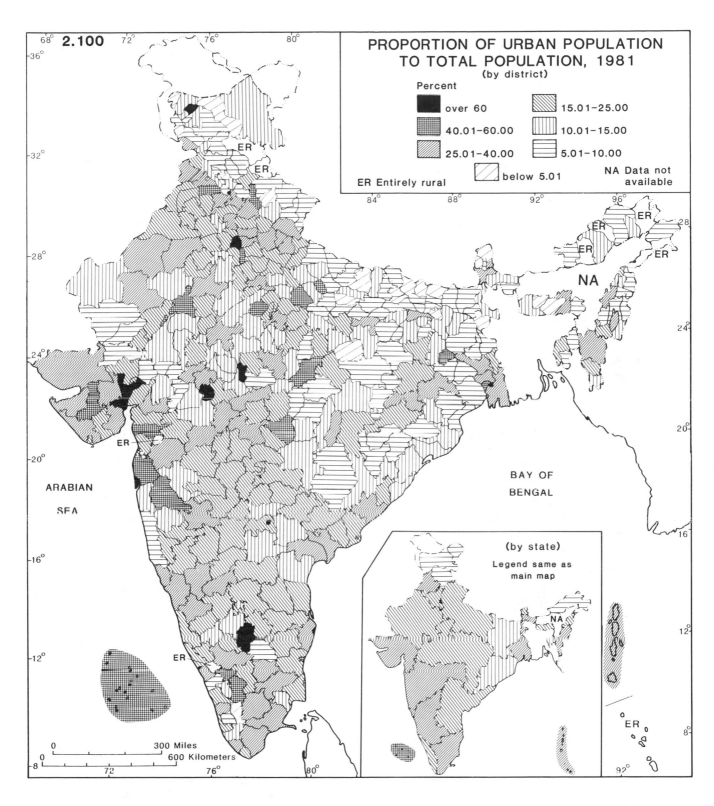

both sectors. In the urban areas, particularly in larger cities such as Calcutta, Bombay, Delhi, and Madras, the increase in height of the buildings has significantly altered the appearance of the skyline. In the rural areas, the introduction of paved roads, rail lines, concrete buildings, and transmission and power lines changed the traditional landscape.

Though the urbanization of India is partly the result of rural migration to the cities, the backwash of urban ideas and forms into the rural areas also takes place continuously, resulting in changes in the political, physical, economic, and social life-styles in both sectors.

LARGE URBAN CENTERS

In 1981, India had 216 urban areas which had a population of 100,000 or more people (called Class I cities), whereas in 1971, it had only 147. According to the 1961 Census, the number of Class I cities was 113; in 1951 it was only 81. Such cities have increased almost 50% during the decade from 1961 to 1971 and 57% from 1971-81. The Class I group has registered the greatest population growth as compared to other smaller-sized groups of cities and towns. Most probably the expansion in this size city is more a reflection of India's development and modernization than of any actual great move toward the urbanization of the population. The percentage of urban to the total population showed a slight increase from 17.98% in 1961 to 20.22% in 1971 to 23.73% in 1981. Class I cities accounted, in 1981, for 60.37% of the total urban population, a clear indication of the fact that India's urbanization is to a great extent a reflection of the growth of its largest cities. Actually, the first 10 of the most highly populated cities (Calcutta, Bombay, Delhi, Madras, Bangalore, Hyderabad, Ahmadabad, Kanpur, Pune and Nagpur) constitute almost 45% of the total population of all Class I cities and 25% of all urban population.

The large cities of India are widely scattered except in the northern Himalayan rim, the central dry uplands, and the western deserts. There are, however, four principal nuclei of urban concentration around Calcutta, Bombay-Ahmadabad, Madras-Bangalore, and Delhi.

No single city in India can be called a primate city, such as London for the United Kingdom, Moscow for the Soviet Union and Buenos Aires for Argentina. India's largest city, with a population of 9.1 million, is Calcutta. It is followed closely by Greater Bombay which has 8.7 million residents. Delhi and Madras have populations of 5.4 million and 4.2 million, respectively. The population growth rate is most rapid in the case of Delhi as compared to other metropolitan areas in recent times. A number of cities combined together exert metropolitan influence over the northern and southern parts of India. Three cities—Calcutta, Delhi, and Bombay—constitute a triangular primacy in north and west India; whereas Hyderabad, Madras, and Bangalore generate a secondary triangular primacy for the southern half of peninsular India. It is the combination of these cities which is engendering a substantial metropolis-oriented cultural and economic development in the country.

The Class I cities of India have a particular type of modern developmental framework that can be viewed as a generator of future growth. India's industrial and economic growth largely depends on the accentuated development of these cities.

MEDIUM- AND SMALL-SIZE URBAN CENTERS IN COMPARISON TO LARGE URBAN CENTERS

Medium- and small-size urban centers in India are classified by Census authorities as Class II, Class III, Class IV, and Class V towns. In 1981 there were 270 Class II towns, 739 Class III towns, 1048 Class IV towns, and 742 Class V towns in India. According to Christaller's pyramidal hierarchy of urban centers, the number of smaller groups of towns multiplies compared to larger cities. In the case of India, such multiplication of small towns does not occur. This is indicative of the fact that the smaller towns are losing population because they are not only uneconomic, but also socially unattractive. As a result, when existing smaller towns are transferred to a higher hierarchical rank due to natural population growth, they are not being replaced.

The national capital and all state capitals are Class I cities excepting for two states: Nagaland (Kohima) and Sikkim (Gangtok). Backwardness, lack of economic activity and generally low population densities in the hinterlands have prevented the formation of

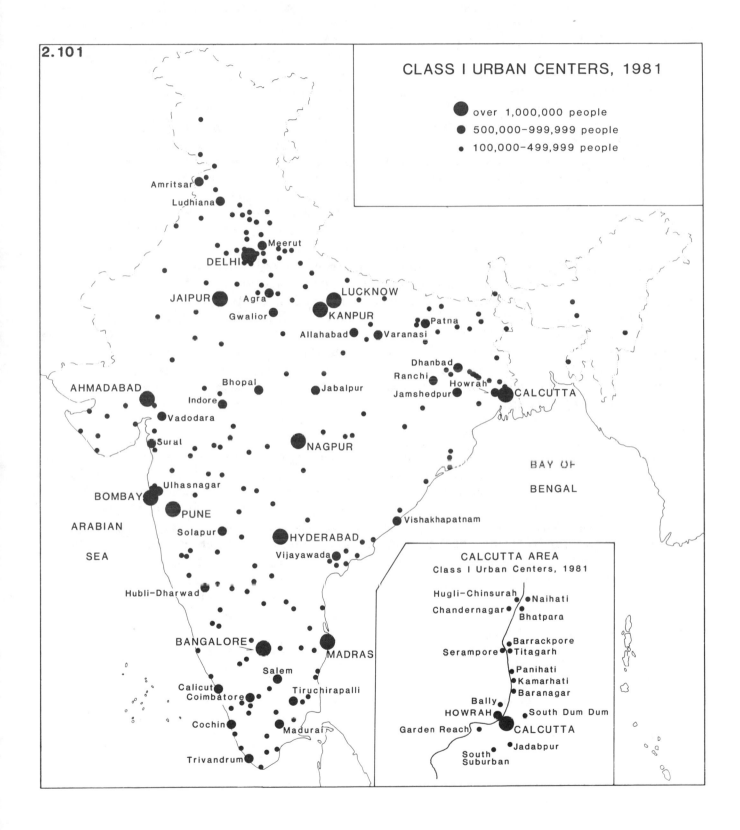

2.101

CLASS I URBAN CENTERS, 1981

- over 1,000,000 people
- 500,000-999,999 people
- 100,000-499,999 people

Amritsar
Ludhiana
Meerut
DELHI
JAIPUR   Agra   LUCKNOW
Gwalior   KANPUR   Patna
Allahabad   Varanasi
Dhanbad
Ranchi
AHMADABAD   Bhopal   Jabalpur   Howrah   CALCUTTA
Indore   Jamshedpur
Vadodara
Surat   NAGPUR
BAY OF
BENGAL
Ulhasnagar
BOMBAY
ARABIAN   PUNE
Solapur   Vishakhapatnam
SEA   HYDERABAD
Vijayawada

CALCUTTA AREA
Class I Urban Centers, 1981

Hubli-Dharwad

Hugli-Chinsurah   Naihati
Chandernagar   Bhatpara

Barrackpore
Serampore   Titagarh
BANGALORE   MADRAS   Panihati
Kamarhati
Salem   Baranagar
Calicut   Bally   South Dum Dum
Coimbatore   Tiruchirapalli   HOWRAH
Garden Reach   CALCUTTA
Cochin   Jadabpur
Madurai   South
Suburban
Trivandrum

Class I cities in these two states. Towns in Classes II through V are generally either district or subdivisional administrative headquarters, trading centers, transport nuclei, educational centers, religious places, industrial centers, or a combination of the above.

Larger towns are better organized than small ones and provide city services under the aegis of a municipal body. As a matter of fact, fewer than one percent of Class I cities lack municipal status, whereas, as town size decreases, an increasing number are not recognized as municipalities. Three percent of the Class II towns, 15% of the Class III towns, 36% of the Class IV towns, and 42% of the Class V towns, do not have civic status. Those towns which do not have civic status are generally provided with a type of rural organization called a *panchayat* which is responsible for arranging town services.

The three states of West Bengal, Maharashtra, and Meghalaya have over 70% of their urban populations in Class I cities, although the national average is 60%. The first two states are highly industrialized and overwhelmingly influenced by their primate cities, Calcutta and Bombay, respectively. Meghalaya has only one Class I city (Shillong) dominating the state. As a result, this city has achieved regional primacy, although the state as a whole has a sparse population.

In Assam, Himachal Pradesh, Manipur, Nagaland, Jammu and Kashmir, and Sikkim all backward and primarily agricultural states, the proportion of urban population in Class V towns is over 10%, while the national proportion is only 3.6%. In general, the more industrialized states have a greater proportion of their population in larger cities as contrasted with a relatively greater proportion of the population being concentrated in the smaller towns in the predominantly agricultural and/or backward states.

The larger cities, which attract a greater immigration from both smaller urban centers and rural areas, have a greater concentration of the working-age population, with a consequently lesser proportion of people under the age of 14 and over the age of 60. In the larger urban centers, particularly in Class I cities, single male migration is substantial. As a result, the sex ratio in Class I cities is 761 females for every 1,000 males, compared to 894 females for every 1,000 males in Class V towns.

The working force participation rate for females increases as the size of the urban area decreases: in 1971, in Class I cities it was 8%, in Class II, 11%, in Class III, 13%, In Class IV, 16% and in Class V, it was 17%. The increasing female working force participation rate in smaller cities is attributable to the changing structure of occupation. In Class I and II cities, less than 1% of the working force is engaged in agriculture, while in the remaining town classifications it increases, becoming as high as 18% in Class V towns. Similarly, in Class I and Class II cities, 50% of the working force is engaged in manufacturing, in contrast to an average of only 31% in the other town classifications.

The average size of Class I cities in 1981 was 437,000 people, an increase of 9% over 1971. Though compared to the national urban growth rate (1971-81) of 46%, Class I (56.83%) and Class II (51.22%) cities grew faster while the Class III (28.41%), Class IV (24.03%) and Class V (15.44%) towns grew much slower.

The size of the town in India determines not only its functional characteristics but also its status, density, and social diversity. Bombay, Calcutta and Madras are the most diverse. Although the urban population of India like other countries is essentially tied to manufacturing and services compared to rural areas the following characteristics occur in the urban areas: higher female literacy, older age at marriage, lesser proportion of male cultivators, greater proportion of household industry workers, larger percentage of males to females, and lower fertility rates.

MEDIUM- AND SMALL-SIZE URBAN CENTERS

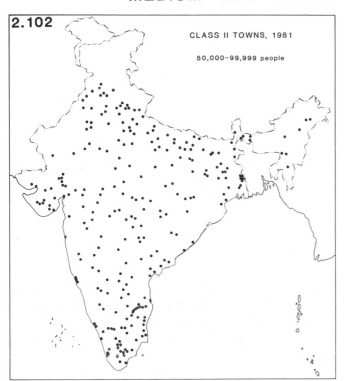

2.102

CLASS II TOWNS, 1981

50,000-99,999 people

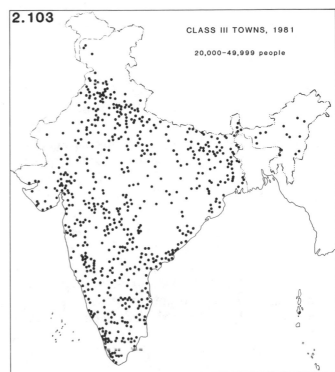

2.103

CLASS III TOWNS, 1981

20,000-49,999 people

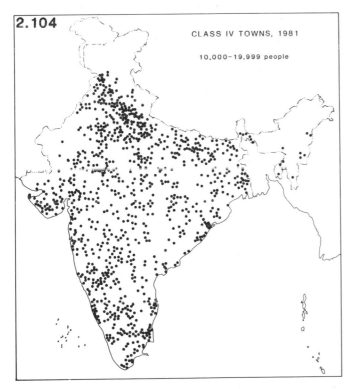

2.104

CLASS IV TOWNS, 1981

10,000-19,999 people

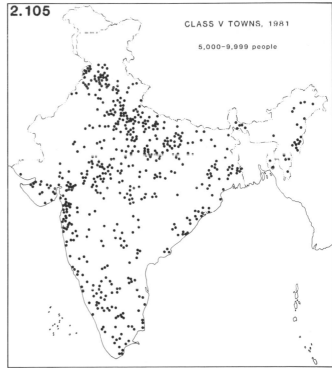

2.105

CLASS V TOWNS, 1981

5,000-9,999 people

CALCUTTA

The founding of Calcutta is traditionally attributed to Job Charnock in 1690, when he, on behalf of the British East India Company, established a military-cum-trading encampment at the village of Sutanuti (present site of Calcutta) on the left bank of the Hooghly River. Actually, it was the Portuguese, beginning in the mid-17th century, who encamped at Sutanuti for trading purposes, followed by the Dutch, who also constructed a diversion canal to overcome the navigation problems of the Hooghly River. They had erected a toll booth as well. Thus, in contradiction to traditional belief, Calcutta's origin dates back about 40 years earlier than 1690. There is, however, no doubt that it was the erection of the British encampment that began the impetus of growth that eventually turned the trading center into a

gigantic metropolis; forming a linear conurbation on both banks of the Hooghly, one of the ten most populous metropolises of the world. In 1981, the city of Calcutta had a population of 3.3 million, while the metropolis had 9.2.

When Calcutta-based British forces, led by Robert Clive, defeated the ruler of Bengal in 1757, the city became the main seat of operation for the northeastern British Indian territory, while Madras remained the capital for operations in British South India. This dual-capital situation ended in 1772, when Calcutta became the sole capital of the British Raj in India. The British needed seaport locations like Calcutta, Madras and Bombay for the convenience of trading and military/ammunition reinformcements from the mother country whenever necessary. Calcutta also enjoyed a unique and significant locational advantage compared with both Madras and Bombay, because it had a command over the huge, densely populated and agriculturally rich hinterland of the Indo-Gangetic Plain. The hinterland, also possessed valuable mineral resources. Initially the hinterland was connected to Calcutta, by an intricate network of rivers, but beginning in the 1850s, an efficient railroad system was introduced accompanied by through and feeder roads. Unlike Calcutta, the hinterlands of neither Madras nor Bombay had an extensive and perennial river system and therefore, they could not take advantage of a strong, inland trading base of support during the 17th through mid-19th centuries, when water transport was the most effective means of long-distance trade.

Until 1911, Calcutta was the capital of the British Empire of India and Burma. From 1911 through 1947, with the removal of the government to Delhi, it was reduced to a capital of a British Indian province and thus, the great national and international significance it had acquired started to wane. Nonetheless, during the British occupation, the city became a typical colonial city with a port, a fort surrounded by a *maidan* for the field of fire, a western style central business district, a planned European town with spacious houses, apartments and modern facilities, and an ill-planned, filthy and unsanitary native town where rich and poor lived clustered together in

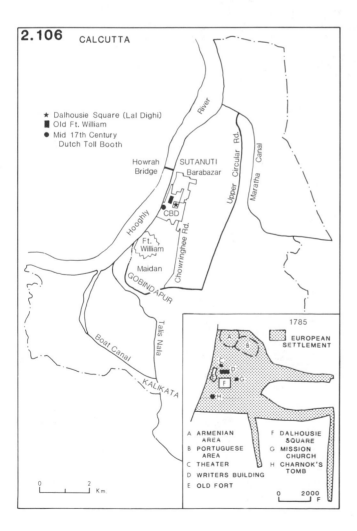

2.106 CALCUTTA

★ Dalhousie Square (Lal Dighi)
■ Old Ft. William
● Mid 17th Century Dutch Toll Booth

River
Howrah Bridge
SUTANUTI
Barabazar
Upper Circular Rd.
Maratha Canal
Hooghly
CBD
Ft. William
Chowringhee Rd.
Maidan
GOBINDAPUR
Boat Canal
Talis Nala
KALIKATA

0   2 Km.

1785
EUROPEAN SETTLEMENT

A ARMENIAN AREA
B PORTUGUESE AREA
C THEATER
D WRITERS BUILDING
E OLD FORT
F DALHOUSIE SQUARE
G MISSION CHURCH
H CHARNOK'S TOMB

0   2000 F

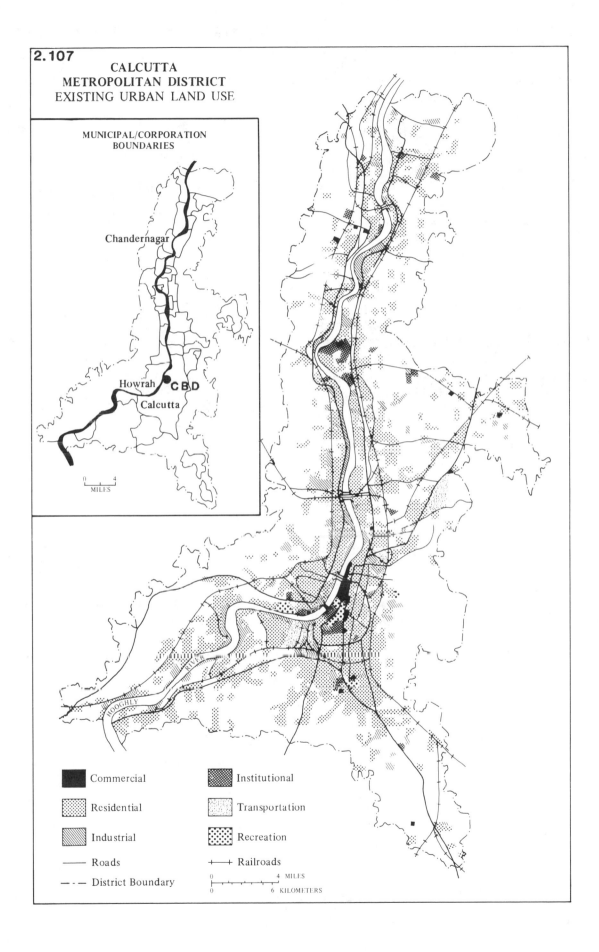

2.107

**CALCUTTA
METROPOLITAN DISTRICT
EXISTING URBAN LAND USE**

MUNICIPAL/CORPORATION
BOUNDARIES

Chandernagar

Howrah ● C B D
Calcutta

0   4
MILES

■ Commercial   ▨ Institutional

▨ Residential   ▨ Transportation

▨ Industrial   ▨ Recreation

— Roads   +—+ Railroads

–·– District Boundary

0   4 MILES
0   6 KILOMETERS

HOOGHLY RIVER

great densities, while the European town and the CBD had minimal densities. The Britons had developed a special affinity for Calcutta; no wonder Kipling, an admirer of English superiority in the 19th century wished its well-being in business and mercantilism. Winston Churchill felt a cool 'westerly' breeze like London, when he was visiting Calcutta. After London, Calcutta was the most populous and important metropolis of the British Empire.

Modern-day Calcutta continues to thrive. Its national importance may be judged from the fact that 1) its port handles a sizeable portion of the nation's exports of manufactured goods, 2) it contains the greatest single concentration of the country's manufacturing activity, 15%, 3) it handles about a third of India's bank clearances, and 4) it provides opportunities for about 13% of all India's students to pursue a college education. In terms of number of students, Calcutta University is the largest in the world.

The Calcutta Metropolitan District (CMD), a planning unit formed in 1961, contains over 500 administrative units, with compactly settled urbanized areas formed into Municipalities and Corporations. The three corporations are the City of Calcutta, Howrah and Chandernagar, a French enclave before 1947. The CMD provides a sound basis for city-regional planning for existing urbanized areas irrespective of the municipal boundaries and for future urbanized areas.

The twin cities of Calcutta and Howrah not only contain about half of the CMD's population, but provide the bulk of employment. The land uses of the District show the following characteristics: industries on both banks of the river and by the side of the railroads; commerce concentrated in the city of Calcutta giving rise to a Central Business District situated in the east-central part, and nucleated around the old British fort site (west of the Writers' Building); residences following a linear pattern along the highlands provided by levees of the Hooghly River and former channels of the Ganges. Such a linear development was necessary because of the swamplands around the levees, a typical feature of deltaic terrain.

The first year for which accurate population

2.108 CALCUTTA POPULATION DENSITY

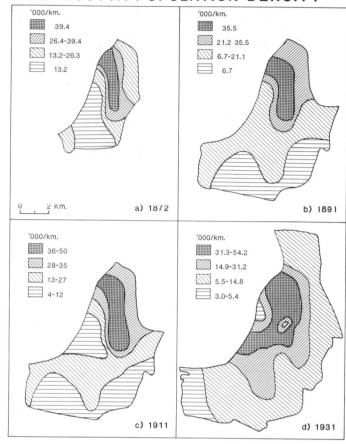

figures are available is 1872. The areal spread of population in Calcutta from that time can be observed on the maps. In all of these years the lowest densities are in the CBD and the highest densities are just to the north and northwest, the former native settlement and now the central bazaar (Barabazar) of high residential and commercial activity. These two areas represent the two old-city components and have served as the core of urban development. The differences in population density, have increased with time. In 1872, half the population lived within two kilometers of the city center. In 1911 and 1931, the radius of mean population was 3 kilometers. After independence, population densities in northern Calcutta grew rapidly, reaching a peak in 1971. This growth was mainly due to an influx of workers in search of employment. These people lived in crowded tenements, close to their place of work, to avoid the cost of using public transportation. By 1981, the highest densities had decreased slightly, as a result of an outward spread of population, following recent extensions in more economical and efficient public transport networks.

The central-crater phenomenon or lower density at the center in population densities in Indian Presidency towns, first identified by John Brush, can be shown to have existed in Calcutta from the earliest period of development. It appears in the first census returns of 1872, and undoubtedly existed almost from the initiation of European settlement because when the colonial settlements of the British were established around the Lal Dighi or Dalhousie Square at the end of the 17th century, the Europeans were housed in spacious houses with provisions for adjacent non-residential facilities.

Such settlement created a dual structure in Calcutta. Low population densities in the European town which grew up in proximity to the safety of the fort, contrasted sharply with the high density Indian town developing on the periphery. This early dichotomy ensured that

the crater effect in population density would become firmly fixed in the urban structure of the colonial city of Calcutta.

Calcutta has many problems: extreme congestion, health hazards, slow traffic, poor housing, and a meager industrial growth rate. Considering the enormity of these continuing problems, the metropolis has been termed by many as the most troubled in the world. The efforts of the Metropolitan planning organizations to solve these problems are handicapped by parallel economic problems, but steps taken for slum improvement, increased water supply and better transport flow, including an underground city rail system, have registered considerable success.

The city of Calcutta has an elitist heritage as it was the pioneer of western education in India. Many Calcutta-educated Bengalis settled all over north India during the British rule. Calcutta is also the seat of Bengali culture. Though the city attracts migrants from different parts of India, Bengali mother-tongue speakers constitute three-fifths of the city population, while Hindi, Urdu, and Oriya mother-tongue speakers make up 23%, 11% and 1%, respectively. Though Hindus constitute 83% of the city population, Moslems (14%) and Christians (1%) are other minorities.

CALCUTTA POPULATION DENSITY

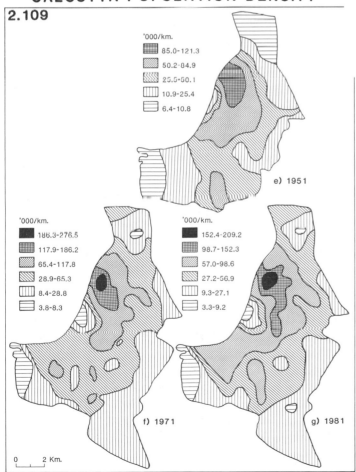

2.109

'000/km.
85.0-121.3
50.2-84.9
25.5-50.1
10.9-25.4
6.4-10.8

e) 1951

'000/km.
186.3-276.5
117.9-186.2
65.4-117.8
28.9-65.3
8.4-28.8
3.8-8.3

f) 1971

'000/km.
152.4-209.2
98.7-152.3
57.0-98.6
27.2-56.9
9.3-27.1
3.3-9.2

g) 1981

0   2 Km.

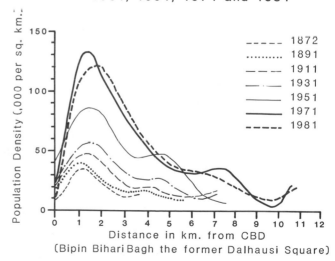

2.110   CALCUTTA CITY

Density Gradient Curves (APL Polyfit)
for the years 1872, 1891, 1911,
1931, 1951, 1971 and 1981

----- 1872
.... 1891
– – – 1911
–·–·– 1931
——— 1951
——— 1971
– – – 1981

Population Density ('000 per sq. km.)

Distance in km. from CBD
(Bipin Bihari Bagh the former Dalhausi Square)

SOURCE: Based on Census Data

BOMBAY

The city of Bombay is an island which forms the southern tip of Greater Bombay. Bandra Creek separates the island from Greater Bombay which came into existence as an administrative unit in 1957. Bombay is not only the capital of one of the most industrialized states of India, Maharashtra, but is the nation's major port for Western contacts.

The origin of Bombay dates back to the year 1664 when Western colonial interests needed the establishment of a trading-cum-military outpost at this site, which was then a group of islands inhabited by fishermen. Bombay eventually attained its fame with growing port activities and cotton textile industries during British rule. Of all the Indian metropolises, Bombay is the most westernized; the imprint quite visible in the building architecture.

Bombay is the "Gateway to India." Its greatest pace of development came during the last half of the nineteenth century. The city became the most important cotton textile manufacturing center of India after its businessmen profited from the American Civil War by exporting huge amounts of raw cotton to the mills in England, temporarily replacing the American supply. Bombay is located near the fertile cotton-producing black soils of western India and this factor added to its industrial localization. The opening of the Suez Canal in 1869 greatly added to Bombay's advantage in handling East-West trade.

The population of Greater Bombay has multiplied almost seven times between 1901-71. Almost two-thirds of the current population (8.7 million in 1981) remains concentrated within the 26 square miles of the island-city of Bombay, raising congestion to over 1,400 persons per acre in some of the slums of the city. A large-scale vertical expansion of buildings both for commercial and residential uses has resulted because of its island site and lack of horizontal expansion. No other city in India has such a large concentration of skyscrapers as has Bombay. Because of an ever-increasing demand for commercial and residential land in the former fort area, initially inhabited by Europeans, many skyscrapers have been erected since the 1960s at Nariman Point, generating a skyline that resembles Manhattan.

Bombay's rich live in the southwestern part of the island in Malabar Hill, Cumballah Hill and Mahalaksmi, where the European lived after moving from the fort area, which became a Western-style CBD starting in the 19th century. The poor and the middle-class are settled mostly in the center and the northern part of the city. Cotton textiles are still the most important industrial activity, employing about half the industrial work-force.

The existing land use pattern is characterized by 1) concentration of commercial activity in the southern part of the city, 2) agglomeration of port-oriented industries near the docks, located on the eastern part of the island, 3) localization of the cotton textile mills, which required large areas of land, in the central part of the present island city (at the edge of the urbanized areas when the mills were established), 4) post-World War II industrial establishments in the eastern sector of Greater Bombay following the proposals of Bombay's 1948 Master Plan, and 5) residential areas spread all over.

The Greater Bombay Landuse Development Plan intends to 1) preserve existing patterns of land uses with a view to protect the best of the present character of the city and 2) redistribute densities, deconcentrate industries from the island city, and 3) provide adequate housing and other facilities.

In accordance with the Regional Plan for Bombay Metropolitan Region, construction of a new satellite town (New Bombay) on the mainland has been started. Old and New Bombay have been connected by a bridge and residential and industrial land uses have already been developed in the latter. In 1985, it was estimated that over 100,000 people lived in New Bombay. Though New Bombay has been planned to divert growth away from Greater Bombay and thus relieve ever-increasing problems of the latter's employment, housing, transportation and density, the former's slow pace of development is no match in diverting the attraction away from already established Greater Bombay.

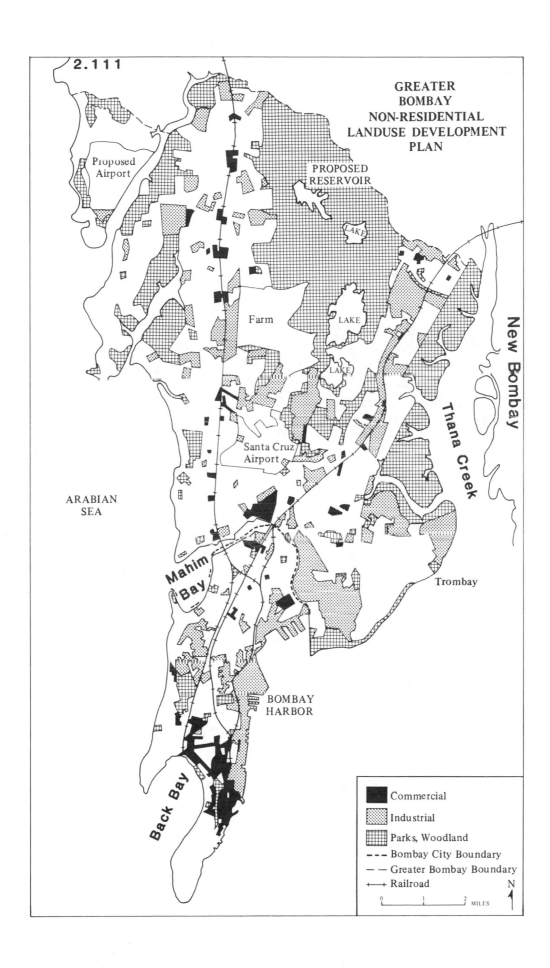

2.111

GREATER
BOMBAY
NON-RESIDENTIAL
LANDUSE DEVELOPMENT
PLAN

Proposed
Airport

PROPOSED
RESERVOIR

LAKE

Farm

LAKE

LAKE

New Bombay

Santa Cruz
Airport

ARABIAN
SEA

Thana Creek

Mahim
Bay

Trombay

BOMBAY
HARBOR

Back Bay

Commercial
Industrial
Parks, Woodland
Bombay City Boundary
Greater Bombay Boundary
Railroad

N

0   1   2
                    MILES

Of all the Indian metropolises, Bombay is not only the most cosmopolitan, but it is the most diverse in religions and linguistic composition. Of its total population, 68.8% are Hindu, 14.1% Moslem, 6.2% Christian, 4.7% Buddhist, 4% Jain and .7% Sikh. Unlike other metropolises of India, no single language is spoken by the majority of the city people. Marathi, the regional language, is the mother tongue of only 42%. People from other linguistic areas have migrated to this city in great numbers, as Gujarati (18%), Urdu (11%), Hindi (10%), Tamil (2.6%), Sindhi (2.6%) and Punjabi (1.5%) mother-tongue speakers accentuate the diversity.

MADRAS

Madras is a typical south Indian city with a colonial base. Madras was purchased by the British East India Company in 1639 from the Vijayanagar empire and a fort (St. George) was built there the following year. It became the main administrative and trading center of British operations in India and continued to enjoy such a position until 1772 when it became merely the regional center for south India. The city developed a 'black town' lived in by the natives in great congestion and unsanitary conditions north of the fort walls, while the whites were spread out towards the west and southwest from the fort, living in bungalows and in garden-like pleasant suburbia. Eventually, by the 19th century, a western-style CBD developed at a point near the fort and between the black and white towns. The CBD, centered around Parry's Corner, is a low density and non-residential area with new and old multi-storied buildings mainly devoted to commercial, administrative and transport uses. From the CBD towards the southwest extends large-scale commercial activities along the Mount Road (now Anna Salai).

Noble, Dutt and Venugopal's land-value study for the city reveals that there is a direct, positive association between land value and commercial area and that is the reason the CBD and the area along the Anna Salai have the maximum value. In general, distance-decay

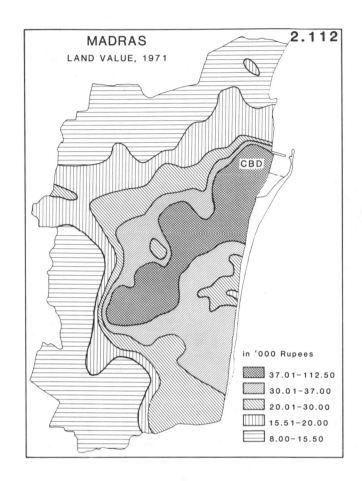

MADRAS
LAND VALUE, 1971

2.112

CBD

in '000 Rupees

37.01–112.50
30.01–37.00
20.01–30.00
15.51–20.00
8.00–15.50

from the CBD is evidenced in land-value, confirming the established concepts of Western cities that peripheral areas have lower land value than that of the center. In contrast to the Western cities, Madras's land value gradient from the CBD towards the outer rim is less steep; indicative of relatively lesser polarization of land values in developing countries.

Madras serves south India not only as the main seaport, but is also the area's largest metropolis. Textiles, tanning, engineering and match-making are some of its leading industries. It had a population of 4.2 million in 1981, three-fourths of which speak the regional language of Tamil, while Telugu- (14%) and Malayalam- (3%) speaking people are important minorities. It is the least diverse linguistically compared to Calcutta, Bombay, and Delhi. As a typical representative of south Indian cities, Madras has relatively balanced male-female ratio, 1000:900, whereas the north Indian metropolises show great imbalances: Calcutta with 1000:780, Bombay with 1000:773; Delhi with 1000:808. In south India,

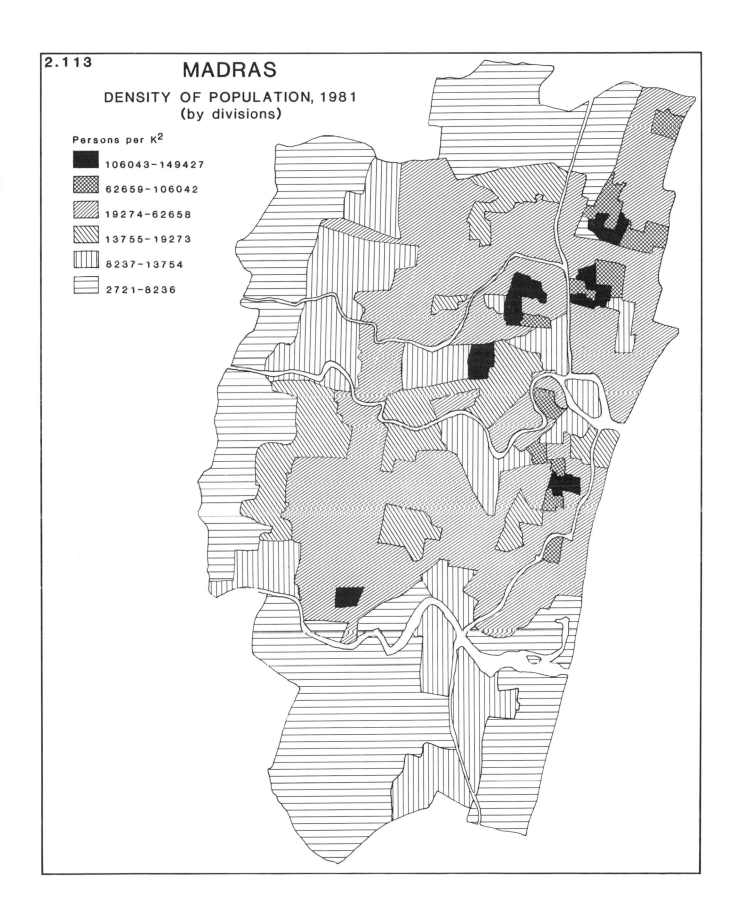

2.113

MADRAS

DENSITY OF POPULATION, 1981
(by divisions)

Persons per K^2

- 106043-149427
- 62659-106042
- 19274-62658
- 13755-19273
- 8237-13754
- 2721-8236

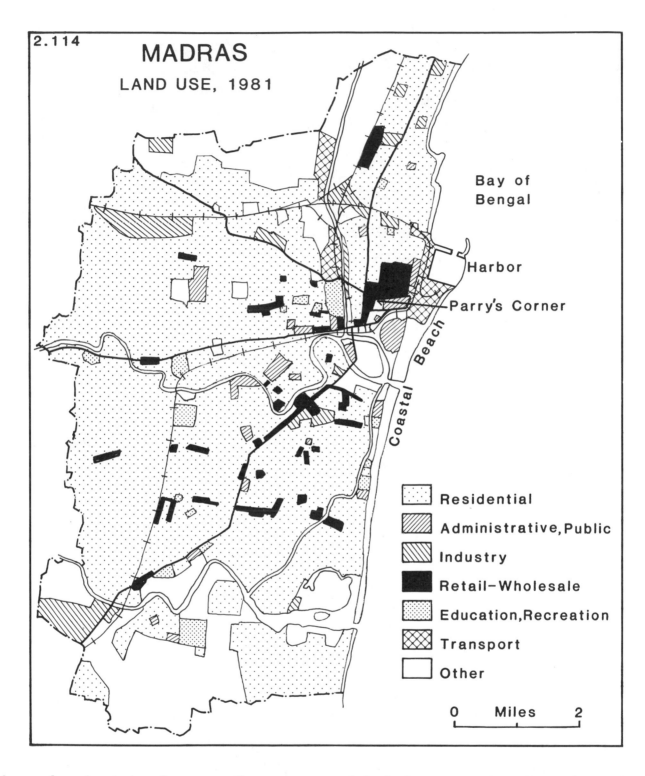

2.114

MADRAS
LAND USE, 1981

Bay of Bengal

Harbor

Parry's Corner

Coastal Beach

Residential

Administrative, Public

Industry

Retail-Wholesale

Education, Recreation

Transport

Other

0   Miles   2

when males migrate to urban areas, the women generally accompany them. Madras also represents regional religious characteristics with 84% Hindu, 8% Moslem, and 7% Christian. Its level of religious diversity is much lower than Bombay and Delhi.

Madras, like other colonial cities of South Asia, had a crater-rim effect of population-density gradient from the time the city was founded; central area low density with a surrounding rim of a very high density and then declining density towards the periphery. Such a pattern of density was entrenched because a handful of white men (the soldiers, officers, merchants and administrators) lived in the low density areas of the center until the 19th century surrounded on two sides by a densely populated 'black town'. When the center became a CBD, it further lost its population, the trend quite visible in the 1960s and 1970s.

DELHI

Delhi, the capital of India, has historic roots of almost 3000 years, which is not only unparalleled among the South Asian metropolises, but very few world metropolises are as old as Delhi. Historical records confirm eighteen different capital sites in the Delhi area and only one of them 'Dilli' dating back to the 1st century has not been identified. Fifteen different names have been given to the various capital sites, most important of which was Shahjahanabad, but the name 'Delhi', derived from 'Dilli' and later 'Dhillika', remained the name of the city.

The attraction for Delhi as the capital site is natural to South Asia's physiography because it occupies a relatively flat water-divide between the two most productive agricultural areas of the subcontinent, the Indus and the Ganges plains, control of which was paramount to the endurance of any Indian empire. North of both these plains and Delhi lie the snow-clad and difficult-to-cross Himalayas while to the southwest lies the extensive Thar (Rajasthan) desert. Most migrants and invaders to India follow the strategic Khyber or other passes in the northwest and thus, entered the Indus plains of Punjab, and for them, a firm hold on Delhi was essential to insure their grip over the north Indian plains. The Delhi site was so vital to the rule of north India that there was a saying: "He who controls Delhi, controls India." Delhi's location on the right bank of the Yamuna, a tributary of the Ganges, gave access to the year-round waterborne traffic of the Ganges system and to the Bay of Bengal. From Delhi, a land route developed (Jaipur-Ajmer-Udaipur to Baroach and Surat) to seaports on the Arabian Sea.

Of all the historic sites, five need mentioning, two of which (Shahjahanabad and New Delhi)

will be considered in detail. The sites of Lal Kot (1050) and Rai Pithora (1180) together formed almost a round fortified city with a surrounding wall and a watch tower (Katub Minar, 238' high) in the southwestern part. Tughluqabad (1320-51), capital of the Tughluq kings, had almost a square shape with the palace at the southwest and high stone walls on all sides.

Shahjahanabad (1638-48), capital of the last Mughals, was planned by the emperor Shah Jahan, who also built the Taj Mahal. The city is the true reflection of Mughal architecture. The royal residence (*Diwani Khas* along with the Pearl Mosque and court *Diwani Am*) were magnificent buildings. The entire palace was included within the walled fort (Red Fort) and formed a parallelogram. Two main roads, Chandni Chawk and Khas Road were the most important. Bernier, a European visitor in 1656-68, described the walled city outside the fort (paraphrased here):

2.115

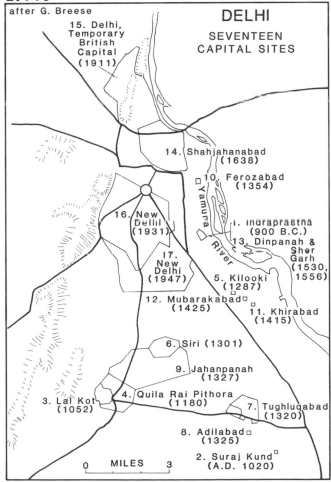

after G. Breese

DELHI
SEVENTEEN CAPITAL SITES

15. Delhi, Temporary British Capital (1911)

14. Shahjahanabad (1638)

10. Ferozabad (1354)

16. New Delhi (1931)

1. Indraprastna (900 B.C.)

13. Dinpanah & Sher Garh (1530, 1556)

17. New Delhi (1947)

5. Kilooki (1287)

12. Mubarakabad (1425)

11. Khirabad (1415)

6. Siri (1301)

9. Jahanpanah (1327)

3. Lal Kot (1052)

4. Quila Rai Pithora (1180)

7. Tughluqabad (1320)

8. Adilabad (1325)

2. Suraj Kund (A.D. 1020)

0   MILES   3

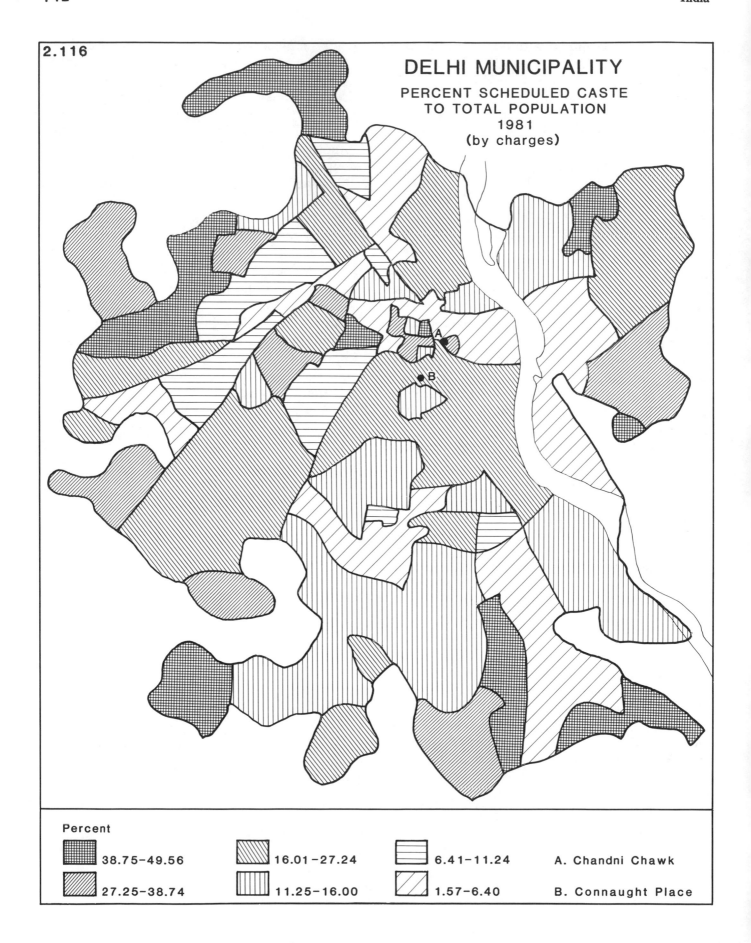

2.116

DELHI MUNICIPALITY
PERCENT SCHEDULED CASTE
TO TOTAL POPULATION
1981
(by charges)

Percent

38.75–49.56	16.01–27.24	6.41–11.24
27.25–38.74	11.25–16.00	1.57–6.40

A. Chandni Chawk

B. Connaught Place

Many streets had arcades but except for the Chandni Chawk and Khas Road, they were asymmetrical. On both sides of the streets lived officers and merchants. Most houses were made of clay and straw, few were brick or stone-built. A large number of common troopers, servants and camp followers lived in much smaller houses with thatch roofs, susceptible to fire. In one summer three fires were recorded which consumed 60,000 roofs because they occurred during the gusty summer winds that are known as *loo*. The Omrahs and the exalted men lived in the suburbs and on the bank of Jumna. The Chandni Chawk (Silver Market) was 150' wide with a canal in the middle and was considered the 'Great Bazaar of the Orient'. Even there the costly merchandise was not displayed, but were kept in warehouses and the shops were 'seldom decked with rich or showy articles'. On the other hand, one could see pots of oil or butter, baskets of rice, barley, chick-peas, wheat and other grains and lentils, as they were always displayed.

Shahjahanabad ceased to be the Mughal capital in 1857, but did not cease to be a functional city. In the first half of the 19th century, the British built a cantonment town at the northwestern end of the city and slowly took control of the kingdom of the Mughals who 'ruled' until 1857 from the confines of the Red Fort without any power, depending completely on the pension granted by the British. When the British moved the capital of India to Delhi in 1911 they housed the capital temporarily north of Shahjahanabad (Old Delhi) while a new capital (New Delhi) was being built to the south. The basic construction of New Delhi was completed in 1930.

New Delhi was an endeavor to show the majestic might of Imperial Britain. It was mainly planned for the British, 'who by shutting out the commonality and the country at large only ended by trapping themselves in their own snare thus hastening their own downfall and that of their city' (Asok Mitra, 1970). New Delhi was planned by British planners Edwin Lutyens and Herbert Baker. It became a func-

tional capital in 1931. The main elements of New Delhi consisted of spacious roads, a magnificent viceroy's residence (now the President's House), a circular council chamber (now Parliament House), imposing secretariat buildings, a western-styled shopping center (Connaught Place) with a large open space in the middle, officers' residences in huge compounds, and a garden-like atmosphere everywhere. The new capital was reserved for the British and their supporting administrative apparatus and was separated from the congested, unsanitary, and the generally poor conditions of Old Delhi by an open space. Old Delhi continued to be a traditional bazaar-type city where the native 'humblest classes were honored, along with the highest of the nobles'. Even in British eyes the congestion was so pathetic that, in 1937, they ordered the formation of the Delhi Improvement Trust to tackle Old Delhi's problems. The implantation of elitist New Delhi by the side of a traditional Old Delhi was so full of contrasts that even after almost four decades of independence they have remained the same, only the main players of New Delhi have changed from British to Indian. Asok Mitra wrote in the 1960s that the "trees, having grown since

144   India

1920, have blurred the secretarial spires...while...dust haze...smudge and blot the grand perspective, conceived in the image of Versailles...".

After India's independence, an increasing demand for housing and space for government offices was created. Immigration of new government employees led to large-scale public housing developments around earlier settlements of New Delhi. Delhi witnessed an unparalleled spatial expansion. The most disturbing feature of such developments was the segregation of large neighborhoods that were sponsored by the government or other related agencies. These neighborhoods housed people according to the rank of the government employees and foreign residents. For example, diplomats and rich Indians were housed in the sparsely settled Chnakyapuri, military officers in Dhaulakuan complex and the lower, middle-class clerks were in the Vinaynagar's (modest town) high density.

After independence, an avalanche of Punjabi refugees from Pakistan beseiged the city and were housed in temporary camps; one in the Kingsway (now Raj Path) alone accommodated 300,000. Such an influx of Punjabi population not only started to change the city's basic Hindi-Urdu linguistic base by the infusion of Punjabi, but the Punjabi Sikhs augmented the religious diversity. Before 1947, despite being the capital of British India, Delhi was essentially a regional city in nature as most of its immigrants came from the area around the city. However, after independence, along with the Punjabi refugees, immigrants came from all over India. Delhi still retains the characteristics of the north Indian city as, in 1971, Hindi (76%), Punjabi (13%), Urdu (6%) and Bengali (1%) mother-tongue speakers dominated Delhi's population. The four south Indian languages combined (Tamil, Malayalam, Kannada and Telugu) accounted for only 1.7% of the population. In terms of religious diversity, Delhi is not as diverse as Bombay with 82.4% Hindu, 7.8% Sikh, 6.9% Moslem, 1.3% Jain and 1.1% Chirstian. In contrast to the great increase of Hindu and Sikh proportions after independence, the Moslems, who accounted for 33% of the population in 1931, have declined significantly in number because of their migration to Pakistan.

Vivid imprints of a traditional city with a high-density center is reflected in Old Delhi, and that of a colonial city with a low density centered around Connaught Place in New Delhi. The modern developments, surrounding Old and New Delhi, are in many ways a continuation of the colonial forms as they polarize the classes/status of people.

With a population of 5.7 million in 1981, the Delhi Urban Area has grown fastest (57% during 1971-81) compared to Calcutta (30%), Greater Bombay (38%) and Madras (35%) because the city has been expanding both its industrial and service basis. Delhi is also becoming India's cultural center as a large number of publishing companies are headquartered there along with a concentration of national fine arts activities. If the process continues, Calcutta and Bombay may be relegated to eastern and western regional centers like Madras is in the south, with Delhi becoming the pace-setting city of the country.

NATIONAL PLANNING

2.118

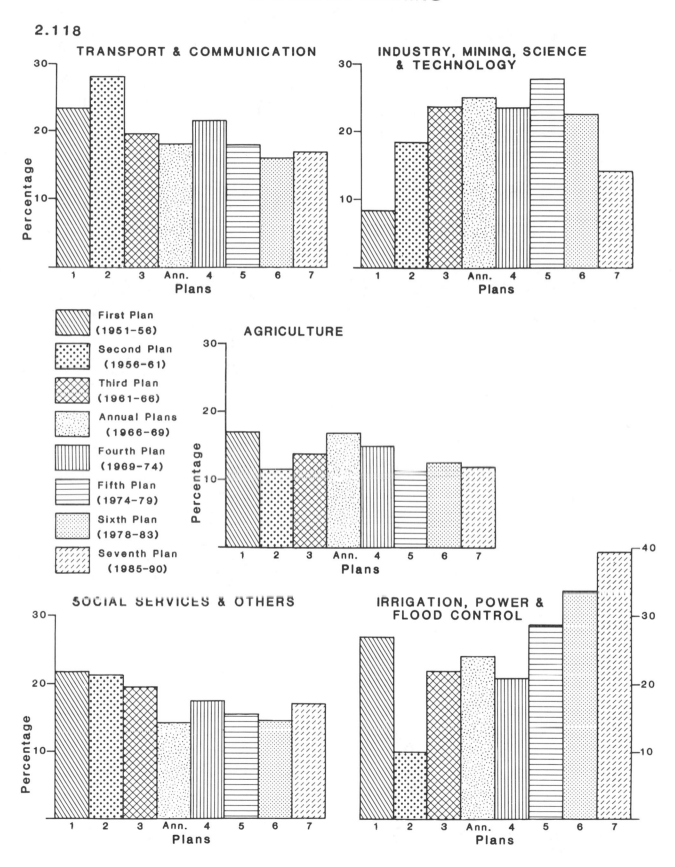

2.119
Fourth Five-Year Plan (1969-74)

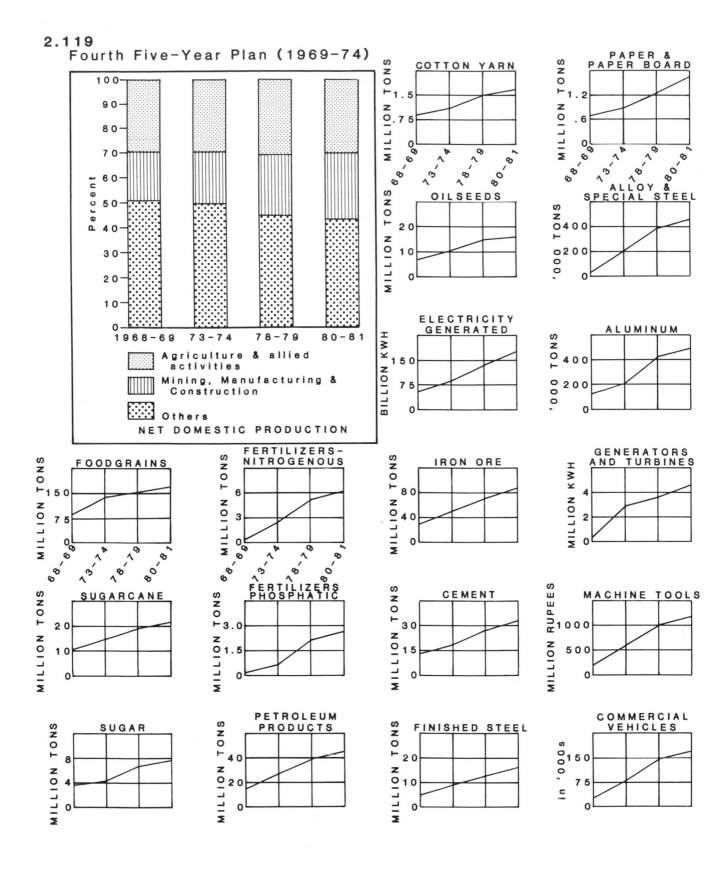

FIFTH FIVE-YEAR PLAN, 1974-79

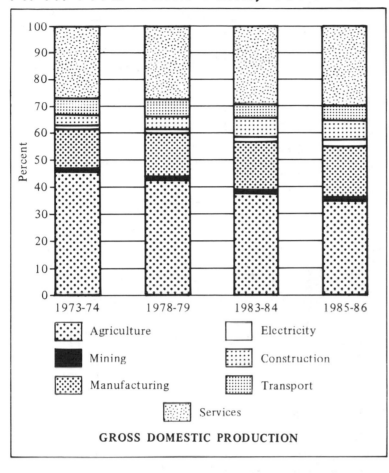

GROSS DOMESTIC PRODUCTION

Legend:
- ⣿ Agriculture
- ■ Mining
- ⣿ Manufacturing
- ⣿ Services
- □ Electricity
- ⣿ Construction
- ⣿ Transport

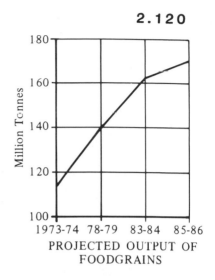

PROJECTED OUTPUT OF
FOODGRAINS

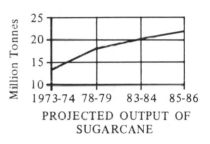

PROJECTED OUTPUT OF
SUGARCANE

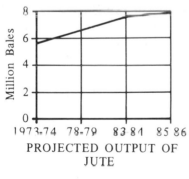

PROJECTED OUTPUT OF
JUTE

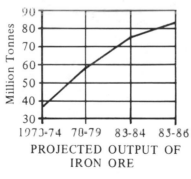

PROJECTED OUTPUT OF
IRON ORE

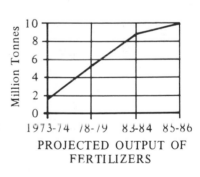

PROJECTED OUTPUT OF
FERTILIZERS

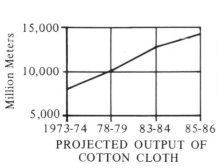

PROJECTED OUTPUT OF
COTTON CLOTH

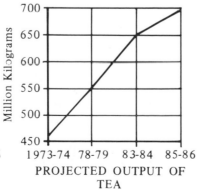

PROJECTED OUTPUT OF
TEA

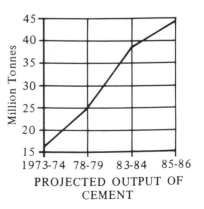

PROJECTED OUTPUT OF
CEMENT

SIXTH-FIVE YEAR PLAN 1980-85

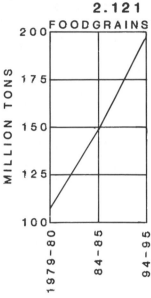

2.121

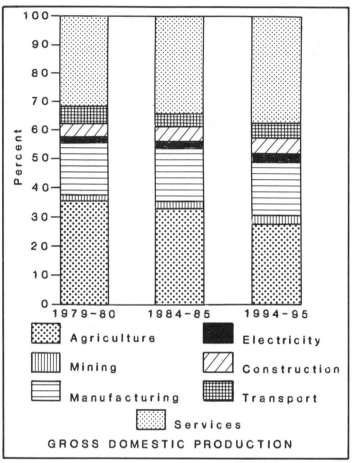

GROSS DOMESTIC PRODUCTION

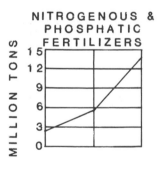

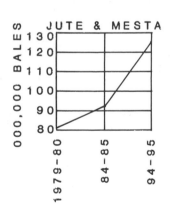

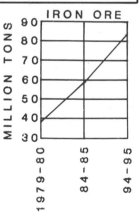

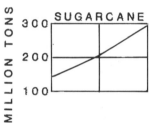

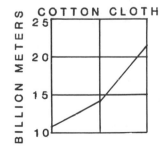

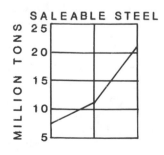

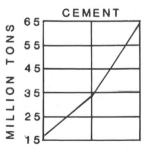

SEVENTH FIVE YEAR PLAN (1985-90)

2.122

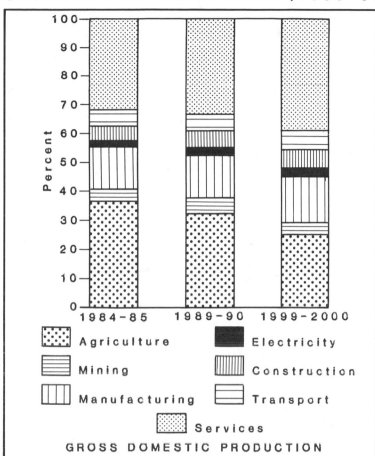

GROSS DOMESTIC PRODUCTION

- Agriculture
- Mining
- Manufacturing
- Electricity
- Construction
- Transport
- Services

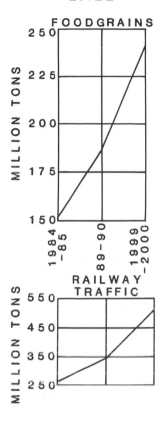

FOODGRAINS

RAILWAY TRAFFIC

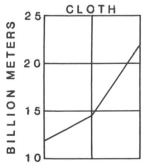

COAL

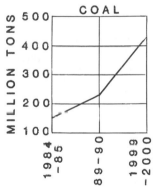

IRON ORE

FERTILIZER

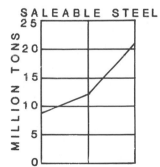

CLOTH

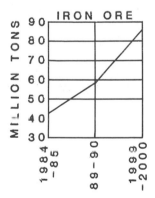

SALEABLE STEEL

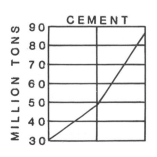

CEMENT

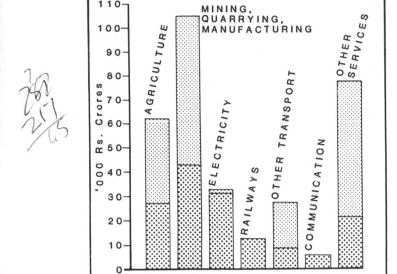

GROSS INVESTMENT BY PUBLIC
AND PRIVATE SECTOR 1985-90

- PUBLIC SECTOR
- PRIVATE SECTOR

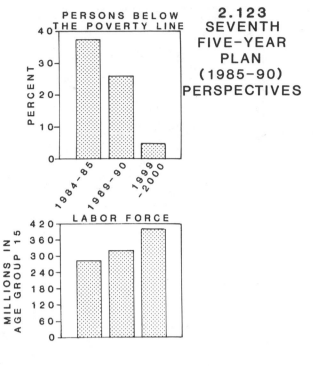

2.123
SEVENTH
FIVE-YEAR
PLAN
(1985-90)
PERSPECTIVES

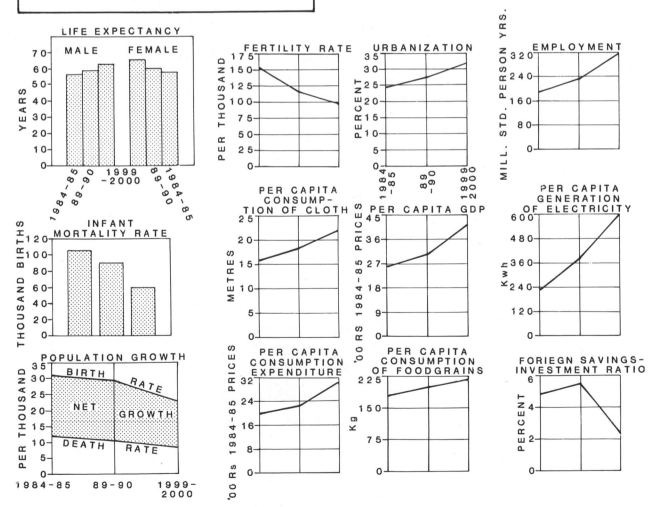

3. BANGLADESH

Bangladesh is the newest independent country of the Indian subcontinent dating back to 1971. The word Bangladesh means 'country of the Bengalis'. As almost all Bangladeshis speak the Bengali language, this is the most linguistically homogeneous country in the subcontinent. The Bengali or Bengal region, defined by the use of the Bengali language, extends beyond the boundaries of Bangladesh into India. In Bangladesh, all areas except the Chittagong Hill Tracts, fall within the region. In India, all of the state of West Bengal except for the district of Darjeeling, two-thirds of the state of Tripura along with the Cachar district of the state of Assam are in the region. This extended Bengali region covers an area of 85,000 sq. miles, 53% larger than Bangladesh and has a population of 140 million (1981), 56% greater than Bangladesh alone. In this defined Bengali region, Moslems and Hindus constitute about 60% and 36% of the population, respectively. Within Bangladesh, however, is to be found a much higher percentage of Moslems (86.6%) than Hindus (12.1%). Over the centuries, the Bengalis, Moslem or Hindu, have developed a common heritage and therefore, any analysis of Bangladesh's history needs to be made in a much broader spatial perspective.

Bangladesh at a Glance

Name: People's Republic of Bangladesh

Borders with: Burma, India

Area: 55,126 mi² (142,776 km²)

Population: 96,539,000 (1983 est.)

Capital: Dhaka

Other Cities: Chittagong, Khulna, Narayanganj

Monetary Unit: Taka (March 1984: 25.2 = 1 U.S. $)

Chief Products: Agriculture - Rice, Jute, Tea

Industries - Cement, Fertilizers

Minerals - Natural gas

Per Capita G.N.P.: U.S. $140 (1982)

Religion: Islam, Hinduism

Languages: Bengali (official), English

Railroads: 3,470 km (2,156 mi)

Roads: 4,044 km (2,513 mi)

As soon as the capital of Bengal was moved to Murshidabad in 1720, the Bengal Nawab (king) found the western part of his realm to be the center of greatest activity, for it was along the river Baghirathi that most Europeans operated their trading forts. Also, it was there that Bengal faced the aggressive Marathas, who later created havoc with their savage raids, the memory of which persists in common Bengali folklore. Though Bengali rulers sent tribute to the Delhi emperors, their regimes were virtually independent. Their territory not only covered all of Bengal and Bihar, but also parts of Orissa and Assam. The last Bengali Nawab, Sirajuddaulla, was defeated by the British in the Battle of Plassey, in 1757, by the treachery of his commander-in-chief.

Before the British came to trade, the Por-

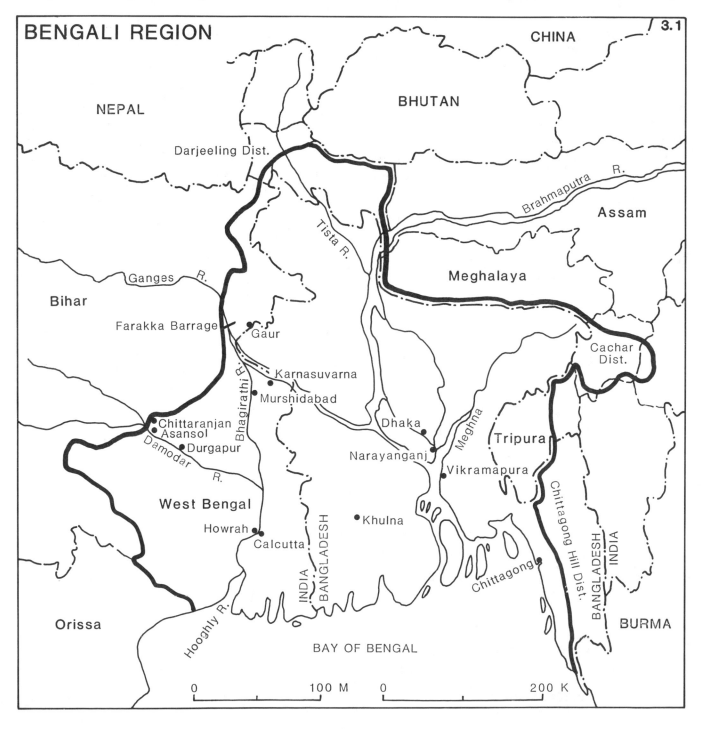

BENGALI REGION   **3.1**

tuguese had established trading and military outposts in Chittagong and Sandwip Island, and had a settlement in Satgaon and later in Hooghly. Out of this contact came certain Portuguese words, such as *almirah* (almary in Bengali) and *balti* (bucket) which became part of the Bengali vocabulary. The Portuguese *Jesu Kristos* (Jesus Christ) became *Jisu Khrista* in Bengali. They introduced new flowers, such as *krishnakali (Mirabilis Jalapa)*, fruits, such as papaya, pineapple and guava, and cashew nuts to the area. However, their missionary activity collapsed because of conflict with the Mughals, who finally drove them out. Some of the Portuguese joined the Mogh tribe residing in Arakan (Burma) and pillaged the Bengal coasts. The association of the Moghs with looting brought a new word into the English language, *mugging*.

The British in Bengal. Calcutta became the capital of the British territories in 1772, but it reverted to being the provincial capital after 1911, when Delhi became the seat of imperial administration. During the British era, a significant aspect of their 'divide and rule' policy was reflected in the effort to partition Bengal into Hindu and Moslem areas. In 1905, parts of Bengal with a Moslem majority were merged with Assam and designated as East Bengal and Assam, with Dhaka as the capital. The Hindu-majority districts of West Bengal, along with Bihar and parts of Orissa, were designated simply as Bengal. This move was taken by the Bengalis as divisive and was thought to be a design to dilute Bengal's participation in the national liberation movement. Mass resistence to this division occurred over all Bengal, and as a result, in 1912, eastern India was divided into three provinces and Bengal was reunited with Calcutta the provincial capital.

Throughout its history, Bengal has displayed several spatial characteristics: i) divided into several regions, ii) united into one administrative unit, iii) expanded to include adjacent territories, or iv) as part of empires ruled by north Indian kings or the British Raj. All those years (6th through 20th centuries) of division, unity, expansion and subjugation witnessed the emergence of core areas in the Gaur region, Murshidabad, Dhaka, and Calcutta. In the course of time, the first two core areas disappeared, whereas Calcutta and Dhaka have persisted and now are the leading political and cultural centers for West Bengal and Bangladesh, respectively.

Bengal has layers of Hindu, Buddhist, Moslem, and Christian influences laid on one over the other, though currently its eastern part is essentially Moslem and the western primarily Hindu. In spite of this heterogeneity, the region is characterized by its unity of language. But even with language, two different directions of evolution can be seen.

Islamization of Bengal. Beginning in the 13th century, Bengalis in large numbers converted from Hinduism to Islam, especially in eastern Bengal. Several reasons account for this movement. First, the Hindu caste strictures and the exploitation of the lower castes and the untouchables (*nomosudras*) by the upper castes, especially the Brahmins, were acute in Bengal. Therefore, when the lower castes were exposed to more egalitarian Islamic principles and practices they embraced the new religion readily. Second, because East Bengal was somewhat isolated from the rest of South Asia, it remained outside the strongest impact of basic Hindu beliefs from the west. Third, East Bengal was strongly influenced first by mystically-based Tantric Buddhism, and later by Tantric Hinduism, which provided a fertile ground for the mystically-oriented Moslem saints, called *sufis*, who came to Bengal in large numbers with the new Moslem rulers. Fourth, a very limited amount of direct force was applied by the new Moslem rulers and the jagirdars for conversion. There were religious tax incentives for converting to Islam. Finally, Moslems received preferential treatment in the matter of government employment and promotion.

The process of Islamization continued through the British period, and, by 1947, over 50% of the Bengalis were Moslems. The largest concentration of Moslems, during the prepartition period, was in the east-central part of the region. The partition caused large numbers of Hindus to migrate primarily westward into India and, at the same time, large numbers of

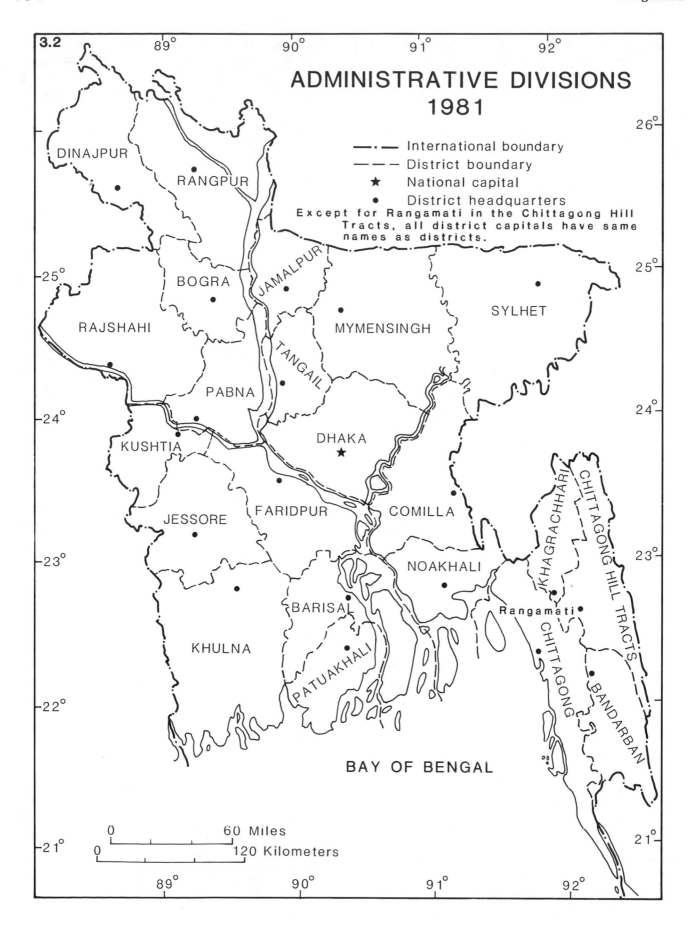

3.2

ADMINISTRATIVE DIVISIONS
1981

—·—·— International boundary
— — — District boundary
★ National capital
● District headquarters
Except for Rangamati in the Chittagong Hill
Tracts, all district capitals have same
names as districts.

DINAJPUR

RANGPUR

BOGRA

JAMALPUR

RAJSHAHI

MYMENSINGH

SYLHET

TANGAIL

PABNA

KUSHTIA

DHAKA

JESSORE

FARIDPUR

COMILLA

NOAKHALI

BARISAL

KHAGRACHHARI

CHITTAGONG HILL TRACTS

Rangamati

KHULNA

CHITTAGONG

BANDARBAN

PATUAKHALI

BAY OF BENGAL

0   60 Miles

0   120 Kilometers

POLITICAL DIVISION OF THE BENGALI REGION

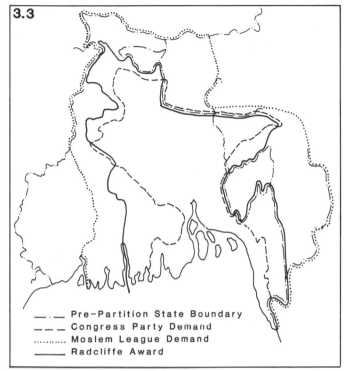

3.3

_._ Pre-Partition State Boundary
_ _ _ Congress Party Demand
.... Moslem League Demand
_____ Radcliffe Award

Moslems to move primarily eastward into East Pakistan, which later became Bangladesh. As a result of these movements, the concentration of Moslems today in Bangladesh reaches over 85%, whereas the concentration of Hindus in the West Bengal state of India is 78%.

Partition of Bengal in 1947. When the British left India in 1947, the former British Indian Empire was partitioned along religious lines. East Pakistan was created by partitioning the Bengali region on the basis of a decision called the Radcliffe Award. The Indian National Congress Party demanded a much greater area for India, while an even larger area, including Calcutta, was claimed by the Moslem League Party for Pakistan. When the British indicated their intention of leaving India, serious thoughts were given to the idea of an independent nation state in the Bengal region. As early as 1940, the Lahore Resolution of the Moslem League (later known as the Pakistan Resolution), moved by a prominent Bengali leader, A.K. Fazlul Huq (who was called "Sher-e-Bangla", the "Tiger of Bengal"), had originally proposed the establishment of *two* sovereign states, in the Moslem-majority northwestern and northeastern parts of the subcontinent.

Subsequent political developments, led to the polarization of the Hindus and Moslems and the partition of India. The partition of Bengal became inevitable. Influenced by the supra-Bengal course of religious separation in Indian society as a whole, the differing regional and religious identities of the Bengali people won out over their combined ethnolinguistic identity.

Even though several notable Moslem League and Congress Party leaders from Bengal continued their campaigns for an independent "Greater Bengal" until as late as mid-1947, and although they had apparently received the blessings of both Gandhi and Jinnah, the scheme was ultimately frustrated by elements interested in either Indian nationalism or Moslem unity within a larger Pakistan. As in 1905, the second partition of Bengal was, in the main, engineered by the British rulers, but ironically, this time they found the strongest support from among the Hindu community, which had fought most vehemently against the first partition. The Calcutta-based, middle class, Hindu leadership proved most agile as they anticipated potential political domination in a united Bengal by the numerically superior Moslem community. To be sure, these leaders supported a united Bengal as long as it remained part of an undivided India. To West Bengalis the appeal of a united India proved stronger than the attraction of a separate, sovereign Bengali state.

Thus, in 1947, the course of Bengali nation-building and state formation received a significant check. It seemed the newly subdivided parts of the ethnolinguistic Bengal were destined to go their separate ways. East Bengal (including the Sylhet district of Assam) with a Moslem majority became a province of Pakistan and eventually transformed itself into a sovereign republic in 1971, after a long political struggle culminating in a national liberation war. Both West Bengal and Tripura with Hindu majorities remained states within the Republic of India. Although presently parts of Assam fall within the ethnolinguistic Bengali region, politically they form minority areas within that state, in the same way that the Chittagong Hill Tracts, the Darjeeling district of West Bengal and the district of North Tripura are also non-Bengali areas.

Independent Bangladesh generated an anti-Pakistani euphoria because, during the period 1947-71, West Pakistanis treated the Bengali East Pakistanis as inferiors, exploited them economically, gave special preference to West Pakistan's development and, in 1971, tried to ruthlessly crush the Bengali nationalists struggle for independence. However, pro-Pakistani elements initially dormant, came to influence Bangladeshi politics from the mid-1970s, giving rise to a mixture of Islamic fundamentalism and Bangladeshi nationalism.

Bangladesh Today

Bangladesh today stands quite in contradiction to what it was thought of until the early 20th century when Bengal was a prosperous land and India's 'rice bowl'. The Bengali poet D.L. Roy referred to it as "a country filled with rice, riches and flowers." The Mughal governors of the 16th century amassed enormous fortunes for themselves and their Emperors from the fertile province of Bengal. The attraction of Bengal was so great that the British initiated their vast Indian colonial adventure from Bengal in the mid-18th century. Bangladesh today is one of the poorest nations of the world with a very low per-capita income. It is a region of extreme political ferment, with a very high population density, primarily dependent upon agriculture, in which farmers continually toil on countless tiny plots of periodically flooded farmland. Though only a part of the region falls in the Ganges-Brahmaputra delta, most of the rest is also low-lying and riverine. Very few regions of the world experience the kind of impact received by Bangladesh from its three principal rivers, the Ganges (Padma), the Brahmaputra, and the Meghna. The lower Meghna, formed by convergence of these rivers, has an average annual discharge of 875 million acre feet. Not only is it

3.4

PHYSIOGRAPHIC REGIONS

Deltaic and Coastal Plain

Tidal Plain

Pleistocene Uplands

Piedmont Plain

Hills

Flood Plain

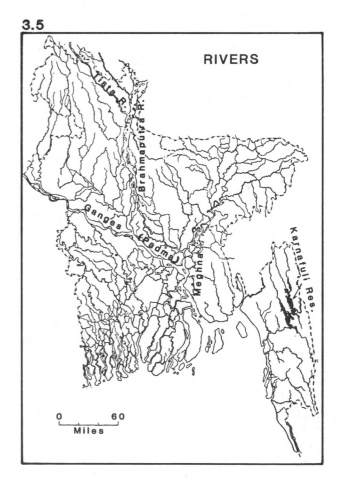

3.5

RIVERS

Tista R.

Brahmaputra R.

Ganges (Padma)

Meghna

Karnafuli Res.

0   60
Miles

LIST OF DISTRICTS AND THANAS

I. DINAJPUR

1. Tetulia
2. Panchagarh
3. Atwari
4. Boda
5. Baliadangi
6. Thakurgaon
7. Debiganj
8. Haripur
9. Ranisankail
10. Pirganj
11. Birganj
12. Bochaganj
13. Kaharole
14. Khansama
15. Birol
16. Kotwali
17. Chirirbandar
18. Parbatipur
19. Fulbari
20. Birampur
21. Nawabganj
22. Hakimpur
23. Ghoraghat

II. RANGPUR

24. Patgram
25. Domar
26. Dimla
27. Hatibandha
28. Jaldhaka
29. Nilphamari
30. Kishoreganj
31. Kaliganj
32. Saidpur
33. Taraganj
34. Gangachara
35. Aditmari
36. Lalmanirhat
37. Fulbari
38. Bhurungamari
39. Nageswari
40. Kotwali
41. Kaunia
42. Rajarhat

43. Kurigram
44. Badarganj
45. Mitha Pukur
46. Pirgachha
47. Ulipur
48. Pirganj
49. Sadullapur
50. Sundarganj
51. Chilmari
52. Char Rajibpur
53. Rahumari
54. Palashbari
55. Gaibandha
56. Fulchhari
57. Gobindaganj
58. Sughatta

III. BOGRA

59. Panchbibi
60. Joypurhat
61. Khetlal
62. Kalai
63. Shibganj
64. Sonatala
65. Akkelpur
66. Dubchanchia
67. Kahaloo
68. Bogra
69. Gabtali
70. Sariakandi
71. Adamdighi
72. Nandigram
73. Sherpur
74. Dhunat

IV. JAMALPUR

75. Dewanganj
76. Bakshiganj
77. Sribardi
78. Jhenaigati
79. Nalitabari
80. Islampur
81. Madarganj
82. Melandah

83. Sherpur
84. Nakhla
85. Sarishabari
86. Jamalpur

V. RAJSHAHI

87. Sapahar
88. Patnitola
89. Dhamoirhat
90. Porsha
91. Bhola Hat
92. Gomastapur
93. Niamatpur
94. Mahadevpur
95. Badalgachhi
96. Shibganj
97. Nachole
98. Tanore
99. Manda
100. Naogaon
101. Nawabganj
102. Godagari
103. Mohanpur
104. Bagmara
105. Atrai
106. Raninagar
107. Paba
108. Boalia
109. Durgapur
110. Puthia
111. Natore
112. Singra
113. Charghat
114. Bagatipara
115. Bagha
116. Lalpur
117. Baraigram
118. Gurudaspur

VI. PABNA

119. Kazipur
120. Tarash
121. Raiganj
122. Sirajganj

123. Chatmohar
124. Ullahpara
125. Kamarkhanda
126. Belkuchi
127. Faridpur
128. Shahzadpur
129. Chowhali
130. Ishurdi
131. Atghoria
132. Santhia
133. Pabna
134. Sujanagar
135. Bera

VII. TANGAIL

136. Madhupur
137. Gopalpur
138. Bhuapur
139. Ghatail
140. Kalihati
141. Tangail
142. Basail
143. Sakhipur
144. Delduar
145. Nagarpur
146. Mirzapur

VIII. MYMENSINGH

147. Haluaghat
148. Dhobaura
149. Durgapur
150. Kalma Kanda
151. Phulpur
152. Purbadhala
153. Netrokona
154. Barhatta
155. Muktagachha
156. Kotwali
157. Gouripur
158. Iswarganj
159. Kendua
160. Atpara
161. Mohanganj
162. Madan

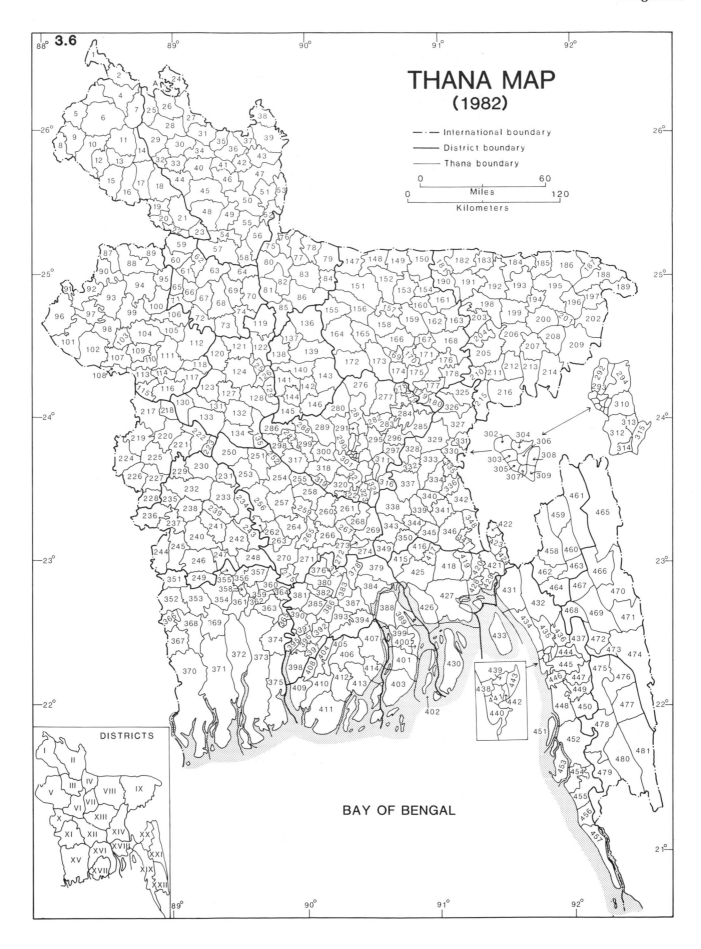

3.6

THANA MAP
(1982)

—·—·— International boundary
———— District boundary
———— Thana boundary

Miles
Kilometers

BAY OF BENGAL

DISTRICTS

Bangladesh

163. Kaliajuri
164. Fulbaria
165. Trishal
166. Nandail
167. Tarail
168. Itna
169. Hossainpur
170. Kishoreganj
171. Karimganj
172. Bhaluka
173. Gaffargaon
174. Pakundia
175. Katiadi
176. Nikli
177. Bajitpur
178. Austagram
179. Kuliarchar
180. Bhairab

IX. SYLHET

181. Madhyanagar
182. Tahirpur
183. Bishwamvarpur
184. Dowarabazar
185. Companiganj
186. Gowainghat
187. Jaintiapur
188. Kanaighat
189. Zakiganj
190. Dharampasha
191. Jamalganj
192. Sunamganj
193. Chhatak
194. Biswanath
195. Kotwali
196. Golapganj
197. Beanibazar
198. Derai
199. Jagannathpur
200. Balaganj
201. Fenchuganj
202. Barlekha
203. Sulla
204. Ajmiriganj
205. Baniachong
206. Nabiganj
207. Moulvibazar
208. Rajnagar
209. Kulaura
210. Lakhai
211. Habiganj
212. Bahubal

213. Srimangal
214. Kamalganj
215. Madhabpur
216. Chunarughat

X. KUSHTIA

217. Daulatpur
218. Bheramara
219. Gangni
220. Mirpur
221. Kushtia
222. Kumarkhali
223. Khoksa
224. Meherpur
225. Alamdanga
226. Damurhuda
227. Chuadanga
228. Jibannagar

XI. JESSORE

229. Harina Kunda
230. Shailkupa
231. Sripur
232. Jhenaidah
233. Magura
234. Mohammadpur
235. Kotchandpur
236. Maheshpur
237. Chowgachha
238. Kaliganj
239. Salikha
240. Kotwali
241. Bagherpara
242. Narail
243. Lohagara
244. Sarsha
245. Jhikargachha
246. Manirampur
247. Abhaynagar
248. Kalia
249. Keshabpur

XII. FARIDPUR

250. Pangsha
251. Rajbari
252. Goalandaghat
253. Baliakandi
254. Kotwali

255. Char Bhadrasan
256. Boalmari
257. Nagarkanda
258. Sadarpur
259. Bhanga
260. Shibchar
261. Zanjira
262. Alfadanga
263. Kasiani
264. Muksudpur
265. Rajoir
266. Madaripur
267. Palong
268. Naria
269. Bhedarganj
270. Gopalganj
271. Kotwalipara
272. Kalkini
273. Damodya
274. Goshairhat
275. Tungipara

XIII. DHAKA

276. Sripur
277. Kapasia
278. Monohardi
279. Belabo
280. Kaliakair
281. Joydebpur
282. Kaliganj
283. Palash
284. Shibpur
285. Raipura
286. Daulatpur
287. Ghior
288. Saturia
289. Dhamrai
290. Savar
291. Tongi
292. Mirpur
293. Cantonment
294. Gulshan
295. Rupganj
296. Narsingdi
297. Araihazar
298. Shivalaza
299. Manikganj
300. Singair
301. Keraniganj
302. Mohammadpur
303. Dhanmondi
304. Tejgaon

305. Lalbagh
306. Ramna
307. Kotwali
308. Motijheel
309. Sutrapur
310. Demra
311. Sonargaon
312. Fatullah
313. Siddhirganj
314. Narayanganj
315. Bandar
316. Gazaria
317. Harirampur
318. Nawabganj
319. Dohar
320. Srinagar
321. Sirajdikhan
322. Louhajang
323. Tongibari
324. Munshiganj

XIV. COMILLA

325. Nasirnagar
326. Sarail
327. Brahmanbaria
328. Banchharampur
329. Nabinagar
330. Kasba
331. Akhaura
332. Homna
333. Muradnagar
334. Debidwar
335. Brahmanpara
336. Burichang
337. Daudkandi
338. Matlab
339. Kachua
340. Chandina
341. Barura
342. Kotwali
343. Chandpur
344. Hajiganj
345. Shahrasti
346. Laksham
347. Langalkot
348. Chouddagram
349. Haim Char
350. Faridganj

XV. KHULNA

351. Kalaroa

352. Satkhira
353. Tala
354. Dumuria
355. Phultala
356. Daulatpur
357. Terokhada
358. Khulna
359. Rupsha
360. Mollahat
361. Batiaghata
362. Fakirhat
363. Bagerhat
364. Chitalmari
365. Kachua
366. Debhata
367. Kaliganj
368. Assasuni
369. Paikgachha
370. Shyamnagar
371. Koyra
372. Dacope
373. Rampal
374. Morrelganj
375. Sarankhola

XVI. BARISAL

376. Gaurnadi
377. Agailjhara
378. Muladi
379. Hizla
380. Wazirpur
381. Nazirpur
382. Banaripara
383. Babuganj
384. Mehendiganj
385. Swarupkati
386. Jhalakati
387. Kotwali

388. Bhola
389. Daulatkhan
390. Perojpur
391. Kaukhali
392. Rajapur
393. Nalchiti
394. Bakerganj
395. Indurkani
396. Bhandaria
397. Kathalia
398. Mathbaria
399. Burhanuddin
400. Tazumuddin
401. Lalmohan
402. Monpura
403. Charfasson

XVII. PATUAKHALI

404. Betagi
405. Mirzaganj
406. Patuakhali
407. Bauphal
408. Bamna
409. Patharghata
410. Barguna
411. Kalapara
412. Amtali
413. Galachipa
414. Dashmina

XVIII. NOAKHALI

415. Raipur
416. Ramgati
417. Chatkhil
418. Begumganj
419. Senbag

420. Daganbhuiyan
421. Feni
422. Parshuram
423. Fulgazi
424. Chhagalnaiya
425. Lakshmipur
426. Ramganj
427. Shudharam
428. Companiganj
429. Sonagazi
430. Hatiya

XIX. CHITTAGONG

431. Mirsharai
432. Fatikchhari
433. Sandwip
434. Sitakunda
435. Hathazari
436. Rauzan
437. Rangunia
438. Pahartali
439. Panchlaish
440. Chittagong Port
441. Double Moorings
442. Kotwali
443. Chandgaon
444. Boalkhali
445. Patiya
446. Anwara
447. Chandanaish
448. Banshkhali
449. Satkania
450. Lohagara
451. Kutubdia
452. Chakaria
453. Maheskhali
454. Cox's Bazar
455. Ramu

456. Ukhia
457. Teknaf

XX. KHAGRACHHARI

458. Matiranga
459. Panchhari
460. Khagrachhari
461. Dighinala
462. Ramgarh
463. Mahalchhari
464. Manikchhari

XXI. CHITTAGONG HILL TRACTS

465. Baghaichhari
466. Langadu
467. Nannerchar
468. Betbunia
469. Rangamati
470. Barkal
471. Juraichhari
472. Chandraghona
473. Rajasthali
474. Belaichhari

XXII. BANDARBAN

475. Bandarban
476. Rowangchhari
477. Ruma
478. Lama
479. Nakhyangchhari
480. Alikadam
481. Thanchi

the foremost among all Asian rivers, but it is surpassed only by the Amazon and the Congo rivers.

Bangladesh Politics Since 1971. Independent Bangladesh had its first national election in 1973 and the Awami League Party, led by Sheikh Mujibur Rahman (Father of Bangladesh), won almost all of the 300 seats of the National Assembly (*Jatiyo Sangsad*). A parliamentary democracy was introduced and Abu Sayeed Choudhury became the president and Mujib, the prime minister. The new democracy was so strained by internal chaos and economic setbacks that by December of

1974, the constitution was amended making Mujib president, who could rule the country by decree, independent of the national assembly. Democracy was subdued in the name of "lawlessness and subversion" and a "national emergency" was proclaimed. In mid-August of 1975, a coup was staged by a handfull of young military men and Mujib was asassinated. A total militarily-backed, authoritarian rule prevailed in Bangladesh. The army chief, Ziaur Rahman, seized control of power in November, 1975, and Abu Sadat Mohammad Sayeem, a civilian, was designated as president. Ziaur became the president after Sayeem's resignation in 1977. He, thus, became the seventh president in the six years of Bangladesh's independence. By the end of 1977, democracy was partially reinstated, Ziaur formed a new Bangladesh Nationalist Party, and became the elected president in 1978. In 1979, martial law, which was in effect since 1975, was annulled and a democratic government, combining a presidential form with a parliament, was restored. Ziaur, on an official visit to Chittagong, was asassinated by some junior army officers in November 1981. Abdus Sattar, the vice president, succeeded to the presidency in accordance with the new constitution. In March 1982, the 52-year-old army chief Hussain Mohammed Ershad, staged a bloodless coup saying that he wanted to "save" Bangladesh from corruption and disasters; yet, even after 3 years, corruption in officialdom and civil life continued unabated. Natural hazards, over which men do not have too much control, at least in Bangladeshi circumstances, ravage the country on a regular basis. Ershad first became the chief administrator and, later, also the president. Martial law was proclaimed and the country was divided into 5 zones, for administration by regional martial law commanders. The country is further divided into 22 districts and over 450 thanas for administrative purposes.

Climate and Rainfall. As Bangladesh has a tropical monsoon climate with heavy summer rain (60"-80" average) and dry winters, large areas along the banks of the three main rivers are seasonally inundated. In general, people have learned to live with this abundance of water and the heavy monsoon rains which may produce as much as 3"-5" a day. Just as heavy snow forces school closings in middle-latitude areas, the heavy rains and flooding in the country cause similar disruptions.

Moisture-laden winds from the Indian Ocean and the Bay of Bengal flow steadily inland from the south and southwest, bringing with them as much as 95% of the annual rainfall between April and October. The real rainy season, which accounts for three-fourths of the annual rainfall, extends from June to September. This is very evident from observing the rainfall occurrence at two stations, Comilla in the wetter

east and Bogra in the not-so-wet west. At both stations, December through March are dry with low relative humidity.

Monsoon rains are erratic. Some years are rainy and others may be relatively dry. Between 1974-83, several centers have shown remarkably low rainfall both in the western and the eastern parts of the country; Bogra, for example, with only 43" in 1978-79 and Comilla with 47". Jessore recorded only 29" in 1979-80 though its average annual rainfall normally totals 53". Droughts are, therefore, not uncommon in Bangladesh.

Natural Hazards. Floods, cyclones and occasional droughts are faced by Bangladesh. Destructive floods occur every two to three years. They are caused by heavier than usual rainfall and snow melt in the Himalayas, the headwater region of the Ganges-Brahmaputra system. In 1974, about two-thirds of the country was under flood waters and as an aftermath several thousand people died of starvation. Except for areas shown as hills, Pleistocene upland and Piedmont Plains on the physiographic map, all areas of Bangladesh are susceptible to flooding. The tidal plain experiences low floods caused by local heavy rainfall, for the low level of relief is no help in draining the water to the sea.

Cyclones or hurricanes originating in the Bay of Bengal, usually before or after the rainy season, devastate the southern part of Bangladesh on a regular basis. Between 1960-78, 31 major cyclonic storms hit the country causing moderate to extensive damage. Some years, such as in 1964, 1968 and 1972, no major storm hit the country, but in 1960 there were three cyclones, one of which, on October 9-10, killed 3,000 people. One most severe cyclone to ever hit Bangladesh was in May 1822, causing death to 40,000 people and loss of 100,000 cattle in the districts of Barisal and Patuakhali.

Agriculture. Bangladesh is primarily dependent on agriculture. In 1981, 80% of the country's employed people worked in the agriculture sector, which is responsible for two-thirds of the gross national product. Nevertheless, the total food production of the nation falls short, requiring the importing of 222,000 tons of rice and 1.1 million tons of wheat annually (1979-81 average).

Though 7% of Bangladesh is covered with water, 36% of its 51,626 square miles of land area is cultivated. Rice (food crop) and jute (cash crop) are the principal agricultural crops. Others are wheat, barley, maize, millet, lentils, grams, beans, vegetables, spices, oil-seeds and sugarcane. Tea plantations are located in the northeastern hilly areas of Sylhet.

The summer and rainy season crop is called *Kharif*. The rainy season's only crop is *Haimantik*. The winter crop is *Rabi*. Should the rainfall be less than 50", rice cultivation is adversely affected. The three principal categories of rice are *Aman, Aus* and *Boro* and they associate with *Kharif, Haimantik* and *Rabi* crops, respectively. Almost two-thirds of the rice acreage is in *Aman*, with average yields of only 1,040 pounds per acre; *Boro* with 1,650 pounds and *Aus* with 800 pounds. Low yields

are caused by lack of modernization and relatively little use of high-yielding varieties (HYV) of rice; in 1981-82, only 37% of the country's rice tonnage came from HYV, which was planted on 22% of the total rice land. The relatively higher yield of *Boro* resulted from the fact that 63% of the *Boro* acreage was planted with HYV in 1981-82 in contrast to only 15% for *Aus* and 16% for *Aman*. Production of winter crops, such as *Boro* rice and wheat, is possible only with the help of irrigation. As temperatures remain in the sixties or above all year, frost does not limit the growing season, thus allowing for multiple cropping. Of the 21.2 million acres of net-cropped area of the country in 1981-82, 54% was cultivated once, 38% twice and 8% three times. Two factors determine multiple croppings: the use of irrigation and freedom from moderate to deep flooding for continued periods of time.

Jute is very important to the economy of

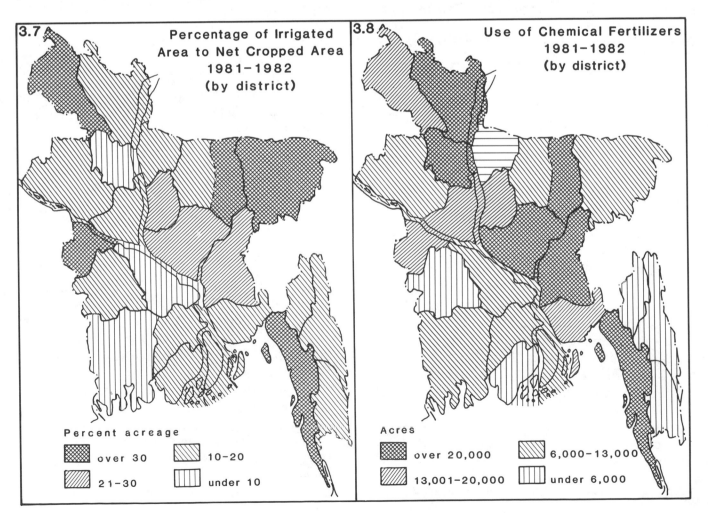

3.7 Percentage of Irrigated Area to Net Cropped Area 1981-1982 (by district)

Percent acreage

▨ over 30   ▧ 10-20
▨ 21-30   ⊞ under 10

3.8 Use of Chemical Fertilizers 1981-1982 (by district)

Acres

▨ over 20,000   ▧ 6,000-13,000
▨ 13,001-20,000   ⊞ under 6,000

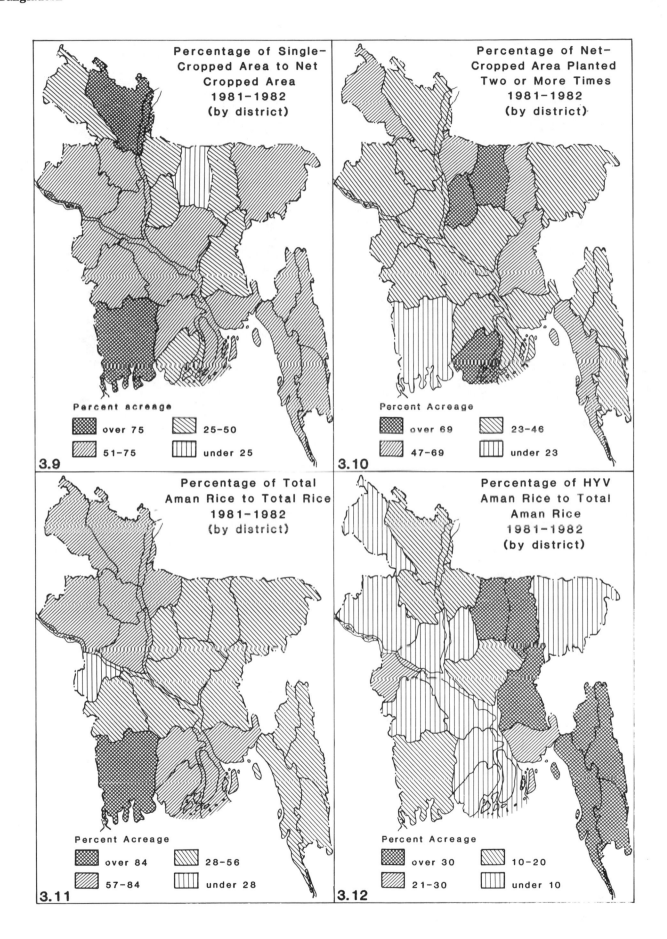

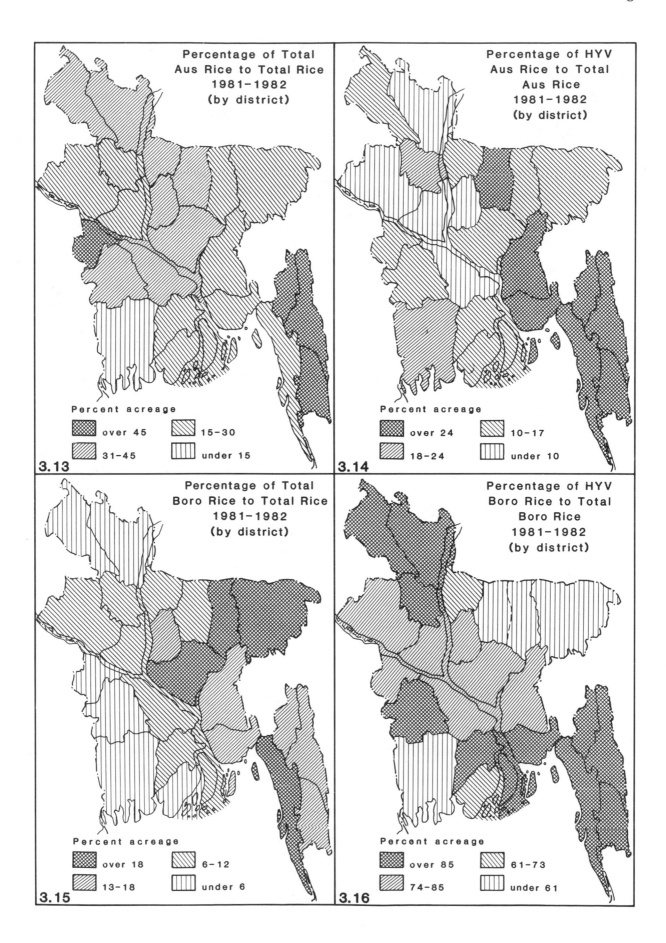

Percentage of Total
Aus Rice to Total Rice
1981–1982
(by district)

Percent acreage
over 45   15–30
31–45   under 15

3.13

Percentage of HYV
Aus Rice to Total
Aus Rice
1981–1982
(by district)

Percent acreage
over 24   10–17
18–24   under 10

3.14

Percentage of Total
Boro Rice to Total Rice
1981–1982
(by district)

Percent acreage
over 18   6–12
13–18   under 6

3.15

Percentage of HYV
Boro Rice to Total
Boro Rice
1981–1982
(by district)

Percent acreage
over 85   61–73
74–85   under 61

3.16

OTHER CROPS

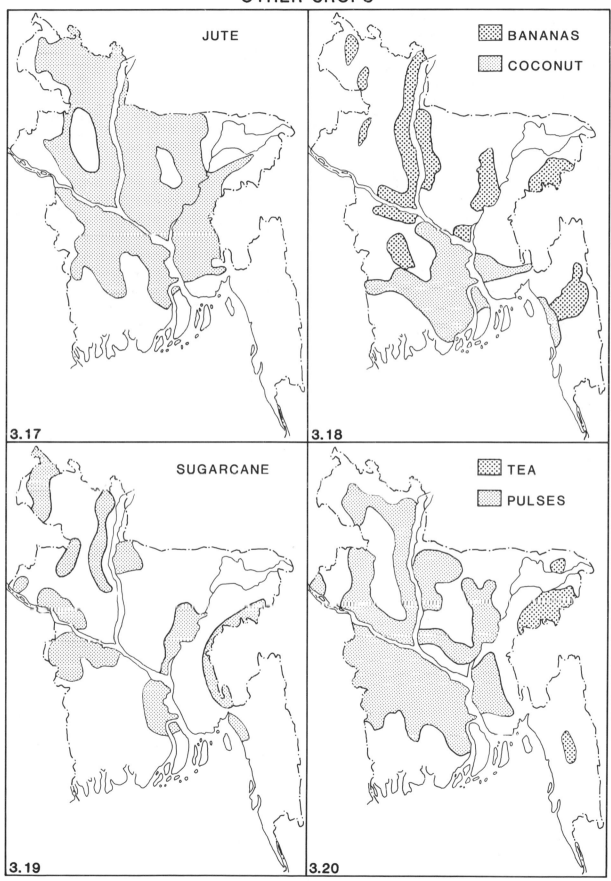

JUTE

BANANAS
COCONUT

3.17
3.18

SUGARCANE

TEA
PULSES

3.19
3.20

Bangladesh; it is the second most important crop in acreage, the main cash earner for farmers and the main export item of the country. About two-fifths of the world's jute is produced in Bangladesh, which is also its leading exporter in the world. Jute fiber is traditionally used for making sturdy packing bags (burlap sacks), but synthetic fibers and paper bags are fast replacing it. As a result, not only jute acreage in Bangladesh, but its total production has declined. Between 1970-74 and 1979-82, the average production and acreage of jute for the country have decreased from 5792 bales to 5184 and 2030 acres to 1618, respectively. Tossa jute is the best variety but it cannot withstand flooding and is, therefore, grown only on high lands; white jute in its later stages of growth is able to withstand up to 5' of flooding. Jute is sown in March through May and is harvested in August, yielding an average of 1316 pounds per acre in 1981-82.

Industry. Industries are classified into five groups: i) agro-based (jute and rice mills); ii) forest-based (saw mills, match factories and paper mills); iii) mineral-based (cement, glass, chemical and fertilizers); iv) engineering-based (including railroad workshops) and v) others. Fewer than 5% of gainfully employed workers in the country were engaged in manufacturing in 1982-83. There were 3214 registered factories, of which food manufacturing accounted for 20%, textiles 18%, chemicals 16% and metal products, including machinery, 13%. Jute fiber, mainly used for the manufacture of sacks, is the specialty of Bangladesh. Over 30% of the laborers engaged in large industries are employed by 77 jute mills, which manufacture about half a million tons of jute products annually.

Transportation and Communication. Railroad, road and water are the principal means of transport, which in 1982-83 combined to transport 84 million tons of goods. Cargo moved by air is negligible.

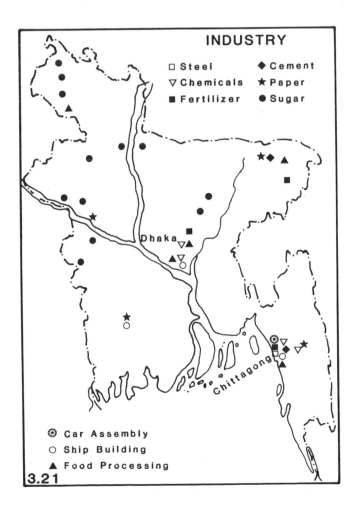

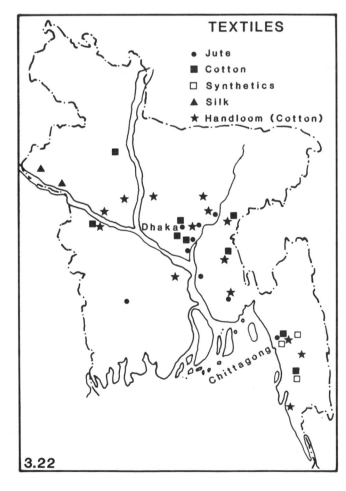

Water transport is of great importance to Bangladesh. During the rainy season boats of ten tons and more can ply 4,000 miles of its waterways. Small country boats can use an additional 11,000 miles. In summer, before the rainy season, only 3,000 miles remain navigable. Passenger and cargo boats total 316,505. The modernized sector of the inland water transport vehicles consist of 172 steamers, 887 motor vessels, 6 oil tankers and 713 barges mainly carrying jute.

Bangladesh Railways, owned by the government, operated 1,792 miles of tracks and 510 stations and had 417 locomotives and 1711 coaches in 1981-82. The railroads carried 90 million passengers in 1981-82. There are 2,969 miles of metalled roads with an additional 58,000 miles of major and minor unmetalled roads. The number of mechanized vehicles on the road in 1981 was 118,240 and the number of bullock carts totalled 5.3 million in 1977.

The official airlines, Bangladesh Biman, operates mainly from its international airport at Dhaka with connections to Chittagong, Jessore, Thakurgaon and Sylhet and carries about half a million passengers annually.

Bangladesh is served by over 7,000 post offices. Telephone connections total 73,000, though the district of Dhaka alone has over half of them. Radio and television transmission is government-owned and transmission centers include Dhaka and Chittagong. Daily newspapers are printed both in Bengali and English.

Foreign Trade. Bangladesh suffers from a chronic imbalance in its balance of trade. Until the mid-1980s, its import-export ratio of commodities stood at 3:1. Except for jute, both as raw material and processed, it does not have too many commodities to offer as export items. Its industrial supplies (primary and processed) constitute about 78% of its total exports and consist of jute and a mixture of other raw materials. On the other hand, its import items

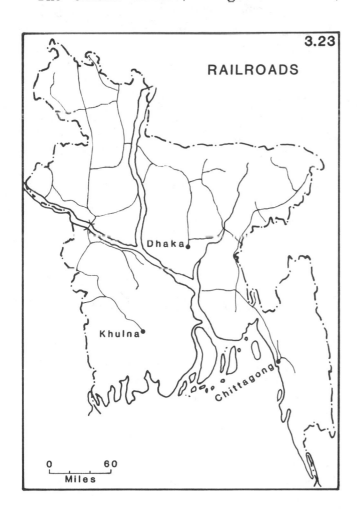

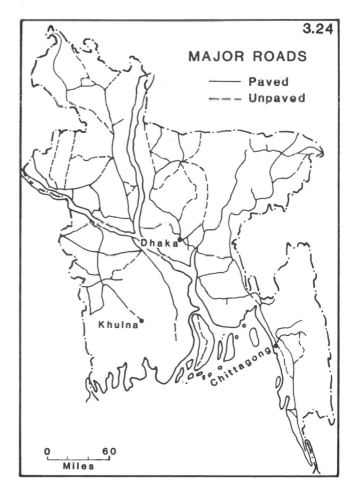

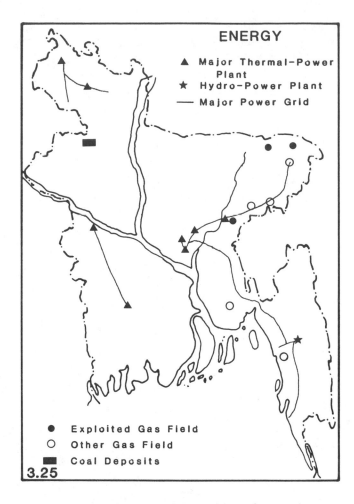

ENERGY

▲ Major Thermal-Power Plant
★ Hydro-Power Plant
— Major Power Grid

● Exploited Gas Field
○ Other Gas Field
▬ Coal Deposits

3.25

are relatively balanced though industrial supplies, mainly processed commodities, constitute about 41% of the total imports. Foreign economic assistance, which totaled 1,345 million dollars in 1982-83 alone, and remittances from Bangladeshi residents abroad, partly make up for the balance of payments deficits. In 1982 alone, over 62,000 Bangladeshis left the country for employment abroad; almost all went to the oil-rich Middle Eastern countries.

People. The main problem of Bangladesh lies in the sheer number and density of people because the country's main resource, agriculture, is not only primitive, but its growth has been meager. In the 20th century, the demographic situation has worsened without any significant helpful change in the geographic correlates. During the eighty-year period (1901-1981), the population of the country has tripled and the Bangladesh Bureau of Statistics projects that by the year 2025 it will

reach a phenomenal 177 million, all in an area slightly smaller than Wisconsin.

During the 19th century and the early 20th century, the Bengalis had earned a reputation for being leisurely and living the good life, because theirs was a land of plenty with a surplus food production. They not only made use of water for productive agriculture, but used the waterways for extensive transportation. Moreover, the public health and anti-famine measures taken by the British prevented the occurrence of high-mortality situations that had been prevalent in the country for so long. This led to a consistent rise in population during the first half of the 20th century with the exception of the period 1941-51.

In 1943, an unprecedented famine occurred in Bengal brought on by drought, worsened by the inevitable hoarding of available grain by native black-marketeers and by British reluctance to use the railroads to transport foodgrains to Bengal from other parts of India. The British thought it more 'advisable' to use these boxcars for carrying war supplies to the Burma front. Some claim that the British reluctance was deliberate and revenge against the Indians for their anti-British, 'Quit India' movement of 1942 in the face of Japanese aggression against the Empire to the east. The results were catastrophic; 5 million dead of starvation, widespread malnutrition among the people who survived and a dislocated rural economy. Both the growth rate and numerical growth of population in the decade 1941-51 were the lowest in the twentieth century.

With the creation of East Pakistan in 1947, there began a 'population explosion' process which continues to the present. In 1931-41, the area's crude death rate was 37 per 1000 people, but a) the introduction of large-scale preventive and curative health-care facilities, b) improvement in sanitation, c) the use of new life-saving drugs, and d) response from the world community with help whenever famine or natural disaster struck have caused a significant drop in the death rate to 11.9 per 1000 in 1982. While the death rate dropped significantly, the birth rate declined only slightly from 47 per 1000 in 1961 to 34.8 per 1000 in 1982, mostly as a result of government-sponsored, family-

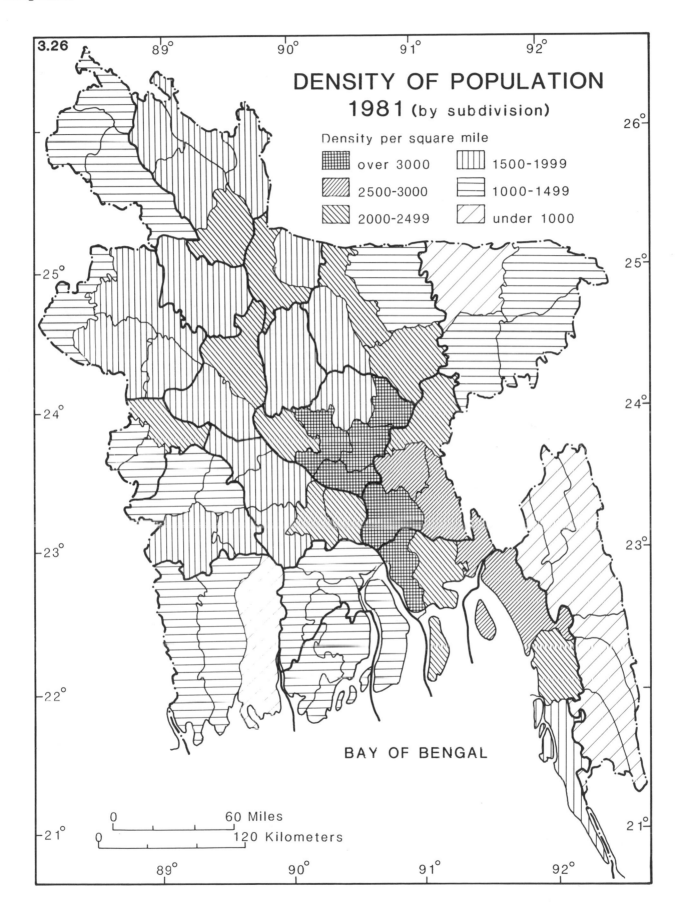

3.26

DENSITY OF POPULATION
1981 (by subdivision)

Density per square mile

- over 3000
- 2500-3000
- 2000-2499
- 1500-1999
- 1000-1499
- under 1000

0   60 Miles
0   120 Kilometers

BAY OF BENGAL

POPULATION BY AGE AND SEX, 1974

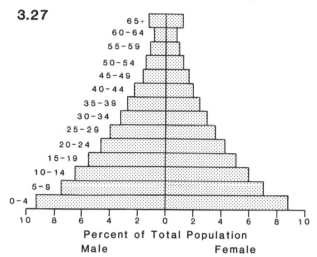

3.27

planning programs. This resulted in a continued net growth of population. Although when compared to world standards, infant mortality remains very high, it nonetheless declined from 205 per 1000 live births in 1911, to 179 in 1951 and to 122 in 1982. All of these improvements, combined with longer life expectancy, have resulted in a high-dependency rate, meaning an increase in the proportion of non-working age-groups, those below 15 years and above 60 years. In 1951, 42% of the population was in the 0-14 year age-group, but, in 1981, it increased to 47%; a similar increase (4% to 6%) was registered for the 60+ age-group for the same years, respectively. A high-dependency rate leads to a greater burden on those who are working and strains the economy as a whole.

With an estimated population of 103 million in 1985, Bangladesh's density amounts to 1853 persons per sq. mile. At the beginning of the century, the density was less than one-third that of the 1985 level. The current population density is the highest in the districts of Dhaka and Comilla, while the lowest is in the Chittagong Hill Tracts. However, the effective land area, from which the river and forest areas are excluded, is only 83% of the total area of the country. When the density is calculated based on this effective land area, it reaches a phenomenal 2239 persons per square mile, a density unmatched by any other country in the world. Until recently, much of the population

increase was absorbed by settling farmers on marginal lands susceptible to periodic floods and cyclonic hazards. Beginning in the 1950s, a large number of farmers, both Hindus and Moslems, migrated to the nearby Indian states of West Bengal and Assam. Assam's recent crusade against 'aliens' resulted from this unwanted migration.

Rice is a common staple with all the meals. The previous day's leftover rice is eaten for breakfast mixed with *gur* (country sugar). Both during the mid-day meal and dinner, boiled rice is eaten with lentil soup (*dal*), a small amount of vegetables and a fish curry, if available. As most village markets (*hats*) take place in the afternoon, the availability of fresh fish is greater for dinner than for the mid-day meal. Although the above food habit is generally true for all, the Moslems tend to supplant fish with meat more often than Hindus, but for both groups, fish consumption is much higher than meat. Moslems start their meals with fish or meat, while the Hindus consume them at the end. Imported wheat, primarily supplied to the urban centers, is changing traditional Bengali eating habits by replacing rice in at least one of the three meals with bread.

Almost 99% of Bangladesh's population consists of Moslems and Hindus. Buddhists, residing in Chittagong Hill Tracts and Banderban, make up only .6% of the total population. There had been a consistent increase in the Moslem population during the 20th century with a reciprocal decline in Hindus. During 1941-51, the Hindu population actually declined by 21.4%, primarily a result of partition and communal riots, resulting in a mass exodus of Hindu refugees to India. Since 1951, the Hindu population has risen at a much lower rate than the national average because they continue to migrate to India, overriding the gains made by natural increase. Hindus, in general, do not feel safe and often feel afraid for their lives. On the other hand, a large number of Moslem refugees migrated to Bangladesh starting in 1947, showing a consistent increase of Moslem proportions in the subsequent years. Although all Bangladeshis have a common Bengali culture, there exist separate subcultures based on religion. One reflection of

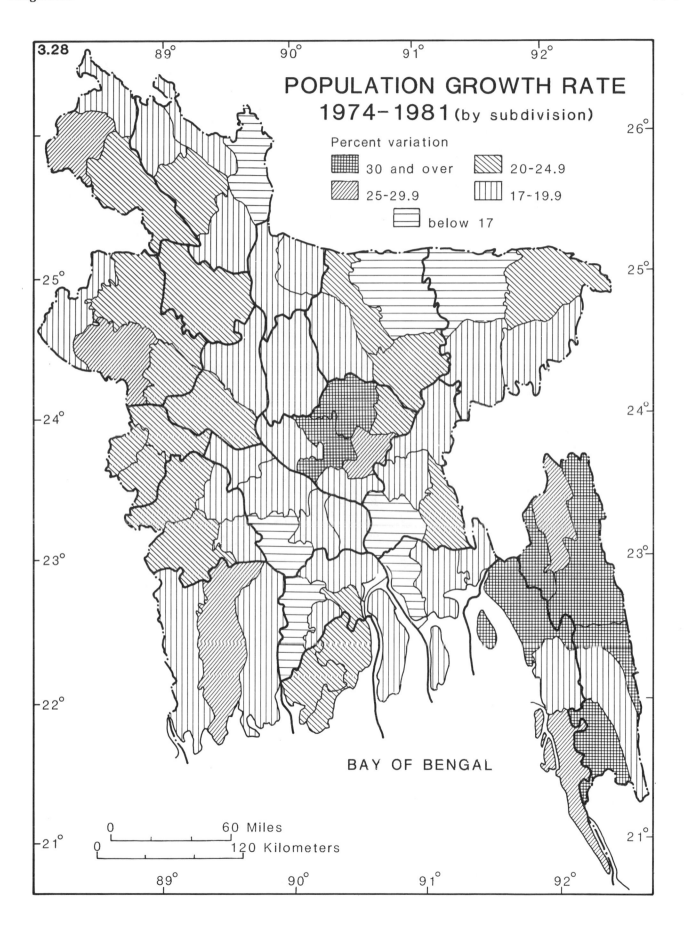

3.28

POPULATION GROWTH RATE
1974–1981 (by subdivision)

Percent variation

30 and over   20–24.9

25–29.9   17–19.9

below 17

BAY OF BENGAL

0   60 Miles

0   120 Kilometers

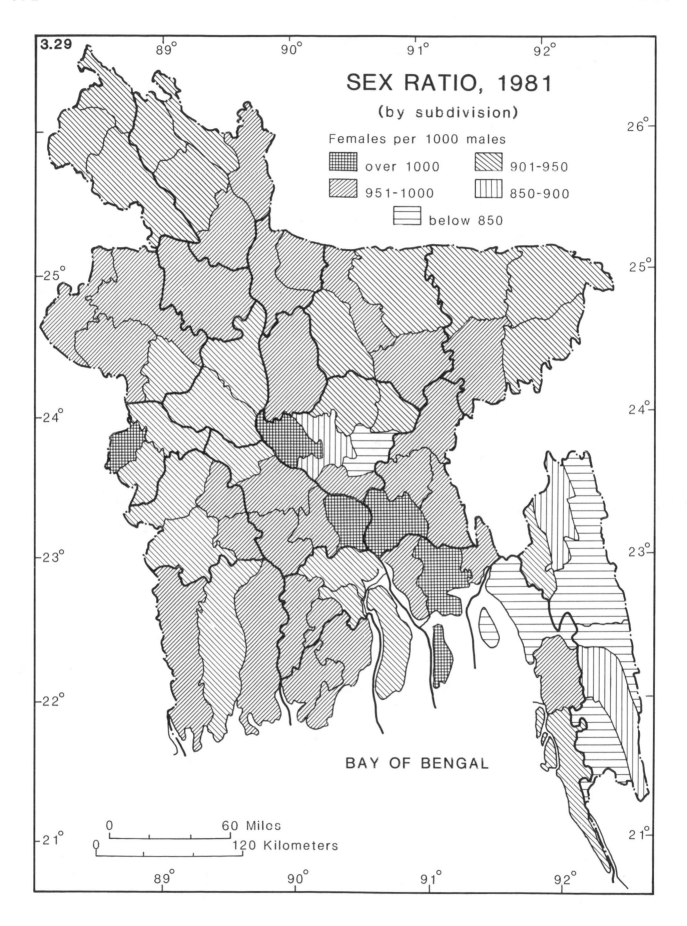

3.29

SEX RATIO, 1981
(by subdivision)

Females per 1000 males

over 1000   901-950

951-1000   850-900

below 850

BAY OF BENGAL

0   60 Miles

0   120 Kilometers

this is found in the language, where the Moslems use more Persian and Arabic words while the Hindus insist on more Sanskrit. Although Bangladesh is not officially an Islamic state, Islam forms an integral part of the government, resulting in a lack of political leadership sharing by the Hindu minority. No Hindu has been appointed as a senior cabinet member during most of the regimes.

Urbanization. Bangladesh's urban population has grown rapidly, from 8.8% of the total population in 1974 to 15% in 1981. In numbers, 6.2 million people lived in urban areas in 1974 and another 6.9 million were added by 1981. Such an enormous rise in urban population does not reflect a similar increase in the pace of economic development, but it is indicative of rural overpopulation and a resultant 'rural push'. The rural migrants, largely unskilled agricultural laborers, swell the urban areas creating slums, bad sanitation and employment problems in the city.

Dhaka, the primate city and capital, with a population of 3.4 million, and Chittagong, the second largest city and principal port, with a population of 1.4 million in 1981, are the primary attractions for the migrants. The two districts of Dhaka (39%) and Chittagong (31%) have the highest percentage of urban population in the country. Only 15 cities have a population over 100,000, with 54 other small- and medium-size towns scattered throughout the country.

Perspectives. Bangladesh's problems hover around its, a) few resources along with a backward agriculture, b) growing population

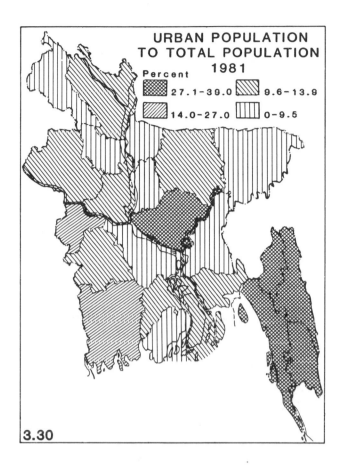

3.30

with limited success in family planning, c) an ever deteriorating law-and-order situation, and, d) dominance of dictatorial administrative regimes preventing an emergence of democratic and secular forces. The problems are linked together and, unfortunately, must be solved simultaneously if Bangladesh is to survive and avoid the bleak prospects predicted by many development planners and demographers.

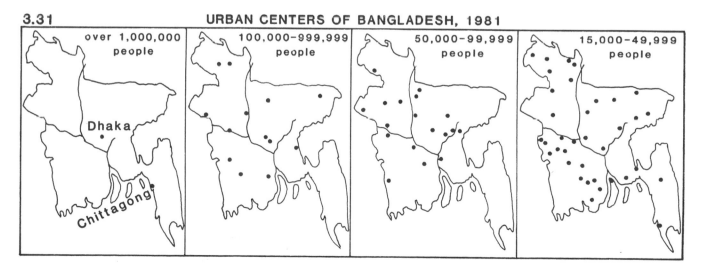

3.31   URBAN CENTERS OF BANGLADESH, 1981

4. PAKISTAN

Pakistan is the "gift of the Indus" and its tributaries just as Egypt is the "gift of the Nile." The arid and semi-arid climate of Pakistan could never support the nation's rich agricultural base if it were not for these rivers. The great Indus Valley civilization was based on the network of these rivers. The ancient cities of Mohenjodaro and Harappa were located on the banks of the Indus and its tributary the Ravi, respectively. Modern canal development, which began during British colonial times in 1859, took advantage of the river system and eventually turned both the upper and lower Indus plains into rich agricultural lands. The long established cities of Lahore, Hyderabad, Multan, and Peshawar are situated beside rivers. Even the port-city of Karachi, the largest metropolis of Pakistan, is located on the margin of the Indus delta.

Pakistan, the third largest Moslem nation in the world with a population of 90 million (1983), is in the northwestern part of South Asia. It extends from the Arabian Sea, 1600 km (1000 miles) northward across the Thar Desert and eastern plains, to the Hindu Kush and the foothills of the Himalaya Mountains. It also has boundaries with Iran and Afghanistan toward the west and north.

Its location, in recent times, has placed it in a position of geo-stragetic significance as

---

Pakistan at a Glance

Name: Islamic Republic of Pakistan

Borders with: Afghanistan, China, India, Iran

Area: 307,374 mi² (796,095 km²) excluding Jammu and Kashmir

Population: 83,782,000 (1981)

Capital: Islamabad

Other Cities: Karachi, Lahore, Peshawar, Rawalpindi, Hyderabad

Monetary Unit: Rupee (March 1984: 13.40 = 1 U.S. $)

Chief Products: Agriculture - Wheat, Rice, Cotton, Tobacco

Industries - Textiles, Food processing, Chemicals

Minerals - Natural Gas, Iron Ore

Per Capita G.N.P.: U.S. $380 (1982)

Religion: Islam

Languages: Urdu (official), Punjabi, Sindhi, Baluchi, Pashto

Railroads: 8,565 km (5,322 mi)

Roads: (1982) 97,488 km (60,579 mi)

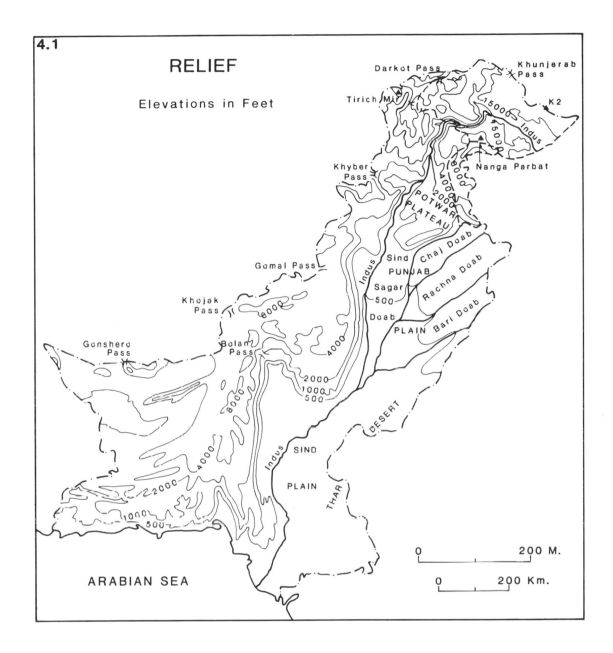

4.1

RELIEF

Elevations in Feet

Darkot Pass
Khunjerab Pass
Tirich Mir
K 2
Khyber Pass
Nanga Parbat
POTWAR PLATEAU
Gomal Pass
Sind
Chaj Doab
PUNJAB
Rachna Doab
Sagar
Doab
Bari Doab
Khojak Pass
PLAIN
Bolan Pass
Gonshero Pass
DESERT
Indus
SIND
PLAIN
THAR
ARABIAN SEA

0   200 M.

0   200 Km.

Pakistan lies as a frontier nation to Afghanistan, which has a Soviet-backed, communist government against which the Afghan nationalistic and religious forces have launched a guerilla war. It is a favorite of the U.S. government as it plays a vital role in the latter's global strategy to halt the advance of communism.

The concept of Pakistan as an independent Moslem nation grew directly from developments in British India in the first half of this century, particularly in the 1930s. On March 23, 1940, Mohammed Ali Jinnah, the leader of the Moslem League, publicly endorsed the concept of a separate Moslem state by a division of British India in an address in Lahore.

At the end of the World War II, the U.K. started to take steps for India's independence. In June 1947, the British Government declared that it would allow either a dominion status or full independence to two successor states—India and Pakistan. Pakistan consisted of the contiguous Moslem majority areas of British India. Bengal and Punjab were partitioned, and the various princely states were free to accede to either India or Pakistan. This resulted in the creation of Pakistan as a 'self-governing

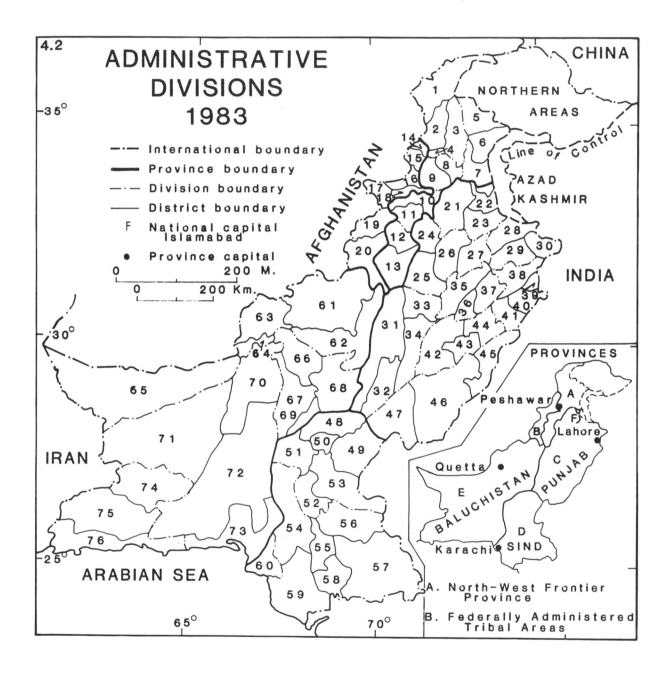

ADMINISTRATIVE DIVISIONS 1983

- —·— International boundary
- —— Province boundary
- —·— Division boundary
- —— District boundary
- F National capital Islamabad
- ● Province capital

0   200 M.
0   200 Km.

CHINA

NORTHERN AREAS

Line of Control

AZAD KASHMIR

AFGHANISTAN

INDIA

IRAN

ARABIAN SEA

PROVINCES

Peshawar

Lahore

Quetta

BALUCHISTAN

PUNJAB

SIND

Karachi

A. North-West Frontier Province
B. Federally Administered Tribal Areas

dominion' within the Commonwealth on August 14, 1947. The name Pakistan was first used in 1933 and can be interpreted as meaning "the land (stan) of the religiously pure (pak)."

The death of Jinnah in 1948, and the assassination of Prime Minister Liaquat Ali Khan in 1951, eliminated two established leaders and dealt a serious blow to the nation's political development based on democracy. On March 23, 1956 following the adoption, by the National Assembly, of a new constitution, Pakistan rejected its "dominion status" and became an "Islamic Republic" within the Commonwealth, becoming formally independent.

On October 7, 1958, President Iskander Mirza, supported by Army Commander-in-Chief

LIST OF PROVINCES, DIVISIONS
AND DISTRICTS

A. NORTH-WEST FRONTIER
PROVINCE
  MALAKAND DIVISION
    1. Chitral
    2. Dir
    3. Swat
    4. Malakand
  HAZARA DIVISION
    5. Kohistan
    6. Mansehra
    7. Abbottabad
  PESHAWAR DIVISION
    8. Mardan
    9. Peshawar
  KOHAT DIVISION
    10. Kohat
    11. Karak
  DERA ISMAIL KHAN
  DIVISION
    12. Bannu
    13. Dera Ismail Khan

B. FEDERALLY ADMINIS-
TERED TRIBAL AREAS
    14. Bajaur
    15. Mohmand
    16. Khyber
    17. Kurram
    18. Orakzai
    19. North Waziristan
    20. South Waziristan

C. PUNJAB PROVINCE
  RAWALPINDI DIVISION
    21. Attock
    22. Rawalpindi
    23. Jhelum
  SARGODHA DIVISION
    24. Mianwali
    25. Bhakkar
    26. Kushab
    27. Sargodha
  GUJRANWALA DIVISION
    28. Gujrat
    29. Gujranwala
    30. Sialkot
  DERA GHAZI KHAN
  DIVISION
    31. Dera Ghazi Khan
    32. Rajanpur
    33. Leiah
    34. Muzaffargar

FAISALABAD DIVISION
    35. Jhang
    36. Tobatek Singh
    37. Faisalabad
LAHORE DIVISION
    38. Sheikupura
    39. Lahore
    40. Kasur
    41. Okara
MULTAN DIVISION
    42. Multan
    43. Vehari
    44. Sahiwal
BAHAWALPUR DIVISION
    45. Bahawalnagar
    46. Bahawalpur
    47. Rahim Yar Khan

D. SIND PROVINCE
  SUKKUR DIVISION
    48. Jacobabad
    49. Sukkur
    50. Shikarpur
    51. Larkana
    52. Nawabshah
    53. Khairpur

HYDERABAD DIVISION
    54. Dadu
    55. Hyderabad
    56. Sanghar
    57. Thar Parker
    58. Badin
    59. Thatta
KARACHI DIVISION
    60. Karachi

E. BALUCHISTAN PROVINCE
  QUETTA DIVISION
    61. Zhob
    62. Loralai
    63. Pishin
    64. Quetta
    65. Chagai
  SIBI DIVISION
    66. Sibi
    67. Kachhi
    68. Kohlu
    69. Nasirabad
  KALAT DIVISION
    70. Kalat
    71. Kharan
    72. Khuzdar
    73. Lasbela
  MAKRAN DIVISION
    74. Panjgur
    75. Turbat
    76. Gawadar

General Ayub Khan, proclaimed a peaceful revolution, and imposed martial law. With the resignation of Mirza on October 27, 1958, General Ayub assumed the presidency. An indirect election confirmed his position and Ayub Khan began a 5-year term on February 17, 1960.

Martial law ended on June 8, 1962 and the new National Assembly convened in accordance with a new constitution promulgated by Ayub on March 23, 1962. The first presidential election under the 1962 constitution took place in January of 1965, with President Ayub Khan selected for another 5 year term. However after several months of political agitation, Ayub gave up the presidency on March 25, 1969. General A.M. Yahya Khan, Commander-in-Chief of the Army, took over as Chief Martial Law Administrator, suspended the constitu-tion of 1962, and reimposed martial law. He assumed the presidency on April 1, 1969.

Full political activity legally resumed on January 1, 1970. Elections for a National Assembly and five provincial legislatures took place in December. The 313-member Assembly was to adopt a constitution for a new civilian government. The major issue of East Pakistan's role in the re-constituted government remained unresolved. The Awami League, led by Bengali Sheikh Mujibur Rahman, had won 167 of the 169 seats alloted to East Pakistan. This gave the Awami League and East Pakistan a majority in the National Assembly. Its emphasis on a large degree of provincial automony created divisions with Pakistan's government.

Last minute efforts at negotiations failed. On the night of March 25, the army began a crackdown on Bengali disobedience. Mujibur Rahman was arrested, and his party was banned. More than 9 million Bengalis crossed into India to escape the fighting which ensued between the Pakistan Army and the insurgents' 'Mukhti Bahini' or 'Liberation Army.' After months of escalating tensions over events in East Pakistan and the cruel repression of East Bengalis by the Pakistan Army, hostilities broke out between India and Pakistan in late November. The combined Indian and Bengali forces soon overwhelmed Pakistan's army in the east. Pakistan surrendered in the east on December 16th resulting in the birth of 'Bangladesh.' The defeat resulted in the fall of Yahya Khan on December 20th, 1971. Zulfikar Ali Bhutto, whose Pakistan People's Party (PPP) had won majority seats in West Pakistan in the 1970 election, replaced Yahya Khan. Bhutto moved decisively on several fronts to restore national confidence.

When Bhutto called for elections in March 1977, nine leading opposition parties joined together and formed the Pakistan National Alliance (PNA). Bhutto won two-thirds of the National Assembly seats. The PNA denounced the election as a fraud, and called for a boycott of provincial assembly elections scheduled for two days later and demanded new elections. A new wave of violence swept the country, the army stepped in and removed Bhutto from power. Bhutto and the PNA leaders were placed under house-arrest.

The Army Chief-of-Staff General Muhammed Zia-ul-Haq became the Chief Martial Law Administrator. He postponed the October elections and began investigations of the senior PPP leadership. Bhutto, released from house-arrest earlier along with other political leaders, was arrested again, tried and then convicted for the "murder" of a political opponent's father and was hanged in April, 1979.

After canceling the elections, Zia began to formalize his regime. On September 16, 1978, Pakistan's President Choudary resigned. Under the terms of the 1973 constitution, the Chief Justice should have assumed the Presidency. Claiming that the Chief Justice was too involved in the ongoing Bhutto case, General Zia became the President. On August

12, 1983, Zia announced his intention to end martial law and hold new elections. Such highly restrictive 'election' took place in 1985.

On December 30, 1985, martial law was lifted and in President Zia's words, the country experienced a "return to democratic government". The amended 1973 constitution was restored along with the restoration of fundamental rights, but the President (meaning Zia) had the right to dissolve the national assembly, declare states of emergency, remain the country's president until 1990, and retain the position of the army Chief-of-Staff. The election in 1985 for the national assembly was conducted on a "partyless" basis with a relative fairness primarily because Zia's leadership and authority was never at stake. However, during 1983-1986, there was a strong and growing opposition against Zia among the people, led by a coalition of eleven banned parties, the Movement for the Restoration of Democracy. Such opposition was spear-headed by increasingly popular Benazir Bhutto, daughter of Zulfikar Bhutto. The fact remained in 1986 that, a) hundreds of political prisoners were still in prison, b) military men still headed important organs of the government, c) with the exception of prime minister's Muslim League no political party was permitted to operate legally and d) a political party had to serve one year's probation and, during that period, satisfy the government's Election Commission about its operation, before being allowed to function freely. Pakistan continues to Islamize the society, particularly in the sphere of the legal system, banking and taxation.

Pakistan's 38-year history, during its independent era, is a repeat of episodes that have prevailed in Bangladesh and many other developing nations; an independent country starts with a democracy, and then a military dictatorship takes over, in which fake elections take place or elusive promises of fair election are made, only to have the dictator resume power. If an elected government is installed, the military sits on the side lines waiting to take over power whenever the opportunity is right for them.

Economic Base. While a part of British India before 1947, Pakistan's economy was integrated with that of India. Accordingly, partition from the rest of the subcontinent truncated regional economic systems, cut across road, rail and irrigation systems, and left most of the subcontinent's manufacturing industries in India while Pakistan was left with a surplus cotton and wheat production capacity.

Pakistan has now a mixed economy but all development programs are carried out within the framework of five-year plans. Agriculture accounts for 30% of the GNP while industry accounts for 17%. Pakistan's economic performance has improved considerably since 1977, with economic growth averaging over 6% per annum.

Tight government fiscal policies have reduced budgetry deficits and government borrowing from the banking system, thereby lowering inflationary pressures. Pakistan's balance of payments, which have deteriorated because of the world recession and an overvalued Pakistani rupee, improved dramatically during the fiscal year of 1983; $433 million, down from the 1982 figure of 1.6 billion.

4.3
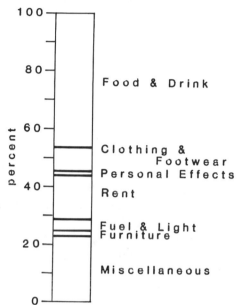
MONTHLY EXPENDITURE PER URBAN HOUSEHOLD, 1979

4.4
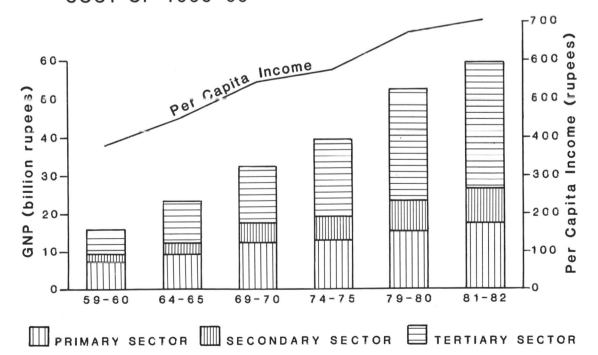
GNP AT CONSTANT FACTOR COST OF 1959-60

Per Capita Consumption. As per capita income in Pakistan has risen since 1947, there has been a concomitant rise in the per-capita consumption of some of the essential food, beverage and clothing items, such as, wheat, meat, refined sugar, oil and cotton cloth. Nonetheless, the people in urban areas spend over 46% of their monthly income in food and drinks and another 33% in other essential items. Thus only 22.6% of their monthly income is left for medical treatment, children's education, luxury items and savings. Pakistan reflects this characteristic of most developing countries, that the greater part of one's income is spent for food, shelter and other essential items.

Agriculture. Agriculture employs about 51% of the total labor force and contributes about 31% of the national income. Having grown at an annual rate of 5% from 1961 to 1970, the growth rate fell to 2.3% in the 1971-77 period. However, the programs initiated in the late 1970s produced positive results and the agricultural growth rates increased from 2.5% in 1978 to 4.3% in 1979, 6.9% in 1980 and 4% in 1981. Approximately 20% of country's land is cultivated, about 80% of it with the aid of irrigation. The country boasts that it possesses one of the largest irrigation systems in the world, fed by the Indus and its tributaries. The major crops are wheat, rice, cotton, and sugar cane. Rapid growth and record output levels during the Fifth Five-Year Plan (1979–83) have led to self-sufficiency in wheat and sugar. A new National Agricultural Policy (NAP) was adopted in 1980. It emphasizes a) a progressive adjustment of input and output prices to reflect real resource crisis, b) a gradual transfer of certain operations from the public to private sector, and c) a reorientation of public recurrent and capital expenditures away from major

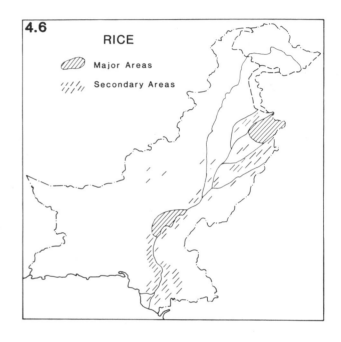

4.6 RICE

Major Areas

Secondary Areas

4.5

WATER AVAILABILITY AT FARM GATE

4.7 WHEAT

Major Areas

Secondary Areas

4.8

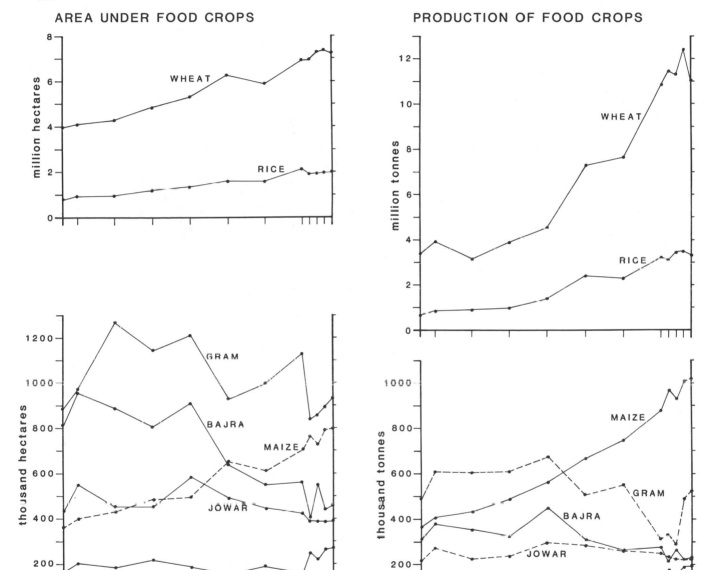

AREA UNDER FOOD CROPS

PRODUCTION OF FOOD CROPS

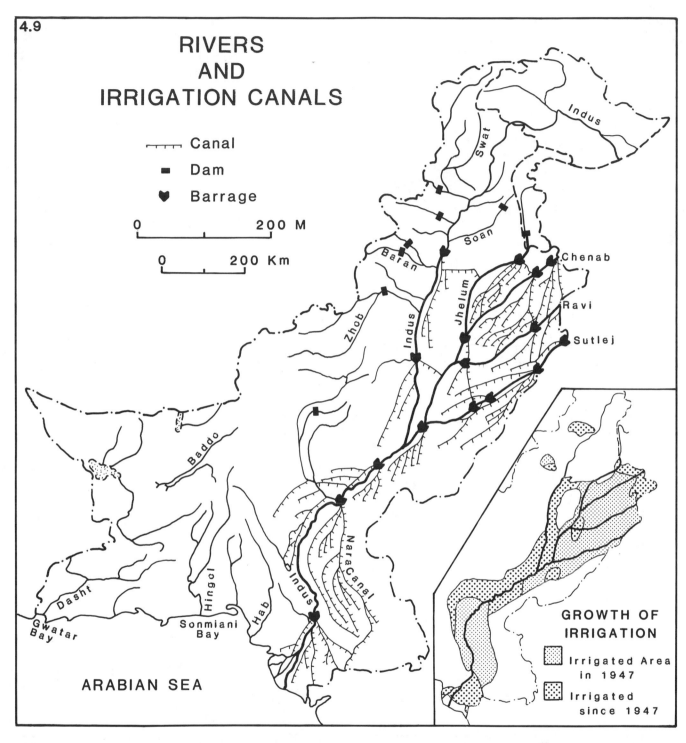

4.9

RIVERS AND IRRIGATION CANALS

Canal
Dam
Barrage

0   200 M

0   200 Km

Indus

Swat

Soan

Baran

Chenab

Zhob

Indus

Jhelum

Ravi

Sutlej

Baddo

Hingol

Hab

Indus

Nara Canal

Dasht

Gwatar Bay

Sonmiani Bay

ARABIAN SEA

GROWTH OF IRRIGATION

Irrigated Area in 1947

Irrigated since 1947

new irrigation works toward improved utilization of the existing system.

Although agricultural activity existed in all areas of Pakistan, the bulk of production came from the Indus Basin—Punjab and Sind provinces. According to United Nations 1981 reports, only 23% of Pakistan's total area of 80 million hectares is claimed as usable for

forestry or agriculture. Since independence in 1947, the amount of cultivated land (Net Area Sown or NAS) increased from 14.7 million hectares to about 15.5 million hectares in 1981. The area under principal crops increased from 13,438 thousand in 1972 to 15,340 thousand hectares in 1982—an increase of 14% over a decade. While the areas under wheat, rice,

4.10

AREA UNDER COMMERCIAL CROPS

PRODUCTION OF COMMERCIAL CROPS

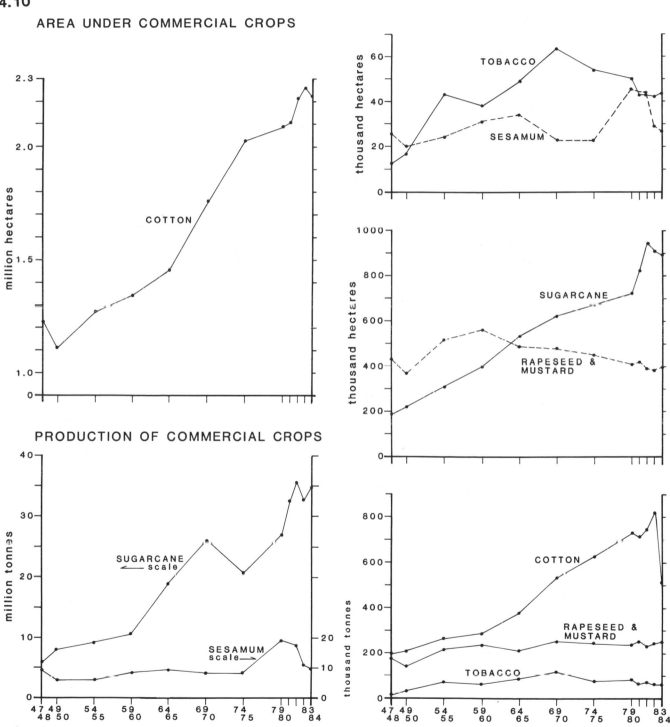

maize and sugarcane increased, the areas under millet, chickpeas and mustard decreased during this period.

The production of principal crops increased from 32,214 thousand metric tons in 1972 to about 54,094 thousand metric tons in 1982—an increase of 70%. Of all the food crops, wheat, rice, and sugarcane are not only the most important crops, consisting 95% of the total crop production, but they have also posted major increases. The production of wheat increased from 6,890 thousand metric tons in 1972 to 11,142 thousand metric tons in 1982 (165%) while the production of rice increased from 2262 to 3430 thousand metric tons (52%) during the same period. Sugarcane, a cash crop, rose 83% from 19,963 thousand metric tons in 1972 to 36,580 in 1982.

All these increases are the result of the application of the Green Revolution technique, combining the use of hybrid seeds, regulated irrigation water, application of chemical and organic fertilizers and spraying with pesticides.

The consumption of fertilizers has increased 30 times between 1962-1984; area irrigated growing from 17 to 18.81 million hectares between 1971-1983; use of improved HYV seeds for all crops rising 3½ times between 1971-83, with wheat alone showing a rise of over 9 times. Though inputs for the above were subsidized to a considerable extent by the government, by 1984, they were greatly reduced. Subsidies on tubewells were completely removed in that year. All the above efforts and increased productions have fulfilled the Fifth Plan's aim of achieving self-sufficiency in all major food crops by 1982-83. Except for edible oils, Pakistan is now a self-sufficient country in food. Inspired by such achievements, the Sixth Plan's objective has been set to a) produce increased surpluses of rice and wheat, mainly for export, b) develop areas of new agricultural export-items, such as, fruits, vegetables and poultry and c) to substitute domestic products of oilseeds and thus, minimize edible oil imports.

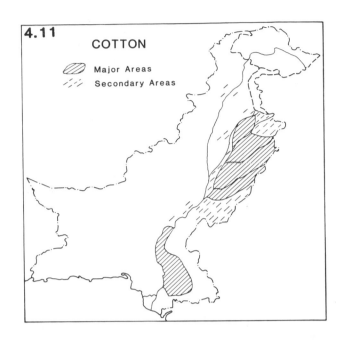

4.11 COTTON
Major Areas
Secondary Areas

4.12

CONSUMPTION OF FERTILIZER

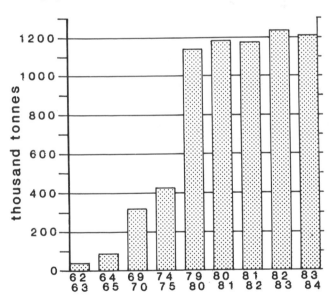

4.13   FARM SIZE AND AREA, 1980

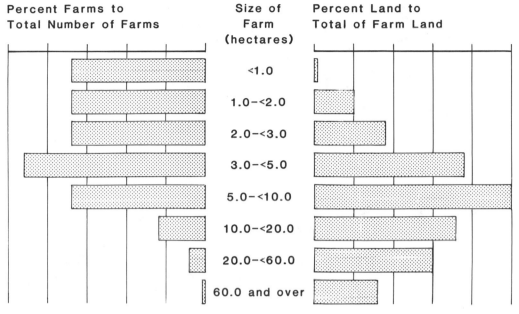

Percent Farms to   Size of   Percent Land to
Total Number of Farms   Farm   Total of Farm Land
                             (hectares)

<1.0

1.0-<2.0

2.0-<3.0

3.0-<5.0

5.0-<10.0

10.0-<20.0

20.0-<60.0

60.0 and over

4.14
YIELD PER HECTARE OF FOOD CROPS

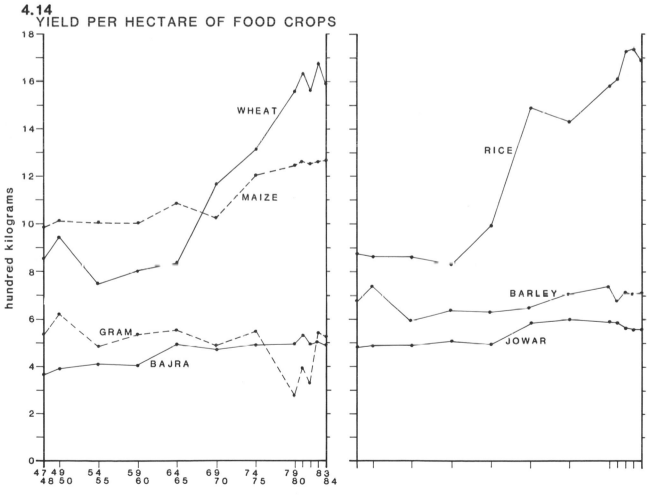

Industry. Pakistan, initially at the time of independence, inherited an economy which, being wholly agricultural, was not dependable because of her undeveloped system of irrigation, lack of industrialization and widely fluctuating world market place. Realizing the vagaries of such economy, the government of Pakistan found it necessary from the very beginning that industrial progress must form the basis of national economy. In order, therefore, to formulate an industrial policy for building up a stable and balanced economy for the country, the first Pakistan Industrial Conference was organized in December, 1947. A statutory body known as the Pakistan Industrial Development Corporation was set up in 1952.

Nearly all of the country's manufacturing capability has been installed since partition. The pace of industrialization has been remarkable. During the fiscal year 1981-82 industry constituted about 17% of GNP and 20%

4.16
MANUFACTURING PRODUCTION
(1980=100)

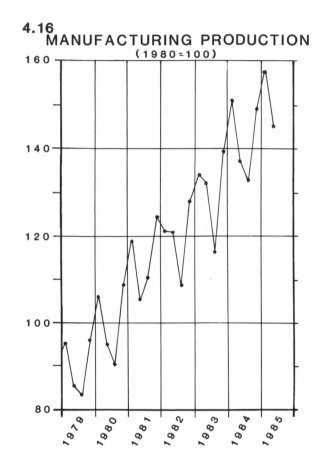

4.15   **COMPOSITION OF INDUSTRIAL ORIGIN OF NET DOMESTIC PRODUCT, 1983-84**

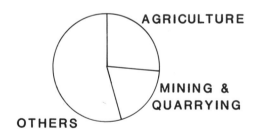

4.17
PRODUCTION OF SELECTED PRODUCTS

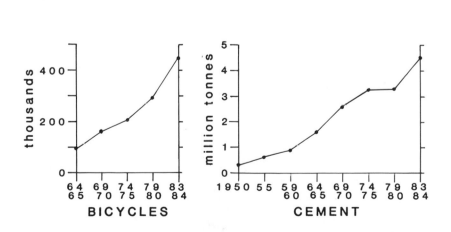

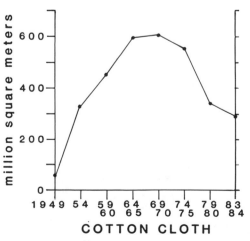

of labor force. In the 1950s the manufacturing sector hardly existed except for the textile industry. During 1960s manufacturing expanded at about 10% a year. Industrial production stagnated during the mid-1970s in reaction to a wave of nationalizations, anti-business government policies, and the general global economic recession. In 1978, a reversal of those policies began and industrial production responded to the improved economic climate. Pakistan averaged an annual economic growth rate of about 10% from 1979-1982.

Today, cotton textiles remain the most important sector of the industrialized economy although diversification has occurred. Pakistan engages in the production of cement, fertilizer, light metals, consumer items and processed food.

Mining-Mineral Production. Exploration of the country's mineral resources is in its initial stages. Petroleum, natural gas, iron ore, chromite and coal are some of the minerals that were produced during 1947. The Geological Survey of Pakistan is responsible for produc-

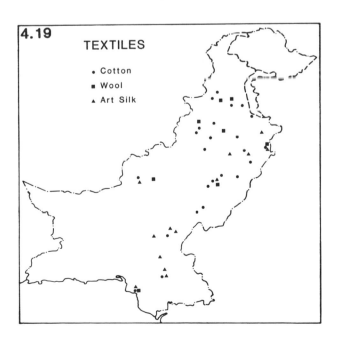

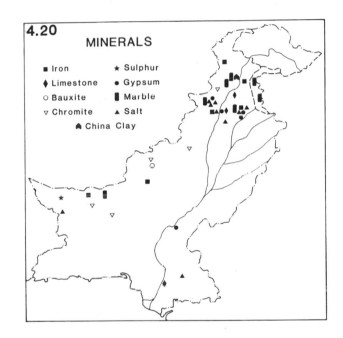

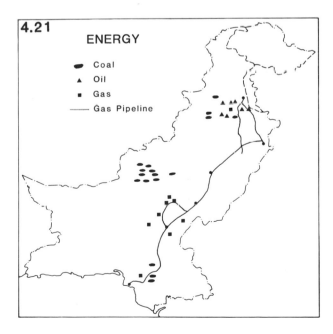

ing geological maps and reports and for systematically searching and evaluating the economic minerals of the country. Mining and quarrying contributed only about 1% of GDP in 1983, although this was also the share a decade earlier.

Trade: Exports and Imports. The first five years of independence saw Pakistan

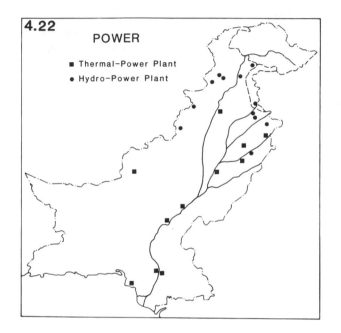

4.22 POWER
■ Thermal-Power Plant
● Hydro-Power Plant

establishing her contacts on a wide scale with almost all nations of the world, setting for herself a definite pattern of trade in both import and export.

Foreign trade has always been important to Pakistan's economy because of need for a variety of imports. Pakistan imports crude oil, capital goods, industrial raw materials, food stuffs, and consumer items. In 1982, petroleum (crude and refined) composing about 30% of total imports, was the major import followed by non-electric machinery (11.5%). The leading suppliers are U.S., Japan, Saudi Arabia, Kuwait, U.A.E. in that order and constituted 50% of the total import value in 1980.

Pakistan's exports have grown by 273% in value between 1970 and 1980. Its major exports are rice, cotton, petroleum products and carpets. This growth resulted not only from the recovery of the textile industry but also from a concerted effort to diversify and enhance exports from other industries.

Cotton and cotton-related goods are the foremost export earners of Pakistan averaging 31% (1979—82) of the total export value; rice, the second most significant export item averaged 18%; carpets, showing a declining trend, averaged 8%; leather also with a declin-

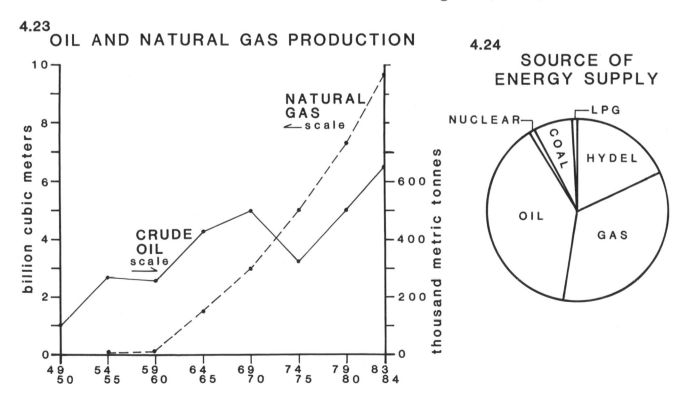

4.23 OIL AND NATURAL GAS PRODUCTION

4.24 SOURCE OF ENERGY SUPPLY

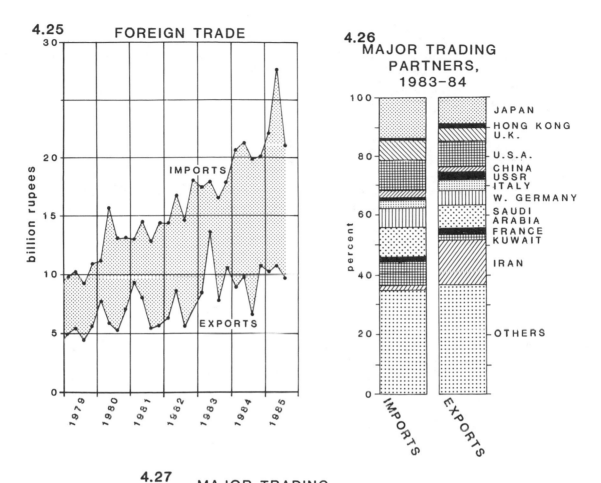

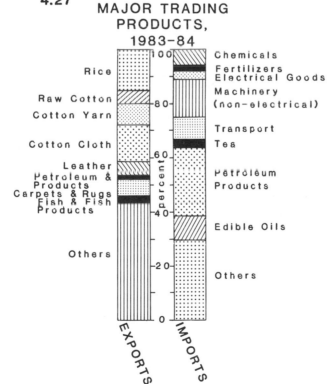

ing trend, 5%. Thus, Pakistan's export base is essentially primary-production oriented, while the industrial goods contribute only a small proportion of its export total. The principal industrial export is petroleum products, averaging only 6% of the export for 1979—82. China, Japan, Iran, Hong Kong and Saudi Arabia were the major export partners in 1980.

More than 2 million Pakistanis work abroad, and their remittances, estimated at about $3 billion annually, have become Pakistan's major single source of foreign currency. The vast majority of these migrants work in the oil-rich Persian Gulf nations, especially Saudi Arabia.

Roads. Pakistan's road system in 1981 had a length of about 41,750 km of which 26,209 km were paved roads (63%) and the rest being gravel or crushed stone or graded earth roads. The length of roads was 30,860 km in 1972, increasing by 35% in 1981. During 1978-83, the roads comprised about 27% of total transport sector development outlays and were projected to compose 46% during 1983—88 (Sixth-Five-Year Plan). The Federal government took over the responsibility for the major interprovincial highways in 1978-79 and 4,200 km are now designated as National Highways. These roads carry about 60% of total road traffic.

There were about 301,200 passanger cars and 111,000 commercial vehicles in Pakistan in 1981. The number of passenger cars increased from 170,600 in 1972 to about 300,000 in 1982—an increase of about 75%.

Absorbing about 1/5 of the total public-sector development expenditures during 1978—83, Pakistan's transport system and traffic densities reflect the concentration of population as economic activity grows around the Karachi and Lahore areas which are 1200 km apart. Movement of goods and passengers is concentrated on a few major routes, especially along the Karachi-Lahore-Rawalpindi-Peshwar axis.

Railroads. The railroad system is operated by Pakistan Railways (PR). A government of Pakistan undertaking with about 130,000 employees, the Pakistan railroad network, in 1982, consisted of about 8,823 route km of which 7,766 km were broad gauge, 446 km were

meter gauge and 611 km were narrow gauge. Pakistan Railways is largely a passenger-oriented operation with 16,235 million passengers in 1982 which indicates about 70% of 23,256 million traffic kilometers. The passenger-kilometers increased from 9,515 million km in 1972 to 16,325 million-km in 1982—an increase of about 72%. During the same period, freight traffic fell from 7,756 million ton-km to 6,931 million ton-km—a decrease of about 11%. Much of this decrease

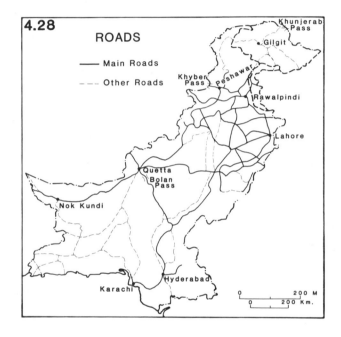

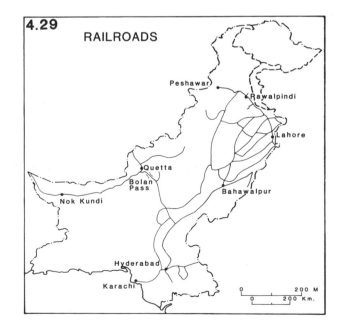

has been atributed to cheaper freight transportation by roads, prevailing emphasis on passenger services and persistent operating inefficiencies. In 1981, Pakistan Railways consisted of about 960 locomotives, 3,032 passenger cars and 36,248 box cars.

Shipping. Karachi is Pakistan's major port and it handles most of its foreign trade. Port Qasim has been recently opened to reduce the congestion of ships waiting at Karachi. The merchant ship fleets increased from 533,000 gross registered tons in 1972 to 580,000 in 1981. During the same time the international sea-borne trade increased from 4,836,000 net registered tons in 1972 to 10,956,000 in 1982.

Air Transport. The Civil Aviation Department is responsible for the development and control of civil aviation in Pakistan. Civil aviation comprises about 20% of transport development outlays during 1978-83. Pakistan International Airlines (PIA) is the national airline. Civil aviation had a total fleet of 33 in 1981 with 23,546 employees. The total kilometers flown increased from 20.1 million in 1974 to 44 million in 1981. Karachi, Lahore and Islamabad are the major international airports.

Population Characteristics. Most Pakistanis live in the Indus Valley in Sind, Karachi, the Punjab plains, and along an area formed by the cities of Lahore, Rawalpindi, and Peshawar.

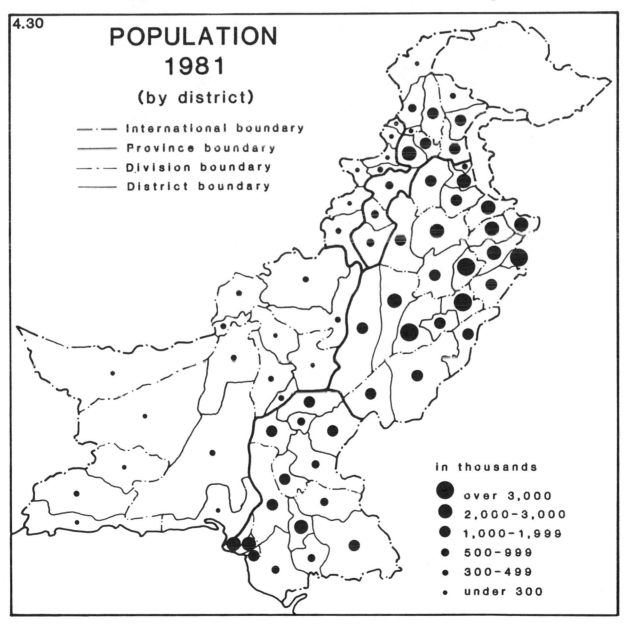

The official language is Urdu, but it is spoken as a first language by only 9% of Pakistanis. English, widely spoken, is used within the government and the military, and is used as a medium of instruction in institutions of higher learning. The literacy rate in 1983 was 24%. According to the March 1, 1981 census there were 43,917,000 males to 39,865,000 females while Islam is the dominant religion with 97% of the country's total. Christians and Hindus exist in insignificant numbers. The same census acknowledged that Pakistan's population registered a 28% rise in 1981 from its 1972 base. During the same period, Punjab Province's share of rise was only 25%, whereas,

Baluchistan, Sind and N.W.F.P. rose by 77%, 30% and 34%, respectively. It seems that the plains of Punjab have reached a saturation point in terms of agricultural potential and therefore, the "push factor" from village-bound agriculture is operational. In 1981, Punjab contained 56% of the country's population, though only 28% of its total population was urban. Sind was the most urbanized with 43% of its total population in urban areas. N.W.F.P. and Baluchistan were less than 16% urbanized and were the most rural provinces in the country.

Twenty-eight percent of total population of the country was urban in 1981. Karachi, with a

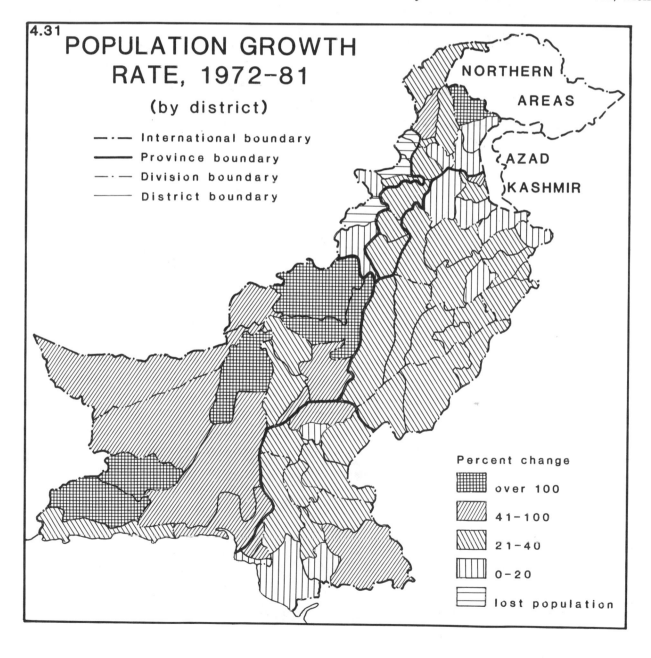

4.31 POPULATION GROWTH RATE, 1972–81
(by district)

—··— International boundary
———— Province boundary
—·—· Division boundary
———— District boundary

NORTHERN AREAS

AZAD KASHMIR

Percent change
▦ over 100
▨ 41–100
▧ 21–40
▥ 0–20
▤ lost population

population of over 5 million, was the largest city. The capital city, Islamabad, a Doxiadis-planned new town, had a population of about 235,000.Karachi grew by 45% during 1972-81. The other important cities, according to the 1981 census were Lahore (2.9 mil), Faisalabad (1 mil), Rawalpindi (.8 mil) and Hyderabad (.79 mill). During 1972-81, two cities grew phenomenally: Islamabad by 161% and Peshawar by 103%. While Islamabad's growth is accredited to the settlement process of a new town and the shifting of the national capital functions from Rawalpindi, Peshawar's growth is the result of the large-scale Afghan refugee influx. Of the 12 largest cities listed in the 1981

census, Rawalpindi registered the lowest growth rate, only 31%, because the shift of the national capital not only reduced its administrative base, but it also entailed the out-migration of government employees and their families to Islamabad.

The people of Pakistan reflect a diverse mix of Dravidian and Aryan races combined with a later infusion of Greeks, Persians, Arabs, Afghans, Turks and Mongols. Ethnically, the Pakistan population consists of five components: Punjabis of Punjab, Sindhis of Sind, Pushtus of the North West Frontier Province, Baluchis of Baluchistan and Kashmiris of Pakistan-occupied Kashmir. Though all five

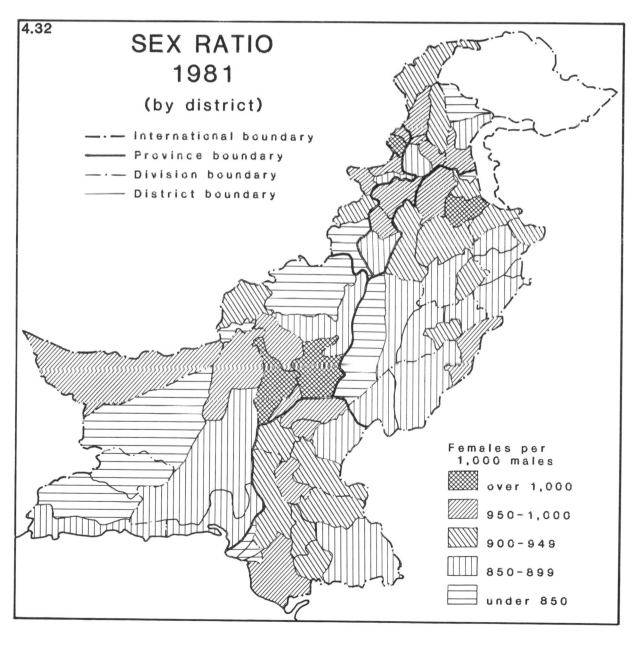

4.32

SEX RATIO
1981
(by district)

—··— International boundary
——— Province boundary
—·— Division boundary
——— District boundary

Females per
1,000 males

over 1,000
950 - 1,000
900 - 949
850 - 899
under 850

4.33 POPULATION TRENDS

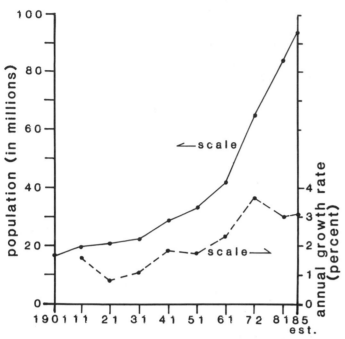

4.35 URBAN POPULATION

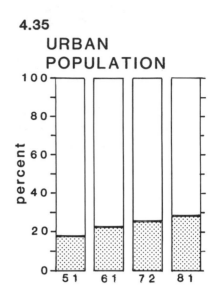

4.34 POPULATION BY PROVINCE, 1981

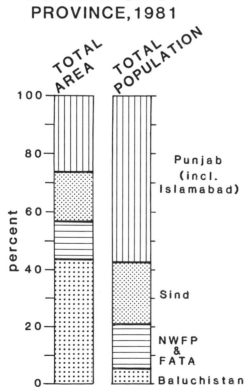

4.36 POPULATION BY AGE AND SEX, 1972

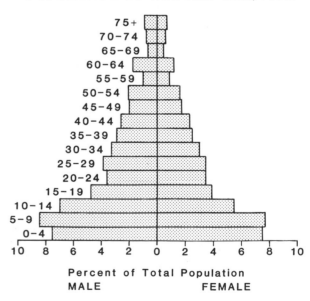

have distinct languages, they are all part of the
Aryan sub-family of the Indo-European family
of languages. Pushtu and Baluchi belong to the
Iranian branch, Kashmiri to Dardic branch,
and Punjabi and Sindhi to the Indo-Aryan
branch. Brahui, a Dravidian language, is
spoken in the southeastern part of
Baluchistan. Punjabis are not only the largest
ethnic group of Pakistan with about 66% of the
total population, but they are the main
decision-makers of the country. Their help and
collaboration is essential for any ruler. Sindhis
constitute 13%, Pusthus 8%, and Baluchis 2%
of the total population.

Karachi. The city of Karachi is the most
populous city of Pakistan and the fastest-
growing metropolis in South Asia. Situated on
the western edge of the Indus delta, it is highly
industrialized and has a busy port with a
Karachi Export Processing Zone (KEPZ),

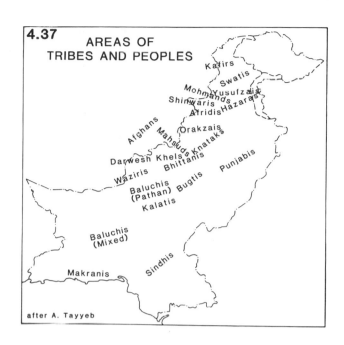

4.37 AREAS OF TRIBES AND PEOPLES

after A. Tayyeb

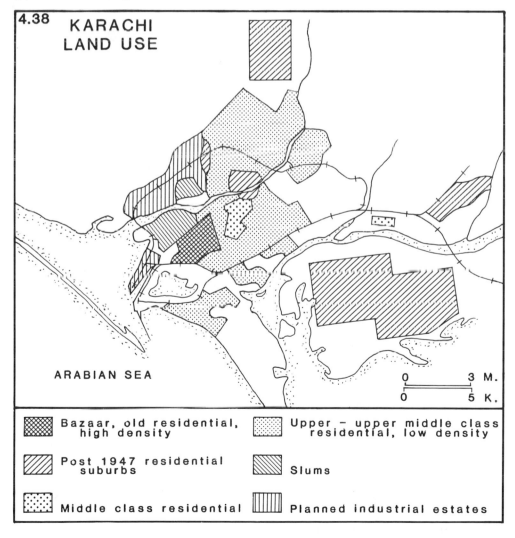

4.38 KARACHI LAND USE

ARABIAN SEA

0   3 M.
0   5 K.

▨ Bazaar, old residential, high density

▨ Post 1947 residential suburbs

▨ Middle class residential

▨ Upper - upper middle class residential, low density

▨ Slums

▨ Planned industrial estates

operational since 1982. After independence, Karachi, for a short period, was the federal capital of Pakistan.

In 1941, Karachi had only a population of 435,000. It registered a very high growth rate of 161% during 1941-1951 and 81% during 1961-1972, mainly resulting from large-scale industrialization. In 1986, the population is nearly 7.5 million. The city's industries, before 1947, consisted of a few servicing workshops and small handicrafts establishments located in and around the traditional bazaar-type center. By the 1960s, more than half of the city's industrial work force was employed in the newly developed, large, planned industrial estates at the periphery of the city.

The rapid industrial growth greatly increased the pull factor of the city. Not only Pakistanis, but Moslem refugees from India flocked to Karachi in large numbers. No other South Asian metropolis has so large a non-native population base as Karachi. In the 1960s, only 16% of Karachi's citizens had been born there, while 18% were in-migrants from different parts of Pakistan and 66% were Indian Moslem refugees. Though the natives of the city and refugees from India have a balanced age-sex pyramid, the in-migrants from West Pakistan, most numerous in the active age group (20 to 35), had a higher ratio of males. Immigration from India and in-migration from Pakistan created a greater religious homogeneity as well as a hetergeneous linguistic composition. After 1947, all but a few thousand Hindus left for India, and Urdu-speaking Moslem immigrants came in large numbers from the north and central parts of India. The in-migrants from Pakistan were largely Punjabi Moslems, who were bilingual, speaking Urdu and Punjabi. Karachi's population became essentially Islamic. Sindhi, the native language, had a minority status because of the much greater influx of Urdu speakers from Punjab and India. After the 1947 partition, Urdu became Pakistan's national language, providing an additional impetus for becoming the majority language of Karachi's citizens. Even prior to 1947, there was a preexistent base of Gujarati speakers, both Moslems and Hindus, further augmented by the Gujarati Moslem refugees

from India. Gujaratis, in keeping with their traditional business acumen, are at present the well-to-do merchants and mill owners of Karachi. Thus, apart from English, a lingua franca of the elites, three languages, Urdu, Sindhi, and Gujarati prevail in the city. Karachi-based newspapers are published in four languages.

The center of Karachi represents a true bazaar model: high population density, high intensity of commercial and small-scale industrial activity, and higher concentration of rich people. Toward the east of the city were the planned cantonment quarters that originated during the British occupation dating back to 1839. The Civil Lines inhabited by the British developed farther to the north after Karachi became the capital of the new Province of Sind. During much of colonial times, Karachi remained confined to a land-use pattern that placed the docks in the southwest, the bazaar in the center, and the Civil Lines and military establishments in the east and toward the north. After independence, new suburban residential developments occurred surrounding the eastern two-thirds of the colonial city, while planned industrial estates were built mainly toward the northern and western fringes. Thus the trends of colonial landscape continued, with the native rich settling toward the east adjacent to the former Civil Lines and cantonment. One study points out that the south-eastern section of the city adjoining the Civil Lines has attained the highest socioeconomic status.

Karachi's problems are many. In 1986, it had a drinking water shortage of 47 million gallons per day. Every year over 200,000 new immigrants swamp the city. The city grows at an annual rate of 6%; only 3% by natural increase. There are hundreds of *katchi abadi* or squatter and slum settlements, where living conditions are at a sub-human level. The city government, in 1986, led by its mayor Abdus Sattar Afghani, planned to solve part of its water and slum problems in cooperation with the World Bank and by prohibiting the development of heavy industries in the city. New industries are encouraged to locate in the rural areas around Karachi, tax free.

Islamabad. It is the capital of Pakistan and situated in the foothills of the Himalayas at an elevation of 1800 feet (540 m.). It has an undulating site of exquisite natural beauty. Islamabad's construction started in 1961, and people started to settle there in 1963. The city plan combines an Islamabad Park toward the northeast, adjacent to which administrative and university centers have been established. Linear blocks or belts of built-up land uses separated from each other by broad boulevards, and a central open space have been designed in such a way that each one of the uses could be extended southwestward toward Rawalpindi, because it is in that direction the city is most likely to grow. Only small-scale industries have been allowed in the inner city to meet the daily needs of the citizens. As these industries do not have any nuisance value, they have been located by the side of the residential blocks. A space has been reserved for the larger and nuisance-causing industries on the south-central periphery of the city. The ad-

ministrative center, the seat of the central government, has been located in the north so that it can be extended along the Himalayan foothills in the future. The residential area comprises neighborhoods linked by a central commericial district and several trading units. Daily requirements such as shopping, schooling, and recreation can be found in the neighborhoods themselves. Pedestrian and vehicular traffic have been separated from each other. The Central Business District (CBD) and special institutions have been designed to contain multistoried buildings. The capital has an area of 350 sq. mi. (907 sq. km.), half of which consists of Islamabad Park. The Islamabad District (Federal Capital Area) had a population of 335,000 in 1981, while Islamabad city had a population of 201,000, 55% of which was male. It is one of the masterpieces of city planning, designed by Doxiadis, and is referred extensively as an example of a new town in the planning literature.

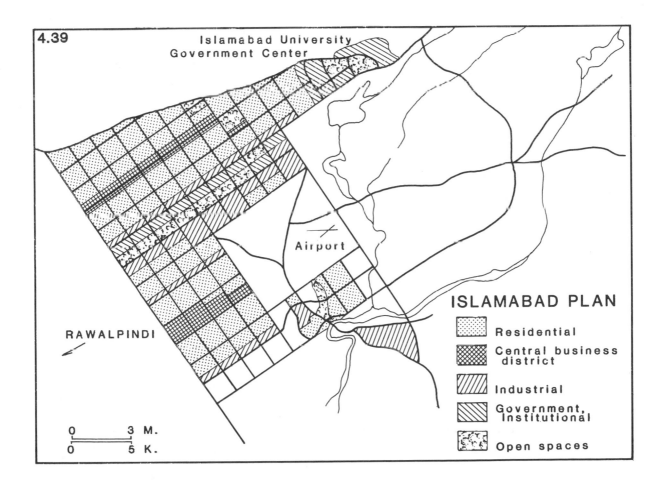

National Plans. Pakistan has had six national plans starting from 1955. The Fourth Plan is considered the non-plan stage. During the eight-year period (1970-78) the country was divided into two parts, and one of them seceded to form independent Bangladesh in 1971. Such a political bifurcation virtually caused the planning process to stop. Regular national planning resumed only since 1978. Though the average annual growth rate of GDP is 5.55% during the six plans, the Second, Third, Fifth and Sixth Plans have performed above average, while the performance of the First was the worst. Ever since the First Plan a greater emphasis has been given to industries and this has resulted in a relatively greater growth rate in this sector throughout the plan period. Both in the Fifth and Sixth Plans, energy development has been considered one of the main pace-setters for further industrialization and expansion of irrigation through the use of electric pumps. The Sixth Plan has allocated 20.2% of its outlay to energy, the maximum single item of allocation of the Plan.

The Fifth Plan is considered to be a success even though it failed to realize a targeted 7% annual growth of real GDP. Actually, the GDP grew 6.4% annually. Agriculture and manufacture grew at an annual rate of 4.4% and 9% respectively, an appreciable growth rate,

though falling short of the planned target. Balance of payments was held in check, self-sufficiency was achieved in basic food production, unnecessary controls that throttled industries were relaxed and backward regions received greater budgetary allocations for development. The Plan, however, failed to a) encourage sufficient private industrial investment and b) augment the pace of rural infrastructure development.

The Sixth Plan, realizing the main weaknesses of country's economy, such as, lower ratio between investment and savings, heavy dependence on imported petroleum, low productivity in agriculture and deep socio-economic inequality set the following objectives: a) GDP to grow at an annual rate of 6.5%, b) extensive rural electrification, c) improved agricultural productivity, d) greater emphasis on oil exploration, e) improved investments by private sector, f) increased spending on health and education and g) raising the saving rate.

The State Bank of Pakistan in its annual report in 1984-85 pointed out the structural weaknesses of the economy: a) large deficits in the fiscal operations, b) a widening gap on the balance of payments and c) deep imbalance between investment and national savings. The other weaknesses include a perennially

4.40   PLAN-PERIOD ANNUAL GROWTH RATES

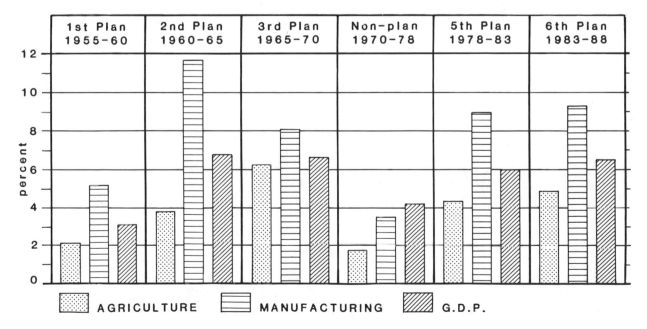

vulnerable base of exports, and irrational tax system which excludes agriculture (the largest single component of the economy), reliance on indirect taxation and lack of substantive incentives to unleash the latent productive forces. Moreover, in the wake of the Islamization process, an inefficient 'interest free' banking system has been introduced because the Islamic law prohibits the earning of interest. If, however, the Islamic fiscal policies are carried to the letter, the government will be able to take full advantage of the two newly enacted taxes: Zakat (a wealth tax) and Ushr (an agricultural tax), both approved by Islamic laws. Thus, the revenue base can be fairly expanded.

The first two years of the Sixth Plan experienced mixed successes. In the first year (1983-84), the real GDP grew by only 3.5% while in the second it reached a phenomenal 8.4% rise. The performance of agriculture was mainly responsible for this rise as compared to 6.1% decline in 1983-84, the value added was up in this sector by 9.9%.

Though the mid-1980s oil glut has forced some Pakistani workers to return home, remittances from overseas workers are substantial and effectively meet part of foreign exchange problem emanating from the excess of imports over exports. However, the advantages that can be earned from the remittances are not fully derived by the Pakistani economy because they are partly diverted through 'black-market' channels and used for nonproductive purposes. In one official survey, it was estimated that only 14% of the remittances are used for productive purposes, while 63% is spent on consumer goods and 23% on purchase of land and houses. Incentives for productive investments and transfer through legal channels will improve the health of the domestic economy and the Five-Year Plans.

4.41
DEVELOPMENT PLAN OUTLAYS

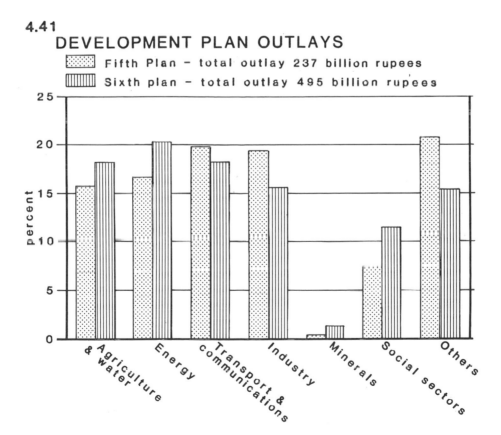

Fifth Plan – total outlay 237 billion rupees
Sixth plan – total outlay 495 billion rupees

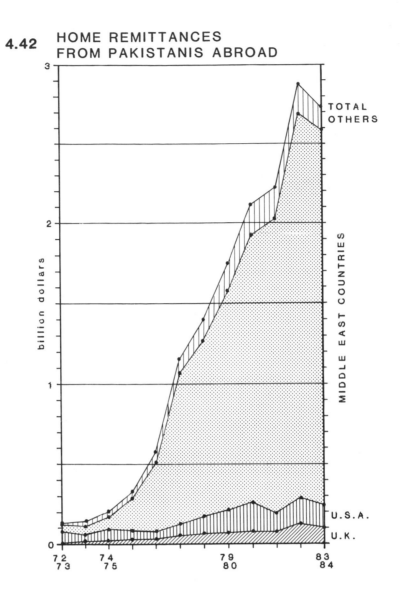

4.42 HOME REMITTANCES
FROM PAKISTANIS ABROAD

Perspectives: Pakistan eventually has to come to terms with its neighbors: Iran, Afghanistan and India. Though Shiite Iran is different from Sunni Pakistan, both emphasize Islamic fundamentalism through their governments. Afghanistan, with communist rulers backed by the Soviets, and U.S. Pakistan-backed anti-communist guerillas, poses a real threat. In the world-revolution strategy of Soviet communism, Pakistan now lies on the first line of defense. India, a democratic country, which has disavowed communism ever since her independence, stands to be the best future ally in forging a common line of defense against communist advancement into the subcontinent. If Pakistan introduces legitimate human rights along with true democracy and makes an alliance with India, the future of the subcontinent will remain guaranteed as a non-communist realm. The geopolitics of the realm, however, could be fundamentally different if Afghanistan were to become Russia's "Vietnam" and the communist puppet government in Kabul were to be toppled by the nationalists and/or religions fundamentalists.

5. SRI LANKA

Sri Lanka has a marked individuality although it is separated from India only by the 22-mile (35 km) wide Palk Strait. K. M. deSilva confirms that its proximity to India has brought forth a great deal of diverse influences throughout the island's history. The influences generated by the Portuguese, Dutch and British during the colonial era (1505 – 1948) are also marked. Moreover, Sri Lanka's maritime location at the middle of the main east-west trade route of the Indian Ocean has subjected it to manifold influences from distant lands, such as Bengal, South India, the Middle East, China and Europe.

This country shares its geological origins with the Gondwanalands of South India. Almost 90% of its land is composed of highly metamorphosed crystalline rocks of the Pre-Cambrian and Paleozoic Eras, the highest core of which lies in the south-central hills and the Hattan Plateau, Uva Basin, Knuckles Massif, Rakwana Massif and the southern mountain wall. It is in the south-central part of the country that the highest peaks, namely Pidurutalagala (8,281'), Kirigalpotha (7,737'), and Totapola (7,733'), are located. Most of the rivers of the country originate in these highlands and flow radially except the largest river, Mahaweli Ganga (335 km or 205 miles long), whose head streams cut across the central mountain system giving rise to an annular pattern of flow.

The present morphology is currently believed to be the result of folding and crumpling during the Pre-Cambrian and Paleozoic Eras, followed by later minor displacement of the

---

Sri Lanka at a Glance

Name: Democratic Socialistic Republic of Sri Lanka

Area: 25,332 mi² (65,610 km²)

Population: 15,300,000 (1983 est.)

Capital: Colombo

Other Cities: Kandy

Monetary Unit: Rupee (March 1984: 25.12 = 1 U.S. $)

Chief Products: Agriculture - Tea, Coconuts, Rice

Industries - Plywood, Paper, Textiles, Milling, Chemicals

Per Capita G.N.P.: U.S. $320 (1982)

Religion: Buddhism, Hinduism, Christianity, Islam

Languages: Sinhala (official), Tamil, English

Railways: (1981) 1,520 km

Roadways: (1981) 152,423 km

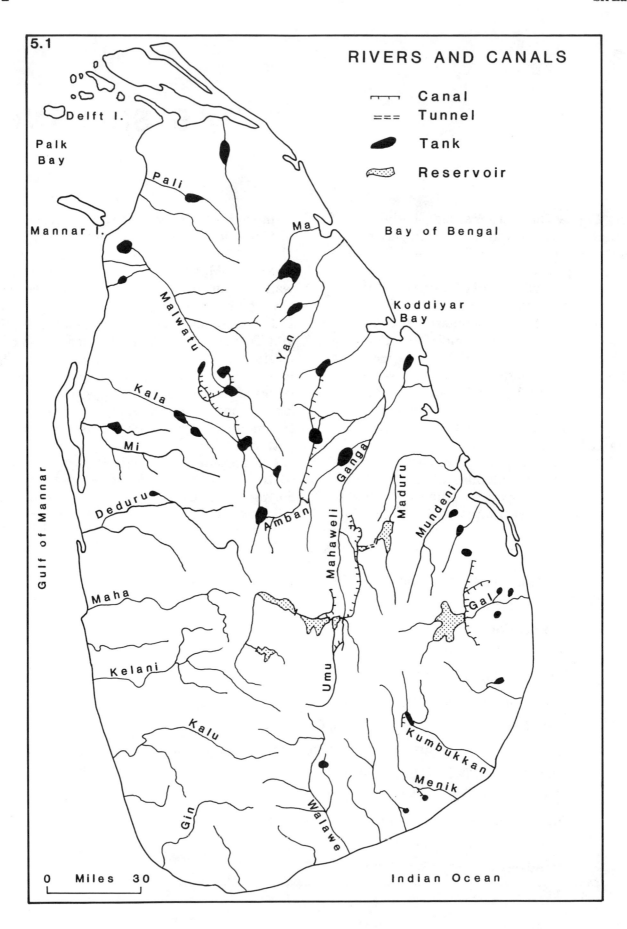

5.1

RIVERS AND CANALS

Canal
Tunnel
Tank
Reservoir

Delft I.

Palk
Bay

Pali

Ma

Bay of Bengal

Mannar I.

Koddiyar
Bay

Malwatu

Kala

Yan

Mi

Deduru

Ganga

Maduru

Mundeni

Amban

Mahaweli

Gal

Maha

Gulf of Mannar

Umu

Kelani

Kalu

Kumbukkan

Gin

Walawe

Menik

0   Miles   30

Indian Ocean

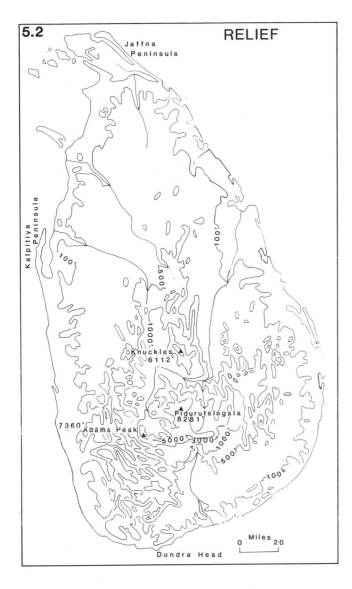

5.2   RELIEF

Jaffna
Peninsula

Kalpitiya
Peninsula

Knuckles
6112'

Pidurutalagala
8281'

7360' Adams Peak

0   Miles   20

Dondra Head

crust and long-continued weathering activity. This view outdates the earlier postulations that the island's morphology resulted from some form of geologic uplift. The island surface has been denuded to the extent that most of its surface has been reduced to a height of less than 1000 feet.

On the basis of rainfall, Sri Lanka is commonly divided into a southwestern *Wet* Zone and the remaining land area as a *Dry* Zone by the 75" rainfall isohyet. But two more zones, the *Intermediate* between the Dry and Wet, and the *Arid* at the extremities of the Dry Zone, are also recognized. The wet zone is characterized by the occurrence of red-yellow podzolic soils. The year-round rainfall gives rise to tropical rain-forests in the lowlands and

subtropical evergreen forests in the higher areas. This is the most densely populated portion of the island. The Dry Zone has a predominance of the infertile reddish brown earths, alternating with alluvial soils in the flood plains of the river. It is the latter soil which provides the main activity centers for cultivation.

History. In spite of its close proximity to India, a long, continued dominance of an Indian Kingdom over Sri Lanka has not occurred. *Mahavamsa*, the ancient Sinhalese chronicle, records that a prince from Bengal, Vijaya (according to Bengali legend, Vijaya Singha), along with his army, conquered Sri Lanka in 543 B.C. He must have taken advantage of the northeastern trade winds in winter to sail his ships from Bengal directly to the northwest coast of Sri Lanka. King Vijaya and his followers were Caucasoid Aryans and introduced sedentary agriculture and Aryan culture, including a Sanskritic language. They vanquished and displaced the Sinhalese aborigines; according to legend the Nagas and Takkas, led by Queen Kuweri, were pushed out of the fertile plains to the forests. *Veddas*, who currently are almost an extinct community living in the forest of the eastern part of the country, lead a primitive way of life and believe in animism. They may be descendents of those aborigines.

The 2000 years that succeeded the arrival of Vijaya witnessed the establishment of a kingdom with its first capital city at Anuradhapura and subsequently, the formation of core areas around Anuradhapura and the present cities of Magampathi, Polonnaruwa, Jaffna, Kandy and Kotte. Tamils from south India (Cholas, Cheras and Pandyas) continuously looked upon Sri Lanka as potential grounds for *lebensraum*, particularly during the 10th through 13th centuries. They not only conquered parts of the northern territory but established a Tamil Kingdom centered on Jaffna, extending control over Anuradhapura and Polonnaruwa. Tamil settlements and language spread not only in the north but in the eastern coastal area as well. The Tamils were Hindus and Dravidians, whereas the Sinhalese were Buddhists and Aryans. The resultant weakening of the central Buddhist powers of Anuradhapura and Polonnaruwa during 1200—1500 A.D. caused the decline of the extensive irrigation system of the north-center (referred to as the hydraulic civilization), on which depended the prosperity of the Dry Zone kingdom. The core of Sinhalese power shifted to the center of the island in gradual stages to Gampola, Kandy and southwest to Kotte. The Hindu Tamil kingdoms of the north further consolidated during this period.

Western colonial contact dates back to 1505-06 when the Portuguese established themselves with a fort in Colombo and were in control of the Kotte Kingdom in 1580; they placed a protege on the throne of Jaffna in 1591. They were interested in the cinnamon trade as Sri Lanka produced this spice in large amounts. This trade was later monopolized by the Portuguese by ousting the Moslems. They also converted a significant number of people to Catholicism in the coastal areas.

The Dutch replaced the Portuguese by 1658, and the coastal areas of Sri Lanka came under Dutch control. The Kingdom of Kandy continued to remain independent during both Portuguese and Dutch presence on the island because its core lay in the hilly, relatively inaccessible, central part of the country where guerilla activity by the natives was most rampant. Actually, neither the Portuguese nor the Dutch had the capability of committing enough manpower in the island to deliver a knockout blow to Kandy. The Dutch control of coastal Sri Lanka lasted until 1801 and during their period of occupation they a) introduced the plantation system to cinnamon production, which was until then collected from wild forests and cultivated by farmers in small holdings, b) popularized the Calvinistic Protestant faith, while persecuting not only the Catholics but also the native religions, and c) codified the customary Hindu (Tamilian) and Moslem laws and introduced Roman/Dutch laws to the Sinhalese population.

The British, who came because of the strategic importance of Trincomalle which belonged to Kandy, assisted the Kandyan empire to get rid of the Dutch. The British not only conquered the Dutch possessions, but turned against Kandy in 1803. The first British ex-

pedition against Kandy failed, but by 1815 the entire Kandyan Empire became British. Their immediate action was to build extensive roads in the Kandyan region for effective control and troop movements. Though Sri Lanka was considered more of a strategic point in the British control of the seas, their rule over a long time unified the island under one political organization with a new administrative system of provinces and districts. Coffee, which was introduced as an effective plantation crop, was later replaced by tea and rubber. Indian Tamil workers were imported to work in the plantations of the south-central part of the country. Efforts were made to restore the old irrigation system. The chief center of activity moved to the Wet Zone centered around Colombo, the capital of British Sri Lanka. A secular, liberal, western system of education was introduced along with the English language. As an effort to a limited self-government, the British introduced universal suffrage in 1931. Such a step, though a novel experience in Asia, coupled with a one-and-a-half century-old British 'divide and rule' policy, encouraged a Buddhist resurgence led by S.W.R.D. Bandaranaike through his *Sinhala Maha Sabha* party. Such religious revivalism of the Buddhist majority divided the nation after the 1948 independence and paved the way for a new Tamil separatist movement in the north.

Independent Sri Lanka. Sri Lanka attained Dominion status within the British Empire in 1948, which meant recognizing the British monarch as head of state. *De facto* sovereignty resided in an elected parliament modelled on a constitution prepared in 1947. In the beginning, the political scene in the country was polarized between the United National Party (UNP), a conservative group, and the leftists. The UNP has remained a potent political force ever since the country's independence. Its charismatic leader, D. S. Senanayake, was elected the first prime minister as a result of the 1947 election in which over 60% of the eligible voters cast their votes.

During the 1950s, two other elements entered the political scene. The first was the formation of an alternative party, the Sri Lankan Freedom Party (SLFP) oriented to the Sinhalese middle class of the rural areas and

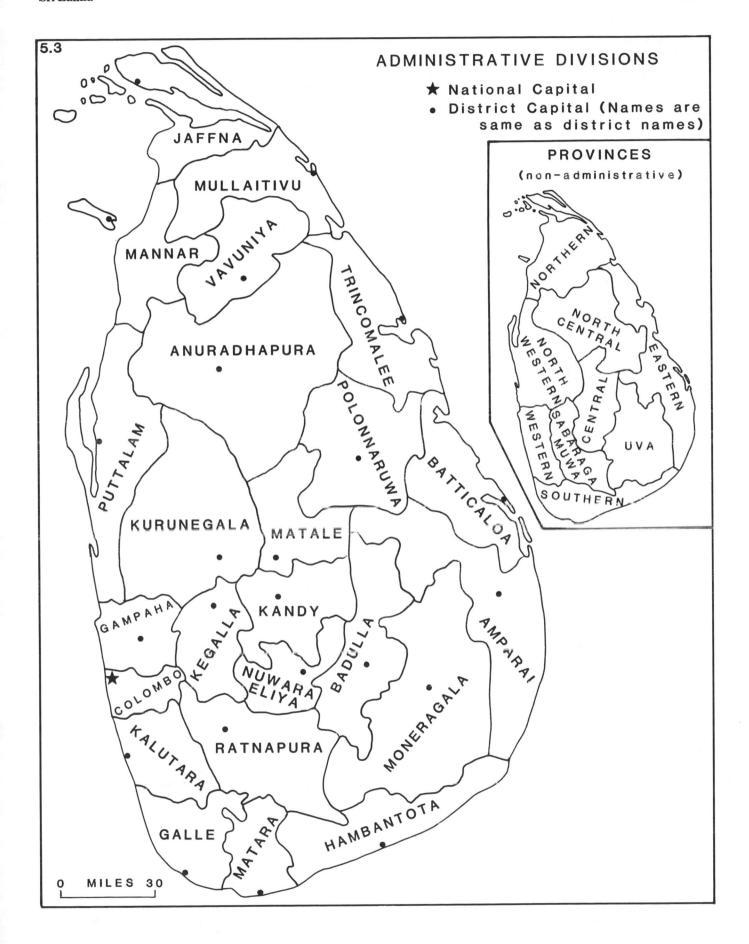

5.3

ADMINISTRATIVE DIVISIONS

★ National Capital
• District Capital (Names are same as district names)

PROVINCES
(non-administrative)

JAFFNA

MULLAITIVU

MANNAR

VAVUNIYA

TRINCOMALEE

ANURADHAPURA

POLONNARUWA

BATTICALOA

PUTTALAM

KURUNEGALA

MATALE

GAMPAHA

KEGALLA

KANDY

BADULLA

AMPARAI

COLOMBO

NUWARA ELIYA

KALUTARA

RATNAPURA

MONERAGALA

GALLE

MATARA

HAMBANTOTA

NORTHERN

NORTH CENTRAL

NORTH WESTERN

EASTERN

CENTRAL

WESTERN

SABARAGAMUWA

UVA

SOUTHERN

0   MILES   30

Buddhist *bhikkhus*. Its leader was S.W.R.D. Bandaranaike and it continues to influence the political arena along with the UNP. The second was the polarization of the Tamils into separate ethnic organizations championing such demands as the declaration of Tamil as a national language in addition to Singhalese, citizenship rights to newly immigrated Indian Tamils and a 50% share for the minorities in the affairs of the government. Until the 1960s, the Tamil cause was partially defended by the UNP. When the SLFP attracted Singhalese ethnic sentiments by turning against the Tamils, the UNP gradually dropped its defense of the Tamil cause to win the support of the Sinhala majority. Then the Tamil groups were gradually polarized and started to work against the system.

Sri Lanka, like India, continues to be democratic with power shifting between two political parties—UNP and SLFP. With the adoption of the 1972 constitution, Sri Lanka became a free sovereign state and the British monarch is no longer considered its head of

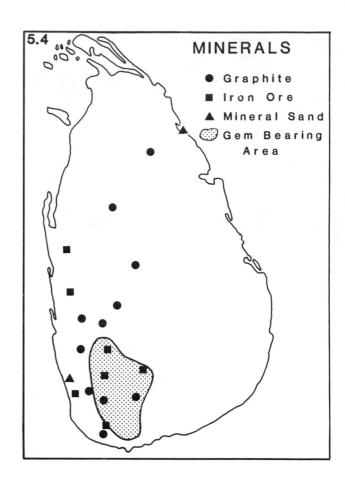

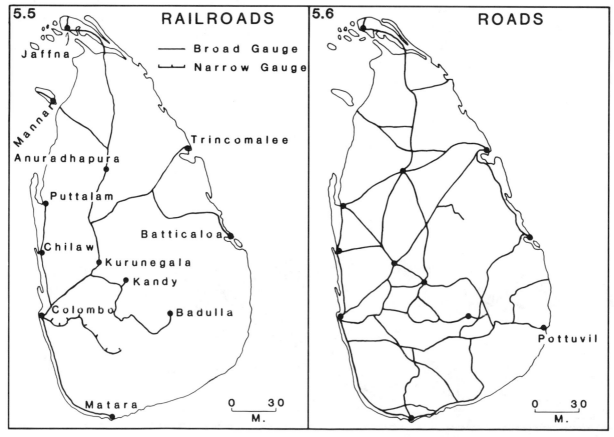

state. The third constitutional change, in 1977, introduced a) a presidential form of government, where the president is directly elected by the people, b) a proportional representation in the parliamentary elections, and c) preservation of 'the status of Sinhalese as the official language while granting constitutional recognition to the Tamil language by making it a National Language along with Sinhalese.' Since 1978, the UNP has held a majority in the parliament and the 1980s are characterized by conflicts between Tamil separatists and those who want to preserve Sri Lanka as one country.

Economy. Sri Lanka is by far the second in South Asia in per capita income. It has a relatively smaller population and therefore, fewer mouths to feed. Nevertheless, it is a food-deficit country and its annual food import constitutes about 15%-20% of total imports. Rice is not only a staple food of the people, but it is cultivated on 56% of the Dry Zone and 44% of the Wet Zone agricultural land. In 1978-79, the country produced about 2 million metric tons of rice, not enough to meet the country's needs.

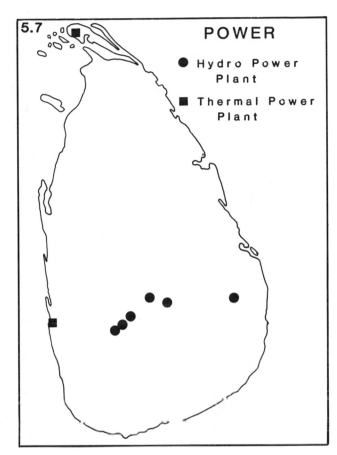

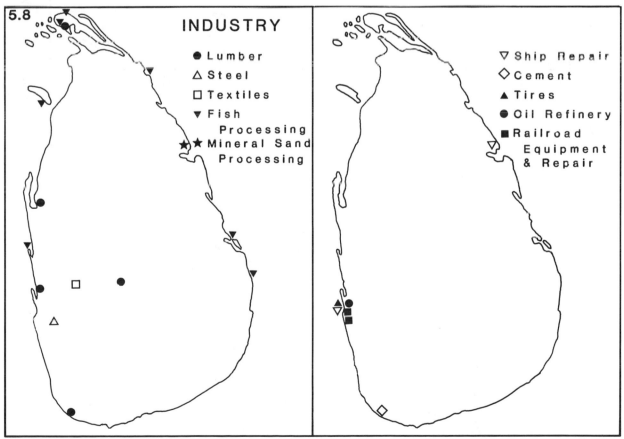

Self-sufficiency in rice had been one of the main goals of Sri Lanka's Five-Year Plans.

Tea, rubber and coconut plantation agriculture constitutes the backbone of the country's prosperity. These products account for about 70% of foreign exchange earnings and 50% of cultivated land of the country. Tea,

the king of the tree crops, grown in the hilly uplands of the south-central part of Sri Lanka, accounts for over two-fifths of the country's exports. Sri Lanka is not only the second largest tea exporter of the world, but its share of total tea trade in the world is 25%. Because of such dependence on tree crops the govern-

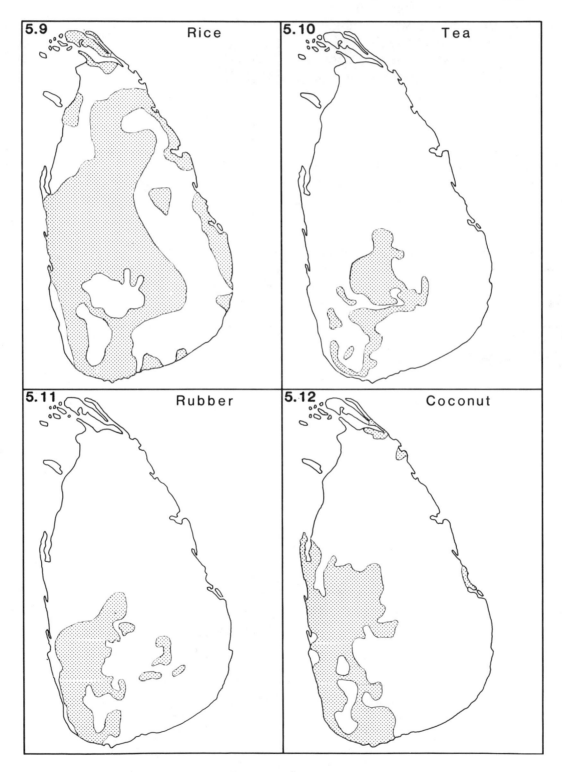

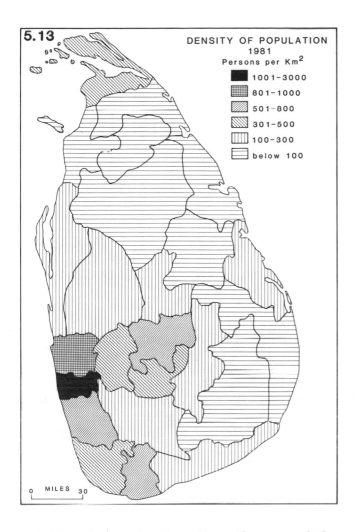

DENSITY OF POPULATION
1981
Persons per Km²

■ 1001-3000
▨ 801-1000
▧ 501-800
▨ 301-500
▥ 100-300
□ below 100

5.13

0 MILES 30

5.14

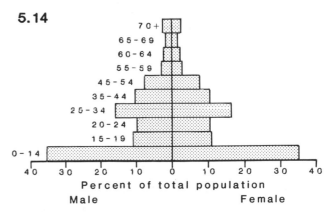

Percent of total population
Male   Female

growth rate of 1.7% per annum (in the 1970s) is the lowest in South Asia with a drop in the birth rate to 28.7 per 1,000 in 1979. It has a diverse ethnic composition: 42.8% Low Country Sinhalese, 29.2% Kandyan Sinhalese, 11.2% Ceylon Tamils, 9.3% Indian Tamils, 6.5% Ceylon Moors (Moslems), 0.2% Indian Moors (Moslems) and 0.8% others. Buddhists comprise 67.3% of the people and are mostly Sinhalese, while 17.6% are Hindus and they are mostly Tamils. The Christians and the Moslems constitute 7.9% and 7.1%, respectively. The essential rivalry, that has developed during the last 30 years, is between the Buddhist Sinhalese who speak Singhalese as their mother tongue and the Hindu Tamils who speak Tamil. The former are of Aryan origin while the latter are Dravidian. Political opportunism for winning the popular vote during elections has also motivated leaders of different parties to instill divisions between the Sinhalese and Tamil, and Buddhist and Hindu. Thus, as time passes, the electoral process, in which the leaders make use of cheap divisionary sentiments, also fosters polarization of ethnic and religious divisions in Sri Lanka.

Prospects. Though self-sufficiency in rice production, stability of plantation agriculture, diversification of the economy and the success of the Mahaweli Project will determine the economic future of the country, the resolution of the Sinhalese-Tamil conflict is essential not only for law and order, but for all effective endeavors directed toward economic development.

ment has been planning diversification of the economy through industrialization and the creation of an export-oriented Free Trade Zone near Colombo. As a result, industrial exports have risen from 16% of the country's total in 1976 to 24% in 1979. The United Kingdom, USA, Japan and the People's Republic of China receive about 30% of Sri Lanka's exports and Japan, India, the United Kingdom and the USA supply about the same percentage of imports.

On the whole, Sri Lanka is striving to develop rapidly, particularly in the production of food. The accelerated program for the completion of the Mahaweli River Valley Project will provide irrigation to 132,000 hectares of new land and 400 MGH of electric power capacity by the end of the 1980s.

Demographic Characteristics. The Sri Lankan population has grown from 2.4 million in 1871 to 14.8 million in 1981. The annual

6. NEPAL

Nepal is a mountain kingdom bordered by Tibet to the north and the Indian states of Sikkim to the east, and Uttar Pradesh and Bihar to the west and south. Lying between the two great countries of communist China and democratic India, Nepal tries to maintain a balance between the two in respect to its foreign policy. Such a strategic position raises Nepal's geopolitical importance. Until the early 1950s, it maintained a self-imposed isolation. In the last three decades the country has opened its doors to the outside world, but its development still remains at a miserably low level.

Physiography. Nepal is basically a mountainous region as more than 75% of its area is covered by hills and mountains. The country extends from west to east with its topography being in linear strips more or less corresponding to the lines of latitude. These strips can be divided into four main physical divisions.

1. The Terai in the south
2. The Churia Hills (Siwaliks) and Inner Terai Zone
3. The mid-mountain region
4. The Great Himalayas in the north

Along with these, the Kathmandu Valley, with the capital Kathmandu, and the Pokhara Valley are very significant features.

The Terai. It is a low-lying, fertile, alluvial plain which, on an average, is 18 miles wide totaling about 9000 square miles, and 200 meters (656 feet) above sea level. It is adjacent to the border of India, and is an extension of

---

Nepal at a Glance

Name: Kingdom of Nepal

Borders with: India, China

Area: 54,362 mi^2 (140,797 km^2)

Population: 16,169,000 (1983 est.)

Capital: Kathmandu

Other Cities: Pathan, Bhadgaon, Kiotipur

Monetary Unit: Rupee (March 1984: 15.75 = 1 U.S. $)

Chief Products: Agriculture - Rice, Grains, Jute

Others - Hides, Drugs, Quartz

Per Capita G.N.P.: U.S. $170 (1982)

Religion: Hinduism, Buddhism

Language: Nepali (official)

Roads: (1979) 4,700 km (2,921 mi)

ADMINISTRATIVE DIVISIONS

EASTERN REGION

A. MECHI
1. Taplejung
2. Panchthar
3. Ilam
4. Jhapa

B. KOSHI
5. Sankhuwasabwa
6. Bhojpur
7. Dhankuta
8. Terhathum
9. Morang
10. Sunsari

C. SAGARMATHA
11. Solukhumbu
12. Okhaldhunga
13. Khotang
14. Udayapur
15. Saptari
16. Siraha

CENTRAL REGION

D. JANAKPUR
17. Dolakha
18. Ramechhap
19. Sindhuli
20. Dhanusa
21. Mahottari
22. Sarlahi

E. BAGMATI
23. Sindhu Palchok
24. Rasuwa
25. Dhading
26. Nuwakot
27. Kathmandu
28. Bhaktapur
29. Kabhre
30. Lalitpur

F. NARAYANA
31. Makawanpur
32. Rautahat
33. Bara
34. Parsa
35. Chitawan

WESTERN REGION

G. GANDAKI
36. Gorkha
37. Manang
38. Kaski
39. Lamjung
40. Tanahun
41. Syangja

H. LUMBINI
42. Gulmi
43. Arghakhanchi
44. Palpa
45. Nawalparasi
46. Rupandehi
47. Kapilbastu

I. DHAWALAGIRI
48. Mustang
49. Myagdi
50. Parbat
51. Baglung

MID WESTERN REGION

J. KARNALI
52. Dolpa
53. Mugu
54. Humla
55. Kalikot
56. Jumla

K. RAPTI
57. Rukum
58. Salyan
59. Rolpa
60. Pyuthan
61. Dangdeukhuri

L. BHERI
62. Jajarkot
63. Dailekh
64. Surkhet
65. Banke
66. Bardiya

FAR WESTERN REGION

M. SETI
67. Bajura
68. Bajhang
69. Achham
70. Doti
71. Kailali

N. MAHAKALI
72. Darchula
73. Baitadi
74. Dadeldhura
75. Kanchanpur

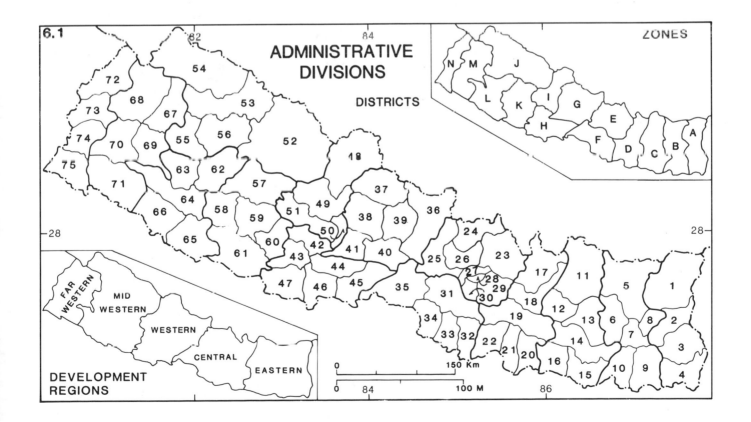

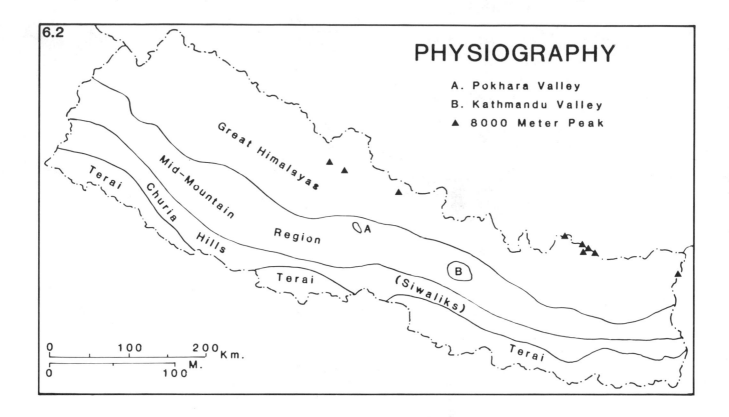

PHYSIOGRAPHY

A. Pokhara Valley
B. Kathmandu Valley
▲ 8000 Meter Peak

India's Gangetic Plain. The southern Terai is a rich agricultural belt where rice, sugarcane and wheat are cultivated. This belt merges to the north into gently rising forested land. These forests are slowly being cleared for agricultural use. The northern part of the Terai is covered with marshes and jungles. In spite of its unhealthy climatic conditions and the endemicity of malaria, it is densely populated and intensively cultivated. In 1981, although Nepal had an over all population density of 102 persons per km^2, the Terai had about 180. It has been estimated that between 1971–85, the Terai's percentile share of national population has risen to 40% from 38%.

The Churia Hills and Inner Terai. Beyond the Terai are the foothills of the Himalayas. These hills attain altitudes of 4000 feet and are heavily forested with a humid subtropical climate. Agriculture is unimportant in this region.

The Mid-Mountain Region. Lying between the Churia Hills and the Great Himalayas, this region presents a complex mountain system 50 miles wide, which ranges up to 14,000 feet. The Kathmandu and Pokhara Valleys, enclosed by mountains, lie here. This region is heavily cultivated in the eastern two-thirds of the country; terracing is widely practiced.

The Great Himalayas. The main Himalayan Range extends along the northern part of Nepal. Nine of the 14 mountain peaks of over 8000 meters (26,246 ft.) lie within or on the country's borders. In the cluster of Everest, Lhotse, Makalu and Lhotse Shar, are four of the six highest mountains in the world. This mountainous area is uninhabited except for scattered settlements.

Political and Administrative System. In its political history, Nepal has experienced a variety of governmental forms and had, in the past, expanded its territory deep into present day India and Tibet. Until the 18th century, Nepal was divided into numerous feuding principalities. In 1769, Nepal was united when the Gurkhas seized power, but by 1846, the Ranas came into ascendency. They continue to be the country's ruling dynasty. By 1814, the Gurkhas had expanded Nepalese territory westwards into Punjab and southwards into present-day Bihar and Uttar Pradesh.

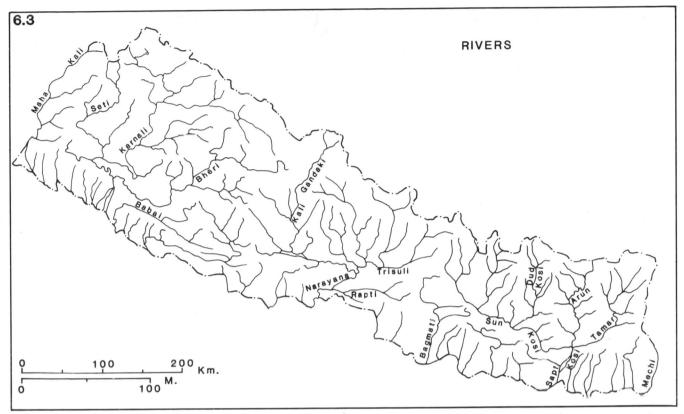

6.3

RIVERS

0   100   200 Km.

0   100 M.

However, defeat at the hands of the British (1814–16) restricted their domain almost to the present boundaries. After India's independence in 1947 and the establishment of a democratic system there, the Nepalese people led by the Congress Party forced the Rana King to adopt a democratically elected parliamentary government, which was fully controlled by a civilian prime minister. Such a democratic system lasted eleven years (1950–60). On December 15, 1960, the King dismissed the elected government and turned the country into an absolute monarchy. The newborn democracy did not survive because of a lack of tradition, selfish intrigues carried out by the ruling politicians and the ingrained myth of the god-king image among the people.

The King rules through a council of ministers and a four-tier system of Panchayats (councils). There is the National Panchayat at the top. Fourteen Zones (Anchal) and 75 development districts, for administrative purposes, largely based on major watersheds and river basins form the second and third tiers. At the bottom are about 4000 village Panchayats.

Agriculture. More than 90% of the population is engaged in agriculture. The material prosperity of Nepal is bound to its agricultural activity. The density of population on the cultivated land is very high and the result is that the average size of holdings is small and insufficient to provide the basic means of livelihood.

Agriculture in Nepal is characterized by a large labor force, primitive conditions of production, an irrational distribution of land and insecurity of tenure. Subsistence farming is most widely practiced, but farms are occasionally threatened by adverse weather conditions. The other types of farming practices are i) nomadic pastoral subsistence farming, ii) pastoral subsistence farming based on villages, iii) rain-fed subsistence farming requiring regular seasonal work, and iv) subsistence farming with irrigation facilties from small mud dams and channels, a common feature of the hills.

The principal crops grown are: rice, corn, millet, wheat, oil seeds, sugarcane, tobacco, jute, fruits and vegetables. Rice, the principal crop of the country, is grown in the Terai region, which is not only a surplus producer, but provides a sizeable export, especially to Bangladesh. In the lower hilly regions, the principal crop is corn; millets are grown at higher altitudes.

Shifting cultivation exists in the hills even today but to a lesser degree than it did in the past. Excessive shifting cultivation in the past and the over-use of forest wood as fuel has resulted in extensive deforestation, which is affecting agricultural development adversely. The denudation of the hills and mountains is leading to some of the most severe erosion anywhere on earth. Whole mountain sides are slumping, the thin soil, no longer held in place, is washing away in the streams. Major flooding is now an annual occurrence, not only in the valleys and Terai of Nepal, but also in the areas of India into which all of Nepal's rivers flow.

Industry. Industrial production in Nepal constitutes a small segment of its economy; less than 10% of the GDP, and half of this is from cottage industries of the informal sector. Most of the industries process agricultural products and are localized in the areas where the raw materials are available. The small-scale cottage industries include cotton and woolen textiles, pottery, bamboo and cane products, leather and wood work, etc., produced mainly for local consumption. With the help of foreign aid, many handicraft industrial centers have been developed. The majority of the people are too poor to buy any factory products, thus the manufactured goods do not have a sufficient local market. The only way the industrial sector can be expanded is by improving agricultural productivity and generating more purchasing power among the people.

In 1971, Nepal was identified as one of the least-developed countries of the world by the United Nations on the basis of a number of economic and social indicators. The economy of Nepal is characterized by extreme poverty as a result of which there exists a large-scale dependence upon its neighbors.

Urbanization. The urbanization process in Nepal is very slow, as there has been a stagnation in the economy since the country depends largely on other nations and external trade for the supply of development materials.

The classification of an urban center in Nepal is based on the functions of that center, mostly relating to trade, education and administration. Most of the towns are basically small market towns with few modern amenities and show a tendency of growth around nodal points of traditional trade routes.

Because of the lack of heavy pressure due to migration, the urban centers in Nepal are

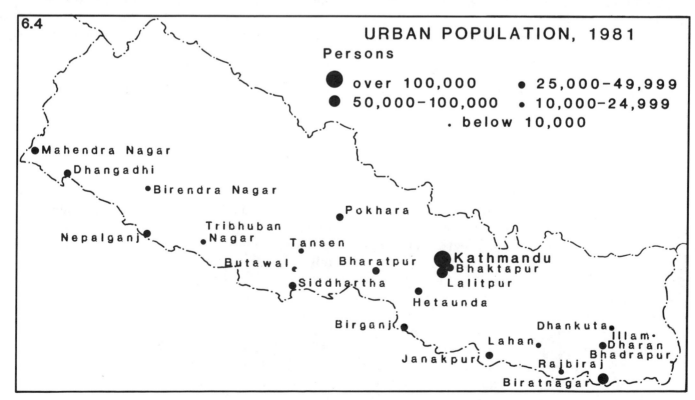

6.4

URBAN POPULATION, 1981

Persons

⬤ over 100,000   • 25,000-49,999
● 50,000-100,000   · 10,000-24,999
                . below 10,000

Mahendra Nagar
Dhangadhi
Birendra Nagar
Pokhara
Nepalganj   Tribhuban Nagar   Tansen
Butawal   Bharatpur   Kathmandu
Siddhartha   Bhaktapur
Hetaunda   Lalitpur
Birganj   Dhankuta
Lahan   Illam
Janakpur   Dharan
Rajbiraj   Bhadrapur
Biratnagar

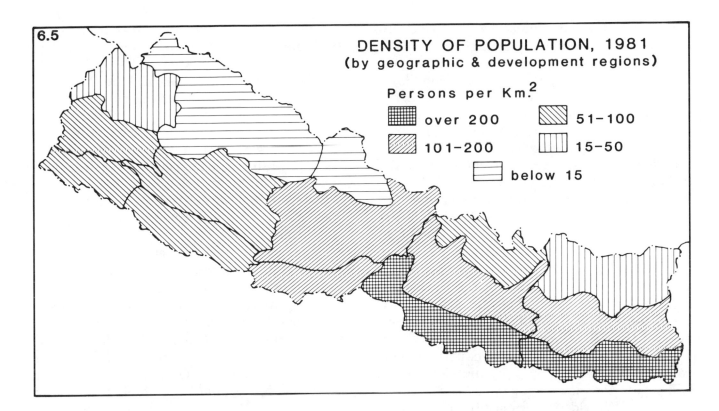

6.5
DENSITY OF POPULATION, 1981
(by geographic & development regions)

Persons per Km.^{2}

▦ over 200   ⧅ 51-100

▨ 101-200   ⊞ 15-50

▭ below 15

somewhat better than other Asian cities. Squatter settlements are almost absent and there is no shortage of housing. This may be because of the slow growth of the towns, which are inhabited basically by the old residents with few incoming migrants.

One development probelm Nepal faces is inter-regional disparity. Apart from the "Kathmandu Valley," a small area but economically the most prosperous region and socially prestigious, the country is still very backward. The per capita income is the highest in the Valley which also has a higher literacy rate, better communications as well as sanitation facilities. The existence of a political capital in Kathmandu for centuries and productive agricultural lands around it in the Valley has turned it into an attractive region.

Culture. Culturally Nepal sits between the influence generated from Tibet to the north and India to the south. Although the founder of the Buddhist religion, Guatama Buddha, was born in the Terai region adjacent to India, in Lumbini, Buddhism disappeared from the country almost 1000 to 1200 years ago, only to return to the northern fringe through Tibetan influence. The region south of the Great

Himalayas reverted back to Hinduism.

The people of Mongoloid origins came to Nepal from the north as well as from Sikkim and thus, the northern and eastern areas of the country are largely inhabited by this race. The Indo-Aryans moved from the south and as a result the Terai peoples are generally Caucasoid. In the mid-mountain region the Mongoloids and Caucasoids are intermingled.

Because of Hindu influence, the caste-system remains entrenched in Nepal even today. Different tribes also continued their distinct existence. Such tribal and caste seperatism has caused continued prevalence of individual ethnic groups, such as the Newars of the Kathmandu Valley, the Gurungs of the western hill areas and the Bhotias or mountain-climbing Sherpas of the north.

Nepal has also been influenced by two different families of languages: Tibeto-Burman and Indo-Aryan. The Nepali language is a subgroup of the Indo-Aryan (Sanskrit) language and is the official language of the state. Maithili, Bhojpuri and Kukaoni, dialects of Hindi, are spoken in the Terai region as extensions of languages whose core areas lie in the Indian states of Bihar and Uttar Pradesh.

The Tibeto-Burman languages of Nepal are Newari, Margarkura and Gurungkura.

Prospects and Potentialities. Nepal's problems lie in her economic stagnation, high population growth rate, lack of internal resource development, ecological imbalance due to deforestation and inability to increase internal market potentialities.

Nepal's economic stagnation can be recognized from the fact that during the 1960s and 1970s the annual growth rate in real terms had remained at around the 2.5% level and the share of agriculture to the GDP about 65%. Although the most recent, the Sixth, Five-Year Plan (1980–85) aimed at raising the growth rate to 4%, the performance of the Fifth Plan (1975–80), which also proposed a growth rate rise of 4–5%, was unsatisfactory. The primary cause of the Fifth Plan's shortfall was the actual decline in agricultural production; food grain production fell by 1% annually during the five-year span.

A 1979 World Bank study designates Nepal's demographic situation "among the worst in the world and is deteriorating steadily." The study also confirms that it has an estimated growth rate of 2.6% annually and its population density with respect to

cultivable land far exceeds that of Bangladesh, India and Pakistan. In 1978, Nepal's density of population was estimated at 331 persons for one square kilometer of arable land. Moreover, the World Bank also estimated that if the population of the country (14.5 million in 1980) grows without any change in the fertility rate, by 2030 it would reach 72.5 million as life expectancy at birth, is expected to rise from 45 in 1980 to 63 in 2030.

In terms of internal resources, the country does not have much to offer other than its agriculture. The Terai region has been a surplus rice producer, meeting the deficits of the hill and mountain production, with some for export. However, static productivity, resulting from the lack of use of hybrid seeds, fertilizers and irrigation, has constrained agricultural development. This has further been accentuated by increased flooding and soil erosion caused by increasing deforestation.

Wood, used primarily for fuel, accounts for about 90% of Nepal's energy use. Fuel wood is an economic necessity as the rural people do not have the means to buy an alternative fuel at the market place. The fuel wood is obtained free from the nearby forests and 95% of rural areas depend on this source. An average Nepali

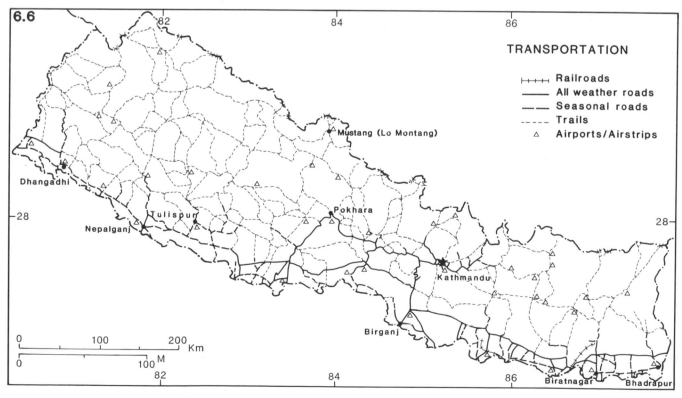

family spends about 11 man days a month on fuel wood collection. At the present rate of forest destruction, it is estimated that all accessible forests in the hills and Terai will disappear by 1990 and 2000, respectively.

Nepal represents one of the most underdeveloped nations in the world. In comparative development studies, it is still referred to as technologically primitive. The Nepalese government officials and planners, however, are aware of this underdevelopment and they have devised strategies to remedy the situation with the help of consecutive Five-Year Plans that started in 1956. The major emphasis of the first four plans (1956–75) was on road construction, both for political unity of the country and accessibility to otherwise isolated population pockets. Such capital-intensive investments did not bring about improvements in the income levels of the people in general.

The Fifth Plan (1975–80) tried to reorient the strategy "towards smaller, quicker-yielding investments and to social services." Such reoriented strategy continued with the Sixth Plan (1980–85). The total percentile share of planned investments in agriculture and irrigation, rose from 23% in the Fourth Plan, to 27% in the Fifth Plan and 29% in the Sixth Plan; similarly the share of industries and power rose from 15% to 17% and 22%, respectively. The transport and communications investments dropped from 43% in the Fourth to 29% in the Fifth and 21% in the Sixth Plan. One still has to assess the results of such a reoriented strategy along with efforts to control population growth, balance the ecology, meet the fuel needs more meaningfully and improve agricultural output. The 1980s are the most crucial for Nepal, for during this time, the country will either embark on a progressive path of development or get more deeply entrenched in the quagmire of underdevelopment and dependence on foreign doles.

7. BHUTAN

Bhutan like Nepal, is a land-locked Himalayan kingdom and is located in the mountains between the China-ruled Tibetan Plateau and the Indian states of Sikkim, West Bengal and Assam, and the union territory of Arunachal Pradesh. Physically it may be divided into three regions; the Great Himalayas, the Lesser or Middle Himalayas, and the Duars Plains.

The northern part of Bhutan lying within the Great Himalayas, has snow-capped peaks over the height of 7,315 m (24,000 ft). The valleys are at heights of 3,657 m - 5,486 m (12,000 ft to 18,000 ft). The land is arid and the climate is dry. A large part of this region remains snow-covered during the entire year.

The Lesser or the Middle Himalayas are in central Bhutan. Valleys range from 1,524 m to 2,743 m (5,000 ft - 9,000 ft). During the summer, this area falls within the southwest monsoon regime and the rain brought by these monsoon winds produces various types of vegetation, from dense forests on the rain swept slopes to alpine vegetation at higher elevations. The valleys are relatively broad and flat and highly productive agriculturally. They receive moderate rainfall, approximately 1,016 mm - 1,250 mm (40 in - 50 in) or less a year. This region possesses valuable timber resources for the country.

Southern Bhutan lies within the subtropical narrow strip of the Duars Plains. This area is 13 km - 16 km (8 mi - 10 mi) wide and experiences excessive rainfall, between 5,080 mm - 7,620 mm (200 in - 300 in) annually. Covered with a dense subtropical forest, the Duars tract is unhealthy, hot and steamy. It also has timber resources.

Bhutan's population is composed of three defined ethnic groups, the Bhote (Ngalops) of north and central Bhutan, Indo-Mongoloids (Sharchops) of eastern Bhutan and the

Bhutan at a Glance

Name: Kingdom of Bhutan

Borders with: India, China

Area: 17,800 mi^2 (45,569 km^2)

Population: 1,386,000 (1983 est.)

Capital: Thimpu

Monetary Unit: Ngultrum (October 1983:10.21 = 1 U.S. $)

Chief Products: Rice, Corn, Wheat, Timber, Handicrafts

Per Capita G.N.P.: U.S. $190 (1978)

Religion: Buddhism, Hinduism

Languages: Dzongkha (official), Nepali

Railroads: None

Roads: (1982) 2,050 km (1,281.21 mi)

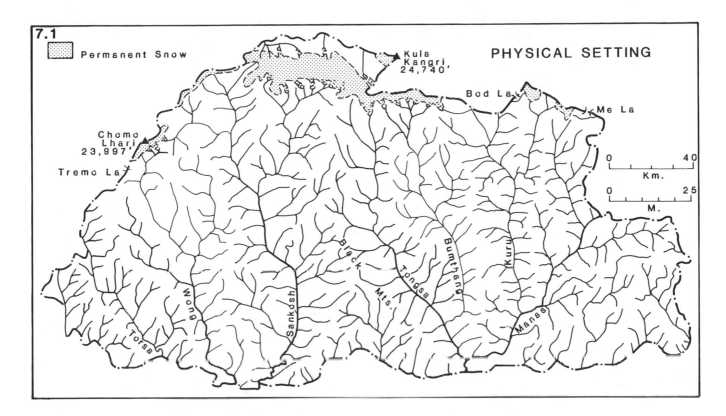

7.1
Permanent Snow

PHYSICAL SETTING

Kula Kangri, 24,740'

Bod La

Me La

Chomo Lhari 23,997'

Tremo La

0   40
Km.
0   25
M.

Torsa

Wong

Sankosh

Black Mts.

Tongsa

Bumthang

Kuru

Manas

Nepalese of southwestern Bhutan. The Bhote, who's origins are Tibetan, arrived in the country from the 8th century through the present century and represent 60% of the total population. They speak Dzongkha, a Tibetan dialect written in classical Ucaen Tibetan script. Their religion is Lamaistic Buddhism. Their traditions are rooted deeply in Tibetan culture. The Sharchops, the earliest settlers of the country, are related to the people of northeast India and Burma and represent 15% of the population. The Nepalese make-up 25% of the population. Originally from Nepal, their language is Nepali and their religion is Hinduism. They arrived in the 19th and 20th centuries to work the foothills of southern Bhutan. Ethnic conflicts between the Bhote and the Nepalese remain a major political problem for Bhutan because, until recently, the Nepalese minority was not so much discriminated against as ignored. Steps are being taken by the government to bring the Nepalese more and more into the national picture, politically and economically. The state religion is Drukpa, a subsect of Kagyupa of Lamaist Mahayana Buddhism. Dzongkha is the official language, although Nepali predominates in the southern region and eleven

vernacular languages prevail in the east. In spite of such linguistic diversity, Dzongkha is taught in all schools, while English is taught in the secular schools. Nepali is taught in the schools of southern Bhutan. Education is available to all. It was slow in coming about, until schools were built and teachers trained, but these major hurdles have been cleared.

Bhutan's historical origin dates back to about the 8th century when Buddhism was brought from Tibet with the introduction of the Niyingmapa sect, who eventually migrated farther south in the major river valleys establishing fortress-like dzongs, the focal points of settlements. The dzongs, or large fortified monasteries, still dominate the river valleys. Two other Tibetan sects (Drukpas and Lpapas) entered Bhutan in the 12th century and eventually it was the Drukpa which dominated both the cultural and political aspects of the country. It became a distinct political entity starting from 1616, when a Tibetan Drukpa lama, Ngawang Namgyal united many Drukpa families and established a firm rule over most of western and eastern Bhutan. At that time the Dharma Raja (king) had both spiritual and secular powers. The suc-

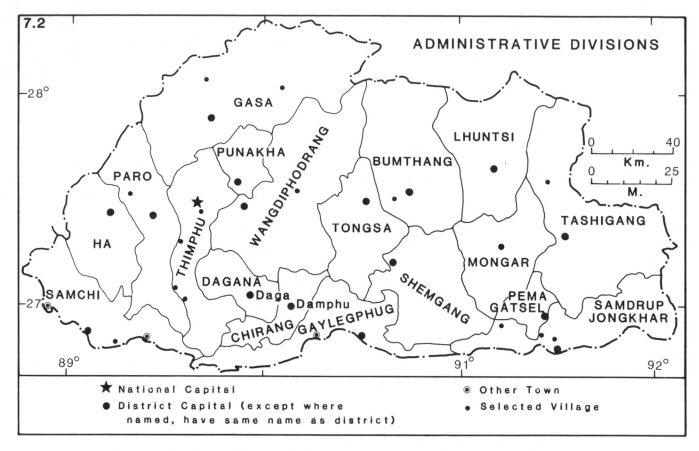

7.2

ADMINISTRATIVE DIVISIONS

—28°

GASA

LHUNTSI

PUNAKHA

BUMTHANG

PARO

0   40
Km.
0   25
M.

THIMPHU

WANGDIPHODRANG

HA

TONGSA

TASHIGANG

DAGANA

MONGAR

SAMCHI

Daga
Damphu

SHEMGANG

PEMA
GATSEL

SAMDRUP
JONGKHAR

—27°

CHIRANG GAYLEGPHUG

89°   91°   92°

★ National Capital   ⊚ Other Town
● District Capital (except where   • Selected Village
   named, have same name as district)

cessor to this king limited the Dharma Raja's role in spiritual matters. An appointed Deb Raja (minister) was given temporal powers and the Dharma Raja remained the spiritual leader.

Bhutan's governmental structure was established with the appointment of *penlops* (provincial governors) and *jungpens* (governors of forts). By the 19th century, the penlops had more power than the Deb Raja. A series of civil wars occurred during this century. In 1885, the Deb Raja requested and received help from the Chinese to defeat the penlops. British presence was encouraged in 1906, by Ugyen Wangchuk, Penlop of the Tongsa district, to neutralize the Chinese threat. In 1907, Ugyen Wangchuk, Penlop of Tongsa, was elected by the other penlops to become Bhutan's first hereditary king. In 1910, the Treaty of Punakha was signed by King Ugyen and the British which granted Bhutan full internal autonomy, but provided that foreign affairs be advised by British India. In 1949, Bhutan signed an Indo-Bhutan Treaty with independent India reinforcing the 1910 treaty and instead of the British, the Indians guide the government of Bhutan in

its external relations.

The king of Bhutan, Jigme Singhye Wanchuk, the great-grandson of Ugyen Wanchuk, rules with the assistance of the *Tsongdu* (National Assembly), composed of 150 members. The Assembly, originally a consultative body, was empowered with final decision-making authority since the constitutional change in 1968. This change in the constitution was, in fact, forced on the Assembly. Later, the Assembly requested that the king take back his former powers. These men felt they were not yet able to rule. The king is, however, highly revered and his decisions are not challenged by the Assembly. He is also determined that before long the Assembly will once again be the ruling authority in the country. The king appoints 40 of the members and the rest are elected. No political parties function within the Bhutanese government structure, however, there is one political party called the Bhutan State Congress. The party's leadership is entirely Nepalese, and its headquarters are in India.

Bhutan's economy is based on its agriculture

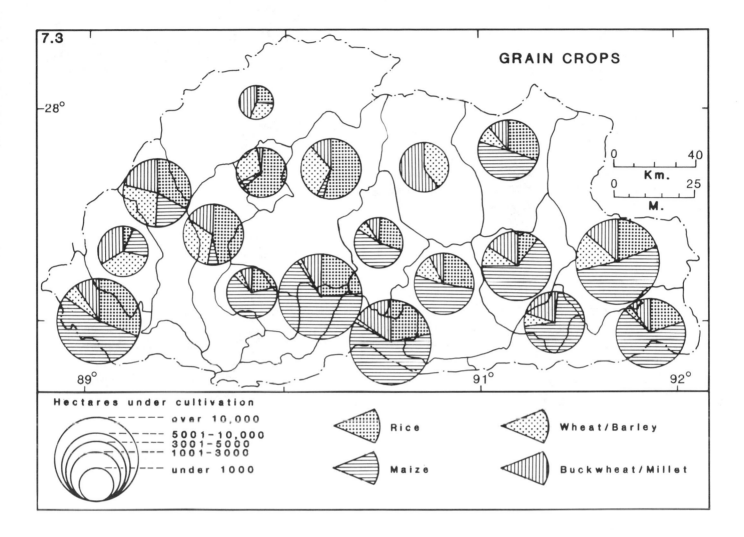

7.3

GRAIN CROPS

-28°

89°   91°   92°

Hectares under cultivation

- over 10,000
- 5001-10,000
- 3001-5000
- 1001-3000
- under 1000

Rice   Wheat/Barley

Maize   Buckwheat/Millet

0   40
Km.
0   25
M.

7.4   LAND USE

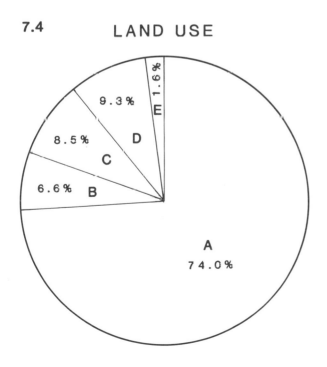

A. Forest
B. Alpine Pasture, Shrub, Clearings
C. Cultivated, Orchards
D. Barren Land, Rocks
E. Permanent Snow, Lakes

The above diagram shows the findings of an aerial survey conducted in 1974-79, which covered 63% of the 46,500 km.^{2} of Bhutan. Not covered were the largely uninhabited northern and northwestern areas of permanent snow and barren land.

resources. Over 47% of the country's GDP (1981) comes from agriculture and animal husbandry. Most cultivated land lies in the low, moist and fertile valleys of central Bhutan. One recent survey puts the average size of a family holding at 3.95 acres. Because of altitude and climatic variations over the topography, a variety of crops are grown including maize, rice, wheat, potatoes, barley, and millet. In 1982, maize accounted for 50% of the country's total cropped area in food grains, rice 25%, and buckwheat/millets, 14%. Orchards have recently been established by the government to increase and diversify agriculture productivity. Though efforts are made to abolish *tsheri* (shifting) cultivation, it is still prevalent especially in the east. Bhutan's Department of Agriculture has calculated that *tsheri* land has the lowest cropping intensity value compared to Wet Land and Dry Land, because 79% of the year it remains fallow compared to 0% for Wet Land and 11% for Dry Land. Rice is the main crop of Wet Land, and maize for both Dry and *tsheri* Lands.

Many of Bhutan's small farms raise yaks, cattle, sheep, and pigs. There are two large sheep breeding farms. Silk worm farms provide raw silk for the weaving industry. There is also a modern fish hatchery which stocks the rivers and lakes with brown trout.

POPULATION BY AGE AND SEX, 1982

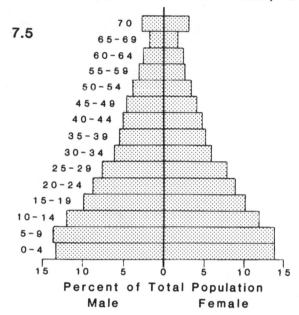

7.5

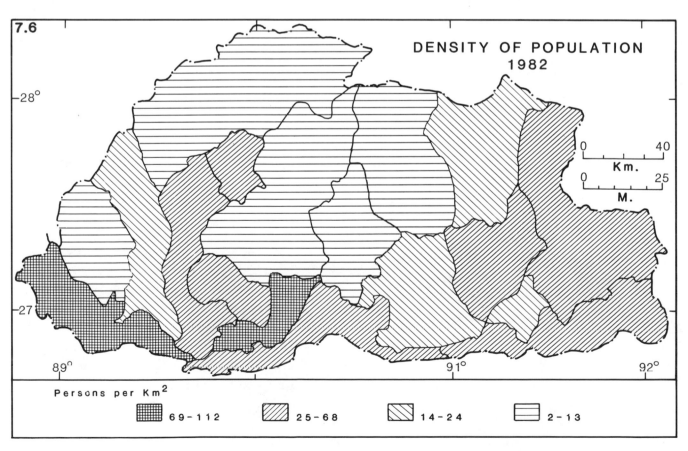

Bhutan's forests cover 70% of the land and contribute 16% of the GDP (1981). As a step towards conservation and regulation of forest exploitation, the Bhutan government, beginning in 1979, has severely restricted the commercial felling of trees and nationalized the activity. The king had seen the effects of uncontrolled deforestation in other developing nations, especially Nepal, and took these steps to prevent such problems from developing in Bhutan. As a result, the logging volume fell from 143,000 cu m in 1976-77 to 28,000 cu m in 1980-81. The forest is a resource for government and private sawmills, furniture manufacturing, and paper. Logs are also exported to India. Located in southern Bhutan is a 62 square mile wildlife sanctuary that has many valuable and rare species of animals.

Handcrafts include weaving of cloth, mats, and baskets; papermaking, and handwork in wood, leather, and metal. Silver, copper, and iron have long been mined for craftsmen. As the manufacturing industry accounts for only

3.3% (1981) of the GDP it is not important for the country's economy.

Bhutan has had Five-Year Plans since 1961. In the First Plan (1961-66), the highest priority was given to transportation in order to integrate the country. The city of Thimpu witnessed the first automobile on its roads in 1962 as a result of the newly constructed, all weather, Indo-Bhutan highway. Sixty-six percent of this Plan outlay was given towards transportation. Since then the overriding emphasis on transport declined within the Plans as only 41% of the outlay in the Second Plan (1966-71), 20% in the Third Plan (1971-76), 12% in the Fourth Plan (1976-81), and about 15% in the Fifth Plan (1981-87) were allocated for transport. The major east-west highway was (after the First Plan) budgeted separately from the Plans. The importance of agriculture has increased considerably with 14.3% of the Fifth-Plan outlay including animal husbandry. The significance of power and industry has also been augmented as 16.5% and 17.4% of the

7.7 DEVELOPMENT PLANNING

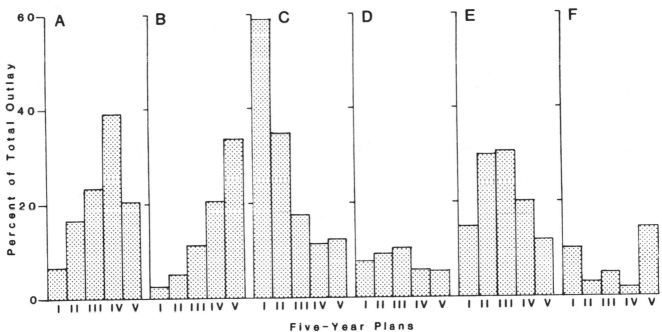

A. Agriculture, Animal Husbandry, Forestry
B. Power & Industry
C. Public Works (in 1st Plan, included transport)
D. Transport, Tourism, Communications
E. Social Services
F. Other

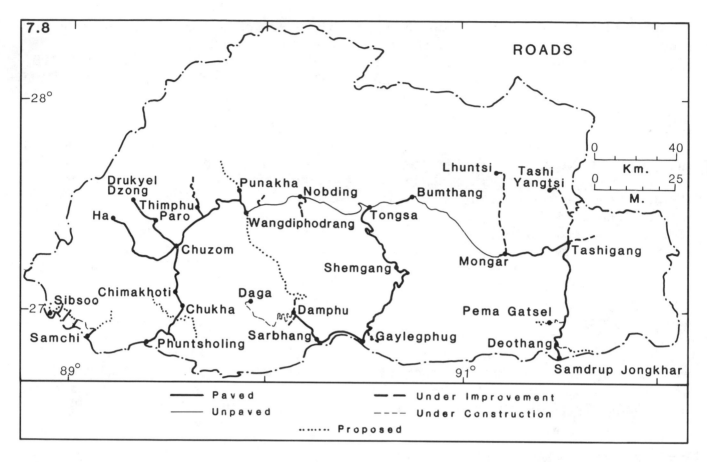

7.8

ROADS

Legend:
- ——— Paved
- ——— Unpaved
- ········ Proposed
- – – – Under Improvement
- - - - - Under Construction

Fifth-Plan outlay are earmarked for them, respectively.

The position of Bhutan is, in many ways, remarkable. The country has moved from absolute isolation in the 1950s to membership in the United Nations and other international bodies by the 1980s. The people, as a whole, have a certain confidence about themselves due in part to centuries of trading with other people—isolation was a one-way street. Another factor is that of all the South Asian countries, Bhutan alone has no real population pressure. With a population of only slightly over one million in 1981, there is little pressure on the land or its resources. There is still new land available for agriculture, although it is limited and the nation has a food surplus. If the population can be held in check and advancement into the 20th century taken slowly, as the government's plan has been, Bhutan could be the one bright light in third-world development. The nation still has a long way to go in its quest for progress but the start has been well made and directed.

Bibliography

Akhtar, Rais. "Geographical Distribution of Cancer in India with Special Reference to Stomach Cancer." *International Journal of Environmental Studies* 20 (1983):291-298.

Akhtar, Rais and Learmonth, A. T. A. ed. *Geographical Aspects of Health and Disease in India*. New Delhi: Concept Publishing Company, 1985

—"Malaria Returns to India," *Geographical Magazine* 54 (1982):135-139.

Aris, Michael. *Bhutan: The Early History of a Himalayan Kingdom*. Warminster, England: Aris & Phillips Ltd., 1979.

Bangladesh Bureau of Statistics *1982 Statistical Yearbook of Bangladesh*. Dhaka: Government of the People's Republic of Bangladesh, 1983.

Basham, A.L. *The Wonder That Was India*. New York: Grove Press, Inc., 1959.

Bhardwaj, S.M. *Hindu Places of Pilgrimage in India: A Study in Cultural Geography*. Berkeley: University of California Press, 1973.

Bose, Ashish, ed. *Pattern of Population Change in India*, 1951-1961. Bombay: Allied Publishers Private, Ltd., 1967.

—"Six Decades of Urbanization in India." *Indian Economic and Social History Review* 2 (January 1967):23-41.

—*Studies In India's Urbanization 1901-1971*. Bombay: Tata-McGraw Hill Publishing Co., 1973.

Breese, Gerald. *Urban and Regional Planning for the Delhi—New Delhi Area*. Princeton, New Jersey: Princeton University Press, 1974.

Brush, John E. "Spatial Patterns of Population in Indian Cities." *Geographical Review* 58 (July 1968):362-391.

Bussagli, M., and Sivaramamurti, C. *5000 Years of the Art of India*. New York: Harry N. Abrams, Inc. n.d.

Calcutta Metropolitan Planning Organization. *Basic Development Plan Calcutta Metropolitan District 1966-1986*. Calcutta: Government of West Bengal, 1966.

Census Commission, Ministry of Home Affairs. *Bangladesh: Census of Population-1974*, Bulletin-2, Publication No. 26. Dacca: Bangladesh Government Press, 1975.

Census Commission, Government of India, Registrar General. *India 1961, Vol. I, India Part IX Census Atlas*. New Delhi, 1970.

—Registrar General. *India 1971, Provisional Population Totals*. New Delhi, 1972.

—Registrar General. *India 1971, Language Handbook on Mother Tongues in Census*. New Delhi, 1972.

—*1971, Religion*, Series 1—India, Paper 2 of 1972. New Delhi: Registrar General of India.

—*1981, Provisional Population Totals and Rural/Urban Totals*. New Delhi: Registrar General of Census.

Chakravarti, A.K. "India's Agriculture." *Focus* 23 (January 1973).

—"India's Land Reform." *Focus* 23 (May 1973)

—"Green Revolution in India." *Annals of Association of American Geographers* 63 (1973):319-330.

—"The Impact of the High-Yielding Varieties Program on Foodgrain Production in India." *The Canadian Geographer* 20 (1976):199-223.

—"Cattle Development Problems and Programs in India: A Regional Analysis." *Geo Journal* 10.1 (1985):21-45.

Chatterji, S.K., and Katre, S.M. "Languages." In *The Gazetteer of India*, vol. 1. New Delhi: Publications Division, Government of India, 1973.

Chatterjee, S.P. "Aspects of the Study of Regional Geographical Structure," *Acta Geologica et Geographica Universitatis Comenianae, Geographica* No. 6. n.d.

Das, Nirmala. *The Dragon Country: The General History of Bhutan.* New Delhi: Orient Longman Ltd., 1974.

Das, P.K. *The Monsoons.* New Delhi: National Book Trust of India, 1968.

Davis, Kingsley. *The Population of India and Pakistan.* Princeton, New Jersey: Princeton University Press, 1951.

Dayal, Edison. "Impact of Irrigation Expansion on Multiple Cropping in India." *Tijdschrift Voor Economische en Sociale Geografie* 68 (1977):100-109.

—"Regional Response to High Yield Varieties of Rice in India." *Singapore Journal of Tropical Geography* 4 (1983):87-98.

—"Agricultural Productivity in India: A Spatial Analysis." *Annals of the Association of American Geographers* 74 (1984):124-137.

DeBary, W.T. ed. *Sources of Indian Tradition.* 2 vols. New York: Columbia University Press, 1958.

Department of Army. *U.S. Army Area Handbook for Nepal, Sikkim, and Bhutan* No. 550-35. Washington, D.C.: U.S. Government Printing Office, 1964.

Department of Census and Statistics. *Sri Lanka Year Book: 1982.* Colombo, Sri Lanka: Department of Government Printing, 1983.

Department of Census and Statistics. *Statistical Pocket Book of the Democratic Socialist Republic of Sri Lanka.* Colombo, Sri Lanka: Department of Government Printing, 1983.

DeSilva, K.M., ed. *Sri Lanka: A Survey.* Honolulu, Hawaii: University Press of Hawaii, 1977.

Dutt, Ashok K. "Daily Shopping in Calcutta." *The Town Planning Review* 37 (October 1966):207-216.

—"Delineation of the Hinterland of Calcutta Port." *The Professional Geographer* 23 (January 1971):22-27.

—"Two Decades of Planning India: An Anatomy of Approach." *The National Geographical Journal of India* 18 (September-December 1972):187-205.

—"Daily Influence Area of Calcutta." *The Journal of Tropical Geography* 35 (December 1972):32-39.

—ed. *India: Resources, Potentialities and Planning.* Dubuque, Iowa: Kendall/Hunt Publishing Company, 1973.

—ed. *Contemporary Perspective on the Medical Geography of South and Southeast Asia.* Oxford: Pergamon Press, 1980.

—"South Asian City." In Brunn, Stanley, and Williams, Jack. ed. *Cities of the World, World Regional Urban Development.* New York: Harper and Row, 1983. pp. 325-370.

—"The National Atlas of India." *Geographical Review* 74 (January 1984):94-100.

Dutt, Ashok K., and Ahmed, Nawajesh. "Population Pressures in Bangladesh." *Focus* 25 (November-December 1974):1-10.

Dutt, Ashok K., and Costa, Frank. "Necessary Inputs for Reducing Population Growth in Bangladesh." in Wakil, Parvez, ed. *South Asia Perspectives and Dimensions* (Ottawa: Canadian Association for South Asian Studies, 1977):153-163.

Dutt, Ashok K., and Davgun, Satish. "Diffusion of Sikhism and Recent Migration Patterns of Sikhs in India." *Geo Journal* 1.5 (1977):81-90.

—"Religious Pattern of India With a Factoral Regionalization," *Geo Journal* 3.2 (1979):201-214.

Dutt, Ashok K., and Dhussa, Ramesh. "Novelist Sarat Chandra's Perception of His Bengali Home Region: A Literary Geographic Study." *Geo Journal* 5.1 (1981):41-53.

—"Novelist Sarat Chandra's Perception of Bengalis in Probash (Foreign Lands): A Literary Geographic Study." *The National Geographical Journal of India* 29 (September-December 1982):188-189.

Dutt, Ashok K., and Dutta, Hiran M. "Diseases in South and Southeast Asia With Special Reference to India." *The Indian Geographical Journal* 59 (June 1984): 141-147.

Dutt, Ashok K., and Noble, Allen G. "Religious Diversity Patterns of Rajasthan Within An Indian Framework." *Asian Geographer* 4 (1985):137-146.

Dutt, Ashok K., and Pyle, G.F. "Dimensions of India's Foreign Trade." in *International Geography 1972*. vol. 1. Toronto: Toronto University Press, 1972: 543-556.

Dutt, Ashok K., and Venugopal G. "Spatial Patterns of Crime Among Indian Cities." *Geoforum* 14 (1983):223-233.

Dutt, Ashok K., Akhtar, Rais, and Dutta, Hiran M. "Malaria in India With Particular Reference to Two West-Central States." *Social Science and Medicine* 14D.3 (September 1980):317-330.

Dutt, Ashok K., Barai, Daksha, and Sami, A. "Changes and Characteristics of Density Gradients of Colonial and Traditional Cities of India." *Asian Geographer* 3.2 (1984):103-109.

Dutt, Ashok K., Chatterjee, S.P., and Geib, M. Margaret. *India in Maps*. Dubuque Iowa: Kendall/Hunt Publishing Co. 1976.

Dutt, Ashok K., Khan, Abdullah A., and Noble, Allen G. "Bengal: A Search for Regional Identity." *Focus* 34 (June 1984):1-12.

Dutt, Ashok K., Khan, Chandrakanta, and Sangwan, Chandralekha. "Spatial Pattern of Languages in India: A Culture-Historical Analysis." *Geo Journal* 10.1 (1985):51-74.

Dutt, Ashok K., Monroe, Charles, and Vakamudi, Ramesh. "Rural-Urban Correlates of Urbanization in India." *Geographical Review* 76 (April 1986):173-183.

Dutt, Ashok K., Noble, Allen G., and Davgun, Satish K. "Socio-Economic Factors Affecting Marriage Distance in Two Sikh Villages of Punjab." *Journal of Cultural Geography* 2 (Fall/Winter 1981):13-26.

Dutt, Ashok K., Noble, Allen G., and D'Sa, Gerardine. "A Historical View of Density Gradients of Calcutta, A Colonial City." *The National Geographical Journal of India* 31 (1985):269-279.

Dutt, Ashok K., Noble, Allen G., and Singh, Sitasaran. "Is There a North Central Subculture of Violence in India?" *The National Geographical Journal of India* 25 (June 1979):101-111.

Dutt, Ashok K., Noble, Allen G., and Sharma, Kamal K. "Variation of the Spatial Patterns of Crime in Ajmer, India." *Indian Journal of Criminology* 13 (January 1985):57-72.

Fox, Richard G. ed. *Urban India: Society, Space and Image*, Monograph and Occasional Series, No. 10. Duke University, 1970.

Gandhi, M.K. *Gandhi's Autobiography: The Story of My Experiments With Truth*. Boston: Beacon Press, 1957.

Government of India. *Economic Survey 1984-85*. New Delhi: Ministry of Finance, 1985.

—*Report of the Official Language Commission*. New Delhi: Government of India Press, 1956.

—Planning Commission. *A Draft Outline—Fourth Five Year Plan*. New Delhi, 1966.

—*India, A Reference Annual 1954-84*. New Delhi: Ministry of Information and Broadcasting, 1954-84.

—*India Languages*. New Delhi: Publications Division, Ministry of Information and Broadcasting, 1970.

—*Sixth Five Year Plan 1980-85*. New Delhi: Government of India Press, 1981.

—*Seventh Five Year Plan 1985-90*. vols. i and ii. New Delhi: Government of India Press, 1985.

—*Temples of North India*. New Delhi: Publications Division, 1968.

—Irrigation Commission, Ministry of Education and Youth Services. *Irrigation Atlas of India*. Calcutta, 1972.

—Planning Commission. *Draft—Fourth Five Year Plan*, 1969-1974. New Delhi, 1969.

—Planning Commission. *Fourth Five Year Plan*, 1969-74. New Delhi, 1969.

—Planning Commission. *Draft—Fifth Five Year Plan*, 1974-79. vol. i. New Delhi, 1973.

—Planning Commission. *Draft—Fifth Five Year Plan*, 1974-79. vol ii. New Delhi, 1974.

India Meteorological Department. *Forecasting Manual*, Part I. *Climatology of India and Neighborhood*. No. 2. Climate of India. Poona: The Deputy Director General of Observations, 1968.

Information Service of the Ministry of Lands and Land Development and the Ministry of Mahaweli Development. *Mahaweli: Projects and Programme, 1983*. Colombo, Sri Lanka: Department of Government Printing, 1983.

Jakobson, Leo, and Prakash, Ved. "Urbanization and Regional Planning in India." *Urban Affairs Quarterly* 2 (March 1967):3.

Johnson, B.L.C. *South Asia: Selective Studies of the Essential Geography of India, Pakistan and Ceylon*. London: Heinemann Educational Books Ltd., 1969.

—*India: Resources and Development*. New York: Barnes & Noble Inc., 1979.

—*Bangladesh*. London: Heinemann Educational Books, Ltd., 1982.

Joint Committee for Diagnostic Survey of Damodar Valley Region. *The Planning Atlas of the Damodar Valley Region*. Calcutta Unit, Technical Advisory Committee of the D.V.C., 1969.

Karan, P.P. *Nepal: A Cultural and Physical Geography*. Lexington: University of Kentucky Press, 1960.

—"Indian Industrial Change." *Journal of the Association of American Geographers* 54 (1964):336-354.

—*Bhutan: A Physical and Cultural Geography*. Lexington: University of Kentucky Press, 1967.

—and Iijima, Shigeru. *Sikkim Himalaya Development in Mountain Environment*. Tokyo: Institute for the Study of Languages and Cultures of Asia and Africa, 1984.

Khan, Abdullah Al-Mamun. "Rural—Urbàn Migration and Urbanization in Bangladesh." *Geographical Review* 72 (October 1982):379-394.

—"Improving Delivery of Health Care in Bangladesh." *Geographical Review* 74 (1984):100-106.

—"Analyzing Spatial Disparities in Access to Health Care: A Methodology With Application in Bangladesh." *Geo Journal* 10.1 (1985):91-107.

King, Anthony D. *Colonial Urban Development Culture, Social Power and Environment*. London: Routledge and Kegan Paul, 1976.

Kosambi, Meera. *Bombay and Poona: A Sociological Study of Two Indian Cities 1650-1900*. Stockholm: University of Stockholm, Department of Sociology, 1980.

Krishnan, M.S. *Geology of India and Burma*. Madras: Madras Law Journal Office, 1949.

Lal, Amrit, and Tirtha, Ranjit. "India's Urbanization." *Focus* 19 (September 1968):1-7.

Lamb, B.P. *India: A World in Transition*. 3rd ed. New York: Praeger Publishers, 1972.

Majumdar, R.C., Raychaudhuri, H.C., and Datta, Kalikinkar. *An Advanced History of India*. 2nd ed. London: Macmillan and Co., 1958.

Ministry of Information and Broadcasting, Publications Divisions. 2nd ed. *Temples of India*. New Delhi: Patiala House, 1968.

Mitra, Asok. *Calcutta, India's City*. Calcutta: New Age Publishers, 1963.

—*Delhi Capital City*. New Delhi: Thomson Press Ltd., 1970.

Mitra, Asok, and Mukherji, Shekhar. *Population, Food and Land Inequality in India 1971*. Bombay: Allied Publishers Private, Ltd., 1980.

Mitra, Asok, Mukherji, Shekhar, and Bose, Ranendranath. *Indian Cities: Their Industrial Structure In Migration and Capital Investment 1961-71.* New Delhi: Abhinav Publications, 1980.

Mitra, Asok, Pathak, Lalit P., and Mukherji, Shekhar. *The Status of Women: Shifts in Occupational Participation 1961-71.* New Delhi: Abhinav Publications, 1980.

Mitra, Asok, Sherry, Surendra B.L., and Dutt, Brahm. *Shifts in the Functions of Cities and Towns of India 1961-71.* New Delhi: Abhinav Publications, 1981.

Mode, Heinz. *The Harappa Culture and the West.* Calcutta: Sanskrit College, 1959.

Mookherjee, Debnath, and Morrill, Richard C. *Urbanization in a Developing Economy: Indian Perspectives and Patterns.* London: Sage Publications, 1973.

Mukerji, A.B., and Ahmad, Aijazudin, eds. *India Culture Society and Economy Geographical Essays in Honour of Professor Asok Mitra.* New Delhi: Inter-India Publications, 1985.

Muller, Robert A., and Oberlander, Theodore M. *Physical Geography Today: A Portrait of a Planet.* 2nd ed. New York: Random House, Inc., 1978.

Munsi, Sunil K. *Calcutta Metropolitan Explosion—It's Nature and Roots.* New Delhi: People's Publishing House, 1975.

National Atlas of India. 8 vols. Calcutta: National Atlas and Thematic Mapping Organization of the Government of India, 1982.

Nehru, Jawaharlal. *The Discovery of India.* Delhi: S. Chand and Co., 1958.

Noble, Allen G., and Dutt, Ashok K., eds. *Urbanization and Planning in India: Vehicles of Modernization.* New Delhi: Tata-McGraw Hill Publishing Co., 1978.

—*India Cultural Patterns and Processes.* Boulder, Colorado: Westview Press, 1982.

Noble, Allen G., Dutt, Ashok K., and Venugopal, G. "Land Value and Land Use: Spatial Relations in Madras, India." In Hanten, Edward and Utano, Jack. eds. *The Urban Environment in a Spatial Perspective* (Akron, Ohio: The Center for Urban Studies, University of Akron, 1979):45-52.

—"Variations in Noise Generation: Bangalore, India." *Geografiska Annaler* 67B (1985):15-19.

Olschak, Blanche C. *Bhutan: Land of Hidden Treasures.* New York: Stein and Day, Publishers, 1971.

Pakistan Economic Survey 1981-82. Islamabad: Government of Pakistan, 1982.

Pandit, P.B. *Language in a Plural Society: The Case of India.* New Delhi: Delhi University Press, 1977.

Paul, Bimal Kanti. "A Note on the Hierarchy of Health Facilities in Bangladesh." *Social Science and Medicine* 17.3 (1983):189-191.

—"Perception of and Agricultural Adjustment of Floods in Jamuna Floodplain, Bangladesh." *Human Ecology.* 12.1 (1984):3-19.

—"Malaria in Bangladesh." *Geographical Review* 74 (January 1984):63-75.

Planning Commission. *Annual Plan: 1974-1975.* New Delhi: Government of India Press.

—*The Approach to the Seventh Five Year Plan 1985-90.* Faridabad, Government of India Press, 1984.

—*The First Five-Year Plan 1973-78.* Dhaka: Government of the People's Republic of Bangladesh, 1973.

Rahul, Ram. *Modern Bhutan.* Delhi: Vikas Publications, 1971.

Ramage, C.S. *Monsoon Meteorology.* New York and London: Academic Press, 1971.

Rao, Y.P., and Ramamurti, K.S. *Forecasting Manual: Climatology of India and Neighbourhood,* Part 1, *Climate of India,* Section 2. FMU Rep. No. 1-2. Poona: India Meteorological Department, 1968.

Rashid, Haroun. *Geography of Bangladesh.* Boulder, Colorado: Westview Press, 1977.

Reiter, R. Elmer. *Jet-Stream Meteorology.* Chicago and London: University of Chicago Press, 1961.

Report on the Development Plan for Greater Bombay, 1964. Bombay: Government Central Press, 1964.

Rose, Leo E. *The Politics of Bhutan.* Ithaca and London: Cornell University Press, 1977.

Roy, Ajit. *Planning in India Achievements and Problems.* Calcutta: National Publishers, 1965.

Roy, B.K. "Indian Census Cartography." *Geo Journal 6.3 (1982):213-224.*

—"Population Regions—A Perspective in Geographic Space of India." *Geo Journal* 6.2 (1982):173-182.

Schenk, Hans. *Views on Alleppey Socio-Historical and Socio-Spatial Perspectives on an Industrial Port Town in Kerala, South India.* Amsterdam: University of Amsterdam, 1985.

Schwartzberg, Joseph E. *A Historical Atlas of South Asia.* Chicago: University of Chicago Press, 1978.

Sen, Surendra Nath. *Eighteen Fifty-Seven.* Calcutta: The Government of India Press, 1958.

Shrestha, Mohan N. "The Measure of Spatial Choice Pattern." *The Himalayan Review* 4 (1971):11-19.

Siddiqi, Akhtar Husain. "Land Reforms and Development in Pakistan." *Asian Profile* 4.1 (February 1976):55-64.

—"Problems and Performance of Agriculture in Pakistan." *Asian Profile* 5 (August 1977):355-370.

—"Spatial Distribution of Livestock in Pakistan." *Geoforum* 8.1 (1977):33-38.

Singh, Nagendra. *Bhutan: A Kingdom in the Himalayas.* New Delhi: Thomson Press, India, Ltd., 1972.

Singh, R.L. ed. *India: A Regional Geography.* Varanasi: National Geographical Society of India, 1971.

Singh, Rana R.B. "Toward Phenomenological Geography of Indian Village: A Dialogue of Space—Time Experiences." Singh, R.L. and Singh, Rana P.B., eds. *Environmental Appraisal and Rural Habitat Transformation.* Varanasi: National Geographical Society of India, 1984. pp. 103-115.

—"The Personality and Lifeworld of Varanasi as Revealed in Shivprasad Singh's Novel: A Study in Literary Geography." *The National Geographical Journal of India* 31 (1985):291-318.

Singh, S., and Dutta, H.M. "Smallpox Pattern and It's Correlates: A Case Study of an Indian City." *Geo Journal* 5.1 (1981):77-82.

Sirinada, K.U. "Some Meteorological and Climatological Indicators of Drought in Sri Lanka." *Asian Geographer* 3.2 (1984):81-102.

Sita, K., Phadke, V.S., and Bannerjee-Guha, S. *The Declining City-Core of an Indian Metropolis—A Case Study of Bombay.* Department of Geography, University of Bombay, 1985.

Sivamurthy, A. "Spatial Pattern of Commuting of Property Offenders in Madras City." *The Indian Geographical Journal* 54.2 (December 1979):79-84.

Sopher, David E. "Pilgrim Circulation in Gujarat." *Geographical Review* 58 (July 1968):392-425.

—ed. *An Exploration of India: Geographical Perspectives on Society and Culture.* Ithaca: Cornell University Press, 1980.

Spate, O.H.K., and Learmonth, A.T.A. *India and Pakistan: A General and Regional Geography.* 3rd ed. London: Methuen and Co., Ltd., 1967.

Spear, Percival. *A History of India.* vol. 2. Harmondsworth, England: Penguin Books Ltd., 1975.

Stamp, L.D. *Asia.* London: Methuen and Co., Ltd., 1967.

Sukhwal, B.L. *India: A Political Geography.* New Delhi: Allied Publishers Pvt., Ltd., 1971.

—*South Asia: A Systematic Geographic Bibliography.* Metuchen, New Jersey: The Scarecrow Press, Inc., 1974.

Sundaram, V.K. *Urban and Regional Planning in India.* New Delhi: Vikas, 1979.

Tayyeb, A. *Pakistan: A Political Geography.* London: Oxford University Press, 1966.

Thapar, Romila. *A History of India.* vol 1. Harmondsworth, England: Penguin Books, 1974.

Tirtha, Ranjit. "Population Problems in India: A Battle with Hydra." *Focus* 24 (May 1974).

Turner, Roy. *India's Urban Future.* Berkeley and Los Angeles: University of California Press, 1962.

U.S. Army Handbook for India. Washington, D.C.: U.S. Government Printing Office, 1964.

Venugopal, V. "Land Value and Land Use in Madras City: A Study of Spatial Patterns." M.A. thesis of the Department of Geography, the University of Akron, 1980.

Wadia, D.N. *Geology of India.* 3rd ed. London: Macmillan and Co., 1953.

Wanmali, Sudhir. "Central Places and Their Tributary Population: Some Observations." *Behavioral Sciences and Community Development* 6 (1972):11-39.

—"Service Provision, Spatial Intervention and Settlement Systems: The Case of Metropolitan Region, India." *Annals of the National Association of Geographers, India* 3.2 (December 1983):27-65.

Wheeler, Mortimer. *Early India and Pakistan.* New York: Praeger Publishers, 1959.

Whittick, Arnold. ed. *Encyclopedia of Urban Planning.* New York: McGraw-Hill Book Company, 1974.

World Bank. *Wages, Capital Rental Values and Relative Factor Prices in Pakistan.* Washington, D.C.: World Bank, June, 1978.

—*Bangladesh Current Trends and Development Issues.* Washington, D.C.: World Bank, 1979.

—*Nepal Development Performance and Prospects.* Washington, D.C.: The World Bank, 1983.

World Bank Country Study. *India: Economic Issues in the Power Sector.* Washington, D.C.: World Bank, 1979.

—*Pakistan: Review of the Sixth Five-Year Plan.* Washington, D.C.: The World Bank, 1984.

—*Bhutan Development in a Himalayan Kingdom.* Washington, D.C.: The World Bank, 1984.

Yadav, R.K. *The Indian Language Problem: A Comparative Study.* Delhi: National Publishing House, 1966.

Yadav, C.S. *Land Use in Big Cities: A Study of Delhi.* Delhi: Inter-India Publications, 1979.

Zachariah, K.C. *The Anomoly of the Fertility Decline in India's Kerala State: A Field Investigation.* no. 700, Series No. 25. Washington, D.C.: World Bank, 1984.